Pentaho Data Integration Cookbook
Second Edition

Over 100 recipes for building open source ETL solutions
with Pentaho Data Integration

Alex Meadows

Adrián Sergio Pulvirenti

María Carina Roldán

[PACKT] open source*
PUBLISHING   community experience distilled

BIRMINGHAM - MUMBAI

Pentaho Data Integration Cookbook
Second Edition

First published: June 2011

Second Edition: November 2013

Production Reference: 2221113

Published by Packt Publishing Ltd.
Livery Place
35 Livery Street
Birmingham B3 2PB, UK.

ISBN 978-1-78328-067-4

www.packtpub.com

Cover Image by Aniket Sawant (aniket_sawant_photography@hotmail.com)

Credits

About the Author

Alex Meadows has worked with open source Business Intelligence solutions for nearly 10 years and has worked in various industries such as plastics manufacturing, social and e-mail marketing, and most recently with software at Red Hat, Inc. He has been very active in Pentaho and other open source communities to learn, share, and help newcomers with the best practices in BI, analytics, and data management. He received his Bachelor's degree in Business Administration from Chowan University in Murfreesboro, North Carolina, and his Master's degree in Business Intelligence from St. Joseph's University in Philadelphia, Pennsylvania.

First and foremost, thank you Christina for being there for me before, during, and after taking on the challenge of writing and revising a book. I know it's not been easy, but thank you for allowing me the opportunity. To my grandmother, thank you for teaching me at a young age to always go for goals that may just be out of reach. Finally, this book would be no where without the Pentaho community and the friends I've made over the years being a part of it.

Adrián Sergio Pulvirenti was born in Buenos Aires, Argentina, in 1972. He earned his Bachelor's degree in Computer Sciences at UBA, one of the most prestigious universities in South America.

He has dedicated more than 15 years to developing desktop and web-based software solutions. Over the last few years he has been leading integration projects and development of BI solutions.

I'd like to thank my lovely kids, Camila and Nicolas, who understood that I couldn't share with them the usual video game sessions during the writing process. I'd also like to thank my wife, who introduced me to the Pentaho world.

María Carina Roldán was born in Esquel, Argentina, in 1970. She earned her Bachelor's degree in Computer Science at UNLP in La Plata; after that she did a postgraduate course in Statistics at the University of Buenos Aires (UBA) in Buenos Aires city, where she has been living since 1994.

She has worked as a BI consultant for more than 10 years. Over the last four years, she has been dedicated full time to developing BI solutions using Pentaho Suite. Currently, she works for Webdetails, one of the main Pentaho contributors. She is the author of *Pentaho 3.2 Data Integration: Beginner's Guide* published by *Packt Publishing* in April 2010.

You can follow her on Twitter at `@mariacroldan`.

I'd like to thank those who have encouraged me to write this book: On one hand, the Pentaho community; they have given me a rewarding feedback after the Beginner's book. On the other side, my husband, who without hesitation, agreed to write the book with me. Without them I'm not sure I would have embarked on a new book project.

I'd also like to thank the technical reviewers for the time and dedication that they have put in reviewing the book. In particular, thanks to my colleagues at Webdetails; it's a pleasure and a privilege to work with them every day.

About the Reviewers

Wesley Seidel Carvalho got his Master's degree in Computer Science from the Institute of Mathematics and Statistics, University of São Paulo (IME-USP), Brazil, where he researched on (his dissertation) Natural Language Processing (NLP) for the Portuguese language. He is a Database Specialist from the Federal University of Pará (UFPa). He has a degree in Mathematics from the State University of Pará (Uepa).

Since 2010, he has been working with Pentaho and researching Open Data government. He is an active member of the communities and lists of Free Software, Open Data, and Pentaho in Brazil, contributing software "Grammar Checker for OpenOffice - CoGrOO" and CoGrOO Community.

He has worked with technology, database, and systems development since 1997, Business Intelligence since 2003, and has been involved with Pentaho and NLP since 2009. He is currently serving its customers through its startups:

- http://intelidados.com.br
- http://ltasks.com.br

Daniel Lemire has a B.Sc. and a M.Sc. in Mathematics from the University of Toronto, and a Ph.D. in Engineering Mathematics from the Ecole Polytechnique and the Université de Montréal. He is a Computer Science professor at TELUQ (Université du Québec) where he teaches Primarily Online. He has also been a research officer at the National Research Council of Canada and an entrepreneur. He has written over 45 peer-reviewed publications, including more than 25 journal articles. He has held competitive research grants for the last 15 years. He has served as a program committee member on leading computer science conferences (for example, ACM CIKM, ACM WSDM, and ACM RecSys). His open source software has been used by major corporations such as Google and Facebook. His research interests include databases, information retrieval, and high performance programming. He blogs regularly on computer science at http://lemire.me/blog/.

Coty Sutherland was first introduced to computing around the age of 10. At that time, he was immersed in various aspects of computers and it became apparent that he had a propensity for software manipulation. From then until now, he has stayed involved in learning new things in the software space and adapting to the changing environment that is Software Development. He graduated from Appalachian State University in 2009 with a Bachelor's Degree in Computer Science. After graduation, he focused mainly on software application development and support, but recently transitioned to the Business Intelligence field to pursue new and exciting things with data. He is currently employed by the open source company, Red Hat, as a Business Intelligence Engineer.

www.PacktPub.com

Support files, eBooks, discount offers and more

You might want to visit www.PacktPub.com for support files and downloads related to your book.

Did you know that Packt offers eBook versions of every book published, with PDF and ePub files available? You can upgrade to the eBook version at www.PacktPub.com and as a print book customer, you are entitled to a discount on the eBook copy. Get in touch with us at service@packtpub.com for more details.

At www.PacktPub.com, you can also read a collection of free technical articles, sign up for a range of free newsletters and receive exclusive discounts and offers on Packt books and eBooks.

http://PacktLib.PacktPub.com

Do you need instant solutions to your IT questions? PacktLib is Packt's online digital book library. Here, you can access, read and search across Packt's entire library of books.

Why Subscribe?

- Fully searchable across every book published by Packt
- Copy and paste, print and bookmark content
- On demand and accessible via web browser

Free Access for Packt account holders

If you have an account with Packt at www.PacktPub.com, you can use this to access PacktLib today and view nine entirely free books. Simply use your login credentials for immediate access.

Table of Contents

Preface

Pentaho Data Integration (also known as Kettle) is one of the leading open source data integration solutions. With Kettle, you can take data from a multitude of sources, transform and conform the data to given requirements, and load the data into just as many target systems. Not only is PDI capable of transforming and cleaning data, it also provides an ever-growing number of plugins to augment what is already a very robust list of features.

Pentaho Data Integration Cookbook, Second Edition picks up where the first edition left off, by updating the recipes to the latest edition of PDI and diving into new topics such as working with Big Data and cloud sources, data analytics, and more.

Pentaho Data Integration Cookbook, Second Edition shows you how to take advantage of all the aspects of Kettle through a set of practical recipes organized to find quick solutions to your needs. The book starts with showing you how to work with data sources such as files, relational databases, Big Data, and cloud sources. Then we go into how to work with data streams such as merging data from different sources, how to take advantage of the different tools to clean up and transform data, and how to build nested jobs and transformations. More advanced topics are also covered, such as data analytics, data visualization, plugins, and integration of Kettle with other tools in the Pentaho suite.

Pentaho Data Integration Cookbook, Second Edition provides recipes with easy step-by-step instructions to accomplish specific tasks. The code for the recipes can be adapted and built upon to meet individual needs.

What this book covers

Chapter 1, Working with Databases, shows you how to work with relational databases with Kettle. The recipes show you how to create and share database connections, perform typical database functions (select, insert, update, and delete), as well as more advanced tricks such as building and executing queries at runtime.

Chapter 2, Reading and Writing Files, not only shows you how to read and write files, but also how to work with semi-structured files, and read data from Amazon Web Services.

Chapter 3, Working with Big Data and Cloud Sources, covers how to load and read data from some of the many different NoSQL data sources as well as from Salesforce.com.

Chapter 4, Manipulating XML Structures, shows you how to read, write, and validate XML. Simple and complex XML structures are shown as well as more specialized formats such as RSS feeds.

Chapter 5, File Management, demonstrates how to copy, move, transfer, and encrypt files and directories.

Chapter 6, Looking for Data, shows you how to search for information through various methods via databases, web services, files, and more. This chapter also shows you how to validate data with Kettle's built-in validation steps.

Chapter 7, Understanding and Optimizing Data Flows, details how Kettle moves data through jobs and transformations and how to optimize data flows.

Chapter 8, Executing and Re-using Jobs and Transformations, shows you how to launch jobs and transformations in various ways through static or dynamic arguments and parameterization. Object-oriented transformations through subtransformations are also explained.

Chapter 9, Integrating Kettle and the Pentaho Suite, works with some of the other tools in the Pentaho suite to show how combining tools provides even more capabilities and functionality for reporting, dashboards, and more.

Chapter 10, Getting the Most Out of Kettle, works with some of the commonly needed features (e-mail and logging) as well as building sample data sets, and using Kettle to read meta information on jobs and transformations via files or Kettle's database repository.

Chapter 11, Utilizing Visualization Tools in Kettle, explains how to work with plugins and focuses on DataCleaner, AgileBI, and Instaview, an Enterprise feature that allows for fast analysis of data sources.

Chapter 12, Data Analytics, shows you how to work with the various analytical tools built into Kettle, focusing on statistics gathering steps and building datasets for Weka.

Appendix A, Data Structures, shows the different data structures used throughout the book.

Appendix B, References, provides a list of books and other resources that will help you connect with the rest of the Pentaho community and learn more about Kettle and the other tools that are part of the Pentaho suite.

What you need for this book

PDI is written in Java. Any operating system that can run JVM 1.5 or higher should be able to run PDI. Some of the recipes will require other software, as listed:

- **Hortonworks Sandbox**: This is Hadoop in a box, and consists of a great environment to learn how to work with NoSQL solutions without having to install everything.

- **Web Server with ASP support**: This is needed for two recipes to show how to work with web services.

- **DataCleaner**: This is one of the top open source data profiling tools and integrates with Kettle.

- **MySQL**: All the relational database recipes have scripts for MySQL provided. Feel free to use another relational database for those recipes.

In addition, it's recommended to have access to Excel or Calc and a decent text editor (like Notepad++ or gedit).

Having access to an Internet connection will be useful for some of the recipes that use cloud services, as well as making it possible to access the additional links that provide more information about given topics throughout the book.

Who this book is for

If you are a software developer, data scientist, or anyone else looking for a tool that will help extract, transform, and load data as well as provide the tools to perform analytics and data cleansing, then this book is for you! This book does not cover the basics of PDI, SQL, database theory, data profiling, and data analytics.

Conventions

In this book, you will find a number of styles of text that distinguish between different kinds of information. Here are some examples of these styles, and an explanation of their meaning.

Code words in text, database table names, folder names, filenames, file extensions, pathnames, dummy URLs, user input, and Twitter handles are shown as follows: "Copy the .jar file containing the driver to the lib directory inside the Kettle installation directory."

A block of code is set as follows:

```
"lastname","firstname","country","birthyear"
"Larsson","Stieg","Swedish",1954
"King","Stephen","American",1947
"Hiaasen","Carl ","American",1953
```

When we wish to draw your attention to a particular part of a code block, the relevant lines or items are set in bold:

```
<request>
  <type>City</type>
  <query>Buenos Aires, Argentina</query>
</request>
```

New terms and **important words** are shown in bold. Words that you see on the screen, in menus or dialog boxes for example, appear in the text like this: "clicking on the **Next** button moves you to the next screen".

Warnings or important notes appear in a box like this.

Tips and tricks appear like this.

Reader feedback

Feedback from our readers is always welcome. Let us know what you think about this book—what you liked or may have disliked. Reader feedback is important for us to develop titles that you really get the most out of.

To send us general feedback, simply send an e-mail to feedback@packtpub.com, and mention the book title via the subject of your message.

If there is a topic that you have expertise in and you are interested in either writing or contributing to a book, see our author guide on www.packtpub.com/authors.

Customer support

Now that you are the proud owner of a Packt book, we have a number of things to help you to get the most from your purchase.

Downloading the example code

You can download the example code files for all Packt books you have purchased from your account at http://www.packtpub.com. If you purchased this book elsewhere, you can visit http://www.packtpub.com/support and register to have the files e-mailed directly to you.

Errata

Although we have taken every care to ensure the accuracy of our content, mistakes do happen. If you find a mistake in one of our books—maybe a mistake in the text or the code—we would be grateful if you would report this to us. By doing so, you can save other readers from frustration and help us improve subsequent versions of this book. If you find any errata, please report them by visiting `http://www.packtpub.com/submit-errata`, selecting your book, clicking on the **errata submission form** link, and entering the details of your errata. Once your errata are verified, your submission will be accepted and the errata will be uploaded on our website, or added to any list of existing errata, under the Errata section of that title. Any existing errata can be viewed by selecting your title from `http://www.packtpub.com/support`.

Piracy

Piracy of copyright material on the Internet is an ongoing problem across all media. At Packt, we take the protection of our copyright and licenses very seriously. If you come across any illegal copies of our works, in any form, on the Internet, please provide us with the location address or website name immediately so that we can pursue a remedy.

Please contact us at `copyright@packtpub.com` with a link to the suspected pirated material.

We appreciate your help in protecting our authors, and our ability to bring you valuable content.

Questions

You can contact us at `questions@packtpub.com` if you are having a problem with any aspect of the book, and we will do our best to address it.

1

Working with Databases

In this chapter, we will cover:

- Connecting to a database
- Getting data from a database
- Getting data from a database by providing parameters
- Getting data from a database by running a query built at runtime
- Inserting or updating rows in a table
- Inserting new rows when a simple primary key has to be generated
- Inserting new rows when the primary key has to be generated based on stored values
- Deleting data from a table
- Creating or altering a table from PDI (design time)
- Creating or altering a table from PDI (runtime)
- Inserting, deleting, or updating a table depending on a field
- Changing the database connection at runtime
- Loading a parent-child table
- Building SQL queries via database metadata
- Performing repetitive database design tasks from PDI

Introduction

Databases are broadly used by organizations to store and administer transactional data such as customer service history, bank transactions, purchases, sales, and so on. They are also used to store data warehouse data used for Business Intelligence solutions.

In this chapter, you will learn to deal with databases in Kettle. The first recipe tells you how to connect to a database, which is a prerequisite for all the other recipes. The rest of the chapter teaches you how to perform different operations and can be read in any order according to your needs.

 The focus of this chapter is on relational databases (RDBMS). Thus, the term *database* is used as a synonym for *relational database* throughout the recipes.

Sample databases

Through the chapter you will use a couple of sample databases. Those databases can be created and loaded by running the scripts available at the book's website. The scripts are ready to run under MySQL.

 If you work with a different DBMS, you may have to modify the scripts slightly.

For more information about the structure of the sample databases and the meaning of the tables and fields, please refer to *Appendix A, Data Structures*. Feel free to adapt the recipes to different databases. You could try some well-known databases; for example, **Foodmart** (available as part of the **Mondrian** distribution at http://sourceforge.net/projects/mondrian/) or the MySQL sample databases (available at http://dev.mysql.com/doc/index-other.html).

Pentaho BI platform databases

As part of the sample databases used in this chapter you will use the **Pentaho BI platform Demo** databases. The Pentaho BI Platform Demo is a preconfigured installation that lets you explore the capabilities of the Pentaho platform. It relies on the following databases:

Database name	Description
hibernate	Administrative information including user authentication and authorization data.
Quartz	Repository for Quartz; the scheduler used by Pentaho.
Sampledata	Data for Steel Wheels, a fictional company that sells all kind of scale replicas of vehicles.

By default, all those databases are stored in **Hypersonic** (**HSQLDB**). The script for creating the databases in HSQLDB can be found at `http://sourceforge.net/projects/pentaho/files`. Under **Business Intelligence Server | 1.7.1-stable** look for **pentaho_sample_data-1.7.1.zip**. While there are newer versions of the actual Business Intelligence Server, they all use the same sample dataset.

These databases can be stored in other DBMSs as well. Scripts for creating and loading these databases in other popular DBMSs for example, MySQL or Oracle can be found in *Prashant Raju's* blog, at `http://www.prashantraju.com/projects/pentaho`.

Beside the scripts you will find instructions for creating and loading the databases.

 Prashant Raju, an expert Pentaho developer, provides several excellent tutorials related to the Pentaho platform. If you are interested in knowing more about Pentaho, it's worth taking a look at his blog.

Connecting to a database

If you intend to work with a database, either reading, writing, looking up data, and so on, the first thing you will have to do is to create a connection to that database. This recipe will teach you how to do this.

Getting ready

In order to create the connection, you will need to know the connection settings. At least you will need the following:

▸ Host name: Domain name or IP address of the database server.

▸ Database name: The schema or other database identifier.

▸ Port number: The port the database connects to. Each database has its own default port.

▸ Username: The username to access the database.

▸ Password: The password to access the database.

It's recommended that you also have access to the database at the moment of creating a connection.

How to do it...

Open Spoon and create a new transformation.

1. Select the **View** option that appears in the upper-left corner of the screen, right-click on the **Database connections** option, and select **New**. The **Database Connection** dialog window appears.

2. Under **Connection Type**, select the database engine that matches your DBMS.

3. Fill in the **Settings** options and give the connection a name by typing it in the **Connection Name:** textbox. Your window should look like the following:

4. Press the **Test** button. A message should appear informing you that the connection to your database is OK.

If you get an error message instead, you should recheck the data entered, as well as the availability of the database server. The server might be down, or it might not be reachable from your machine.

How it works...

A database connection is the definition that allows you to access a database from Kettle. With the data you provide, Kettle can instantiate real database connections and perform the different operations related to databases. Once you define a database connection, you will be able to access that database and execute arbitrary SQL statements: create schema objects like tables, execute SELECT statements, modify rows, and so on.

In this recipe you created the connection from the **Database connections** tree. You may also create a connection by pressing the **New...** button in the **Configuration** window of any database-related step in a transformation or job entry in a job. Alternatively, there is also a wizard accessible from the **Tools** menu or by pressing the *F3* key.

Whichever method you choose, a **Settings** window, like the one you saw in the recipe, shows up, allowing you to define the connection. This task includes the following:

- ▸ Selecting a database engine (**Connection Type:**)
- ▸ Selecting the access method (**Access:**)

 Native (JDBC) is the recommended access method, but you can also use a predefined ODBC data source, a JNDI data source, or an Oracle OCI connection.

- ▸ Providing the Host name or IP
- ▸ Providing the database name
- ▸ Entering the username and password for accessing the database

A database connection can only be created with a transformation or an opened job. Therefore, in the recipe you were asked to create a transformation. The same could have been achieved by creating a job instead.

There's more...

The recipe showed the simplest way to create a database connection. However, there is more to know about creating database connections.

Avoiding creating the same database connection over and over again

If you intend to use the same database in more than one transformation and/or job, it's recommended that you share the connection. You do this by right-clicking on the database connection under the **Database connections** tree and clicking on **Share**. This way the database connection will be available to be used in all transformations and jobs. Shared database connections are recognized because they appear in bold. As an example, take a look at the following sample screenshot:

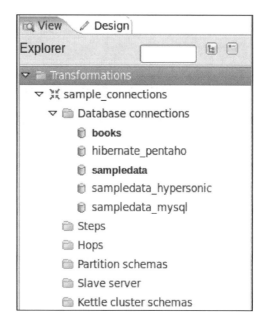

The databases **books** and **sampledata** are shared; the others are not.

The information about shared connections is saved in a file named `shared.xml` located in the Kettle home directory.

No matter what Kettle storage method is used (repository or files), you can share connections. If you are working with the file method, namely `ktr` and `kjb` files, the information about shared connections are not only saved in the `shared.xml` file, but also saved as part of the transformation or job files even if they don't use the connections.

 You can avoid saving all the connection data as part of your transformations and jobs by selecting the option **Only save used connections to XML?** in the **Kettle options** window under **Tools | Options**.

Avoiding modifying jobs and transformations every time a connection changes

Instead of typing fixed values in the database connection definition, it's worth using variables. Variables live in either of the two places: in the `kettle.properties` file, which lives in the Kettle home directory, or within the transformation or job as a named parameter. For example, instead of typing `localhost` as the hostname, you can define a variable named `HOST_NAME`, and as the host name, type its variable notation as `${HOST_NAME}` or `%%HOST_NAME%%`. If you decide to move the database from the local machine to a server, you just have to change the value of the variable and don't need to modify the transformations or jobs that use the connection.

 To edit variables stored in the `kettle.properties` file, just open the `kettle.properties` editor, which can be found under **Edit | Edit the kettle.properties file**.

This is especially useful when it's time to move your jobs and transformations between different environments: development, test, and so on.

Specifying advanced connection properties

The recipe showed you how to provide the general properties needed to create a connection. You may need to specify additional options; for example, a preferred schema name, or supply some parameters to be used when the connection is initialized. In order to do that, look for those options in the extra tab windows under the **General** tab of the **Database Connection** window.

Connecting to a database not supported by Kettle

Kettle offers built-in support for a vast set of database engines. The list includes commercial databases (such as Oracle), open source (such as PostgreSQL), traditional row-oriented databases (such as MS SQL Server), modern column-oriented databases (such as Infobright), disk-storage based databases (such as Informix), and in-memory databases (such as HyperSQL). However, it can happen that you want to connect to a database that is not in that list. In that case, you might still create a connection to that database. First of all, you have to get a JDBC driver for that DBMS. For Kettle versions previous to 5.0, copy the JAR file containing the driver to the `libext/JDBC` directory inside the Kettle installation directory. For versions after 5.0, copy the JAR file containing the driver to the `lib` directory. Then create the connection. For databases not directly supported, choose the **Generic** database connection **type**. In the **Settings** frame, specify the connection string (which should be explained along with JDBC), the driver class name, and the username and password. In order to find the values for these settings, you will have to refer to the driver documentation.

Checking the database connection at runtime

If you are not sure that the database connection will be accessible when a job or transformation runs from outside Spoon, you might precede all database-related operations with a Check DB connection job entry. The entry will return `true` or `false` depending on the result of checking one or more connections.

Getting data from a database

If you're used to working with databases, one of your main objectives while working with PDI must be getting data from your databases for transforming, loading in other databases, generating reports, and so on. Whatever operation you intend to achieve, the first thing you have to do after connecting to the database is to get that data and create a PDI dataset. In this recipe, you will learn the simplest way to do that.

Getting ready

To follow these instructions, you need to have access to any DBMS. Many of the recipes in this chapter will be connecting to a MySQL instance. It is recommended that to fully take advantage of the book's code, (which can be found on the book's website) you have access to a MySQL instance.

How to do it...

1. Create a transformation and drop a **Table Input** step into the canvas. You will find it in the **Input** category of steps.

2. From the **Connection** drop-down list, select the connection to the database where your data resides, or create it if it doesn't exist.

3. In the **SQL** textarea, type the SQL statement that returns the data you need. So far, you should have something like the following:

4. Click on **Preview**. This will bring a sample list of rows so you can confirm that the data is as expected.

5. Click on **OK** to close the **Table Input** configuration window, and you'll be ready to use the data for further manipulation.

How it works...

The **Table Input** step you used in the recipe is the main Kettle step to get data from a database. When you run or preview the transformation, Kettle executes the SQL and pushes the rows of data coming from the database into the output stream of the step. Each column of the SQL statement leads to a PDI field and each row generated by the execution of the statement becomes a row in the PDI dataset.

Once you get the data from the database, it will be available for any kind of manipulation inside the transformation.

There's more...

In order to save time, or in case you are not sure of the name of the tables or columns in the database, instead of typing the SQL statement, click on the **Get SQL select statement...** button. This will bring the **Database Explorer** window. This window allows you to explore the selected database. By expanding the database tree and selecting the table that interests you, you will be able to explore that table through the different options available under the **Actions** menu.

Double-clicking on the name of the table will generate a SELECT statement to query that table. You will have the chance to include all the field names in the statement, or simply generate a SELECT * statement. After bringing the SQL to the **Table Input** configuration window, you will be able to modify it according to your needs.

By generating this statement, you will lose any statement already in the SQL textarea.

See also

▸ *Connecting to a database*

▸ *Getting data from a database by providing parameters*

▸ *Getting data from a database by running a query built at runtime*

Getting data from a database by providing parameters

If you need to create a dataset with data coming from a database, you can do it just by using a **Table Input** step. If the SELECT statement that retrieves the data doesn't need parameters, you simply write it in the **Table Input** setting window and proceed. However, most of the times you need flexible queries—queries that receive parameters. This recipe will show you how to pass parameters to a SELECT statement in PDI.

Assume that you need to list all products in Steel Wheels for a given product line and scale.

Getting ready

Make sure you have access to the sampledata database.

How to do it...

Perform the following steps to connect to a database with parameters:

1. Create a transformation.

2. Before getting the data from the database, you have to create the stream that will provide the parameters for the statement.

3. Create a stream that builds a dataset with a single row and two columns: the product line parameter and the scale parameter. For this exercise, we will be using a **Data Grid** step, but other steps like the **Generate Rows** step will also work. Opening the **Data Grid** step, add the `productline_par` and `productscale_par` lines to the **Meta** tab. They should both be of type **String**:

4. Switch to the **Data** tab. Notice how the fields created in the **Meta** tab build the row for data to be added to. Create a record with `Classic Cars` as the value for `productline_par` and `1:10` as the value for `productscale_par`:

5. Now drag a **Table Input** step to the canvas and create a hop from the **Data Grid** step, which was created previously, towards this step.

6. Now you can configure the **Table Input** step. Double-click on it, select the connection to the database, and type in the following statement:

```
SELECT  PRODUCTLINE
      ,  PRODUCTSCALE
      ,  PRODUCTCODE
      ,  PRODUCTNAME
FROM    PRODUCTS  p
WHERE   PRODUCTLINE  = ?
AND     PRODUCTSCALE = ?
```

Downloading the example code

You can download the example code files for all Packt books you have purchased from your account at `http://www.packtpub.com`. If you purchased this book elsewhere, you can visit `http://www.packtpub.com/support` and register to have the files e-mailed directly to you.

7. In the **Insert data from step** list, select the name of the step that is linked to the **Table Input** step. Close the window.

8. Select the **Table Input** step and do a preview of the transformation. You will see a list of all products that match the product line and scale provided in the incoming stream:

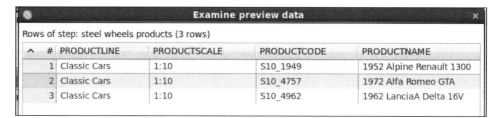

How it works...

When you need to execute a `SELECT` statement with parameters, the first thing you have to do is to build a stream that provides the parameter values needed by the statement. The stream can be made of just one step; for example, a data grid with fixed values, or a stream made up of several steps. The important thing is that the last step delivers the proper values to the **Table Input** step.

Then, you have to link the last step in the stream to the **Table Input** step where you will type the statement. What differentiates this statement from a regular statement is that you have to provide question marks. When you preview or run the transformation, the statement is prepared and the values coming to the **Table Input** step are bound to the placeholders; that is, the place where you typed the question marks.

Note that in the recipe the output of the stream was a single row with two fields, which is exactly the same number of question marks as in the statement.

> The number of fields coming to a **Table Input** step must be exactly the same as the number of question marks found in the query.

Also note that in the stream, the product line was in the first place and the product scale in the second place. If you look at the highlighted lines in the recipe, you will see that the statement expected the parameter values to be exactly in that order.

> The replacement of the markers respects the order of the incoming fields.
>
> Any values that are used in this manner are consumed by the **Table Input** step. Finally, it's important to note that question marks can only be used to parameterize value expressions just as you did in the recipe.
>
> Keywords or identifiers (for example; table names) cannot be parameterized with the question marks method.

If you need to parameterize something different from a value expression, you should take another approach, as explained in the next recipe.

There's more...

There are a couple of situations worth discussing.

Parameters coming in more than one row

In the recipe you received the list of parameter values in a single row with as many columns as expected parameter values. It's also possible to receive the parameter values in several rows. If, instead of a row you had one parameter by row, as shown in the following screenshot, the behavior of the transformation wouldn't have changed:

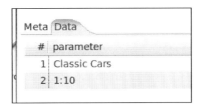

The statement would have pulled the values for the two parameters from the incoming stream in the same order as the data appeared. It would have bound the first question mark with the value in the first row, and the second question mark with the value coming in the second row.

Note that this approach is less flexible than the previous one. For example, if you have to provide values for parameters with different data types, you will not be able to put them in the same column and different rows.

Executing the SELECT statement several times, each for a different set of parameters

Suppose that you not only want to list the Classic Cars in 1:10 scale, but also the Motorcycles in 1:10 and 1:12 scales. You don't have to run the transformation three times in order to do this. You can have a dataset with three rows, one for each set of parameters, as shown in the following screenshot:

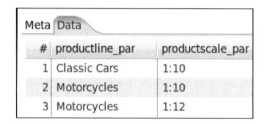

Then, in the **Table Input** setting window you have to check the **Execute for each row?** option. This way, the statement will be prepared and the values coming to the **Table Input** step will be bound to the placeholders, once for each row in the dataset coming to the step. For this example, the result would look like the following:

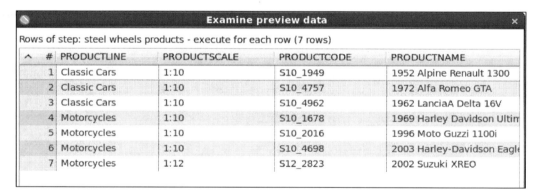

See also

▶   *Getting data from a database by running a query built at runtime*

Getting data from a database by running a query built at runtime

When you work with databases, most of the time you start by writing an SQL statement that gets the data you need. However, there are situations in which you don't know that statement exactly. Maybe the name of the columns to query are in a file, or the name of the columns by which you will sort will come as a parameter from outside the transformation, or the name of the main table to query changes depending on the data stored in it (for example `sales2010`). PDI allows you to have any part of the SQL statement as a variable, so you don't need to know the literal SQL statement text at design time.

Assume the following situation: you have a database with data about books and their authors, and you want to generate a file with a list of titles. Whether to retrieve the data ordered by title or by genre is a choice that you want to postpone until the moment you execute the transformation.

Getting ready

You will need a book database with the structure as explained in *Appendix A, Data Structures*.

How to do it...

1. Create a transformation.
2. The column that will define the order of the rows will be a named parameter. So, define a named parameter named `ORDER_COLUMN`, and put `title` as its default value.

> Remember that named parameters are defined in the **Transformation** setting window and their role is the same as the role of any Kettle variable. If you prefer, you can skip this step and define a standard variable for this purpose.

3. Now drag a **Table Input** step to the canvas. Then create and select the connection to the book's database.
4. In the **SQL** frame, type the following statement:

```
SELECT * FROM books ORDER BY ${ORDER_COLUMN}
```

5. Check the option **Replace variables in script?** and close the window.
6. Use an **Output** step such as a **Text file output** step to send the results to a file, save the transformation, and run it.
7. Open the generated file and you will see the books ordered by title.
8. Now try again. Press the *F9* key to run the transformation one more time.
9. This time, change the value of the `ORDER_COLUMN` parameter typing `genre` as the new value.

10. Click on the **Launch** button.

11. Open the generated file. This time you will see the titles ordered by genre.

How it works...

You can use Kettle variables in any part of the SELECT statement inside a **Table Input** step. When the transformation is initialized, PDI replaces the variables by their values provided that the **Replace variables in script?** option is checked.

In the recipe, the first time you ran the transformation, Kettle replaced the variable ORDER_COLUMN with the word title and the statement executed was as follows:

```
SELECT * FROM books ORDER BY title
```

The second time, the variable was replaced by genre and the executed statement was as follows:

```
SELECT * FROM books ORDER BY genre
```

 As mentioned in the recipe, any predefined Kettle variable can be used instead of a named parameter.

There's more...

You may use variables not only for the ORDER BY clause, but in any part of the statement: table names, columns, and so on. You could even hold the full statement in a variable. Note however that you need to be cautious when implementing this.

 A wrong assumption about the metadata generated by those predefined statements can make your transformation crash.

You can also use the same variable more than once in the same statement. This is an advantage of using variables as an alternative to question marks when you need to execute parameterized SELECT statements.

Named parameters are another option to store parts of statements. They are part of the job or transformation and allow for default values and clear definitions for what the parameter is. To add or edit named parameters, right-click on the transformation or job, go into its settings, and switch to the **Parameters** tab.

See also

▶ *Getting data from a database by providing parameters*

Inserting or updating rows in a table

Two of the most common operations on databases, besides retrieving data, are inserting and updating rows in a table.

PDI has several steps that allow you to perform these operations. In this recipe you will learn to use the **Insert/Update** step. Before inserting or updating rows in a table by using this step, it is critical that you know which field or fields in the table uniquely identify a row in the table.

> If you don't have a way to uniquely identify the records, you should consider other steps, as explained in the *There's more...* section.

Assume this situation: you have a file with new employees of Steel Wheels. You have to insert those employees in the database. The file also contains old employees that have changed either the office where they work, the extension number, or other basic information. You will take the opportunity to update that information as well.

Getting ready

Download the material for the recipe from the book's site. Take a look at the file you will use:

```
EMPLOYEE_NUMBER, LASTNAME, FIRSTNAME, EXTENSION, OFFICE, REPORTS,
TITLE
1188, Firrelli, Julianne,x2174,2,1143, Sales Manager
1619, King, Tom,x103,6,1088,Sales Rep
1810, Lundberg, Anna,x910,2,1143,Sales Rep
1811, Schulz, Chris,x951,2,1143,Sales Rep
```

Explore the Steel Wheels database, in particular the employees table, so you know what you have before running the transformation. Execute the following MySQL statement:

```sql
SELECT
    EMPLOYEENUMBER ENUM
  , CONCAT(FIRSTNAME,' ',LASTNAME) NAME
  , EXTENSION EXT
  , OFFICECODE OFF
  , REPORTSTO REPTO
  , JOBTITLE
FROM EMPLOYEES
WHERE EMPLOYEENUMBER IN (1188, 1619, 1810, 1811);
```

```
+-------+------------------+---------+------+--------+-----------+
| ENUM  | NAME             | EXT     | OFF  | REPTO  | JOBTITLE  |
+-------+------------------+---------+------+--------+-----------+
| 1188  | Julie Firrelli   | x2173   | 2    | 1143   | Sales Rep |
| 1619  | Tom King         | x103    | 6    | 1088   | Sales Rep |
+-------+------------------+---------+------+--------+-----------+
2 rows in set (0.00 sec)
```

How to do it...

Perform the following steps to insert or update rows in a table:

1. Create a transformation and use a **Text File input** step to read the file `employees.txt`. Provide the name and location of the file, specify comma as the separator, and fill in the **Fields** grid.

 Remember that you can quickly fill the grid by clicking on the **Get Fields** button.

2. Now, you will do the inserts and updates with an **Insert/Update** step. So, expand the **Output** category of steps, look for the **Insert/Update** step, drag it to the canvas, and create a hop from the **Text File** input step toward this one.

3. Double-click on the **Insert/Update** step and select the connection to the Steel Wheels database, or create it if it doesn't exist. As target table, type EMPLOYEES.

4. Fill the grids as shown in the following screenshot:

^	#	Table field	Comparator	Stream field1	Stream field2
	1	EMPLOYEENUMBER	=	EMPLOYEE_NUMBER	

Update fields:

^	#	Table field	Stream field	Update
	1	EMPLOYEENUMBER	EMPLOYEE_NUMBER	N
	2	LASTNAME	LASTNAME	N
	3	FIRSTNAME	FIRSTNAME	N
	4	EXTENSION	EXT	Y
	5	OFFICECODE	OFFICE	Y
	6	REPORTSTO	REPORTS	Y
	7	JOBTITLE	TITLE	Y

5. Save and run the transformation.

6. Explore the `employees` table by running the query executed earlier. You will see that one employee was updated, two were inserted, and one remained untouched because the file had the same data as the database for that employee:

```
+------+----------------+-------+-----+-------+--------------+
| ENUM | NAME           | EXT   | OFF | REPTO | JOBTITLE     |
+------+----------------+-------+-----+-------+--------------+
| 1188 | Julie Firrelli| x2174 | 2   |  1143 |Sales Manager |
| 1619 | Tom King       | x103  | 6   |  1088 |Sales Rep     |
| 1810 | Anna Lundberg  | x910  | 2   |  1143 |Sales Rep     |
| 1811 | Chris Schulz   | x951  | 2   |  1143 |Sales Rep     |
+------+----------------+-------+-----+-------+--------------+
4 rows in set (0.00 sec)
```

How it works...

The **Insert/Update** step, as its name implies, serves for both inserting or updating rows. For each row in your stream, Kettle looks for a row in the table that matches the condition you put in the upper grid—the grid labeled **The key(s) to look up the value(s):**. Take for example the last row in your input file:

```
1811, Schulz, Chris,x951,2,1143,Sales Rep
```

When this row comes to the **Insert/Update** step, Kettle looks for a row where EMPLOYEENUMBER equals 1811. When it doesn't find one, it inserts a row following the directions you put in the lower grid. For this sample row, the equivalent INSERT statement would be as follows:

```
INSERT INTO EMPLOYEES (EMPLOYEENUMBER, LASTNAME, FIRSTNAME,
         EXTENSION, OFFICECODE, REPORTSTO, JOBTITLE)
     VALUES (1811, 'Schulz', 'Chris',
            'x951', 2, 1143, 'Sales Rep')
```

Now look at the first row:

```
1188, Firrelli, Julianne,x2174,2,1143, Sales Manager
```

When Kettle looks for a row with EMPLOYEENUMBER equal to 1188, it finds it. Then, it updates that row according to what you put in the lower grid. It only updates the columns where you put Y under the **Update** column. For this sample row, the equivalent UPDATE statement would be as follows:

```
UPDATE EMPLOYEES SET EXTENSION = 'x2174'
                   , OFFICECODE = 2
                   , REPORTSTO = 1143
                   , JOBTITLE = 'Sales Manager'
WHERE EMPLOYEENUMBER = 1188
```

Note that the name of this employee in the file (Julianne) is different from the name in the table (Julie), but, as you put N under the column **Update** for the field FIRSTNAME, this column was not updated.

 If you run the transformation with the log level **Detailed**, in the log you will be able to see the real prepared statements that Kettle performs when inserting or updating rows in a table.

There's more...

Here there are two alternative solutions to this use case.

Alternative solution if you just want to insert records

If you just want to insert records, you shouldn't use the **Insert/Update** step but the **Table Output** step. This would be faster because you would be avoiding unnecessary lookup operations; however, the **Table Output** step does not check for duplicated records. The **Table Output** step is really simple to configure; just select the database connection and the table where you want to insert the records. If the names of the fields coming to the **Table Output** step have the same name as the columns in the table, you are done. If not, you should check the **Specify database fields** option, and fill the **Database fields** tab exactly as you filled the lower grid in the **Insert/Update** step, except that here there is no **Update** column.

Alternative solution if you just want to update rows

If you just want to update rows, instead of using the **Insert/Update** step, you should use the **Update** step. You configure the **Update** step just as you configure the **Insert/Update** step, except that here there is no **Update** column.

Alternative way for inserting and updating

The following is an alternative way for inserting and updating rows in a table.

 This alternative only works if the columns in the **Key** field's grid of the **Insert/Update** step are a unique key in the database.

You may replace the **Insert/Update** step by a **Table Output** step and, as the error handling stream coming out of the **Table Output** step, put an **Update** step.

 In order to handle the error when creating the hop from the **Table Output** step towards the **Update** step, select the **Error handling of step** option.

Alternatively, right-click on the **Table Output** step, select **Define error handling...**, and configure the **Step error handling settings** window that shows up. Your transformation would look like the following:

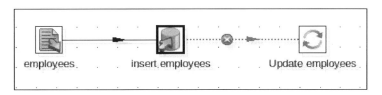

In the **Table Output** step, select the table EMPLOYEES, check the **Specify database fields** option, and fill the **Database fields** tab just as you filled the lower grid in the **Insert/Update** step, except that here there is no **Update** column.

In the **Update** step, select the same table and fill the upper grid—let's call it the Key fields grid—just as you filled the **Key fields** grid in the **Insert/Update** step. Finally, fill the lower grid with those fields that you want to update, that is, those rows that had Y under the **Update** column.

In this case, Kettle tries to insert all records coming to the **Table Output** step. The rows for which the insert fails go to the **Update** step, and get updated.

If the columns in the **Key fields** grid of the **Insert/Update** step are not a unique key in the database, this alternative approach doesn't work. The **Table Output** would insert all the rows. Those that already existed would be duplicated instead of getting updated.

This strategy for performing inserts and updates has been proven to be much faster than the use of the **Insert/Update** step whenever the ratio of updates to inserts is low. In general, for best practice reasons, this is not an advisable solution.

See also

▸ *Inserting new rows where a simple primary key has to be generated*

▸ *Inserting new rows where the primary key has to be generated based on stored values*

Inserting new rows where a simple primary key has to be generated

It's very common to have tables in a database, where the values for the primary key column can be generated by using a database sequence (in those DBMSs that have that feature; for example, Oracle) or simply by adding 1 to the maximum value in the table. Loading data into these tables is very simple. This recipe teaches you how to do this through the following exercise.

There are new offices at Steel Wheels. You have the data of the offices in a file that looks like the following:

```
CITY;PHONE;ADDRESS;COUNTRY;POSTALCODE
Sao Paulo;11 3289-3703;Avenida Paulista 1330;Brazil;01310-200
Sao Paulo;11 3104-1116;Rua Boa Vista, 51;Brazil;01014-001
Buenos Aires;11 4582-6700;Cabildo 2127;Argentina;C1428AAT
```

You have to insert that data into the Steel Wheels database.

Getting ready

For this recipe, you will use the Pentaho sample database. If you don't have that database, you'll have to follow the instructions in the introduction of this chapter.

As you will insert records into the office table, it would be good if you explore that table before doing any insert operations. The following is a sample query:

```
SELECT
      OFFICECODE
    , ADDRESSLINE1
    , CITY
    , COUNTRY
FROM    OFFICES
ORDER BY OFFICECODE;
```

```
+------------+------------------------+---------------+-----------+
| OFFICECODE | ADDRESSLINE1           | CITY          | COUNTRY   |
+------------+------------------------+---------------+-----------+
| 1          | 100 Market Street      | San Francisco | USA       |
| 2          | 1550 Court Place       | Boston        | USA       |
| 3          | 523 East 53rd Street   | NYC           | USA       |
| 4          | 43 Rue Jouffroy D'abbans | Paris       | France    |
| 5          | 4-1 Kioicho            | Tokyo         | Japan     |
| 6          | 5-11 Wentworth Avenue  | Sydney        | Australia |
| 7          | 25 Old Broad Street    | London        | UK        |
+------------+------------------------+---------------+-----------+
7 rows in set (0.00 sec)
```

How to do it...

1. Create a transformation and create a connection to the `sampledata` database.

2. Use a **Text file input** to read the `offices.txt` file with data about the new offices.

3. From the **Data Warehouse** category drag-and-drop a **Combination lookup/update** step and create a hop from the previous step towards this one.

4. Double-click on the step, select the connection to the `sampledata` database, and type `offices` as the **Target table**.

5. Fill the **Key fields** grid as shown:

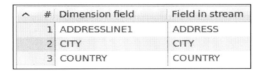

^	#	Dimension field	Field in stream
	1	ADDRESSLINE1	ADDRESS
	2	CITY	CITY
	3	COUNTRY	COUNTRY

6. In the **Technical key** field type `OFFICECODE`. For the **Creation of technical key** fields, leave the default values. Close the window.

7. From the **Output** category of steps, add an **Update** step.

8. Double-click on the step, select the connection to the `sampledata` database, and type `OFFICES` as the **Target table**.

9. In the first grid, add rows with the text `OFFICECODE` both under **Table field** and under **Stream field1**. As **Comparator** choose =. This way, you will update the rows where `OFFICECODE` is equal to the office code in your stream.

10. In the lower grid, add a row and type `PHONE` both under **Table field** and **Stream field**. Add a second row and type `POSTALCODE` in both columns.

11. Close the window.

12. It's time to save the transformation and run it to see what happens.

13. As you might guess, three new offices have been added, with primary keys `8`, `9`, and `10`. The results are as follows:

```
SELECT
    OFFICECODE
  , ADDRESSLINE1
  , CITY
  , COUNTRY
FROM    OFFICES
ORDER BY CAST(OFFICECODE AS UNSIGNED);
```

```
+------------+-------------------------+---------------+-----------+
| OFFICECODE | ADDRESSLINE1            | CITY          | COUNTRY   |
+------------+-------------------------+---------------+-----------+
| 1          | 100 Market Street       | San Francisco | USA       |
| 10         | Cabildo 2127            | Buenos Aires  | Argentina |
| 2          | 1550 Court Place        | Boston        | USA       |
| 3          | 523 East 53rd Street    | NYC           | USA       |
| 4          | 43 Rue Jouffroy D'abbans | Paris        | France    |
| 5          | 4-1 Kioicho             | Tokyo         | Japan     |
| 6          | 5-11 Wentworth Avenue   | Sydney        | Australia |
| 7          | 25 Old Broad Street     | London        | UK        |
| 8          | Avenida Paulista 1330   | Sao Paulo     | Brazil    |
| 9          | Rua Boa Vista, 51       | Sao Paulo     | Brazil    |
+------------+-------------------------+---------------+-----------+
10 rows in set (0.01 sec)
```

How it works...

In many situations, before inserting data into a table you have to generate the primary key. If the primary key is a simple sequence or the maximum primary key plus one, you can generate it by using a **Combination lookup/update** step.

In the recipe, for each row in your file, with the **Combination lookup/update** step, you look for a record in the `offices` table with the same values for `address`, `city`, and `country`.

Because the offices are new, (there aren't offices in the table with the same combination of `address`, `city`, and `country` values) the lookup fails. As a consequence, the step generates a key value as the maximum `OFFICECODE` in the table, plus 1. Then, it inserts a row with the generated primary key and the fields you typed in the grid.

Finally, the step adds the generated primary key value to the stream.

As a last task, we used that key to update the other fields coming into the file: `POSTALCODE` and `PHONE`.

There's more...

The **Combination lookup/update** step is within the **Data Warehouse** category, because it is mainly used for loading **junk dimension tables**. But, as you could see, it can also be used in the particular situation where you have to generate a primary key.

In this recipe you generated the primary key as the maximum plus 1, but, as you can see in the settings window, a database sequence can also be used instead.

When you use the **Combination lookup/update** step for inserting, make sure that the columns that are not part of the list of key fields are nullable or have default values.

Using the Combination lookup/update for looking up

In the recipe the **Combination lookup/update** step just inserted new rows. Now suppose that you have a row that existed in the table. In that case, the lookup would have succeeded and the step wouldn't have inserted a new row. Instead, it would just have returned the found `OFFICECODE`. That field would have been added to the stream, ready to be used further in the transformation, for example, for updating other fields, as you did in the recipe, or for being used for inserting data in a related table.

Note that this is a potentially slow step, as it uses all the values for the comparison.

See also

 ▸ *Inserting new rows where the primary key has to be generated based on stored values*

Inserting new rows where the primary key has to be generated based on stored values

There are tables where the primary key is not a database sequence nor a consecutive integer, but a column which is built based on a rule or pattern that depends on the keys already inserted. For example, imagine a table where the values for the primary key are A00001, A00002, and A00003. In this case, you can guess the rule: putting an A followed by a sequence. The next in the sequence would be A00004. This seems too simple, but doing it in PDI is not trivial. This recipe will teach you how to load a table where a primary key has to be generated based on existing rows.

Suppose that you have to load author data into the book's database. You have the main data for the authors, and you have to generate the primary key as in the previous example.

Getting ready

Run the script that creates and loads data into the books database. You'll find it at http://packtpub.com/support. If the book's earlier example from this chapter has been run, the database and author data should already have been created.

Before proceeding, verify the current values for the primary keys in the table where you will insert data:

```
SELECT MAX(id_author)
FROM authors;
+-----------------+
| MAX(id_author)  |
+-----------------+
| A00009          |
+-----------------+
1 row in set (0.00 sec)
```

How to do it...

Perform the following steps to generate keys for inserted database records:

1. Create a transformation and create a connection to the book's database.

2. Use a **Text file input** step to read the authors.txt file.

 For simplicity, the authors.txt file only has new authors, that is, authors who are not in the table.

3. To generate the next primary key, you need to know the current maximum. So, use a **Table Input** step to get it. In this case, the following statement will give you that number:

```
SELECT
CAST(MAX(RIGHT(id_author, 5)) AS UNSIGNED) max_id
FROM authors
```

 Alternatively, you can simply get the `id_author` field and transform the field with the Kettle steps until you get the current maximum. You will have a simple clear transformation, but it will take several Kettle steps to do it.

4. By using a **Join Rows (Cartesian product)** step, join both streams. Your transformation should look like the following:

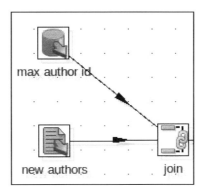

5. Add an **Add sequence** step. Replace the default value `valuename` with `delta_value`. For the rest of the fields in the setting window, leave the default values.

6. Add a **Calculator** step to build the keys. You do it by filling the setting window as shown:

Fields:									
New field	Calculation	Field A	Field B	Fie	Value type	Len	Pl	Remove	Conver:
new_id	A + B	max_id	delta_value		String			N	00000
prefix	Set field to constant value A	A			String			N	
new_author_id	A + B	prefix	new_id		String			N	

7. In order to insert the rows, add a **Table output** step, double-click on it, and select the connection to the `books` database.

8. As **Target table** type `authors`.

9. Check the option **Specify database fields**.

10. Select the **Database fields** tab and fill the grid as follows:

Fields to insert:

^	#	Table field	Stream field
	1	id_author	new_author_id
	2	lastname	lastname
	3	firstname	firstname

11. Save and run the transformation.

12. Explore the `authors` table. You should see the new authors:

```
SELECT * FROM authors ORDER BY id_author;

+-----------+-----------+-------------+-----------+----------+
| lastname  | firstname | nationality | birthyear | id_author|
+-----------+-----------+-------------+-----------+----------+
| Larsson   | Stieg     | Swedish     |      1954 | A00001   |
| King      | Stephen   | American    |      1947 | A00002   |
| Hiaasen   | Carl      | American    |      1953 | A00003   |
| Handler   | Chelsea   | American    |      1975 | A00004   |
| Ingraham  | Laura     | American    |      1964 | A00005   |
| Ramsey    | Dave      | American    |      1960 | A00006   |
| Kiyosaki  | Robert    | American    |      1947 | A00007   |
| Rowling   | Joanne    | English     |      1965 | A00008   |
| Riordan   | Rick      | American    |      1964 | A00009   |
| Gilbert   | Elizabeth | unknown     |      1900 | A00010   |
| Franzen   | Jonathan  | unknown     |      1900 | A00011   |
| Collins   | Suzanne   | unknown     |      1900 | A00012   |
| Blair     | Tony      | unknown     |      1900 | A00013   |
+-----------+-----------+-------------+-----------+----------+
13 rows in set (0.00 sec)
```

How it works...

When you have to generate a primary key based on the existing primary keys, there is no direct way to do it in Kettle, unless the new primary key is simple to generate by adding one to the maximum. One possible solution is the one shown in the recipe—getting the last primary key in the table, combining it with your main stream, and using those two sources for generating the new primary keys. This is how it worked in this example.

First, by using a **Table Input** step, you found out the last primary key in the table. In fact, you got only the numeric part needed to build the new key. In this exercise, the value was 9. With the **Join Rows (Cartesian product)** step, you added that value as a new column in your main stream.

Taking that number as a starting point, you needed to build the new primary keys as A00010, A00011, and so on. You did this by generating a sequence (1, 2, 3, and so on), adding this sequence to the max_id (that led to values 10, 11, 12, and so on), and finally formatting the key with the use of the calculator.

Note that in the **Calculator** step, the first A+B performs an arithmetic calculation. It adds the max_id with the delta_value sequence. Then it converts the result to a String giving it the format with the mask 0000. This led to the values 00010, 00011, and so on.

The second A+B is a string concatenation. It concatenates the literal A with the previously calculated ID.

Note that this approach works as long as you have a single user scenario. If you run multiple instances of the transformation, they can select the same maximum value and try to insert rows with the same PK leading to a primary key constraint violation.

There's more...

The key in this exercise is to get the last or maximum primary key in the table, join it to your main stream, and use that data to build the new key. After the join, the mechanism for building the final key would depend on your particular case.

See also

▶ *Inserting new rows where a simple primary key has to be generated*

Deleting data from a table

Sometimes you might have to delete data from a table. If the operation to do it is simple, for example:

```
DELETE FROM LOG_TABLE WHERE VALID='N'
```

Or

```
DELETE FROM TMP_TABLE
```

You could simply execute it by using an **SQL** job entry or an **Execute SQL script** step. If you face the second of the above situations, you can even use a **Truncate table** job entry.

For more complex situations, you should use the **Delete** step. Let's suppose the following situation: you have a database with outdoor products. Each product belongs to a category: tools, tents, sleeping bags, and so on. Now you want to delete all the products for a given list of categories, where the price is less than or equal to $50.

Getting ready

In order to follow the recipe, you should download the material for this chapter: a script for creating and loading the database, and an Excel file with the list of categories involved.

After creating the outdoor database and loading data by running the script provided, explore the database before following the recipe. In particular, execute the following statement:

```
SELECT   category
    , COUNT(*) quantity
FROM     products p
JOIN     categories c ON p.id_category=c.id_category
WHERE    price<=50
GROUP BY p.id_category;
+----------------+----------+
| category       | quantity |
+----------------+----------+
| kitchen        |       19 |
| lights         |       14 |
| sleeping bags  |        5 |
| tents          |        4 |
| tools          |        8 |
+----------------+----------+
5 rows in set (0.00 sec)


SELECT   category
    , COUNT(*) quantity
FROM     products p
JOIN categories c ON p.id_category=c.id_category
WHERE    price>50
GROUP BY p.id_category;
+----------------+----------+
| category       | quantity |
```

```
+----------------+----------+
| kitchen        |        5 |
| lights         |        1 |
| sleeping bags  |        1 |
| tents          |        8 |
| tools          |        2 |
+----------------+----------+
5 rows in set (0.00 sec)
```

The highlighted lines belong to the products that you intend to delete.

How to do it...

1. Create a transformation.

2. The value to which you will compare the price before deleting will be stored as a **named parameter**. So right-click within the transformation and select **Transformation settings**. Switch to the **Parameters** tab and create a parameter named MAX_PRICE. Set the default value to 50.

3. Drag to the canvas an **Excel Input** step to read the Excel file with the list of categories.

4. Drag to the canvas a **Get Variables** step to get the named variable as a field named max_price with type Number.

5. After that, add a **Database lookup** step. Configure it to get the id_category fields based on the category descriptions in the Excel file. So far, the transformation looks like the following:

For higher volumes, it's better to get the variable just once in a separate stream and join the two streams with a **Join Rows (Cartesian product)** step.

6. Select the **Database lookup** step and do a preview. You should see the following:

∧	#	category	max_price	id_category
	1	tents	50.00	4
	2	tools	50.00	5
	3			

Rows of step: lk category (2 rows)

7. Finally, add a **Delete** step. You will find it under the **Output** category of steps.

8. Double-click on the **Delete** step, select the outdoor connection, and fill in the key grid as follows:

The key(s) to look up the value(s):

∧	#	Table field	Comparator	Stream field1	Stream field2
	1	id_category	=	id_category	
	2	price	<=	max_price	

9. Save and run the transformation.

10. Explore the database. If you run the same statements that you ran before starting the recipe, you'll note that all products belonging to the categories in the Excel file with price less than or equal to $50 have been deleted. The following is what you will see:

```
SELECT   category
     , COUNT(*) quantity
FROM     products p
JOIN     categories c ON p.id_category=c.id_category
WHERE    price<=50
GROUP BY p.id_category;
+----------------+----------+
| category       | quantity |
+----------------+----------+
| kitchen        |       19 |
| lights         |       14 |
| sleeping bags  |        5 |
+----------------+----------+
3 rows in set (0.00 sec)
```

```
SELECT    category
       , COUNT(*) quantity
FROM      products p                          '
JOIN   categories c ON p.id_category=c.id_category
WHERE     price>50
GROUP BY p.id_category;
+---------------+----------+
| category      | quantity |
+---------------+----------+
| kitchen       |        5 |
| lights        |        1 |
| sleeping bags |        1 |
| tents         |        8 |
| tools         |        2 |
+---------------+----------+
5 rows in set (0.00 sec)
```

How it works...

The **Delete** step allows you to delete rows in a table in a database based on certain conditions. In this case, you intended to delete rows from the table `products` where the price was less than or equal to 50, and the category was in a list of categories, so the **Delete** step is the right choice. This is how it works:

PDI builds a prepared statement for the `DELETE` operation. Then, for each row in your stream, PDI binds the values of the row to the variables in the prepared statement.

Let's see it by example. In the transformation you built a stream where each row had a single category and the value for the price.

If you run the transformation with the log level **Detailed** and look at the log, you will see the statement that is executed:

```
DELETE FROM products
WHERE price < ?
AND id_category = ?
```

The `WHERE` clause is built based on the conditions you entered in the **Delete configuration** window. For every row, the values of the fields you typed in the grid—`max_price` and `id_category`—are bound to the question marks in the prepared statement.

Note that the conditions in the **Delete** step are based on fields in the same table. In this case, as you were provided with category descriptions and the `products` table that does not have the descriptions but the ID for the categories, you had to use an extra step to get that ID—a Database lookup.

Suppose that the first row in the Excel file had the value `tents`. As the ID for the category `tents` is 4, the execution of the prepared statement with the values in this row has the same effect as the execution of the following SQL statement:

```
DELETE FROM products
WHERE price < 50
AND id_category = 4
```

See also

▸ The *Looking for values in a database table* recipe in *Chapter 6, Looking for Data*

Creating or altering a database table from PDI (design time)

It's not uncommon that someone asks you to load a table that doesn't exist yet. The following are some use cases:

▸ You receive a flat file and have to load the full content in a temporary table

▸ You have to create and load a dimension table with data coming from another database

You could write a `CREATE TABLE` statement from scratch and then create the transformation that loads the table, or you could do all that in an easier way from Spoon.

In this case, suppose that you received a file with data about countries and the languages spoken in those countries. You need to load the full content into a temporary table. The table doesn't exist and you have to create it based on the content of the file.

Getting ready

In order to follow the instructions, you will need the `countries.xml` file available for downloads from the book's site.

How to do it...

Perform the following steps to create or alter a database table:

1. Create a transformation and create a connection to the database where you will save the data.

2. In order to read the `countries.xml` file, use a **Get data from XML** step. As **Loop XPath** type `/world/country/language`.

3. Fill the **Fields** grid as follows:

| File | Content | Fields | Additional output fields |

∧	#	Name	XPath	Element	Result type	Type	Fo	Le	Pre	C	De	Gr	Trim type	Repeat
	1	country	../name	Node	Value of	String							none	N
	2	capital	../capital	Node	Value of	String							none	N
	3	language	name	Node	Value of	String							none	N
	4	isofficial	@isofficial	Attribute	Value of	String							none	N

 The @ symbol preceding the field `isofficial` is optional. By selecting **Attribute** as **Element**, Kettle automatically understands that this is an attribute.

4. From the **Output** category, drag-and-drop a **Table Output** step into the transformation.

5. Create a hop from the **Get data from XML** step to this new step.

6. Double-click on the **Table Output** step and select the connection you just created.

7. In the **Target table** textbox type `countries_stage`.

8. Click on the **SQL** button. A window will appear with the following script:

```
CREATE TABLE countries_stage
(
  country TINYTEXT
, capital TINYTEXT
, language TINYTEXT
, isofficial TINYTEXT
)
;
```

 The syntax may be different for different DBMSs.

9. Because you know that `isofficial` is just a simple flag with values `Y/N`, replace `isofficial TINYTEXT` with `isofficial CHAR(1)`.

10. After clicking on **Execute**, a window will show up telling that the statement has been executed, that is, the table has been created.

11. Save and run the transformation. All the information coming from the XML file is saved into the table just created.

How it works...

PDI allows you to create or alter tables in your databases depending on the tasks implemented in your transformations or jobs. To understand what this is about, let's explain the previous example.

A **Table Output** step causes Kettle to execute an INSERT statement against the database. The insert is made based on the data coming to the **Table Output** and the data you put in the **Table Output** configuration window, for example, the name of the table or the mapping of the fields.

When you click on the **SQL** button in the **Table Output setting** window, this is what happens: Kettle builds the statements needed to execute that insert successfully. As in this example, the table doesn't exist, and hence the statement generated by clicking on the button is a CREATE TABLE statement.

When the window with the generated statement appeared, you executed it. This caused the table to be created, so you could safely run the transformation and insert into the new table the data coming from the file to the step.

There's more...

The **SQL** button is present in several database-related steps. In all cases, its purpose is the same: to determine the statements to be executed in order to run the transformation successfully. In the recipe, the statement was a CREATE TABLE, but there are other situations. The following are some examples:

- ▶ If you use an **Insert/Update** step and fill the **Update fields:** grid with a field that doesn't exist, Kettle generates an ALTER TABLE statement in order to add that field as a new column in the table.

- ▶ If you use an **Update** step and use the names of columns that are not indexed in the **The key(s) to look up the value(s):** grid type, Kettle generates a CREATE INDEX statement.

> Note that in this case, the execution of the statement is not mandatory but recommended.

- ▶ If you use a **Dimension Lookup/Update** step in order to load a *slowly changing dimension*, Kettle generates a CREATE TABLE statement including all the fields that are needed in order to keep that kind of dimension updated. **Slowly changing dimensions** are a data warehousing construct that stores historical data and keeps versions of the data in the same table.

You can execute the SQL as it is generated, you can modify it before executing it (as you did in the recipe), or you can just ignore it. Sometimes the SQL generated includes dropping a column just because the column exists in the table but is not used in the transformation. In that case you shouldn't execute it.

[💡 Read the generated statement carefully, before executing it.]

Finally, you must know that if you run the statement from outside Spoon, in order to see the changes inside the tool you either have to clear the cache by right-clicking on the database connection and selecting the **Clear DB Cache** option, or restart Spoon.

See also

▸ *Creating or altering a database table from PDI (runtime)*

Creating or altering a database table from PDI (runtime)

When you are developing with PDI, you know (or have the means to find out) if the tables you need exist or not, and if they have all the columns you will read or update. If they don't exist or don't meet your requirements, you can create or modify them, and then proceed. Assume the following scenarios:

▸ You need to load some data into a temporary table. The table exists but you need to add some new columns to it before proceeding.

▸ You have to load a dimension table. This task is part of a new requirement, so this table doesn't exist.

While you are creating the transformations and jobs, you have the chance to create or modify those tables. But, if these transformations and jobs are to be run in batch mode in a different environment, nobody will be there to do these verifications or create or modify the tables. You need to adapt your work so these things are done automatically.

Suppose that you need to do some calculations and store the results in a temporary table that will be used later in another process. As this is a new requirement, it is likely that the table doesn't exist in the target database. You can create a job that takes care of this.

How to do it...

1. Create a job, and add a **Start job** entry.

2. From the **Conditions** category, drag-and-drop a **Table exists** entry, an **SQL** entry from **Scripting**, and a **DUMMY** entry from **General**.

3. Link all the entries as shown:

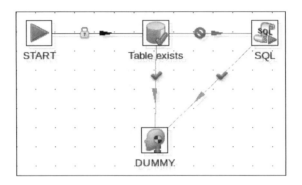

4. Double-click on the **Table exists** entry, choose the books database connection, and as **Table name** type my_tmp_table.

5. Double-click on the **SQL** entry, choose the same database connection, and in the **SQL Script:** type the following:

```
CREATE TABLE my_tmp_table (
CALC_1 NUMERIC(10,2),
CALC_2 NUMERIC(10,2),
CALC_3 NUMERIC(10,2)
);
```

 The preceding statement is written with MySQL syntax. Please review and fix it if needed, because you are using a different DBMS.

6. Save the job and run it.

7. The table my_tmp_table should have been created.

8. Run the job again.

9. Nothing should happen.

How it works...

The **Table exists** entry, as implied by its name, verifies if a table exists in your database. As with any job entry, this entry either succeeds or fails. If it fails, the job creates the table with an **SQL** entry. If it succeeds, the job does nothing.

There's more...

The **SQL entry** is very useful, not only for creating tables as you did in the recipe, but also for executing very simple statements, as for example, setting a flag before or after running a transformation. Its main use, however, is executing DDL statements.

On the other side, in order to decide if it was necessary to create the table or not, you used a **Table exists** entry. In addition to this entry and before verifying the existence of the table, you could have used the **Check Db connections**. This entry allows you to see if the database is available.

Now, let's suppose the table exists, but it is an old version that doesn't have all the columns you need. In this case you can use an extra useful entry: **Columns exist in a table**. If you can detect that a column is not present, you can alter the table by adding that column, also with an **SQL** job entry.

 Creating or altering tables is not a task that should be done as part of a regular ETL process. Kettle allows you to do it but you should be careful when using these features.

See also

▶ *Creating or altering a database table from PDI (design time)*

Inserting, deleting, or updating a table depending on a field

PDI allows you to perform basic operations that modify the data in your tables, that is: insert, update, and delete records. For each of those operations you have at least one step that allows you to do the task. It may happen that you have to do one or another operation depending on the value of a field. That is possible with a rather unknown step named **Synchronize after merge**.

Suppose you have a database with books. You received a file with a list of books. In that list there are books you already have and there are books you don't have.

For the books you already have, you intend to update the prices.

Among the other books, you will insert in your database only those which have been published recently. You will recognize them because they have the text NEW in the **Comment** field.

Getting ready

For this recipe, you will need the database which can be created and filled by running the script books_2.sql. You also will need the file books_news.txt that accompanies the material for this chapter.

As the recipe will modify the data in the database, before proceeding, explore the database to see what is inside. In particular, run the following statements and pay attention to the results:

```
SELECT count(*)
FROM    books;
+----------+
| count(*) |
+----------+
|       34 |
+----------+
1 row in set (0.00 sec)


SELECT id_title, title, price
FROM    books
WHERE   author_id='A00001';
+----------+-----------------------------------------+-------+
| id_title | title                                   | price |
+----------+-----------------------------------------+-------+
| 123-400  | The Girl with the Dragon Tattoo         |    37 |
| 123-401  | The Girl who Played with Fire           |  35.9 |
| 123-402  | The Girl who Kicked the Hornett's Nest  |    39 |
+----------+-----------------------------------------+-------+
3 rows in set (0.00 sec)


SELECT *
FROM    books
WHERE   title="Mockingjay";


Empty set (0.00 sec)
```

How to do it...

1. Create a new transformation and create a connection to the `books` database.

2. Drop a **Text file input** step to the canvas and use the step to read the `books_news.txt` file. As separator, type `|`. Read all fields as `String` except the price that has to be read as a `Number` with `0.00` as the **Format**.

3. Do a preview to verify you have read the file properly. You should see the following:

Rows of step: book_news (10 rows)

#	code	genre	title	author	comment	price
1	123-400	Fiction	The Girl with the Dragon Tattoo	Larsson, Stieg	In Stock	34.98
2	123-401	Fiction	The Girl Who Played with Fire	Larsson, Stieg	In Stock	35.99
3	123-402	Fiction	The Girl Who Kicked the Hornet's Nest	Larsson, Stieg	In Stock	37.99
4	123-602	Fiction	Freedom: A Novel	Franzen,Jonathan	In Stock	28.00
5	223-655	Non-fiction	Eat, Pray, Love: One Woman's Search fo	Gilbert, Elizabeth	NEW	36.00
6	223-701	Non-fiction	A Journey: My Political Life	Blair,Tony	NEW	35.00
7	323-609	Non-fiction	The Business of the 21st Century	Kiyosaki,Robert	NEW	24.45
8	523-110	Teens	Mockingjay	Collins, Suzanne	NEW	37.99
9	523-111	Teens	Catching Fire	Collins, Suzanne	In Stock	37.99
10	523-112	Teens	The Hunger Games	Collins, Suzanne	In Stock	37.99

4. Use a **Split Fields** step to split the name field into two: `firstname` and `lastname`.

5. Use a **Database lookup** step to look up in the `authors` table for an author that matches the `firstname` and `lastname` fields. As the value for **Values to return from the lookup table:** add `id_author`.

6. Check the option **Do not pass the row if the lookup fails** and close the window.

7. From the **Output** category of steps drag-and-drop a **Synchronize after merge** step to the canvas and create a hop from the last step toward this one. Your transformation looks like the following:

8. Double-click on the step. For the **Connection** field, select the **books** connection. As **Target table**, type `books`.

9. Fill the grids as shown:

The key(s) to look up the value(s):

#	Table field	Comparator	Stream field1	Stream field2	
1	id_title	=	code		Get fields
2	id_author	=	id_author		

Update fields:

#	Table field	Stream field	Update	
1	id_title	code	N	Get update fields
2	id_author	id_author	N	Edit mapping
3	genre	genre	N	
4	title	title	N	
5	price	price	Y	

Remember that you can avoid typing by clicking on the **Get Fields** and **Get update fields** buttons to the right-hand side.

10. Select the **Advanced** tab.

11. As **Operation fieldname**, select **comment**. As **Insert when value equal**, type NEW. As **Update when value equal**, type In Stock. Leave the other fields blank.

12. Close the window and save the transformation.

13. Then run the transformation.

14. Explore the database again. In particular, run for the second time the same statements you ran before doing the recipe. Now you will get the following:

```
SELECT count(*)

FROM    books;

+----------+
| count(*) |
+----------+
|       38 |
+----------+
1 row in set (0.00 sec)


SELECT id_title, title, price

FROM    books
```

```
WHERE   author_id='A00001';
+----------+-------------------------------------+-------+
| id_title | title                               | price |
+----------+-------------------------------------+-------+
| 123-400  | The Girl with the Dragon Tattoo     | 34.98 |
| 123-401  | The Girl who Played with Fire       | 35.99 |
| 123-402  | The Girl who Kicked the Hornett's Nest | 37.99 |
+----------+-------------------------------------+-------+
3 rows in set (0.00 sec)


SELECT *
FROM    books
WHERE   title="Mockingjay";
+----------+------------+-----------+-------+-------+
| id_title | title      | id_author | price | genre |
+----------+------------+-----------+-------+-------+
| 523-110  | Mockingjay | A00012    | 37.99 | Teens |
+----------+------------+-----------+-------+-------+
1 row in set (0.00 sec)
```

How it works...

The **Synchronize after merge** step allows you to insert, update, or delete rows in a table based on the value of a field in the stream. In the recipe, you used the **Synchronize after merge** step both for inserting the new books (for example, `Mockingjay`) and for updating the prices for the books you already had (for example, `The Girl with the Dragon Tattoo`).

In order to tell PDI whether to execute an insert or an update, you used the field `comment`. Under the **Advanced** tab, you told PDI that it should insert the records where the comment was equal to `NEW`, and update those where the comment was `In Stock`.

Note that, because you didn't intend to delete rows, you left the **Delete when value equal** option blank. However, you could also have configured this option in the same way you configured the others. An example of that, could be deleting the books that will stop being published. If there are books that match the `out of market criteria`, you could type `out of market` in the **Delete when value equal** option and those books would be deleted.

The inserts and updates were made based on the fields you entered in the grids under the **General** tab, which work exactly as the grids in an **Insert/Update** or an **Update** step.

There's more...

Let's see a little more about the step you used in this recipe.

Insert, update, and delete all-in-one

The **Synchronize after merge** step is like an all-in-one step. It allows you to insert, update, and delete rows from a table all in a single step, based on a field present in the dataset. For each row, Kettle uses the value of that column to decide which of the three basic operations to execute. This happens as follows.

Suppose that the **Operation fieldname** is called op and the values that should cause an insert, update, or delete are NEW, In Stock, and Discontinued respectively:

Operation	How it works
Insert	The insert is made for all rows where the field op is equal to NEW. The insert is made based on the key fields just like in an **Insert/Update** step.
Update	The update is made for all rows where the field op is equal to the value In Stock. The update is made based on the key fields just like in an **Insert/Update** or an **Update** step.
Delete	The delete is made for all rows where the field op is equal to the value Discontinued. The delete is made based on the key fields just like in a **Delete** step. For delete operations, the content of the lower grid is ignored.

Synchronizing after merge

You may wonder what the name **Synchronize after merge** has to do with this, if you neither merged nor synchronized anything. The fact is that the step was named after the **Merge Rows (diff)** step, as those steps can perfectly be used together. The **Merge Rows (diff)** step has the ability to find differences between two streams, and those differences are used later to update a table by using a **Synchronize after merge** step.

See also

▸ *Deleting data from a table*

▸ The *Comparing two streams and generating differences* recipe in *Chapter 7, Understanding and Optimizing Data Flows*

Changing the database connection at runtime

Sometimes, you have several databases with exactly the same structure serving different purposes. These are some situations:

▶ A database for the information that is being updated daily and one or more databases for historical data.

▶ A different database for each branch of your business.

▶ A database for your sandbox, a second database for the staging area, and a third database fulfilling the production server purpose.

In any of those situations, it's likely that you need access to one or the other depending on certain conditions, or you may even have to access all of them one after the other. Not only that, the number of databases may not be fixed; it may change over time (for example, when a new branch is opened).

Suppose you face the second scenario: your company has several branches, and the sales for each branch are stored in a different database. The database structure is the same for all branches; the only difference is that each of them holds different data. Now you want to generate a file with the total sales for the current year in every branch.

Getting ready

Download the material for this recipe. You will find a sample file with database connections to three branches. It looks like the following:

```
branch,host,database
0001 (headquarters),localhost,sales2010
0002,183.43.2.33,sales
0003,233.22.1.97,sales
```

If you intend to run the transformation, modify the file so it points to real databases.

How to do it...

Perform the following steps to dynamically change database connections:

1. Create a transformation that uses a **Text file input** step that reads the file with the connection data.

2. Add a **Copy rows to results** step to the transformation. Create a hop going from **Text file input** to **Copy rows to results**.

3. Create a second transformation and define the following **named parameters**: BRANCH, HOST_NAME, and DATABASE_NAME. Named parameters can be created by right-clicking on the transformation and selecting **Transformation settings**. Switch to the **Parameters** tab and enter the named parameters.

4. Create a database connection. Choose the proper **Connection Type:**, and fill the **Settings** data. Type a value for the **Port Number:**, the **User Name:**, and the **Password** fields. As **Host Name:** type ${HOST_NAME}, and as **Database Name:** type ${DATABASE_NAME}.

5. Use a **Table Input** step for getting the total sales from the database. Use the connection just defined.

6. Use a **Text file output** step for sending the sales summary to a text file. Don't forget to check the option **Append under the Content** tab of the setting window.

7. Create a job with two **Transformation** job entries, linked one after the other.

8. Use the first entry to call the first transformation you created and the second entry to call the second transformation. The job looks like the following:

9. Double-click on the second transformation entry, select the **Advanced** tab, and check the **Copy previous results to parameters?** and the **Execute for every input row?** checkboxes.

10. Select the **Parameters** tab and fill it as shown:

11. Save both transformations. Save the job and run it.

12. Open the generated text file. It should have one line with sales information for each database in the file with the list of databases.

How it works...

If you have to connect to several databases, and you don't know in advance which or how many databases you will have to connect to, you can't rely on a connection with fixed values or variables defined in a single place, for example, in the `kettle.properties` file (which is located in the Kettle home directory). In those situations, the best you could do is to define a connection with variables and set the values for the variables at runtime.

In the recipe, you created a text file with a summary sales line for each database in a list.

The transformation that wrote the sales line used a connection with variables defined as **named parameters**. This means that whoever calls the transformation has to provide the proper values.

The main job loops on the list of database connections. For each row in that list, it calls the transformation copying the values from the file to the parameters in the transformation. In other words, each time the transformation runs, the **named parameters** are instantiated with the values coming from the file.

There's more...

In the recipe, you changed the host and the name of the database. You could have parameterized any of the values that made up a database connection, for example, the username and password.

See also

- ▸ *Connecting to a database*
- ▸ The *Executing part of a job once for every row in a dataset* recipe in *Chapter 8, Executing and Re-using Jobs and Transformations*

Loading a parent-child table

A **parent-child table** is a table in which there is a self-referencing relationship. In other words, there is a hierarchical relationship among its rows. A typical example of this is a table with employees, in which one of the columns contains references to the employee that is above each employee in the hierarchy.

In this recipe you will load the parent-child table of the employees of Steel Wheels. The hierarchy of roles in Steel Wheels is as follows:

  ▸   A sales representative reports to a sales manager

  ▸   A sales manager reports to the vice-president

  ▸   A vice-president reports to the president

  ▸   The president is the highest level in the hierarchy. There is a single employee with this role

You will load all employees from a file. The following are the sample rows in that file:

```
EMPLOYEENUMBER|LASTNAME|FIRSTNAME|EXTENSION|EMAIL|OFFICECODE|JOBTITLE
|REP_TO

1002|Murphy|Diane|x5800|dmurphy@classicmodelcars.com |1|President|

1056|Patterson|Mary|x4611|mpatterso@classicmodelcars.com |1|VP
Sales|dmurphy@classicmodelcars.com

1076|Firrelli|Jeff|x9273|jfirrelli@classicmodelcars.com |1|VP
Marketing|dmurphy@classicmodelcars.com

1088|Patterson|William|x4871|wpatterson@classicmodelcars.com |6|Sales
Manager (JAPAN, APAC)|mpatterso@classicmodelcars.com

. . .
```

As you can see, among the fields you have the e-mail of the employee who is above in the hierarchy. For example, `Gerar Bondur` is a `Sales Manager`, and reports to the employee with e-mail `mpatterso@classicmodelcars.com`, that is, `Mary Patterson`.

Getting ready

In order to run this recipe, either truncate the `employees` table in Steel Wheels, or create the table `employees` in a different database.

How to do it...

1. Create a transformation that inserts the record for the president who is first in the hierarchy and doesn't report to anyone. The transformation should read the file, filter the record with `JOBTITLE=President`, and insert the data into the `employees` table.

2. Create another transformation to load the rest of the employees. Define a named parameter named `LEVEL` that will represent the role of the employees being loaded.

3. Use a **Text file input** step to read the file of employees.

4. Use a **Get Variables** step to add the variable LEVEL as a new field named level.

5. Use a **Join rows** step to merge the employee data with the level the transformation will be filtering on. Leave the **condition** field empty so that the level from the **Get Variables** step will be added to each record.

6. Add a **Filter rows** step to filter the employees to load based on their role. In order to do that, enter the following condition: JOBTITLE REGEXP level.

7. Add a **Database lookup** step to find out the employee number of the employee who is one above in the hierarchy. In the upper grid, add a row with the condition EMAIL = REP_TO. Use the lower grid to get the field EMPLOYEENUMBER and rename it to REPORTSTO.

8. Add a **Dummy** step to send employee records that do not have an employee record parent to. This step will act as an **error handling** step.

9. Add a **Table Output** step and use it to insert the records in the table employees. Your final transformation looks like the following:

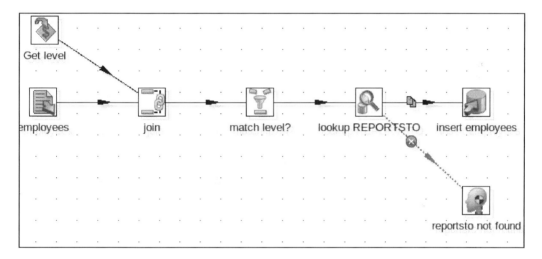

10. Finally, create a job to put everything together. Drag a **START** entry and four **Transformation** job entries to the work area. Link all of them in a row.

11. Use the first **Transformation** entry to execute the transformation that loads the president.

12. Double-click on the second **Transformation** entry and configure it to run the transformation that loads the other employees. Under the **Parameters** tab, add a parameter named LEVEL with value VP.*.

13. Repeat step 12 for the third **Transformation** entry, but this time, type .*Manager.* as the value for the LEVEL parameter.

14. Repeat step 12 for the fourth **Transformation** entry, but this time, type `Sales Rep.*` as the value for the `LEVEL` parameter.

15. Save and run the job. The table should have all employees loaded, as you can see in the following query:

```
SELECT
    EMPLOYEENUMBER N
  , LASTNAME
  , REPORTSTO
  , JOBTITLE
FROM employees;
```

```
+------+-----------+-----------+---------------------------+
| N    | LASTNAME  | REPORTSTO | JOBTITLE                  |
+------+-----------+-----------+---------------------------+
| 1002 | Murphy    |      NULL | President                 |
| 1056 | Patterson |      1002 | VP Sales                  |
| 1076 | Firrelli  |      1002 | VP Marketing              |
| 1088 | Patterson |      1056 | Sales Manager (JAPAN, APAC)|
| 1102 | Bondur    |      1056 | Sale Manager (EMEA)       |
| 1143 | Bow       |      1056 | Sales Manager (NA)        |
| 1165 | Jennings  |      1143 | Sales Rep                 |
| 1166 | Thompson  |      1143 | Sales Rep                 |
| 1188 | Firrelli  |      1143 | Sales Rep                 |
| ...  | ...       |      ...  | ...                       |
+------+-----------+-----------+---------------------------+
23 rows in set (0.00 sec)
```

How it works...

If you have to load a table with parent-child relationships, loading all at once is not always feasible. Look at the `sampledata` database. There is no physical foreign key from the `REPORTSTO` column to the `EMPLOYEENUMBER` column, but if the foreign key had existed, it would fail because of the foreign key constraint. Not only that; in this case loading all at once would be impossible because in the file you missed the ID of the parent employee loading all records needed for the `REPORTSTO` column.

So, in this recipe there was one possible solution for loading the table. We loaded all employees, one role at a time, beginning with the president and followed by the roles below in the hierarchy. The transformation that loaded the other roles simply read the file, kept only the employees with the role being loaded, looked for the ID of the parent employee in the hierarchy, and inserted the records. For the roles you could have used fixed values, but you used regular expressions instead. In doing so, you avoided calling the transformation once for each different role. For example, for loading the vice-presidents you called the transformation once with the regular expression VP.* which matched both VP Sales and VP Marketing.

See also

▸   *Inserting or updating rows in a table*

Building SQL queries via database metadata

While working with source database systems, developers have to remain constantly vigilant for new system changes as they happen. Utilizing the source metadata that can be found within the database system can help generate SQL statements that remain constantly up-to-date. This will allow for source data to be captured even if the rest of an ETL transformation fails due to the new changes.

In this recipe you will create a dynamic data extracting transformation that will extract data from the books database created earlier in the chapter.

Getting ready

For this recipe you will need the database which can be created and filled by running the script books.sql. This can be found in the code for this chapter.

As the recipe will read metadata from the books database, before proceeding, explore the database's metadata repository to see what is inside. In particular, run these statements and pay attention to the results:

```
SELECT
    TABLE_NAME
  , TABLE_TYPE
  , ENGINE
  , VERSION
  , ROW_FORMAT
  , TABLE_ROWS
  , AVG_ROW_LENGTH
  , DATA_LENGTH
```

```
FROM information_schema.TABLES
WHERE TABLE_SCHEMA = 'books';
```

TABLE_NAME	TABLE_TYPE	ENGINE	VERSION	ROW_FORMAT	TABLE_ROWS	AVG_ROW_LENGTH	DATA_LENGTH
authors	BASE TABLE	InnoDB	10	Compact	13	1260	16384
books	BASE TABLE	InnoDB	10	Compact	34	481	16384

```
2 rows in set (0.00 sec)

SELECT
    TABLE_NAME
    , COLUMN_NAME
    , ORDINAL_POSITION
    , COLUMN_DEFAULT
    , IS_NULLABLE
    , DATA_TYPE
FROM information_schema.COLUMNS
WHERE TABLE_SCHEMA = 'books';
```

TABLE_NAME	COLUMN_NAME	ORDINAL_POSITION	COLUMN_DEFAULT	IS_NULLABLE	DATA_TYPE
authors	lastname	1	NULL	NO	tinytext
authors	firstname	2	NULL	NO	tinytext
authors	nationality	3	unknown	YES	varchar

authors int	birthyear	4	1900	YES
authors char	id_author	5	NULL	NO
books char	id_title	1	NULL	NO
books tinytext	title	2	NULL	NO
books tinytext	id_author	3	NULL	NO
books double	price	4	0	YES
books varchar	genre	5	unknown	YES

```
+--------------+-----------+------------------+---------------+-------
------+----------+
```

10 rows in set (0.00 sec)

The preceding statement is written with the MySQL syntax. Please review and fix it if needed if you are using a different DBMS.

Compare how the data in the `information_schema` database matches the `CREATE DDL` statements found in the `books.sql` file. Notice how the same parameters in the statements used to create the tables translate into the `TABLES` and `COLUMNS` tables.

How to do It...

1. Create a new transformation and add a **Table Input** step that can connect to the `information_schema` database.

2. Create a query that selects the `TABLE_NAME` and `COLUMN_NAME` columns from the `COLUMNS` table, making sure to filter only on the `books TABLE_SCHEMA`.

3. Add a constant value using the **Add constants** step found under the **Transform** category. The value should be named `grouper` with type `Integer` and value of `1`. Create a hop from the **Table Input** step to the **Add constants** step:

4. Add a **Denormaliser** step found under the **Transform** category. The **Key field** should be the **grouper** column created in the last step. The **Group field** should be TABLE_NAME. Fill in the **Target fields:** information like the following:

The fields that make up the grouping:		
^	#	Group field
	1	TABLE_NAME

Target fields:													
^	#	Target fieldname	Value fieldname	Key	Type	Fo	Le	Pr	Cu	De	G	N	Aggregation
	1	TABLE_COLUMNS	COLUMN_NAME	1	String								Concatenate strings separated by ,

5. Preview the **Denormaliser** step. For each table in the books database, you should see a record with a comma-separated list of column names.

Rows of step: Row denormaliser (3 rows)		
^	#	TABLE_NAME	TABLE_COLUMNS
	1	authors	lastname,firstname,nationality,birthyear,id_author
	2	books	genre,price,id_author,title,id_title

6. Now finish this transformation by adding a **Copy rows to result** step and create a hop from the **Row denormaliser** step to the **Copy rows to result** step.

7. Since we will be building a SQL query from these columns, the simplest way will be to use them as variables. Variables can not be used in the same transformation as they are set, plus we will have multiple sets of variables, so we need to create a sub job and a parent job. Sub jobs are jobs within other jobs. Let's continue building the transformations needed and then we will build the two jobs required to run this process.

8. Create a second transformation. Add a **Table Input** step that will use the variables we will be creating from the data in the first transformation. Be sure to select the **Replace variables in script?** checkbox. The query should look like the following:

```
SELECT ${column_list_par}
FROM ${table_name_par}
```

9. Add a **Text file output** step. For the **Filename** field, point to a location where the database table extracts can be dumped to. The **Filename** can also use parameters. Use the table_name_par as the file's name. The **Text file output** step will store whatever data is in the stream without declaring any **Fields**, so leave the **Fields** tab empty.

10. Create one last transformation that will use the **Get rows from result** step and load the variables `column_list_par` and `table_name_par` with the **Set Variables** step. The **Set Variables** step should be filled in like the following:

Field values:

∧	#	Field name	Variable name	Variable scope type
	1	TABLE_NAME	table_name_par	Valid in the root job
	2	TABLE_COLUMNS	column_list_par	Valid in the root job

11. Create a job. This will be the sub job that will take each record and execute a query. Bring over a **START** step, two **Transformation** steps, and a **Success** step. The first **Transformation** step should point to the transformation that sets the parameters used in the query. The second **Transformation** step should point to the transformation that uses the parameters and extracts the query output into a text file. This job should look similar to the following:

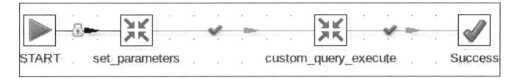

12. Create another job. This will be the parent job to the whole process. Bring over a **START** step, a **Transformation** step, a **Job** step, and a **Success** step. The **Transformation** step should point to the transformation that is extracting data from the `information_schema` database. The **Job** step will be pointing to the job we created previously. Make sure that the **Execute for every input row?** checkbox is checked under the **Advanced** tab for the job. Your final job should look similar to the following:

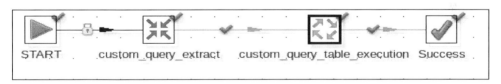

13. Now execute the parent job. There should be a number of text files with an output equal to the number of tables in the `books` database.

How it works...

Most databases have a metadata repository that details tables and columns. This can be used to build dynamic queries to extract data for further processing. In this instance, once the `books` database was created, the database application stored the metadata inside the `information_schema` database. We then queried that database and used a **Row denormaliser** step to merge the column details into a single field so that our query would execute properly.

See also

> ▸ *Getting data from a database by providing parameters*

> ▸ *Getting data from a database by running a query built at runtime*

> ▸ *Performing repetitive database design tasks from PDI*

> ▸ The *Executing part of a job once for every row in a dataset* recipe in *Chapter 8, Executing and Re-using Jobs and Transformations*

Performing repetitive database design tasks from PDI

While we have cautioned that database design tasks should not normally be performed using PDI, sometimes there are certain tasks that are very repetitive and it can save a lot of time by creating a simple transformation to execute such tasks. For instance, maybe there are some new auditing columns that need to be added to all the tables of a given database. With PDI, and using a database's metadata repository, it is very straightforward to add the columns.

In this recipe we will be creating a transformation that will read a list of tables from the `books` database in the database's metadata repository and build dynamic queries for each table.

Getting ready

For this recipe you will need the database which can be created and filled by running the script `books.sql`. This can be found in the code for this chapter.

As the recipe will read metadata from the `books` database, before proceeding, explore the database's metadata repository to see what is inside. In particular, run the following statement to see what tables are available in the `books` database:

```
SELECT
    TABLE_NAME
  , TABLE_TYPE
  , ENGINE
```

```
        , VERSION
        , ROW_FORMAT
        , TABLE_ROWS
        , AVG_ROW_LENGTH
        , DATA_LENGTH
FROM information_schema.TABLES
WHERE TABLE_SCHEMA = 'books';
```

```
+--------------+------------+--------+---------+------------+-----------
+----------------+------------+
| TABLE_NAME   | TABLE_TYPE | ENGINE | VERSION | ROW_FORMAT | TABLE_ROWS
| AVG_ROW_LENGTH | DATA_LENGTH |
+--------------+------------+--------+---------+------------+-----------
+----------------+------------+
| authors      | BASE TABLE | InnoDB |      10 | Compact    |         13
|           1260 |      16384 |
| books        | BASE TABLE | InnoDB |      10 | Compact    |         34
|            481 |      16384 |
+--------------+------------+--------+---------+------------+-----------
+----------------+------------+
2 rows in set (0.00 sec)
```

 The preceding statement and the following tutorial is written with MySQL syntax. Please review and fix it if needed because you are using a different DBMS.

How to do It...

1. Create a transformation. Add a **Table Input** step that reads the TABLE_NAME from the TABLES table from MySQL's information_schema database.

2. From the **Scripting** category, add an **Execute SQL script** step. Check the option **Execute for each row?** and add TABLE_NAME to the **Parameters:** section. For the **SQL script to execute**, use the following:

```
ALTER TABLE ?
    ADD COLUMN create_date DATETIME DEFAULT '1900-01-01 00:00:00',
    ADD COLUMN update_date TIMESTAMP DEFAULT CURRENT_TIMESTAMP ON
UPDATE CURRENT_TIMESTAMP
```

3. Create a hop between the **Table Input** and **Execute SQL script** steps. Save and run the transformation. When completed, check the tables in the `books` database. All of them should now have a `create_date` and an `update_date` column added.

How it works...

Using a database's metadata repository is a very powerful and effective way to know the structure of a given source database. With this transformation we took advantage of that by reading out a list of all the tables from the `books` database and ran a variable-based query that added two columns to each table based on the table name.

Try adding additional filters to specify certain tables from the `books` database. MySQL's `information_schema` database also has a table that details the columns of each table (aptly named COLUMNS). For larger databases, you may want to filter just a subset of tables based on given columns or types.

 While it has been stated before, it bears mentioning again that this technique must be used with extreme caution since it can drastically alter your database depending on the type of query executed!

See also

▸ *Getting data from a database by running a query built at runtime*

▸ The *Executing part of a job once for every row in a dataset* recipe in *Chapter 8, Executing and Re-using Jobs and Transformations*

▸ *Building SQL queries based on database metadata*

2
Reading and Writing Files

In this chapter we will cover:

- ▶ Reading a simple file
- ▶ Reading several files at the same time
- ▶ Reading semi-structured files
- ▶ Reading files having one field per row
- ▶ Reading files having some fields occupying two or more rows
- ▶ Writing a simple file
- ▶ Writing a semi-structured file
- ▶ Providing the name of a file (for reading or writing) dynamically
- ▶ Using the name of a file (or part of it) as a field
- ▶ Reading an Excel file
- ▶ Getting the value of specific cells in an Excel file
- ▶ Writing an Excel file with several sheets
- ▶ Writing an Excel file with a dynamic number of sheets
- ▶ Reading data from an AWS S3 Instance

Introduction

Files are the most primitive, but also the most used format to store and interchange data. PDI has the ability to read data from all kinds of files and different formats. It also allows you to write back to files in different formats as well.

Reading and writing simple files is a very straightforward task. There are several steps under the input and output categories of steps that allow you to do it. You pick the step, configure it quickly, and you are done. However, when the files you have to read or create are not simple—and that happens most of the time—the task of reading or writing can become a tedious exercise, if you don't know the tricks. In this chapter, you will learn not only the basics for reading and writing files, but also all the how-tos for dealing with them.

> This chapter covers plain files (`.txt`, `.csv`, and fixed width) and Excel files. For recipes on reading and writing XML files, refer to *Chapter 4, Manipulating XML Structures*.

Reading a simple file

In this recipe, you will learn the use of the *Text file input* step. In the example, you have to read a simple file with a list of authors' information like the following:

```
"lastname","firstname","country","birthyear"
"Larsson","Stieg","Swedish",1954
"King","Stephen","American",1947
"Hiaasen","Carl ","American",1953
"Handler","Chelsea ","American",1975
"Ingraham","Laura ","American",1964
```

Getting ready

In order to continue with the exercise, you must have a file named `authors.txt` similar to the one shown in the introduction section of this recipe.

How to do it...

Carry out the following steps:

1. Create a new transformation.

2. Drop a **Text file input** step to the canvas.

3. Now, you have to type the name of the file (`authors.txt`) with its complete path. You do it in the **File or directory** textbox.

Alternatively, you can select the file by clicking on the **Browse** button and looking for the file. The textbox will be populated with the complete path of the file.

4. Click on the **Add** button. The complete text will be moved from the **File or directory** textbox to the grid.

5. Select the **Content** tab and fill in the required fields, as shown in the following screenshot:

Filetype	CSV
Separator	,
Enclosure	"
Allow breaks in enclosed fields?	☐
Escape	
Header	☑ Number of header lines 1

 Depending on what operating system the file was created on, your format type will have to be changed. DOS is the default format, with Unix being for any of the *nix based operating systems. The format type can be changed on the **Content** tab under **Format**.

6. Select the **Fields** tab and click on the **Get Fields** button to get the definitions of the fields automatically. The grid will be populated, as shown in the following screenshot:

^	#	Name	Type
	1	lastname	String
	2	firstname	String
	3	country	String
	4	birthyear	String

 Kettle doesn't always guess the data types, size, or format as expected. So, after getting the fields, you may change the data to what you consider more appropriate.

When you read a file, it's not mandatory to keep the names of the columns as they are in the file. You are free to change the names of the fields as well.

7. Click on the **Preview** button and you will see some sample rows built with the data in your file.

How it works...

You use **Text file input** in order to read text files, in this case, the `authors.txt` file.

Looking at the content of the file, you can see that the first line contains the header of the columns. In order to recognize that header, you have to check the **Header** checkbox under the **Content** tab, and type `1` in the **Number of header lines** textbox. You also have to indicate the field's separator. The separator can be made of one or more characters; the most used being the semicolon, colon, or a tab. Finally, you can indicate the **Enclosure** string, in this case, **"**.PDI takes all that information and uses it to parse the text file and fill the fields correctly.

There's more...

To work with these kinds of delimited text files, you could choose the **CSV file input** step. This step has a less powerful configuration, but it provides a better performance.

If you explore the tabs of the **Text file input** setting window, you will see that there are more options to set, but the ones just explained are, by far, the most used. But, there are a couple of additional features that may interest you:

Alternative notation for a separator

Instead of typing the separator for the fields, you can use the following notation:

```
$[H1, H2, ...]
```

Where the values `H1`, `H2`, `...` are the hexadecimal codes for the separators. For example, for specifying a tilde (~) as the separator instead of typing it, you could type `$[7E]`. However, this notation makes more sense when your separators are non printable characters.

For the enclosure string, the hexadecimal notation is also allowed. Just follow the same rules listed for hexadecimal codes for separators.

About file format and encoding

If you are trying to read a file without success, and you have already checked the most common settings, that is, the name of the file, the header, the separator, and the fields, you should take a look at and try to fix the other available settings. Among those, you have **Format** and **Encoding**. Format allows you to specify the format of your file(s): **DOS** (default value) or **UNIX**. If your file has a Unix format, you should change this setting. If you don't know the format but you cannot guarantee that the format will be DOS, you can choose the **mixed** option. Encoding allows you to specify the character encoding to use. If you leave it blank, Kettle will use the default encoding on your system. Alternatively, if you know the encoding and it is different from the default, you should select the proper option from the drop-down list.

About data types and formats

When you read a file and tell Kettle which fields to get from that file, you have to provide at least a name and a data type for those fields. In order to tell Kettle how to read and interpret the data, you have more options. Most of them are self-explanatory, but the format, length, and precision deserve an explanation:

If you are reading a number, and the numbers in your file have separators, dollar signs, and so on, you should specify a format to tell Kettle how to interpret that number. The format is a combination of patterns and symbols, as explained in the Oracle Java API documentation at the following URL: `http://docs.oracle.com/javase/7/docs/api/java/text/DecimalFormat.html`.

If you don't specify a format for your numbers, you may still provide a length and precision. Length is the total number of significant figures, while precision is the number of floating point digits.

 If you don't specify format, length, or precision, Kettle will do its best to interpret the number, but this could lead to unexpected results.

In the case of dates, the same thing happens. When your text file has a date, you have to select or type a format mask, so Kettle can recognize the different components of the date in the field. For a complete reference on date formats, check the Oracle Java API documentation, located at the following URL: `http://docs.oracle.com/javase/7/docs/api/java/text/SimpleDateFormat.html`.

Altering the names, order, or metadata of the fields coming from the file

If you want to reorder or delete some of the columns you read, you have to add another step to the transformation. Suppose you want to move the `country` name to the end of the list of columns, changing it to a more suitable field name, such as `nationality`.

In this case, add a **Select values** step. The **Select values** step allows you to select, rename, reorder, and delete fields, or change the metadata of a field.

Under the **Select & Alter** tab, select all the fields and manipulate those according to your needs, as shown in the following example:

> If you just want to rename the columns, you don't need a **Select values** step. You can do it in the **Text file input** step by typing the names manually:

Fields :

∧	#	Fieldname	Rename to	Length	Precision
	1	lastname			
	2	firstname			
	3	birthyear			
	4	country	nationality		

Reading files with fixed width fields

In the example, you read a **CSV (Comma Separated Values)** file type. This is the default value for the type of file, as you can see under the **Content** tab. You have another option here named **Fixed** for reading files with fixed-width columns. If you choose this option, a different helper GUI will appear when you click on the **Get fields** button. In the wizard, you can visually set the position for each of your fields.

There is also another step named **Fixed file input** in the **Input** category to apply in these cases. It provides better performance and has a simpler, but less flexible configuration.

Reading several files at the same time

Sometimes, you have several files to read, all with the same structure, but different data. In this recipe, you will see how to read those files in a single step. The example uses a list of files containing names of museums in Italy.

Getting ready

You must have a group of text files in a directory, all with the same format. In this recipe, the names of these files start with `museums_italy_`, for example, `museums_italy_1`, `museums_italy_2`, `museums_italy_roma`, `museums_italy_genova`, and so on.

Each file has a list of names of museums, one museum on each line.

How to do it...

Carry out the following steps:

1. Create a new transformation.

2. Drop a **Text file input** step onto the work area.

3. Under the **File or directory** tab, type the directory where the files are.

4. In the **Regular Expression** textbox, type `museums_italy_.*\.txt`.

5. Then, click on the **Add** button. The grid will be populated, as shown in the following screenshot:

^	#	File/Directory	Wildcard (RegExp)
	1	${Internal.Transformation.Filename.Directory}\museums\	museums_italy_.*\.txt

> `${Internal.Transformation.Filename.Directory}` is a variable that will be replaced at runtime with the full path of the current transformation. Note that the variable will be undefined until you save the transformation. Therefore, it's necessary that you save before running a preview of the step. If you are running a script in multiple environments, it is recommended to set variables for the path instead of using `${Internal.Transformation.Filename.Directory}`. You don't have to type the complete name of the `${Internal.Transformation.Filename.Directory}` variable. It can be selected from a list automatically created when pressing *Ctrl + Space*.
>
> To set a variable, you can create a variable/value pair in the `kettle.properties` file, which is located in the Kettle home directory.

6. Under the **Fields** tab, add one row; type `museum` for the **Name** column and `String` under the **Type** column.

7. Save the transformation in the same place, where the `museum` directory is located. Previewing the step, you will obtain a dataset with the content of all files with the names of museums.

How it works...

With Kettle, it is possible to read more than one file at a time using a single **Text File Input** step.

In order to get the content of several files, you can add names to the grid row by row. If the names of files share the path and some part of their names, you can also specify the names of the files by using regular expressions, as shown in the recipe. If you enter a regular expression, Kettle will take all the files whose names match it. In the recipe, the files that matched `museums_italy_.*\.txt` were considered as input files.

`museums_italy_.*\.txt` means all the files starting with `museum_italy_` and having the TXT extension. You can test if the regular expression is correct by clicking on the **Show filename(s)...** button. That will show you a list of all files in that folder that match the expression. If you fill the grid with the names of several files (with or without using regular expressions), Kettle will create a dataset with the content of all of those files one after the other.

To learn more about regular expressions, you can visit the following URLs: `http://www.regular-expressions.info/quickstart.html` and `http://docs.oracle.com/javase/tutorial/essential/regex/`.

There's more...

In the recipe you read several files. It might happen that you have to read just one file, but you don't know the exact name of the file. One example of that is a file whose name is a fixed text followed by the current year and month as in `samplefile_201012.txt`. The recipe is useful in cases like that as well. In this example, if you don't know the name of the file, you will still be able to read it by typing the following regular expression: `samplefile_20[0-9][0-9](0[1-9]|1[0-2])\.txt`.

Reading semi-structured files

The simplest files for reading are those where all rows follow the same pattern: Each row has a fixed number of columns, and all columns have the same kind of data in every row. However, it is common to have files where the information does not have that format. On many occasions, the files have little or no structure. This is also called "semi-structured" formatting. Suppose you have a file with roller coaster descriptions, and the file looks like the following:

```
JOURNEY TO ATLANTIS
SeaWorld Orlando

Journey to Atlantis is a unique thrill ride since it is ...
Roller Coaster Stats
Drop: 60 feet
```

```
Trains: 8 passenger boats
Train Mfg: Mack

KRAKEN
SeaWorld Orlando

Named after a legendary sea monster, Kraken is a ...
Kraken begins with a plunge from a height of 15-stories ...
Roller Coaster Stats
Height: 151 feet
Drop: 144 feet
Top Speed: 65 mph
Length: 4,177 feet
Inversions: 7
Trains: 3 - 32 passenger
Ride Time: 2 minutes, 2 seconds

KUMBA
Busch Gardens Tampa
...
```

As you can see, the preceding file is far from being the typical structured file that you can read simply by configuring a **Text file input** step. Following this recipe, you will learn how to deal with this kind of file.

Getting ready

When you have to read an unstructured file, such as the preceding sample file, the first thing to do is to take a detailed look at it. Try to understand how the data is organized; despite being unstructured, it has a hidden format that you have to discover in order to be able to read it.

So, let's analyze the sample file, which is available for download from Packt's site.

The file has data about several roller coasters. Let's take note of the characteristics of the file:

 As a useful exercise, you could do this yourself before reading the following list.

Each roller coaster spans several lines. There are blank lines, which should be eliminated.

What allows us to distinguish the first line for each roller coaster from the rest, is that it is written in uppercase letters.

The first line below the name of the roller coaster is the name of the amusement park where it is located.

Most of the lines have a property of the roller coaster in the format of `code:description`, as for example `Drop: 60 feet`.

Above the properties, there is a line with the text `Roller Coaster Stats`, which doesn't add any information. It should be discarded.

There are lines with additional information about the roller coaster. There is nothing that distinguishes these lines. They simply do not fall into any of the other kinds of lines (lines with the name of the park, lines with properties of the roller coaster, and so on). Once you understand the content of your file, you are ready to read it, and parse it.

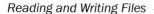
How to do it...

Carry out the following steps:

1. Create a transformation and drag a **Text file input** step.

2. Use that step to read the file named `rollercoasters_II.txt`. Under the **Content** tab, uncheck the **Header** option and under the **Separator** tab, type `|`. Under the **Fields** tab, enter a single field named `text` of type **String**. As the character `|` is not present in any part of the file, you are sure that the whole line will be read as a single field.

> Picking the right separator when building files can be tricky. Try to find the right character or characters that are never used within the dataset that is being stored.

3. From the **Scripting** category of steps, add a **Modified Java Script Value** step, double-click it, and under the Main tab window, type the following snippet of code:

```
var attraction;
trans_Status=CONTINUE_TRANSFORMATION;

if (getProcessCount('r') == 1) attraction = '';
if (text == upper(removeDigits(text))) {
    attraction = text;
    trans_Status=SKIP_TRANSFORMATION;
    }
else if (text == 'Roller Coaster Stats')
    trans_Status=SKIP_TRANSFORMATION;
```

4. Click on the **Get variables** button to populate the grid with the variable `attraction`.

5. From the **Transform** category, add an **Add value fields changing sequence** step. Create a hop from **Modified Java Script Value** to the step **Add value fields changing sequence**.

6. Double-click the step. As **Result field** type `line_nr`. In the first row of the grid, type `attraction`.

7. Do a preview on this last step. You will see the following:

#	text	attraction	line_nr
1	Disney's Magic Kingdom	BIG THUNDER MOUNTAIN RAILROAD	1
2	Height: 45 feet	BIG THUNDER MOUNTAIN RAILROAD	2
3	Top Speed: 30 mph	BIG THUNDER MOUNTAIN RAILROAD	3
4	Length: 2,780 feet	BIG THUNDER MOUNTAIN RAILROAD	4
5	Trains: 6 - 30 passenger	BIG THUNDER MOUNTAIN RAILROAD	5
6	Train Mfg: Walt Disney Imagineering	BIG THUNDER MOUNTAIN RAILROAD	6
7	Busch Gardens Tampa	CHEETAH CHASE	1
8	Busch Gardens' family roller coaster, Cheetah Chase, is located in	CHEETAH CHASE	2
9	Height: 46 feet	CHEETAH CHASE	3
10	Top Speed: 28 mph	CHEETAH CHASE	4
11	Length: 1,214 feet	CHEETAH CHASE	5

So far, you've read the file, and identified all the rows belonging to each roller coaster. It's time to parse the different lines. In the first place, let's parse the lines that contain properties:

1. Add a **Filter rows** step and enter the condition `text REGEXP (.+):(.+)`.

2. From the **Scripting** category, add a **Regex Evaluation** step. Create a hop from the **Filter rows** step to the **Regex Evaluation** step and make the hop be of the type **Main output of step.** This will pass all rows that match the condition in the **Filter rows** step.

3. Configure the step as follows: As **Field to evaluate** select **text**. Check the **Create fields for capture groups** option. As **Regular expression**: type `(.+):(.+)`.

4. Fill the lower grid with two rows: as **New field** type `code` in the first row and `desc` in the second. In both rows, under **Type**, select **String**, and under **Trim** select **both**.

5. Finally, add a **Select values** step to select the fields: `attraction`, `code`, `desc`, and `line_nr`.

> In order to do a preview to see how the steps are transforming your data, you can add a *Dummy* step and send the false rows of the *Filter rows* step towards it. The only purpose of this is to avoid the transformation crashing before the preview can complete.

Now, you will parse the other lines: the lines that contain the park name, and the additional comments:

1. Add another **Filter rows** step, and send the false rows of the other **Filter rows** step toward this one.

2. Add two **Add constants** steps, and a **Select values** step, and link all the steps, as shown in the following diagram:

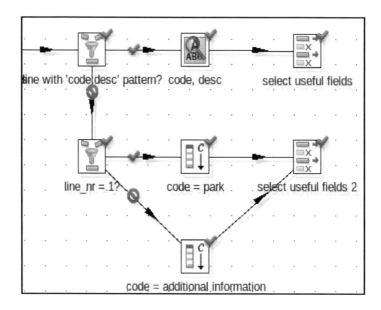

3. In the **Filter rows** enter the condition `line_nr=1`. Open the first **Add constants** step and add a String field named `code` with the value `park`. Make sure the true rows of the **Filter rows** step go toward this step.

4. In the other **Add constants** step, add a String field named `code` with the value `additional_information`. Make sure the false rows of the **Filter rows** step go toward this step. Use the **Select values** step that joins the two **Add constants** steps to select the fields `attraction`, `code`, `text`, and `line_nr`. In the same step, rename `text` as `desc`.

 Make sure that the fields are in this exact order. The metadata of both **Select values** steps must coincide.

Now that you have parsed all the types of rows it's time to join the rows together:

1. Join both **Select values** with a **Sort rows** step. Sort the rows by `attraction` and `line_nr`.

2. Select the **Sort rows** step and do a preview. You should see the following:

^	#	attraction	code	desc	line_nr
	1	BIG THUNDER MOUNTAIN RAILROAD	park	Disney's Magic Kingdom	1
	2	BIG THUNDER MOUNTAIN RAILROAD	Height	45 feet	2
	3	BIG THUNDER MOUNTAIN RAILROAD	Top Speed	30 mph	3
	4	BIG THUNDER MOUNTAIN RAILROAD	Length	2,780 feet	4
	5	BIG THUNDER MOUNTAIN RAILROAD	Trains	6 - 30 passenger	5
	6	BIG THUNDER MOUNTAIN RAILROAD	Train Mfg	Walt Disney Imagineering	6
	7	CHEETAH CHASE	park	Busch Gardens Tampa	1
	8	CHEETAH CHASE	additional_information	Busch Gardens' family roller coaster,	2
	9	CHEETAH CHASE	Height	46 feet	3
	10	CHEETAH CHASE	Top Speed	28 mph	4
	11	CHEETAH CHASE	Length	1,214 feet	5

How it works...

When you have a semi-structured file (a file with little to no real formatting), the first thing to do is understand its content, in order to be able to parse the file properly.

If the entities described in the file (roller coasters in this example) are spanned over several lines, the very first task is to identify the rows that make up a single entity. The usual method is to do it with a **JavaScript** step. In this example, with the JavaScript code, you used the fact that the first line of each roller coaster was written with uppercase letters, to create and add a field named `attraction`. In the same code, you removed unwanted lines.

In this example, as you needed to know which row was the first in each group, you added an **Add value fields changing sequence** step.

After doing this, which as noted is only necessary for a particular kind of file, you have to parse the lines. If the lines do not follow the same pattern, you have to split your stream in as many streams as kind of rows you have. In this example, you split the main stream into three, as follows:

1. One for parsing the lines with properties, for example, `Drop: 60 feet`.
2. One for setting the name of the amusement park where the roller coaster was.
3. One for keeping the additional information.

In each stream, you proceeded differently according to the format of the line.

The most useful step for parsing individual unstructured fields is the **Regexp Evaluation** step. It both validates if a field follows a given pattern (provided as a regular expression) and optionally, it captures groups. In this case, you used that step to capture a code and a description. In the preceding example (`Drop: 60 feet`), the **Regexp Evaluation** step allowed you to build two fields: `code` with value `Drop`, and `desc` with value `60 feet`.

Once you parsed the line with **Regexp Evaluation** or the step of your choice, you can continue transforming or modifying the fields according to your needs and the characteristics of your particular file. In the same way, depending on the purpose of your transformation, you can leave the streams separated or join them back together as you did in the recipe.

There's more...

There are some common kinds of files that can be parsed in the way you parsed the roller coasters' file:

Master/detail files

Suppose that you have a file of invoices such as the following:

```
INV.0001-0045;02/28/2010;$323.99
CSD-031;2;$34.00
CSA-110;1;$100.99
LSK-092;1;$189.00
INV.0001-0046;02/28/2010;$53.99
DSD-031;2;$13.00
CXA-110;1;$40.99
INV.0001-0047;02/28/2010;$1149.33
...
```

The lines beginning with `INV.` are the invoice headers; the lines following the headers are the details of those invoices.

Files like these are not uncommon. If you have a file like this with records that represent headers followed by records that represent details about those headers, and the header and detail records have different structures, you could parse it as explained in the recipe.

Read the file, do whatever is necessary to find out if a row is a header or a detail, and split the stream in two. After that, parse header rows and detail rows accordingly.

Logfiles

Logfiles are among the most common kinds of unstructured files. They are typically used to monitor processes, click-stream analysis, user downloads, and so on. Being able to process through the mountain of details produced can help identify what customers are looking at or what users are frequently doing on given websites. For example, let us look at the following sample lines belonging to a Pentaho Server log:

```
...
2010-09-30 13:01:30,437 DEBUG [org.pentaho.platform.engine.
    services.solution.SolutionEngine] fd386728-ccab-11df-9...
2010-09-30 13:01:30,484 INFO  [org.pentaho.platform.reposit
    ory.solution.SolutionRepositoryBase] Solution Reposito...
```

```
2010-09-30 13:01:30,484 INFO   [org.pentaho.platform.reposit
   ory.solution.SolutionRepositoryBase] Solution Reposit...
2010-09-30 13:01:30,515 INFO   [org.pentaho.platform.reposit
   ory.solution.SolutionRepositoryBase] Could not find d...
2010-09-30 13:01:30,531 ERROR [org.pentaho.platform.engine.
   services.solution.SolutionEngine] fd386728-ccab-11df-...
2010-09-30 13:01:42,515 WARN   [org.hibernate.cache.EhCacheP
   rovider] Could not find configuration [file]; using d...
```

In this case, all lines begin with a timestamp, followed by the level of log (DEBUG, INFO, and so on), and then the details of the log.

Despite being unstructured, the lines in a logfile—the one shown above—have some text that lets you know what kind of data is in those lines. Using that knowledge, you can parse different lines, as explained in the recipe.

In this particular example, you could read the file as containing two fields: one for the timestamp, the other with the rest of the line. Then, you can parse the second field splitting it in two: the kind of log (DEBUG, INFO, and so on) and the detail. Optionally, if you wanted to treat each level of log differently, you could split the stream with a **Switch case** step or nested **Filter rows** steps and proceed.

See also

▶   *Executing part of a job several times until a condition is true* recipe in *Chapter 8, Executing and Re-using Jobs and Transformations*

Reading files having one field per row

When you use one of the Kettle steps meant for reading files, Kettle expects the data to be organized in rows, where the columns are the fields. Suppose that instead of having a file with that structure, your file has one attribute per row, as in the following example:

```
Mastering Joomla! 1.5 Extension and Framework Development
Published: November 2007
Our price: $30.99

CakePHP 1.3 Application Development Cookbook: RAW
Expected: December 2010
Our price: $24.99

Firebug 1.5: Editing, Debugging, and Monitoring Web Pages
Published: April 2010
Our price: $21.99

jQuery Reference Guide
...
```

This file contains book information. In the file, each book is described in three rows: one for the title, one for the published or expected publishing date, and one row for the price.

There is no direct way to tell Kettle how to interpret these rows, but a simple transformation can do the trick.

Getting ready

Create a file containing the preceding text or download the sample file from Packt's site.

How to do it...

Carry out the following steps:

1. Create a transformation and use a **Text file input** step to read the file `packt_books.txt`. Under the **Content** tab, uncheck the **Header** option and as **Separator**, type |. Under the **Fields** tab, enter a single String field named `text`.

2. From the **Transform** category, add a **Row flattener** step.

3. Double-click the step. As **The field to flatten** type or select **text**. Fill the grid with three rows with values `title`, `publishing_date`, and `price`.

4. Do a preview on the last step. You'll see the following:

#	title	publishing_date	price
1	jQuery 1.4 Reference Guide	Published: January 2010	Our price: $24.99
2	Agile Web Application Development with Y	Published: August 2010	Our price: $24.99
3	Learning jQuery 1.3	Published: February 2009	Our price: $24.99
4	CodeIgniter 1.7	Published: November 2009	Our price: $24.99
5	Learning jQuery : Better Interaction Desig	Published: July 2007	Our price: $24.99
6	Magento 1.3: PHP Developer's Guide	Published: January 2010	Our price: $24.99
7	Joomla! 1.5: Beginner's Guide	Published: March 2010	Our price: $27.99
8	Building Powerful and Robust Websites wit	Published: April 2008	Our price: $27.99
9	YUI 2.8: Learning the Library	Published: July 2010	Our price: $27.99
10	WordPress Plugin Development: Beginner'	Published: February 2009	Our price: $24.99
11	Joomla! Template Design: Create your own	Published: June 2007	Our price: $27.99

You already have the fields as columns! Now, you can go a little further and do some cleansing, as follows:

1. From the **Scripting** category, add a **Regexp Evaluation** step.

2. Configure the step as follows: As **Field to evaluate** type or select **publishing_date**. Check the option **Create fields for capture groups**. As **Regular expression**: type `(Published|Expected):(.+)`.

3. In the **Capture Group Fields** grid, add two rows. In the first row, create a new **String** field named `status`. In the second, create a **Date** field named `pub_date` with **Format** MMM yyy. In both rows, under the **Trim** column, select **both**.

4. From the **Transform** category, add a **Replace in string** step. In the grid, add a row with the value `price` under the column **In stream field**, and `Our price:` under the column **Search**.

5. Finally, use a **Select values** step to change the metadata of the **Price** field: Change it to `Number`. As **Format**, type `$#.00`. Do a preview and you'll see the following:

^	#	title	publishing_date	price	result	status	pub_date
	1	jQuery 1.4 Reference Guide	Published: January 2010	$24.99	Y	Published	Jan 2010
	2	Agile Web Application Developme	Published: August 2010	$24.99	Y	Published	Aug 2010
	3	Learning jQuery 1.3	Published: February 2009	$24.99	Y	Published	Feb 2009
	4	CodeIgniter 1.7	Published: November 2009	$24.99	Y	Published	Nov 2009
	5	Learning jQuery : Better Interacti	Published: July 2007	$24.99	Y	Published	Jul 2007
	6	Magento 1.3: PHP Developer's Gu	Published: January 2010	$24.99	Y	Published	Jan 2010
	7	Joomla! 1.5: Beginner's Guide	Published: March 2010	$27.99	Y	Published	Mar 2010
	8	Building Powerful and Robust Web	Published: April 2008	$27.99	Y	Published	Apr 2008
	9	YUI 2.8: Learning the Library	Published: July 2010	$27.99	Y	Published	Jul 2010
	10	WordPress Plugin Development: E	Published: February 2009	$24.99	Y	Published	Feb 2009
	11	Joomla! Template Design: Create	Published: June 2007	$27.99	Y	Published	Jun 2007

In the sample file, the months are written in English. Therefore, you put the mask MMM yyy when capturing groups. If you get an error because of the Date format, there is a high possibility that you do not have English as the preferred language in your regional settings. Consequently, Kettle is not able to parse those dates.

How it works...

The **Row flattener** step is a simple step intended to flatten consecutive rows and is perfect for reading files such as the one in the recipe. In this case, you had a file with book information, each book occupying three consecutive rows. The **Row flattener** step flattened the field `text` into three different new fields: `title`, `publishing_date`, and `price`.

This way, after every three rows, it generated a single one.

Note that if one book has a different number of rows (for example, if it lacks the price row), then you get unexpected results.

The **Row flattener** step flattens the rows as indicated in its setting window, no matter the content of the field being flattened.

There's more...

If you are not sure about the content of the file, you'd best avoid this simple solution and go for a more sophisticated one, for example, a solution that uses a **Row denormalizer** step. Row denormalizer takes a normalized data stream (like a key/value pairing) and denormalizes it so that the data for a given entity will be part of one row. A great example and overview of this step can be found on the Pentaho wiki at `http://wiki.pentaho.com/display/EAI/Row+De-normalizer`.

See also

▸ *Reading semi-structured files*

Reading files with some fields occupying two or more rows

When you use one of the Kettle steps devoted for reading files, Kettle expects one entity per row. For example, if you are reading a file with a list of customers, then Kettle expects one customer per row. Suppose that you have a file organized by rows, where the fields are in different columns, but some of the fields span several rows, as in the following example containing data about roller coasters:

```
Roller Coaster        Speed       Location                    Year
Kingda Ka             128 mph     Six Flags Great Adventure
                                  Jackson, New Jersey         2005
Top Thrill Dragster   120 mph     Cedar Point
                                  Sandusky, Ohio              2003
Dodonpa               106.8 mph   Fuji-Q Highland
                                  FujiYoshida-shi             2001
                                  Japan
Steel Dragon 2000     95 mph      Nagashima Spa Land
                                  Mie                         2000
                                  Japan
Millennium Force      93 mph      Cedar Point
                                  Sandusky, Ohio              2000
Intimidator 305       90 mph      Kings Dominion
...
```

The first row for each roller coaster has the name of the attraction, the speed, and the location in three different columns. The location, however, spans over two or three rows. Finally, the year is not in the first row as you would expect, but in the second one. How to read this file? Not with just a single Text file input, but by combining it with a couple of extra steps, as you will learn in this recipe.

Getting ready

Create a file containing the preceding text or download the sample file from Packt's website.

How to do it...

Carry out the following steps:

1. Create a transformation and use a **Text file input** step to read the file
    `rollercoasters.txt`. Under the **Content** tab, select **Fixed** as **Filetype**.

2. Fill in the **Fields** tab. You can either click on **Get Fields** to use the wizard that lets you
    configure the fixed-width columns, or you can type the fields' properties directly into
    the grid. Under **Trim type**, select **both** for all rows. Under **Repeat**, select **Y** for the first
    two fields: `Roller_Coaster` and `Speed`. Configure the `Year` field with **Format #**.

3. From the **Statistics** category, add a **Group by** step. In the grid **The fields that make
    up the group:** enter two rows with values `Roller_Coaster` and `Speed`. Fill the
    Aggregates: grid, as shown in the following screenshot:

^	#	Name	Subject	Type	Value
	1	Location	Location	Concatenate strings separated by	|
	2	Year	Year	Concatenate strings separated by	

 The **Type** field is **Concatenate string separated by** in both rows. The separators are | and space respectively. Do not confuse this type with **Concatenate string separated by** "," where the separator is a comma.

4. From the **Transform** category, add a **Split Fields** step. Double-click on it and configure
    it as follows: As **Field to split** type, select **Location**. For **Delimiter**, type | . Fill the
    Fields grid with three rows. Under **New field** type `park`, `location`, and `country`.

5. Close the window and do a preview on it. You will see the following:

Rows of step: Split location (20 rows)

^	#	Roller_Coaster	Speed	park	location	country
	1	Kingda Ka	128 mph	Six Flags Great Adventure	Jackson, New Jersey	
	2	Top Thrill Dragster	120 mph	Cedar Point	Sandusky, Ohio	
	3	Dodonpa	106.8 mph	Fuji-Q Highland	FujiYoshida-shi	Japan
	4	Steel Dragon 2000	95 mph	Nagashima Spa Land	Mie	Japan
	5	Millennium Force	93 mph	Cedar Point	Sandusky, Ohio	
	6	Intimidator 305	90 mph	Kings Dominion	Doswell, Virginia	
	7	Goliath	85 mph	Six Flags Magic Mountain	Valencia, California	
	8	Titan	85 mph	Six Flags Over Texas	Arlington, Texas	
	9	Phantom's Revenge	85 mph	Kennywood	West Mifflin, Pennsylvania	

How it works...

If you have to read a file and some of the fields in your file span over several rows, you have to find a way to group all those fields together. The word group makes you think about the **Group by** step. First of all, in order to group rows, the rows should have a field or fields in common. In the sample file, you know that the rows following the one containing the name of the roller coaster belong to the same roller coaster, but Kettle does not. So, you selected **Y** under the **Repeat** field; this makes Kettle repeat the value of the `Roller_Coaster` and `Speed` fields in the rows, where the field is empty. If you do preview the data in the **Text file input** step, you see the following:

#	Roller_Coaster	Speed	Location	Year
1	Kingda Ka	128 mph	Six Flags Great Adventure	
2	Kingda Ka	128 mph	Jackson, New Jersey	2005
3	Top Thrill Dragster	120 mph	Cedar Point	
4	Top Thrill Dragster	120 mph	Sandusky, Ohio	2003
5	Dodonpa	106.8 mph	Fuji-Q Highland	
6	Dodonpa	106.8 mph	FujiYoshida-shi	2001
7	Dodonpa	106.8 mph	Japan	
8	Steel Dragon 2000	95 mph	Nagashima Spa Land	
9	Steel Dragon 2000	95 mph	Mie	2000
10	Steel Dragon 2000	95 mph	Japan	

Rows of step: roller coasters (45 rows)

This way, you are able to group all rows that share the same values for the `Roller_Coaster` and `Speed` fields. With the **Group by** step, you do that and concatenate the different values for the `Location` and `year` fields.

You know that the different rows for the `Location` field belong to the name of the park, where the attraction is located, the city or state, and the country. Therefore, the last thing you do is to split the location into three fields: `park`, `location`, and `country`.

See also

▸ *Reading files having one field per row*

Writing a simple file

In this recipe, you will learn the use of the **Text file output** step for writing text files.

Let's assume that you have a database with outdoor products and you want to export a catalog of products to a text file.

Getting ready

For this recipe, you will need a database with outdoor products with the structure explained in *Appendix A, Data Structures*.

How to do it...

Carry out the following steps:

1. Create a new transformation.

2. Drop a **Table input** step into the canvas. Enter the following SQL statement:

   ```
   SELECT innerj.desc_product, categories.category, innerj.price FROM
   products innerj
   INNER JOIN categories
   ON innerj.id_category = categories.id_category
   ```

3. From the **Output** category, add a **Text file output** step.

4. In the **Filename** textbox under the **File** tab, type or browse to the name of the destination file.

5. In the **Extension** textbox, leave the default value `txt`.

6. Check the **Do not create file at start** checkbox. This checkbox prevents the creation of the file when there is no data to write to it.

> If you want to create the file anyway, uncheck the **Do not create file at start** checkbox and a file with at least 0 bytes will be created.

7. Under the **Content** tab, leave the default values.

> If you want to add lines to an existing file, select the **Append** check box.

8. Under the **Fields** tab, fill in the grid, as shown in the following screenshot:

#	Name	Type	Format
1	Product	String	
2	category	String	
3	price	Number	$0.00

9. Run the transformation, a new text file will be created containing the list of products.

How it works...

The **Text file output** step allows you to generate files. In this recipe, you used it to generate a CSV file with data coming from a database.

Under the **File** tab, you entered the path and name of the file. Here, you also have several options to include the date or time in different formats as part of the name of the file. For this example, you didn't have to use those textboxes.

In the generated file you can see that the first column contains a line with the headers. Those headers are generated when the **Header** option from the **Content** tab is checked.

Under the **Fields** tab of this step, you must include the destination fields, including their types and formats. If you need it, you can include a field more than once.

> If you don't specify any field, the step will write all the fields from the previous step. This could be useful when you don't know the exact names of the fields or when these fields change dynamically.

Under this same tab, the **Null** column specifies the string that will be written in case of a null value.

Finally, if you specify the **Length** field of each column, a fixed width file will be created.

There's more...

Here are some considerations that make the process of writing files more flexible.

Changing headers

If you want to change the name of a header, you could insert a **Select values** step from the **Transform** category just before the **Text file output** step. Under the **Select & Alter** tab, select the fields you want to rename and give them a better description. For example, you could select the desc_product fieldname and rename the field as Product.

In order to send all the other fields toward the **Text file output** step, you also have to check the **Include unspecified fields, ordered by name** option.

Giving the output fields a format

When you write a file and tell Kettle which fields to write to that file, you have the option of specifying the format to apply to those fields. That is particularly useful when you have numeric or date fields.

In both cases, you may specify a format using a mask of patterns and symbols.

In the case of numeric fields, you can find more information about formats at the following URL: `http://docs.oracle.com/javase/7/docs/api/java/text/DecimalFormat.html`.

In the case of date fields, you will find a complete reference at the following URL: `http://docs.oracle.com/javase/7/docs/api/java/text/SimpleDateFormat.html`.

Writing a semi-structured file

A standard file generated with Kettle is a file with several columns, which may vary according to how you configured the **Fields** tab of the **Output** step and one row for each row in your dataset, all with the same structure. If you want the file to have a header, the header is automatically created with the names of the fields. What if you want to generate a file somehow different from that? Suppose that you have a file with a list of topics for a writing examination. When a student has to take the examination, you take that list of topics and generate a sheet like the following:

```
Student name: Mary Williams
-----------------------------------------------------------
Choose one of the following topics and write a paragraph about it
(write at least 300 words)

1. Should animals be used for medical research?
2. What do you think about the amount of violence on TV?
3. What does your country mean to you?
4. What would happen if there were no televisions?
5. What would you do if you found a magic wand?
```

Getting ready

Create a file with a list of topics or download the sample file from Packt's site.

How to do it...

Carry out the following steps:

1. Create a transformation and read the file `writing_topics.txt using a Text file input step`. Under the **Content** tab, uncheck the **Header** option, check the **Rownum in output?** option and as **Rownum fieldname**, type `topic_num`. Under the **Fields** tab, enter a single field named `text`.

2. From the **Scripting** category, drag a **User Defined Java Expression** (**UDJE**). Use it to replace the `text` field with this: `topic_num +". " + text`. Create a hop from the **Text file input** step to the **User Defined Java Expression** step.

3. With a **Select rows** step, select the **text** field and you have the list of topics. Now, you need to add the custom header. Create a hop from the **User Defined Java Expression** step to the **Select rows** step.

4. With a **Get System Info** step, get the student name from the command line. Under **Name** type `text` and under **type** select **command line argument 1**.

5. Add a **UDJE** for replacing the `text` field with the following: `"Student name: " + text`.

6. From the **Input** category, add a **Data Grid** step. Under the **Meta** tab, add a String field named `text`. Fill in the **Data** tab, as shown in the following screenshot (including the empty fourth line):

7. From the **Flow** category, add the two **Append streams** steps and link them to the already created streams, as shown in the following screenshot:

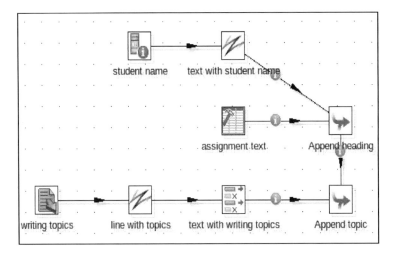

8. Double-click on the first **Append streams** step, as **Head hop**, select the name of the **UDJE** step, as **Tail hop**, select the name of the **Data Grid** step.

9. Double-click on the second **Append streams** step, as **Head hop**, select the name of the previous **Append streams** step, as **Tail hop** select the name of the **Select values** step.

10. After this last **Append streams** step, add a **Text file output** step, enter a path and name for the output file, and as fields, type the name of the only field that exists: the field named `text`.

11. Run the transformation. Don't forget to provide a student name as the first command-line argument. For instance, running the job from the terminal in the Kettle install directory would look like `sh pan.sh /file:<file_path_and_name_here>.ktr <Student Name>`. See the generated file; it should look exactly as the one shown in the introduction.

How it works...

When you generate a file with any of the Kettle output steps, the rows have to be homogeneous, that is, all of them have to have the same format, the same number of columns, the same type of data, and so on. This recipe showed you one of the ways for creating a file with rows that differ in structure. In this case, you had a main stream with two columns: a number and a writing topic. However, you also had several lines that made up a header for those topics. What you did was to build separate streams; in each stream you concatenated the different fields that you wanted to send to the file, creating a single field named `text`. Then, you joined the streams by using **Append streams** steps, and sent the final dataset to a file with a single column.

There's more...

The approach used in the recipe is useful for creating files with custom headers or footers. Now, suppose that you face any of the following scenarios:

▶ You have to generate a file with a custom header, but your main dataset has multiple columns and you want to take advantage of the formatting capabilities of the Kettle **Output** steps.

▶ You have more than one dataset, all with a different structure (different number or type of columns) and you want to send all of them to the same file, one after each other.

In these situations, the problem can be addressed in a different way: create a different transformation for each stream (one for the header, one for each different dataset), and call them one after the other from a main job. Every transformation should append the rows to the same file (don't forget to check the **Append** option in the **Text file output** step). Creating this takes a little more time, but gives you much more flexibility.

Providing the name of a file (for reading or writing) dynamically

Sometimes, you don't have the complete name of the file that you intend to read or write in your transformation. That can be because the name of the file depends on a field or on external information. Suppose you receive a text file with information about new books to process. This file is sent to you on a daily basis and the date is part of its name (for example, `newBooks_20100927.txt`).

Getting ready

In order to follow this recipe, you must have a text file named `newBooks_20100927.txt` with sample book information such as the following:

```
"Title","Author","Price","Genre"
"The Da Vinci Code","Dan Brown","25.00","Fiction"
"Breaking Dawn","Stephenie Meyer","21.00","Children"
"Foundation","Isaac Asimov","38.50","Fiction"
"I, Robot","Isaac Asimov","39.99","Fiction"
```

How to do it...

Carry out the following steps:

1. Create a new transformation.

2. Drop a **Get System Info** step from the **Input** category into the canvas. Add a new field named `today`, and in the **Type** listbox, select `System date (variable)`.

3. From the **Transform** category, add a **Selected values** step, in order to give the date the desired format. Click on the **Meta-data** tab and fill in the first row as follows:

   - As **Fieldname**, type or select `today`
   - As **Type** select **String**
   - As **Format** type `yyyyMMdd`

4. In the recipe, the file is saved in the same directory as the transformation. In order to get this directory, you have to get it as a field in your dataset. That's the purpose of the next step. Add the **Get Variables** step from the **Job** category. In the grid, add a new field named `path`. In the **Variable** column, press *Ctrl + Space* in order to show the list of possible variables, and select **Internal.Transformation.Filename.Directory**.

5. From the **Scripting** category, add a **User Defined Java Expression** step from now on.

6. In the step setting window, add a field named `filename` (type it in the **New field** column), and type `path + "/newBooks_" + today +".txt"` in the **Java Expression** column. Previewing this step, you will obtain the complete path for the file, for example, `file:///C:/myDocuments/newBooks_20100927.txt`.

 The recipe uses the UDJE for its simplicity and performance. However, you can obtain this calculated field in other ways, for example, using the **Calculator** step from the **Transform** category or the **Formula** step from the **Scripting** category.

7. Now that you have the filename, let's read the file. Add a **Text file input** step. Your transformation should look like the one shown in the following screenshot (except possibly for the step names):

Get date   Formatting date   Get path   Get filename   Read new Books

8. Double-click on the step. Under the **File** tab, go to the bottom section and check on the **Accept filenames from previous step** checkbox.

9. In the **Step to read filenames from** textbox, type or select the name of the **UDJE** step created earlier. In the **Field in input to use as filename** textbox, type `filename`.

10. Select the **Content** tab. Type `,` in the **Separator**, and set the header to 1 line.

11. Under the **Fields** tab, add the following **Names** and **Types**: `Title` (`String`), `Author` (`String`), `Price` (`Number`), and `Genre` (`String`).

 You can't use the **Get Fields** button in this case because the name of the file will be set dynamically. In order to obtain the headers automatically, you can fill the **File** tab with the name of a sample file. Then, clicking on the **Get Fields** button, the grid will be populated. Finally, you must remove the sample file from the **File** tab and set the **Accept filenames from previous step** section again.

Run the transformation, you will obtain a data source with the text file information whose name was resolved dynamically.

How it works...

When you have to read a file and the filename is known only at the moment you run the transformation, you cannot set the filename explicitly in the grid located under the **File** tab of the **Input** step. However, there is a way to provide the name of the file.

First, you have to create a field with the name of the file including its complete path.

Once you have that field, the only thing to do is to configure the **Accept filenames from previous step** section of the **Input** step, specifying the step from which that field comes and the name of the field.

In the recipe, you didn't know the complete name because part of the name was the system date, as for example, `C:/myDocuments/newBooks_20100927.txt`. In order to build a field with that name, you did the following:

- ▸ Getting the date of today (**Get System Info** step)
- ▸ Formatting this date as `yyyyMMdd` (**Selected values** step)
- ▸ Getting the path where the file were located (**Get Variables** step)
- ▸ Concatenating the path and the formatted date (**UDJE** step), generating the final field named `filename`

These steps are among the most used for these situations. However, the steps and the way of building the field will depend on your particular case.

In the recipe, you used a **Text file input** step, but the same applies for other **Input** steps: **Excel Input**, **Property Input**, and so on.

It may happen that you want to read a file with a **CSV file input** step, but notice that it doesn't have the option of accepting the name of the file from a previous step. Don't worry! If you create a hop from any step toward this step, the textbox named **The filename field (data from previous steps)** will magically show up, allowing the name to be provided dynamically.

This method for providing the name of the file also applies when you write a file by using a **Text file output** step.

There's more...

What follows is a little background about the **Get System Info** step used in the recipe. After that, you will see how the **Accept file name from field?** feature can be used in the generation of files.

Get System Info

You can use the **Get System Info** step to retrieve information from the PDI environment. In the recipe, it was used to get the system date, but you can use it for bringing and adding to the dataset other environmental information, for example, the arguments from the command line, the transformation's name, and so on.

You can get further information about this step at the following URL: `http://wiki.pentaho.com/display/EAI/Get+System+Info`.

Generating several files simultaneously with the same structure, but different names

Let's assume that you want to write files with book information, but a different file for each genre. For example, a file named `fiction.txt` with all the fiction books, another file named `children.txt` with the children's books, and so on. To do this, you must create the name of the file dynamically, as shown in the recipe. In this case, supposing that your dataset has a field with the genre of the book, you could create a Java expression that concatenates the path, the field that has the genre, and the string `.txt`. Another solution could be concatenating the path, genre field, and `.txt` via the **Calculator** step. Then, in the **Text file output** step, you should check the check box named **Accept file name from field?** and in the **File name field** listbox, select the field just created.

Running this transformation will generate different text files with the book's information; one file for each genre.

Using the name of a file (or part of it) as a field

There are some occasions where you need to include the name of a file as a column in your dataset for further processing. With Kettle, you can do it in a very simple way.

In this example, you have several text files about camping products. Each file belongs to a different category and you know the category from the filename. For example, `tents.txt` contains tent products. You want to obtain a single dataset with all the products from these files including a field indicating the category of every product.

Getting ready

In order to run this exercise, you need a directory (`campingProducts`) with text files named `kitchen.txt`, `lights.txt`, `sleeping_bags.txt`, `tents.txt`, and `tools.txt`. Each file contains descriptions of the products and their price separated with a `|`. Consider the following example:

```
Swedish Firesteel - Army Model|$19.97
Mountain House #10 Can Freeze-Dried Food|$53.50
Coleman 70-Quart Xtreme Cooler (Blue)|$59.99
Kelsyus Floating Cooler|$26.99
Lodge LCC3 Logic Pre-Seasoned Combo Cooker|$41.99
Guyot Designs SplashGuard-Universal|$7.96
```

How to do it...

Carry out the following steps:

1. Create a new transformation.

2. Drop a **Text file input** step into the work area and use it to read the files. Under the **File** tab, type or browse to the `campingProducts` directory in the **File or directory** textbox, and use `.*\.txt` as **Regular Expression**. Click on the **Add** button.

3. Under the **Content** tab, type | as the **Separator** and complete the **Fields** tab as follows:

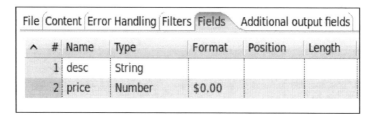

4. Under the **Additional output fields** tab, type `filename` in the field **Short filename field**.

5. Previewing this step, you can see that there is a new field named `filename` with the name of the file (for example: `kitchen.txt`).

6. Now, you must split the filename text to get the category. Add a **Split Fields** from the **Transform** category, double-click on it and fill the setting windows, as shown in the following screenshot:

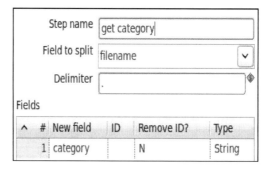

7. Previewing the last step of the transformation, you will see a dataset with the camping products, their price, and also a column named `category` with the proper product category.

How it works...

This recipe showed you the way to convert the names of the files into a new field named `category`. The source directory you entered in the **Text file input** step contains several files whose names are the categories of the products. Under the **Additional output fields** tab, you incorporated the **Short filename** as a field (for example `tents.txt`); you could also have included the extension, size, or full path among other fields. The next step in the transformation, a **Split Fields** step uses a period (`.`) as the **Delimiter** value to use from the field only the first part, which is the category (`tents` in the example). It eliminates the second part, which is the extension of the filename (`.txt`). If you don't want to discard the extension, you must add another field in the grid (for example, a field named `fileExtension`). Note that for this field, you set the type, but you can also specify a format, length, and so on.

Reading an Excel file

Kettle provides the **Excel input** step, in order to read data from Excel files. In this recipe, you will use this step to read an Excel file regarding museums in Italy. The file has a sheet with one column for the name of the museum and an other for the city where it is located. The data starts in the C3 cell (as shown in the screenshot in the next section).

Getting ready

For this example, you need an Excel file named `museumsItaly.xls` with a `museums` sheet, as shown in the following screenshot:

	A	B	C	D	E
3			name	city	
4			Uffizi Gallery	Florence	
5			Casa Buonarroti	Florence	
6			Florence Museums	Florence	
7			Galleria dell'Accademia	Florence	
8			Galleria Palatina	Florence	
9			Marino Marini Museum	Florence	
10			Museo di San Marco	Florence	
11			Museo Nazionale del Bargello	Florence	
12			Opera di Santa Maria del Fiore	Florence	
13			Palazzo Medici Riccardi	Florence	
14			Palazzo Vecchio (Museo Ragazzi)	Florence	
15			Pinacoteca Regionale	Florence	
16			Pitti Palace	Florence	
17			Palazzo Bianco	Genoa	
18			Palazzo Rosso	Genoa	
19			Galleria Nazionale Palazzo Spinola	Genoa	
20			Musei di Genova	Genoa	
21			Museo dell'Accademia Ligustica di Be▶	Genoa	

\museums /

You can download a sample file from Packt's website.

How to do it...

Carry out the following steps:

1. Create a new transformation.

2. Drop an **Excel input** step from the **Input** category.

3. Under the **Files** tab, browse to the `museumsItaly.xls` file and click on the **Add** button. This will cause the name of the file to be moved to the grid below.

4. Under the **Sheet** tab, fill in the first row as follows: type `museums` in the **Sheet name** column, `2` in the **Start row**, and `2` in the **Start column**.

> The rows and columns are numeric values (you cannot define the column with the identification letter you see in Excel). These values are zero-based (they start at the number 0).

5. Under the **Content** tab, leave the **Header** checked.

6. Under the **Fields** tab, click on the **Get fields from header row...** button to obtain the `name` and `city` fields.

7. Previewing the step, you will obtain a dataset with the museums data coming from the Excel sheet.

How it works...

The **Excel input** step allows you to read Excel files. Starting with Kettle 4.1.0, you can also use this step to read **OpenOffice** calc files.

This recipe showed you the way to read a simple Excel file, with a single sheet. However, the **Excel input** step allows you to read several Excel files at the same time. You do it just by adding more filename specifications to the grid located under the **File** tab. The step also allows you to read multiple sheets. You can click on the **Get Sheetname(s)** button to select from the list of sheets to read. If you don't specify any sheet in the grid, the step will read all of them.

> Take care when you leave the sheet name blank or when you select more than one sheet, because if the sheets have different structures, you will get an error.

Except for the sheet information, configuring an **Excel input** step for reading an Excel file is quite the same as configuring a **Text file input** step. You should not have any troubles making it work.

See also

- *Reading a simple file*
- *Using the name of a file (or part of it) as a field*
- *Getting the value of specific cells in an Excel file*

Getting the value of specific cells in an Excel file

One of the good things about Excel files is that they give you the freedom to write anywhere on the sheets, which sometimes is good if you want to prioritize the look and feel. However, that could cause troubles when it's time to automatically process the data in those files. Suppose that you have an Excel file with values for a couple of variables you'd like to set, as shown in the following screenshot:

	A	B	C	D	E
1					
2			Parameters to be used:		
3					
4			Year	2010	
5			ProductLine	Motorcycles	
6			Origin	Japan	
7					

In this example, you want to set values for three variables: Year, ProductLine, and Origin. The problem is, that you don't know where in the sheet that table is. It can be anywhere, near the upper left corner of the sheet. As you cannot ask Kettle to scan somewhere near the upper-left corner, you will learn in this recipe how to get that data with a simple transformation.

Getting ready

Create an Excel file with the preceding table. Feel free to write the values anywhere within the first rows and columns, as long as the labels and values are in adjacent columns.

How to do it...

Carry out the following steps:

1. Create a transformation and drag an **Excel Input** step into the canvas.
2. Double-click on the step and type or browse to the path and name of the Excel file you just created.

3. Under the **Content** tab, uncheck the **Header** option, just in case one of the variables is in the very first row.

4. Select the **Field** tab, and add 10 rows. As **Name** type a, b, c, ..., j. As **Type**, select **String** for the 10 rows.

5. From the **Transform** category of steps, drag into the canvas **Row Normalizer** and a **Row denormalizer** step.

6. From the **Statistics** category, drag **Analytic Query**, and link all the steps, as shown in the following screenshot:

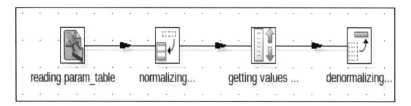

7. Double-click on **Row Normalizer**; click on **Get Fields** and the grid will be filled automatically with 10 rows. Fill the last column, **new field**, typing in all rows the value cell.

8. Double-click on the **Analytic Query** step. In the lower grid, add a row with the following values:

   ❑ Under **New field Name**, type value.

   ❑ Under **Subject** type or select cell.

   ❑ Under **Type**, select **LEAD "N" rows FORWARD and get Subject**.

9. Under **N** type 1. Double-click on **Row denormalizer**. In the **Key** field, type or select cell. Fill the lower grid as follows:

^	#	Target fieldname	Value fieldname	Key value	Type	Format
	1	year	value	Year	String	#
	2	productline	value	ProductLine	String	
	3	origin	value	Origin	String	

10. Do a preview on the last step. You should see the following:

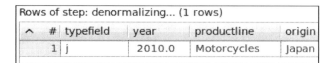

Rows of step: denormalizing... (1 rows)

^	#	typefield	year	productline	origin
	1	j	2010.0	Motorcycles	Japan

How it works...

The trick for getting data from an Excel sheet, if you don't know exactly where in the sheet the data is located, is to get rid of the leading rows and columns. Getting rid of rows is easy: just leave the **No empty rows** option on. The problem is getting rid of the columns.

In this recipe, you had an Excel file with some values: year, product line, and origin. You didn't know where exactly in the sheet the values were, but you had two clues: They were somewhere in the first cells and the values were next to the labels that identified them.

So, in order to find what you were looking for, you read the first 10 columns by using generic names a, b, c, and so on. By normalizing the cells, you put the cells row by row. This way, each value remained in the row just beneath its label. For example, if the cell with the value YEAR remained in the tenth row, the cell with value 2010 was in row 11. You can confirm this by doing a preview on the **Row Normalizer** step.

For each row, the **Analytic Query** step went forward to get the value of the row below and brought it in as a new field in the current row. This way, the labels and the values were again next to each other, as shown in the following screenshot:

#	typefield	cell	value
11	a		
12	b		Year
13	c	Year	2010.0
14	d	2010.0	
15	e		
16	f		
17	g		
18	h		
19	i		
20	j		
21	a		
22	b		ProductLine
23	c	ProductLine	Motorcycles
24	d	Motorcycles	
25	e		
26	f		
27	g		
28	h		
29	i		
30	j		
31	a		
32	b		Origin
33	c	Origin	Japan
34	d	Japan	

Rows of step: getting values ... (40 rows)

The result of combining these two steps was to remove the leading columns both to the right and to the left of our table.

Now, you could just remove the useless rows by keeping only those with labels equal to `Year`, `ProductLine`, or `Origin`, or do what was done in the recipe: denormalize the data to get just one row. This row is ready to be used for setting the variables `Year`, `ProductLine`, and `Origin` just by adding a **Set Variables** step at the end of the stream.

There's more...

As you don't know which columns will hold which kind of data, the advice is to read all as string. This way, you avoid unexpected errors. However, after getting the data, you can change the metadata accordingly by using a **Select values** step.

 You only read the first 10 columns. If you cannot be sure that the values are going to be in this range of cells, feel free to increase that value.

The following are the two use cases related to the main example.

Labels and values are horizontally arranged. What if, instead of having the labels and values as in the recipe, you have them horizontally arranged, as shown in the following screenshot?:

	A	B	C	D	E	F
1						
2			*Parameters to be used:*			
3						
4						
5			Year	ProductLine	Origin	
6			2010	Motorcycles	Japan	
7						

The recipe still works if you make a simple modification. Edit the **Analytic Query** step and change the `1` to `10`. This is how it works: when you denormalize the rows, the labels and their values remain 10 rows apart from each other. So, instead of looking for the next row, the **Analytic Query** step has to look 10 rows forward and get the values on those rows. You can see it in the following screenshot, which is the result of a preview on this step:

Rows of step: getting values ... (30 rows)			
^ #	typefield	cell	value
13	c	Year	2010.0
14	d	ProductLine	Motorcycles
15	e	Origin	Japan
16	f		
17	g		
18	h		
19	i		
20	j		
21	a		
22	b		
23	c	2010.0	
24	d	Motorcycles	
25	e	Japan	

Looking for a given cell

If you just have to look for a specific cell, for example D5, the solution is quite different, but fortunately pretty straightforward. Firstly, you have to know the number of the column and row where your data is. As Excel starts counting at zero, you conclude that the sample cell D5 is in the third column, fourth row. Then, you take an **Excel input** step and enter the name of the Excel file to read. In the grid located under the **Sheets** tab, add a row. Under the **Start row** and **Start column** type, the number of the row and column of interest are 4 and 3 in this case. Under the **Content** tab, uncheck the **Header** and the **No empty rows** options, checked by default, and in the **Limit** textbox, type 1. Under the **Fields** tab, add a single field to hold your value. You are done. Do a preview of the Excel file and you will see the following:

Rows of step: reading 1 cell (1 rows)	
^ #	a
1	Motorcycles

Writing an Excel file with several sheets

Writing an Excel file with Kettle has a lot in common with writing a text file. Except for a couple of settings specific to Excel files, configuring an **Excel Output** step is quite similar to configuring a **Text file output** step. One of the differences is that when you write an Excel file, you add a sheet to the file. What if you want to write more than one sheet in the same file?

Suppose you have a data source containing books and their authors and you want to create an Excel file with two sheets. In the first sheet, you want the authors and in the second, the books' titles. This recipe teaches you how to do this.

Getting ready

In order to run this recipe, you will need a database with books and authors with the structure described in *Appendix A, Data Structures*.

How to do it...

Carry out the following steps, in order to create the sheet with the authors' details:

1. Create a new transformation.

2. Drop a **Table Input** step into the canvas, in order to read the author information:
   ```
   SELECT * FROM Authors order by lastname
   ```

3. Add an **Excel Output** step.

4. In the **Filename** textbox under the **File** tab, write the destination path and the name of the file (Books).

5. As the **Extension**, leave the default value xls.

6. Under the **Content** tab, make sure the **Header** checkbox is selected.

7. In the **Sheet name** textbox, type Authors. Select the **Fields** tab and click on the **Get fields** button to fill the grid with the author data. The grid should look like the one shown in the following screenshot:

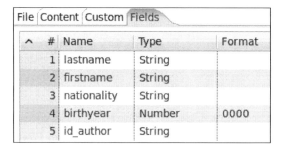

	#	Name	Type	Format
	1	lastname	String	
	2	firstname	String	
	3	nationality	String	
	4	birthyear	Number	0000
	5	id_author	String	

 If you find that the default types or formats of the fields are not correct, you can fix them manually.

Carry out the following steps, in order to create the sheet with the books' details:

1. Create a new transformation.

2. Drop a **Table Input** step into the canvas, in order to read the book's title's information:
   ```
   SELECT * FROM Books order by title
   ```

3. Add an **Excel Output** step and set the same filename and extension configured in the previous transformation (`Books` and `xls`).

> Alternatively, you can use a new step named **Excel Writer**. You will find it in the **Experimental** category in Kettle 4.2 or later. This step allows writing Excel spreadsheets with more flexibility. One of its main features is the support for template files or sheets.

4. Under the **Content** tab, make sure the **Header** checkbox is selected.

5. In the **Sheet name** textbox, type `Titles`.

6. Under the same tab, make sure to check the **Append** checkbox. Select the **Fields** tab and press the **Get fields** button to fill the grid with book titles. The grid should look like the one shown in the following screenshot:

^	#	Name	Type	Format
	1	title	String	
	2	id_author	String	
	3	price	Number	
	4	id_title	String	
	5	genre	String	

(File | Content | Custom | Fields)

7. Create a job and drop a **Start** job entry into the canvas.

8. Then, add two **Transformation** job entries and configure them for running the two transformations you created in the previous steps. The job should look like the following:

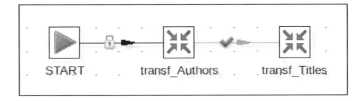

9. Run the job. It will generate an Excel file with two sheets: one for authors and the other for titles. It should look like the following screenshot:

	A	B	C	D	E
1	lastname	firstname	nationality	birthyear	id_author
2	Handler	Chelsea	American	1975	A00004
3	Hiaasen	Carl	American	1953	A00003
4	Ingraham	Laura	American	1964	A00005
5	King	Stephen	American	1947	A00002
6	Kiyosaki	Robert	American	1947	A00007
7	Larsson	Stieg	Swedish	1954	A00001
8	Ramsey	Dave	American	1960	A00006
9	Riordan	Rick	American	1964	A00009
10	Rowling	Joanne	English	1965	A00008

Authors / Titles / +

How it works...

The intuitive way to generate an Excel file with two sheets would be to create a single transformation with the two **Excel Output** steps, one for each sheet. However, that approach does not work because Kettle cannot manage concurrent access to the same Excel file in a single transformation.

One way to avoid this issue is to create different transformations, one for each sheet, and then calling these transformations from a job. With this approach, the transformations are executed sequentially, which means that the sheets are generated one at a time, avoiding the concurrency problem.

There's more...

Another way to assure the sequential generation of the sheets would be using the **Block this step until steps finish** step from the **Flow** category. Using this step, the writing of the second sheet will wait for the first sheet to complete its writing process. For our recipe, the transformation should look like the following:

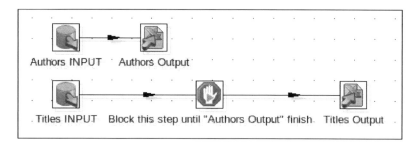

See also

▸ *Writing an Excel file with a dynamic number of sheets*

Writing an Excel file with a dynamic number of sheets

When you generate an Excel file, you usually generate it with a single sheet. You can, however, generate a file with more sheets. With PDI, you can generate an Excel file with several sheets, even if you don't know in advance how many sheets you will generate, or the name of those sheets.

In this recipe, you will create such an Excel file. Your file will have book title information separated in different sheets depending on the genre of the books.

Getting ready

You will need a database containing books and authors with the structure described in *Appendix A*, *Data Structures*.

How to do it...

Carry out the following steps:

1. Create a new job.

2. From the **File Management** category, drop a **Delete file** job entry into the work area.

3. In the **File name** textbox, type the path and name of the Excel file you will create, in order to remove the file if it exists.

4. Then, you have to add the two **Transformation** entries: one for selecting the book's categories (`Transf_Categories`) and another to write the specific sheet for each category (`Trans_BookByCategory`). The job should look like the following:

5. Create the transformation named `Transf_Categories`.

6. In this transformation, drop a **Table input** step, in order to obtain the different book's categories. The SQL statement, should be similar to the following:

```
SELECT DISTINCT genre FROM Books ORDER BY genre
```

7. Add a **Copy rows to result** from the **Job** folder and create a hop from the **Table input** step towards this one.

8. Create the second transformation called `Trans_BookByCategory`. In **Transformation settings** (*Ctrl + T*), go to the **Parameters** tab, and add a new parameter named `GENRE` without default.

9. Drop a **Table input** step into the canvas. In the **SQL** frame, type the following statement, in order to select the books depending on the `GENRE` parameter:

```
SELECT * FROM Books WHERE genre='${GENRE}'
```

10. In this step, check the prompt **Replace variables in script?**.

11. Add an **Excel output** step.

12. In the **Filename** textbox under the **File** tab, type the destination path and file. In the **Extension** textbox, leave the default value `xls`.

13. Under the **Content** tab, be sure to check **Append**.

14. Also here, in the **Sheet name** textbox, type `${GENRE}`.

15. Under the **Field** tab, click on the **Get Fields** button.

16. Come back to the job; edit the job entry details for the transformation `Trans_BookByCategory`. Go to the **Advanced** tab and check the **Copy previous result to parameters?** and **Execute for every input row?** checkboxes.

17. Under the **Parameters** tab, add a new value: type `GENRE` in the **Parameter** column, and `genre` for the **Stream column name**.

18. When you run the job, the Excel file created should have a different sheet for each category, as shown in the following screenshot:

	A	B	C	D	E
1	title	author_id	price	title_id	genre
2	Carrie	A00002	$41.00	123-346	Fiction
3	Salem's Lot	A00002	$33.00	123-347	Fiction
4	The Shining	A00002	$31.00	123-348	Fiction
5	The Dead Zone	A00002	$37.00	123-349	Fiction
6	Pet Sematary	A00002	$41.00	123-351	Fiction
7	The Tommyknockers	A00002	$39.00	123-352	Fiction
8	Bag of Bones	A00002	$40.90	123-353	Fiction
9	The Girl with the Dragon Tatoo	A00001	$34.98	123-400	Fiction
10	The Girl who Played with Fire	A00001	$35.99	123-401	Fiction

Business / Childrens \ **Fiction** / Non-fiction / Teens /

How it works...

When you have to execute the same task over and over again, the solution is to create a loop that executes a single transformation or job, as many times as needed. In this case, the goal was to create a new Excel sheet for each book category. So, the solution was as follows:

- Creating a transformation (`Transf_Categories`) that builds the list of categories
- Creating another transformation (`Trans_BookByCategory`) that appends a single sheet to the Excel file
- Calling the second transformation once for each category in the list by copying the rows to result in the first transformation, and checking the **Execute for every input row** checkbox in the **Job** entry belonging to the second transformation

> The main task was in the second transformation. In order to know which book categories to write each time, in that transformation, you defined a parameter named GENRE. Then, you used the GENRE parameter for filtering in the SQL statement and also for naming the Excel file sheet. The parameter is sent to the transformation because in the job, you set the **Copy previous result to parameters?** checkbox, and configured the **Parameters** tab properly. Note that in the **Excel Output** step, you checked the **Append** option, so that every time the transformation is executed, it creates a new sheet without losing the sheets previously generated. Also note that you deleted the file at the beginning for cleaning purposes.

See also

- *Writing an Excel file with several sheets*
- The *Executing part of a job once for every row in the dataset* recipe in *Chapter 8, Executing and Re-using Jobs and Transformations*

Reading data from an AWS S3 Instance

Amazon Web Services has helped to reshape server management by providing infinite flexibility with virtual machines that can be spun up or shut down almost as fast as a simple command. S3 is a scalable storage space that can be shared across virtual instances and is a common location for files to be processed. With this recipe, we will be reading information out of a file in an S3 instance.

> This recipe will require access to AWS, which does have a free tier for new users. If you have already used AWS in the past and do not have access to the free tier, the recipe will not deal with large transfers of data so the expense will be minimal.

Getting ready

You will need to have access to the files for this recipe, which are available on Packt's website. You will also need to create an S3 bucket to upload the files to.

1. Go to `http://aws.amazon.com` and create an account or log in.

2. Once logged in, you should now see the AWS Console. Click on **S3** under the **Storage and Content Delivery** option.

3. Click on **Create Bucket** and give the bucket a unique name. For the recipe, we will be using the naming convention `<yourname>.pdicb2.test.bucket`.

4. Select a region that is closest to you.

> Pricing will be different per region.

5. Click on the **Create** button. Your S3 bucket will be created and we can load our test files into it.

6. Click on your bucket's name. The contents of the bucket will now be displayed. Click on the **Upload** button and load the `books.csv` file into the bucket.

Security keys are required to access the S3 storage space. Use the following steps to access your keys.

> We are using the root account keys for this recipe. Please follow the AWS documentation regarding best practices with security accounts when setting this up outside of learning and testing.

1. Go to the **Security** page of the AWS Console: `https://console.aws.amazon.com/iam/home?#security_credential`.

2. Click through the pop ups regarding the AWS best practices (but note the links for setting this up in a live environment).

3. Under the section labeled **Access Keys**, find the **S3 Access key** and copy it for later use.

4. The **S3 CSV Input** step requires an S3 secret key. This can be obtained using the legacy page: `https://portal.aws.amazon.com/gp/aws/securityCredentials`. Also copy it for later use.

How to do it...

Carry out the following steps:

1. Create a new transformation.

2. From the **Input** category, bring over an **S3 Input** step onto the canvas.

3. Open the **S3 Input** step. Copy the **S3 Access key** and **S3 Secret key** into their matching fields.

4. Click on the **Select bucket** button. If the keys are active, a listing of available buckets should appear. Select `<yourname>/pdicb2.test.bucket` from the list.

5. Click on the **Browse** button to find the `books.csv` file.

6. Click on the **Get Fields** button. This will pull the field metadata from the file and load it into the **Fields** grid.

7. Click on **Preview** to see the data in the `books.csv` file.

How it works...

The **S3 CSV Input** step works very similarly to the **CSV Input** or **Text File Input** steps, in that it parses data out based on the format of the CSV file. The biggest difference is that to access the file, not only does the file have to be located, but the bucket name and the dual keys to access the bucket must be provided before the data can be pulled into the transformation.

Another powerful feature of the step is that it allows for files to be retrieved in parallel—meaning that very large files can be broken down into much more manageable chunks to be processed. The **S3 CSV Input** step does not allow for compressed files or for processing multiple files. Potential solutions for this could include storing the file name field value of the step into a parameter and looping over the list or mounting the S3 bucket directly into a file system that Kettle can access.

See also

▶ *Reading a simple file*

3
Working with Big Data and Cloud Sources

In this chapter, we will cover:

- ▶ Loading data into Salesforce.com
- ▶ Getting data from Salesforce.com
- ▶ Loading data into Hadoop
- ▶ Getting data from Hadoop
- ▶ Loading data into HBase
- ▶ Getting data from HBase
- ▶ Loading data into MongoDB
- ▶ Getting data from MongoDB

Introduction

While flat files and databases are the most common type of source that developers using Kettle interact with, there are many other types of data sources that are capable of being used. Data warehouses are now starting to leverage the capabilities of tools such as Hadoop, NoSQL databases, and cloud services such as Amazon Web Services and SalesForce.

In this chapter, you will learn to interact with these Big Data sources in Kettle. The recipes in this chapter are grouped into various data sources, with each grouping covering how to connect, read data from, and load data into the given data source.

The focus of this chapter is on data sources that are usually larger than can be set up for working through exercises. For each data source, the recipe *Connecting to a database* in *Chapter 1, Working with Databases,* will cover how to connect to the given data source, as well as recommendations for setting up a test environment in which to work in.

Loading data into Salesforce.com

Salesforce.com is best known for their customer relationship management suite, making it an increasingly common data source to work with. This type of data source utilizes a web API, that developers can interface with the data within the massive cloud service.

Sometimes, the data that is generated from within Salesforce.com is only part of the story around managing customer relationships, and greater benefit can be had by loading in data from other sources to aid in generating sales. This recipe will teach you how to set up and connect to a development Salesforce.com instance and load data into it.

Getting ready

Before we can cover how to interact with Salesforce.com, you will need to register for a developer environment that looks and feels like a full-blown production environment, albeit on a smaller scale. Navigate to `http://www.developerforce.com/events/regular/ registration.php` and fill out the form to register. We will be using the already constructed applications of the developer environment for the recipe. The data we will be loading can be found in the code for this chapter.

Any time you want to create a connection to Salesforce.com, you will need the following:

- ► Username
- ► Password
- ► Security token
- ► Salesforce Webservice URL (a default is entered, but can be changed if a different version of the API is being used)

It is also recommended that you have the development environment up, so that you can troubleshoot if needed.

 Every account that connects through the Salesforce.com API must use both the account password and a security token. Tokens can be generated through **Account | Setup | My Personal Information | Reset My Security Token**. Any time the account password is reset, a new token is generated.

How to do it...

Perform the following steps to load data into Salesforce.com:

1. Open Spoon and create a new transformation.

2. Add a **Text file Input** option from the **Input** category. Browse to the `accounts.csv` file found in the code for this chapter.

3. Make sure on the **Content** tab that the **Separator** field matches the separator of the file downloaded. Also make sure that **Format** matches the file.

4. On the **Fields** tab, click on **Get Fields**. The step will try and make a best guess on the column names, or bring over the column headers if there is a header row.

5. Click on **OK** and close the step.

6. Add a **Salesforce Insert** step from the **Output** category and connect the **Text file Input** step to it via a hop.

7. Open the **Salesforce Insert** step. Enter your Salesforce.com username in the **Username** field and your password with security token in the **Password** field.

 It is recommended that for steps that require login information (such as the **Salesforce Input**, **Insert**, **Upsert**, and **Delete** steps), that those details be stored in parameters, so that when they change, you don't have to remember every place that they are in use.

8. Click on **Test Connection** to verify that the step can connect to Salesforce.com.

9. In the **Settings** section, select **Account** in the **Module** listbox. Since this dataset is small, we can leave the **Batch Size** field set to **10**. The maximum number of records that can be loaded into a batch is 200, as per the Salesforce.com API documentation (`http://www.salesforce.com/us/developer/docs/apexcode/Content/apex_gov_limits.htm`).

10. In the **Fields** grid, click on **Edit mapping** and map the stream fields to the object fields. Click on **OK** to save the mapping and **OK** again to exit the step.

11. Save and launch the step. The account data should now load into the Salesforce.com Account object.

How it works...

The Salesforce steps in Kettle take advantage of the web API to interface with the backend data structure. We can take data from outside of the Salesforce.com environment and load it in, to perform more advanced analytics on the data that lives both within the customer relationship management aspect, as well as the new data from outside. The only limits, as to how much data that can be stored and accessed are, the number of API calls available, and how much space has been allocated to the Salesforce.com account.

See also

▸   *Getting data from Salesforce.com*

Getting data from Salesforce.com

In the previous recipe, we loaded data into the Account object. Pulling data back out from Salesforce.com becomes a bit more complicated, when going for filtered data instead of an entire object's dataset. Fortunately, the Salesforce.com API allows for querying data in a similar manner to the WHERE clauses in SQL. For this recipe, we will be filtering the Account object to get a subset of the records.

 While this recipe does not deal with a large amount of data, keep in mind that API calls are limited to the caps on the account being used.

Getting ready

While we can perform more filtering if the `account.csv` data is loaded as per the *Loading data into Salesforce.com* recipe, there is enough dummy data in the developer environment's Account object, for us to dig into. It will be handy to also have the developer environment open in case any troubleshooting is necessary.

How to do it...

1. Create a new transformation.
2. From the **Input** category, select the **Salesforce Input** step and bring it onto the canvas.
3. On the **Settings** tab, fill in the **Username** and **Password** fields with your username, password, and security token.
4. Click on **Test Connection** to verify the connection to Salesforce.com.
5. Under the **Settings** section, choose **Account** in the **Module** listbox.

6. For **Query condition**, enter `billingStreet != null`. We want to make sure that we get customers that have a billing address entered.

7. Switch to the **Fields** tab and click on **Get fields**. All of the fields for the object should be populated into the grid.

8. Click on **Preview rows** to see the dataset that is returned from the query. Click on **OK**.

9. Add a **Text File Output** step from the **Output** category. Add a hop from the **Salesforce Input** to the **Text File Output** step.

10. Open the **Text File Output** step and for the **Filename** field, choose a location for the text file to be created.

11. Switch to the **Fields** tab and click on **Get fields**. All the stream fields should populate the grid.

12. Run the transformation and the text file should be populated with the dataset.

How it works...

The Salesforce API includes a query language that has similar logic to SQL, called SOQL, that allows for complex querying of data objects to filter out data for specific use. The **Salesforce Input** step allows for the use of these filters to enter data into a normal Kettle data stream. The data can be further cleansed and processed as needed to integrate into a data warehouse, report, or other end user tool.

 To learn more about SOQL, check out the Salesforce. com docs at `http://www.salesforce.com/us/developer/docs/soql_sosl/`.

See also

▶ *Loading data into Salesforce.com*

▶ The recipe *Writing a simple file* in *Chapter 2, Reading and Writing Files*

Loading data into Hadoop

Hadoop is at the heart of the Big Data movement. Being derived from Google's white papers on MapReduce and Google File System, Hadoop is able to scale up beyond petabytes of data and provide the backbone for fast and effective data analysis.

Pentaho was one of the first companies to provide support for Hadoop and has open sourced those capabilities, along with steps for other Big Data sources.

There are a lot of great tutorials and videos on Pentaho's Big Data wiki available at `http://wiki.pentaho.com/display/BAD/Pentaho+Big+Data+Community+Home`.

Getting ready

Before we actually try to connect to Hadoop, we have to set up an appropriate environment. Companies like Hortonworks and Cloudera have been at the forefront of providing new features and functionality to the Hadoop ecosystem, including Sandbox environments, to learn about the various tools. We will be using Hortonworks' Sandbox environment for this chapter's Hadoop recipes.

 Hortonworks' Sandbox environment is available at `http://hortonworks.com/products/hortonworks-sandbox/` after registering with their site. These recipes are applicable to any Hadoop cluster, but there are not that many ways to set up a local cluster that quickly.

Once you have the sandbox set up and ready to run, we have to provide Kettle with a configuration setup. These setups are called **shims**, which give Kettle all the necessary drivers to communicate with a given Hadoop or other Big Data stack. An overview of which versions of Hadoop are officially supported, can be found at `http://wiki.pentaho.com/display/BAD/Configuring+Pentaho+for+your+Hadoop+Distro+and+Version`.

To build a custom shim for Kettle, we start with the basic **hadoop-20** shim provided by Pentaho (which can be located in Kettle's `plugin directory` | `pentaho-big-data-plugin` | `hadoop-configurations`). The `.jar` files under the `lib` directory have to be updated to match the versions of the various tools within the Hortonworks' Sandbox.

 More details on how to set up shims in Kettle can be found at Matt Burgess' blog at `http://funpdi.blogspot.com/2013/03/pentaho-data-integration-44-and-hadoop.html`. We have also provided a working shim for the sandbox out on GitHub at `https://github.com/dbaAlex/hortonworks_pentaho_shim`. It is likely with Version 5.0 that Kettle should work with the Hortonworks' Sandbox without having to build a custom shim.

Now we only need a dataset in which to load our newly minted Hadoop environment. Fortunately, there are quite a few large datasets for us to play with. For the exercises in this chapter, we will be using the Baseball Database found at `http://seanlahman.com/files/database/lahman2012-csv.zip`.

Sean Lahman's Baseball Database goes all the way back to 1871 and is one of the most complete baseball statistics sets available to the public. As an added plus, this data is also used for some of the tutorials provided as part of the Hortonworks Sandbox VM.

How to do it...

Perform the following steps to load the data into Hadoop:

1. Open Spoon and create a new job.

2. Bring a **Start** step and from the **Big Data** section. Bring over a **Hadoop Copy Files** step. Connect the two steps together with a hop going from the **Start** step to the **Hadoop Copy Files** step.

3. Open the **Hadoop Copy Files** step. Tick the **Create destination folder** checkbox.

4. Add the location where you downloaded the baseball data in the **File/Folder source** text field. Be sure to uncompress the dataset so that Kettle will grab the actual file.

5. The Hortonworks Sandbox will try to use a local IP address, which should have displayed on startup of the box. The **File/Folder destination** text field will have the connection of the sandbox and will tell Kettle where to load the data. Use the connection string: `hdfs://<your_sandbox_ip_address>:8020/user/sandbox/baseball/raw`. Your step should look similar to the following screenshot:

General \ Result files name

Settings

Include Subfolders	☑
Destination is a file	☐
Copy empty folders	☐
Create destination folder	☑
Replace existing files	☐
Remove source files	☐
Copy previous results to args	☐

File/Folder source [ ] Add
File/Folder destination [ ]
Wildcard (RegExp) [ ]

Files/Folders:

#	File/Folder source	File/Folder destination
1	file:///${data_location_par}/baseball_dataset	hdfs://192.168.56.101:8020/user/sandbox/baseball/raw

While the sandbox will not require a username or password, production environments will likely need one. It is better to store those values in parameters, since they are displayed in plain text.

6. Save and run the job. The Baseball database is now loading into your sandbox environment. You can monitor the process of the job via the command line from the sandbox:

```
hadoop fs -ls /user/sandbox/baseball/raw
```

If you receive an error message from PDI, ensure that the sandbox is operational and that there are no connectivity issues.

How it works...

Kettle's **Hadoop Copy Files** step provides an easy to use interface to push data into the **Hadoop File System** (**HDFS**). The connection string used in step 5 actually does several things:

- ▸ Declare the protocol being used (HDFS)
- ▸ Identify the Hadoop server (192.168.56.101)
- ▸ Identify the port (8020)
- ▸ Define where the data will be stored (/user/sandbox/baseball/raw)

All of the data gets loaded into that location for further processing, or using it through other tools such as Hive, HBase, and so on.

There's more...

While this step is designed to load the Hadoop File System with data, it can also load data directly into Hive (a SQL-like layer for Hadoop). There is a great tutorial on this functionality at http://wiki.pentaho.com/display/BAD/Loading+Data+into+Hive. Hive is a translation layer used to interface with data stored in Hadoop, allowing users to write queries that are similar to SQL in a custom language called HiveQL. While **Hadoop Copy Files** makes loading massive quantities of data easier, we can also use more traditional means like **Table Output**, **Insert/Update**, and **Update** with a database connection.

See also

- ▸ *Getting data from Hadoop*
- ▸ *Loading data into HBase*

Getting data from Hadoop

Just as Kettle simplifies loading data into Hadoop, pulling data back out from the Hadoop File System is just as easy. In fact, we can treat it just like any other data source that is a flat file.

Getting ready

For this recipe, we will be using the Baseball Dataset loaded into Hadoop in the recipe *Loading data into Hadoop* (also in this chapter). It is recommended that this recipe is performed before continuing.

We will be focusing on the `Salaries.csv` and the `Master.csv` datasets. Let us find out just how much money each player earned over the course of their careers.

How to do it...

Perform the following steps to retrieve the baseball data from Hadoop:

1. Open Spoon and create a new transformation.

2. In the **Design** tab, under the **Big Data** section, select and bring over two **Hadoop File Input** steps. We will use one for each of the `.csv` files we wish to merge together.

3. Edit one of the **Hadoop File Input** steps. This will be used to pull in the `Salaries.csv` information.

4. For the **File or directory** text field, enter the connection information to get to the `Salaries.csv` data. For instance, if the data was stored under the sandbox user's `baseball/raw` folder, use `hdfs://<your_sandbox_ip_address>:8020/user/sandbox/baseball/raw/Salaries.csv`.

5. Switch to the **Content** tab and change the **Separator** from `;` to `,`.

6. Switch to the **Fields** tab and click on **Get Fields**. Click on **OK** on the **Number of lines to sample** prompt. Kettle provides a best guess to the fields in the file.

7. Click on **Preview rows** to view the data stored in the file.

8. Repeat steps 3 through 7 for the `Master.csv` file.

9. Now we need to filter out the fields we do not need. From the **Transform** section, bring over two **Select Values** steps. Connect one to each of the **Hadoop File Input** steps.

10. For the `Salaries` data, we want to remove the `yearID`, `teamID`, and `lgID` fields.

11. For the `Master` data, we want to remove all but the `playerID`, `nameFirst`, and `nameLast` fields.

12. Add a **Sort rows** step and sort the `Salaries` data on `playerID`. We also need to add another **Sort rows** step for the `Master` data and also sort on `playerID`.

13. Under **Statistics**, select and bring over a **Group by** step from the **Statistics** section. For the **Group** field, add `playerID`. Under the **Aggregates:** section, add the following details:

   ❑ **Name**: `salary_sum`

   ❑ **Subject**: `salary`

   ❑ **Type**: `Sum`

   The **Group by** step should now look similar to the following screenshot:

14. Now the two datasets can be merged with a **Merge Join** step. Add hops to bring both streams into the **Merge Join** step. The **Key** field for both steps will be **playerID**. The **Join Type** will be **INNER**. The step should now look similar to the following screenshot:

15. Finally, add a **Text File Output** step and connect it to the **Merge Join** step. Your transformation should look similar to the following screenshot:

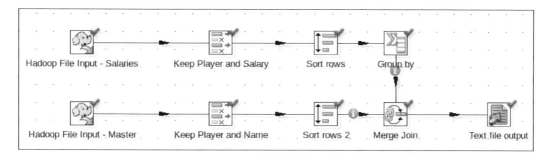

16. Run the transformation and look at the `csv` file created. Just like the source `csv` files were stored locally, we were able to access them and build a small aggregated dataset in Kettle.

How it works...

Hadoop is a giant distributed filesystem. In this recipe, we read data from the Hadoop File System and used Kettle's data integration capabilities to aggregate the data by player, and merge it with the players' names. While the two **Hadoop File Input** steps were calling on a specific file, if the data were across many files, we could just as easily have added a Regular Expression to bring in the files we needed. The data could effectively live throughout the Hadoop cluster, but we only have to call out to the cluster with our request and the step does the rest.

See also

▸ _Loading data into HBase_

▸ The recipe _Writing a simple file_ in _Chapter 2, Reading and Writing Files_

▸ The recipe _Joining two or more streams based on given conditions_ in _Chapter 7, Understanding and Optimizing Data Flows_

Loading data into HBase

HBase is another component in the Hadoop ecosystem. It is a columnar database, which stores datasets based on the columns, instead of the rows that make it up. This allows for higher compression and faster searching, making columnar databases ideal for the kinds of analytical queries that can cause significant performance issues in traditional relational databases.

 For this recipe we will be using the Baseball Dataset loaded into Hadoop in the recipe *Loading data into Hadoop*, (also in this chapter). It is recommended that the recipe *Loading data into Hadoop* is performed before continuing.

Getting ready

In this recipe, we will be loading the `Schools.csv`, `Master.csv`, and `SchoolsPlayers.csv` files. The data relates (via the `SchoolsPlayers.csv` file) schools (found in the `Schools.csv` file) to players (found in the `Master.csv` file). This data is designed for a relational database, so we will be tweaking the data to take advantage of Hbase's data store capabilities. Before we can load anything into HBase, we need to create the schema in which the data will be stored. Let us first look at the relational model for these three datasets:

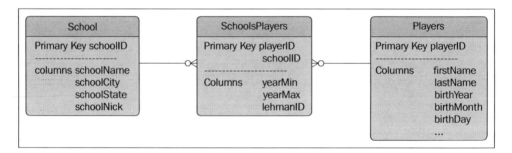

The relationship can be classified as a Many to Many. There are many players, and many schools, with some players going to more than one school. The challenge with using tools like HBase are that they do not have a concept of relational modeling. Joining datasets can become quite cumbersome both for developers, as well as for performance. The solution is to denormalize the data so that it will meet our query demands. It is important to architect the model for the kinds of queries we are going to be running. For this recipe, we want to find the players who attended at a school for a given year. With that in mind, our data model turns into the following:

We now have a flat dataset in which to answer our queries. The schema script to run within the HBase Shell is the following:

```
create 'school', 'key', 'schoolID',
'schoolName', 'schoolCity', 'schoolState',
'schoolNick', 'playerID', 'nameFirst', 'nameLast', 'nameNick', 'yearMin',
'yearMax'
```

This is HBase shorthand to create a table named `school`, with a key column named `key`, and 11 column families (`schoolID`, `schoolName`, `schoolCity`, `schoolState`, `schoolNick`, `playerID`, `nameFirst`, `nameLast`, `nameNick`, `yearMin`, and `yearMax`). Another way to model the data would be to take advantage of an advanced feature of HBase, which is the ability to nest datasets together. This somewhat mimics the Many to Many relationship modeled in the relational database, but can make it a challenge to query data if the nested data goes more than one or two levels in. The model would look like the following figure:

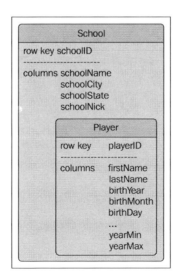

Where the `Player` object would just be another column family within the `School` table.

 Ian Varley created an awesome presentation covering Hbase's schema model for HBase Con 2012. It is definitely a recommended read, that goes into detail about nested objects, column families, and other advanced options. The presentation is available at `http://ianvarley.com/ coding/HBaseSchema_HBaseCon2012.pdf`.

How to do it...

Perform the following steps to load the baseball data into HBase:

1. Open Spoon and create a new transformation.

2. Bring over three **Hadoop File Input** steps from the **Big Data** category to load the `Master.csv`, `School.csv`, and the `SchoolsPlayers.csv` files.

3. Before we can join the datasets together, we must sort each dataset with a **Sort rows** step per file. Sort the data based on the keys for that dataset. For `School`, the key would be `SchoolID`, `Master` would have `playerID`, and so on.

4. Now to merge the datasets together, starting with the `Master` and `SchoolsPlayers` datasets. The two sets can be merged via `playerID`.

5. The `Master/SchoolsPlayers` dataset needs to be sorted by `schoolID` so that it can be merged with the `School` data. Add another **Sort rows** step to sort the data.

6. Add another **Merge Join** step to merge the `Master/SchoolsPlayers` dataset with the `School` data. The two sets can be merged via `schoolID`.

7. Add a **Calculator** step from the **Transform** category. This step will create the values for the key field by combining the `schoolID` and `playerID` fields with a **|** delimiter. Add two rows in the **Fields:** grid, as shown in the following screenshot:

Fields:

#	New field	Calculation	Field A	Field B ^	Field C	Value type	Le	Pr	Remove
1	partition	Set field to constant value A					String			Y
2	key	A + B + C	schoolID	partition	playerID	String			N

8. Before we load data into HBase, we need to remove any fields that we do not want to store into the database. Bring over a **Select Values** step from the **Transformation** section. Select the **Remove** tab and click on **Get fields to remove**. This will add all the stream fields into the **Fields to remove:** grid. We need to keep the fields that match the column family names listed earlier (CschoolID, schoolName, and so on).

9. Finally, add an **HBase Output** step, which can be found under the **Big Data** category. On the **Configure connection** tab, enter the sandbox's IP address and port. The default should be 2181 for the port.

10. Switch to the **Create/Edit mappings** tab. Click on **Get table names** and select the School table from the dropdown.

11. In the **Mapping name** field, enter player.

12. Click on **Get incoming fields**. This will bring the stream fields into the mapping. Find the **key** row and change the **Key** value to Y, leaving the **Column family** and **Column name** fields blank. The **Type** field should be changed to String.

13. All of the other fields (schoolCity, schoolName, schoolNick, and so on) can be added to the column families of the same name. The mapping should look similar to the following screenshot:

#	Alias	Key	Column family	Column name	Type
1	key	Y			String
2	nameFirst	N	nameFirst	nameFirst	String
3	nameLast	N	nameLast	nameLast	String
4	nameNick	N	nameNick	nameNick	String
5	playerID	N	playerID	playerID	String
6	schoolCity	N	schoolCity	schoolCity	String
7	schoolID	N	schoolID	schoolID	String
8	schoolName	N	schoolName	schoolName	String
9	schoolNick	N	schoolNick	schoolNick	String
10	schoolState	N	schoolState	schoolState	String
11	yearMax	N	yearMax	yearMax	Integer
12	yearMin	N	yearMin	yearMin	Integer

14. Click on **Save mapping**. A prompt will appear asking to save the mapping for the School table. Click on **Yes** and switch back to the **Configure connection** tab.

15. For the **HBase table name** field, enter `school`. Select **player** for the **Mapping name** field. Click on **OK**. The final transformation should look similar to the following screenshot:

How it works...

Building on the recipe, *Loading data into Hadoop*, we take the data from Hadoop and use Kettle's built in capabilities to sort and join the data and build a denormalized dataset that can help us to answer queries regarding player statistics based on schools.

It is important to note that HBase is not like typical databases; in that it can be quite difficult to join across tables and column families. As new requirements for given datasets come in, it is very likely that the same data will be restructured across multiple tables and many column families.

There's more...

While we took advantage of the work done in the recipe, *Loading data into Hadoop* we could just as easily have used the original `csv` files, another database, or even spreadsheets to load into HBase. Just like with any of the more common data sources, once the data is part of a PDI stream, it is treated all the same.

See also

▸ *Getting data from HBase*

▸ *Getting data from Hadoop*

▸ The recipe *Joining two or more streams based on given conditions* in Chapter 7, *Understanding and Optimizing Data Flows*

Getting data from HBase

Sources like HBase are dynamically loaded and can have data structured in very different ways than what typical sources are known for. Unlike flat files or traditional relational databases, where there is a somewhat rigid data model, tables in a NoSQL database can be free form. There are several ways in which to query such a database, from writing Java code, using Hive to translate a SQL-like statement into an executable plan, or using a tool like Kettle to extract the needed data. For this recipe, we will be utilizing the **HBase Input** step to load data from HBase.

Getting ready

In order to follow this recipe, you will need to perform the *Loading data into HBase* recipe. We will be using the dataset created in HBase with that recipe, to answer the question posed while designing the data model—which players attended what school at a given year?

How to do it...

Perform the following steps to get the baseball data from HBase:

1. Create a new transformation.

2. Place an **HBase Input** step from the **Big Data** category into the canvas. On the **Configure query** tab, enter the IP address of the **Zookeeper host(s)** and the port for the **Zookeeper port**. For the sandbox, enter in your sandbox's IP address and the port number `2181` respectively.

3. Find the **HBase table name** field and click on **Get mapped table names**. This will provide a drop-down list of tables from HBase. Select the **school** table.

4. Click on the **Get mappings for the specified table** button beside the **Mapping name** field and select the **player** mapping.

5. Click on **Get Key/Fields Info**. All the fields for the school player mapping should populate in the grid on this tab. The grid should match the following screenshot:

#	Alias	Key	Column fami	Column nam	Type	Form:	Index
1	key	Y			String		N
2	nameFirst	N	nameFirst	nameFirst	String		N
3	nameLast	N	nameLast	nameLast	String		N
4	nameNick	N	nameNick	nameNick	String		N
5	playerID	N	playerID	playerID	String		N
6	schoolCity	N	schoolCity	schoolCity	String		N
7	schoolID	N	schoolID	schoolID	String		N
8	schoolName	N	schoolName	schoolName	String		N
9	schoolNick	N	schoolNick	schoolNick	String		N
10	schoolState	N	schoolState	schoolState	String		N
11	yearMax	N	yearMax	yearMax	Integer	#;-#	N
12	yearMin	N	yearMin	yearMin	Integer	#;-#	N

6. Switch to the **Filter result set** tab. Add filters for `yearMax` and `yearMin` so that it matches the following screenshot:

#	Alias	Type	Operator	Comparison	F ^	Signed
1	yearMin	Integer	<=	1989		N
2	yearMax	Integer	>=	1989		N

7. Make sure that **Match all** is selected and then click on **OK** to close the step.

8. Add a **Sort rows** step and connect the **HBase input** step to it with a hop.

9. In the **Sort rows** step, sort the data in ascending order by **schoolName, nameLast,** and **nameFirst**. This will provide an ordered list by both school and player.

10. Bring a **Text file output** step over. Under the **Fields** tab, click on **Get Fields** and add all the stream fields. The final transformation should look like the following screenshot:

HBase Input 2   Sort rows   Text file output

11. Execute the transformation. You should see a text file produced with all of the players that were at a school during the year 1989. You can rerun the transformation with different filter criteria and receive matching result sets.

How it works...

By combining the datasets into one flat structure, we are able to use HBase to quickly query the data for the given filter criteria. We can query the same table against many different mappings to best suite the types of queries we wish to run. The mapping shown in the **Configure query** tab is based on the mappings created or edited on the **Create/Edit mappings** tab. This same functionality can be found in the **HBase Output** step. The **Filter result set** tab allows for complex filtering of the dataset.

See also

- ▸ *Loading data into MongoDB*
- ▸ *Loading data into HBase*
- ▸ The recipe *Writing a simple file* in *Chapter 2, Reading and Writing Files*

Loading data into MongoDB

MongoDB is a type of NoSQL database, called a **document store**. Data is stored in JSON-like arrays in a format called BSON (binary JSON), which allows for quick and scalable queries. **Java Script Object Notation** (**JSON**), are name/value pairs that can be nested to store complex data. Another way of thinking of a MongoDB document is that they are akin to a multidimensional array. Like many NoSQL databases, the schema structure is dynamic. This means that the descriptors of a dataset can be added, removed, or not even required for records to be stored into a given document.

Getting ready

We will continue to use the Lahman's Baseball Database mentioned earlier in the chapter to load MongoDB and later use it to query for specific data. Before we can do anything else though, we need to make sure that we have an instance of MongoDB to play with, either locally on a virtual machine or elsewhere. To download a copy of MongoDB, check out the website at `http://www.monodb/org/downloads`. There is also some great documentation there if you wish to advance beyond the basics.

How to do it...

Follow the steps to load the baseball data into MongoDB:

1. Create a new transformation.
2. Bring a **CSV file input** step over and open the step.
3. **Browse** to the `Batting.csv` file from the Lahman Baseball dataset. Click on **Get Fields** to add all the fields to the data grid. Click on **OK** to exit the step.

4. Add a **MongoDb Output** step from the **Big Data** category. Connect the **CSV file input** step to it with a hop. Open the step.

5. Point to your MongoDB instance by entering the **Host name or IP address** and **Port** that MongoDB is running on.

6. For the **Database** field, enter `baseball`.

7. For the **Collection** field, enter `batting`.

8. Switch to the **Mongo document fields** tab and click on **Get fields**. The stream fields will be populated into the grid. Click on **OK**.

9. Run the transformation. The Batting data should load into the baseball database.

How it works...

By using the **MongoDB Output** step, Kettle is able to define the data stream into a MongoDB document structure, even if the data is nested in a complex manner. To ensure that the data structure matches the schema of an already existing document store, there is an extra feature on the **Mongo document fields** tab called **Preview document structure** that will show the document's data structure, so that if the **Mongo document path** column needs to be tweaked beforehand, the developer can do so. Remember, the step will not necessarily fail if the document structure does not match. It will load a bad structure right alongside the good structure, because MongoDB only sees data. Also note that most NoSQL databases are not defined as an ACID compliant. ACID is the standard used to determine if data will be lost, overwritten, or otherwise manipulated in a controlled manner. While MongoDB and other NoSQL databases provide huge boosts in performance for querying huge datasets, it does come at some cost.

See also

▸ *Getting data from MongoDB*

Getting data from MongoDB

Moving data out of MongoDB is a tad trickier than putting data into the NoSQL database. Fortunately, we are able to filter out data to produce a smaller subset of a source document store.

Getting ready

We will be pulling a subset of data from the batting dataset loaded from the Lahman's Baseball Database in the recipe, *Loading data into MongoDB*. It will also be beneficial to read more on MongoDB's data model. There is a good overview provided by the MongoDB website at `http://docs.mongodb.org/manual/core/data-modeling/`.

How to do it...

1. Open a new transformation.

2. Under the **Big Data** category, select the **MongoDb input** step and bring it over to the canvas.

3. Open the step and add the MongoDB instance connection information to the **Host name or IP address** and **Port**.

4. Enter `baseball` for the **Database** field and `batting` for the **Collection** field.

5. For the **Query expression (JSON)** field, enter `{ "$query" : {"G_batting" : {"$gte" : 10 }}, "$orderby" : {"playerID" : 1, "yearID": 1} }`. This is telling MongoDB to find any players who batted at least 10 games in a given year, and sort the data by `playerID` and `yearID` in ascending order.

6. For the **Fields expression (JSON)** field, enter `{"playerID":1, "yearID":1,"G_batting":1}`. This is telling MongoDB to only include the `playerID`, `yearID`, `teamID`, and `G_batting` fields.

7. Click on **Preview** to view a sample of the filtered dataset. Notice that the data is returning in JSON format. Click on **OK** to exit the field.

8. The data must be translated from JSON for Kettle to be able to do more with it. Under the **Input** category, find the **Json Input** step and add it to the canvas. Add a hop from the **MongoDB Input** step to the **Json Input** step.

9. Open the **Json Input** step. Click on the **Source is defined in a field?** checkbox to true. The **Get source from field** dropdown should have the **json** field selected that was created with the **MongoDB Input** step.

10. Switch to the **Fields** tab and enter the stream data as shown in the following screenshot:

#	Name	Path	Type	Form	Ler	Pre	Cui	Decin	Groi	Trim type	Repe
1	playerID	playerID	String							none	N
2	yearID	yearID	String							none	N
3	teamID	teamID	String							none	N
4	G_batting	G_batting	String							none	N

11. Click on **OK**. Add a **Text File Output** step and add a hop between the **Json Input** step and the **Text File Output** step.

12. Open the **Text File Output** step and give a file path for the output file.

13. Switch to the **Fields** tab and click on **Get Fields**. This will populate the grid with the stream fields.

14. Save and run the transformation. You now have a file listing the `playerID`s and the years in which they batted at more than 10 games.

How it works...

The **MongoDB Input** step is able to translate JSON queries (which are the standard way of querying MongoDB) and pull the data back into the stream. The result set is also a JSON array that needs just a touch more interpretation before it can be further used by Kettle, so a **Json Input** step is required to turn the JSON array into something more manageable. From there, we can use all of Kettle's capabilities to transform and cleanse the data to match our requirements.

For more details on how to query and filter MongoDB, check out the documentation at `http://docs.mongodb.org/manual/core/read-operations/`.

See also

▶ *Loading data into MongoDB*

▶ *Getting data from HBase*

▶ The *Writing a simple file* recipe in *Chapter 2, Reading and Writing Files*

4
Manipulating XML Structures

In this chapter, we will cover:

- ▶ Reading simple XML files
- ▶ Specifying fields by using the Path notation
- ▶ Validating well-formed XML files
- ▶ Validating an XML file against DTD definitions
- ▶ Validating an XML file against an XSD schema
- ▶ Generating a simple XML document
- ▶ Generating complex XML structures
- ▶ Generating an HTML page using XML and XSL transformations
- ▶ Reading an RSS Feed
- ▶ Generating an RSS Feed

Introduction

XML (Extensible Markup Language) is a markup language used to describe data in a format that both humans and machines can understand; the opposite of **HTML** which was designed only to display data in a web browser. It is a self-descriptive language because its tags are not predefined. XML documents are not only used to store data, but also to exchange data between systems.

XML is recommended by **W3C (World Wide Web Consortium)**. You will find the details at the following URL: `http://www.w3.org/XML/`. **PEDI (Pentaho Data Integration)** has a rich set of steps and job entries for manipulating XML structures. The recipes in this chapter are meant to teach you how to read, write, and validate XML using those features.

> Most of the recipes are based on a database with books and authors. To learn more about the structure of that database, see the *Appendix A, Data Structures*, or the examples in *Chapter 1, Working with Databases*.

The recipes assume that you know the basics of XML, that is, you know what XML is, what an attribute is, and so on. If you don't, you should start by reading something about it before proceeding. The following tutorial is a good start: `http://www.w3schools.com/xml/`.

Reading simple XML files

PEDI has a step named **Get XML Data** used to read XML structures. This recipe shows how to read an XML file containing information about museums using this step.

Getting ready

In this exercise, you will use a file named `museum.xml` with the following structure:

```
<museums>
    <museum id_museum= '...'>
        <name>...</name>
        <city>...</city>
        <country>...</country>
    </museum>
</museums>
```

We will be making use of Path, which is used to query XML documents to retrieve and compute information. If you are new to Path, it is recommended to check out the excellent tutorials over at `http://www.w3schools.com/xpath/` to get a better understanding of Path before digging into the recipe.

How to do it...

Perform the following steps:

1. Create a new transformation.

2. Drop a **Get data from XML** step from the **Input** category into the canvas.

3. Under the **File** tab, you must select the XML document. Browse for the file `museums.xml` and click on the **Add** button.

4. Under the **Content** tab, type `/museums/museum` in the Loop Path textbox. This will be the current `node.text` box

 Alternatively, you can click on the **Get Path nodes** and select it.

Under the **Fields** tab, you need to specify the fields by using Path notation. Use the **Get Fields** button to get them automatically. You should get a result similar to the following:

File | Content | Fields | Additional output fields

^	#	Name	XPath	Element	Result type	Type
	1	name	name	Node	Value of	String
	2	city	city	Node	Value of	String
	3	country	country	Node	Value of	String
	4	id_museum	@id_museum	Attribute	Value of	Integer

In the case of XML attributes, if you include the @ character in the Path as a prefix (for example, `@id_museum`), it is not necessary to select **Attribute** under the **Element** column. The @ character is used in Path to denote that an attribute is being queried for:

Doing a preview on this step, you will obtain the following results:

Rows of step: Get data from museums XML (113 rows)

^	#	name	city	country	id_museum
	1	Fundacion Federico Klemm	Buenos Aires	Argentina	1
	2	Fundacion Proa	Buenos Aires	Argentina	2
	3	Museo de Arte Latinoamericano	Buenos Aires	Argentina	3
	4	Museo Nacional de Bellas Artes	Buenos Aires	Argentina	4
	5	Xul Solar Museum	Buenos Aires	Argentina	5
	6	Museu de Arte Contemporanea de Niteroi	Niteroi	Brazil	6
	7	Museu de Arte Contemporanea do Parana	Parana	Brazil	7
	8	Museu de Arte Moderna	Rio de Janeiro	Brazil	8
	9	Museu Nacional de Belas Artes	Rio de Janeiro	Brazil	9
	10	Carlos Costa Pinto Museum	Salvador	Brazil	10
	11	Itau Cultural	Sao Paulo	Brazil	11

How it works...

The **Get XML Data** step allows reading data in XML format by using a Path specification. In this recipe, you read a single file. However, as in any input step, you have the option to read a whole directory, multiple files, or even use a regular expression to specify which files to read. Alternatively, you can use this step to read XML structures from other sources, such as fields or URLs. For more details, see the section *XML data in a field* later in this recipe.

In order to tell Kettle where to get the fields from, the first thing you have to do is to fill the **Loop Path** textbox. You can do that by typing it or by clicking on the **Get Path nodes** button and selecting it from the list of available nodes. For generating the dataset, Kettle will loop over the selected node.

 For each element that matches the selected node, Kettle will generate a new row.

The **Path** and **Element** columns in the **Field** grid are the fields used to define the origin of the fields. The Path should be relative to the current node. The **Element** column simply tells Kettle if the element is a node or an attribute. The rest of the columns in the grid should be filled just as you would in any input step, providing the type, format, and so on. If you are using this step for reading a file, you have the option to fill this grid automatically, by clicking on the **Get fields** button.

There's more...

By default, XML files are interpreted through unicode encoding. If none is specified, you have the option of selecting the encoding under the **Content** tab. For more on encoding, follow the link at http://en.wikipedia.org/wiki/Character_encoding.

If you have large XML files, then see the recommendations at http://wiki.pentaho.com/display/EAI/Get+Data+from+XML+-+Handling+Large+Files.

XML data in a field

In some situations, you don't have the XML as a file, but as a field in your dataset. An example of this is a transformation, where you call a web service that returns the result in XML format. In these situations, instead of specifying the name of the file, you must complete the section **XML source from field** under the **File** tab of the **Get data from XML** step. Checking the option **XML source is defined in a field?** will enable the dropdown list named **get XML source from** a field. From that list, you have to select the field that contains the data in XML format.

The rest of the tabs should be filled exactly as when you read a file. The main difference is that the **Get fields** button will not be enabled. Consequently, you will have to fill the grid manually, or follow this tip:

> Copy the content of the field that contains the XML structure and save it in a file. Read that file by using the **Get data from XML** step, and use the **Get fields** button to fill the **Fields** grid automatically. Finally, change the settings under the **File** tab, in order to read the structure from the desired field.

XML file name in a field

It may happen that your XML structure is in a file, but you don't know its name in advance. If the name of the file is in a field, you still may read it by using the **Get data from XML** step. For reading the file, you must complete the section **XML source from field** under the **File** tab of the **Get data from XML** step. Check the two options: **XML source is defined in a field?** and **XML source is a filename?**. The get **XML source from a field** dropdown list will be filled with the names of the incoming fields. From that list, select the field that contains the name of the file. As in the previous section, the **Get fields** button will be disabled. For advice on filling the **Fields** grid, read the preceding tip.

See also

- ▸ *Specifying fields by using the Path notation*

Specifying fields by using the Path notation

If you intend to read or write XML structures, it's mandatory that you understand at least the basics of Path, the language for finding information in an XML document, or defining parts of an XML document. In this recipe you will be introduced to the Path notation, so that you will find it easier to work with the rest of the recipes in the chapter. Suppose you have an XML structure such as the following:

```
<wound>
  <data>
    <request>
      <type>City</type>
      <query>Buenos Aires, Argentina</query>
    </request>
    <current_condition>
      <observation_time>08:12 PM</observation_time>
      <temp scale="C">19</temp>
      <temp scale="F">66</temp>
      <weatherDesc>Sunny</weatherDesc>
```

```
            <windspeed unit="Miles">8</windspeed>
            <windspeed unit="Kmph">13</windspeed>
            <dirDegree>70</dirDegree>
            <dir16Point>ENE</dir16Point>
            ...
        </current_condition>
        <weather>
            <date>2010-10-24</date>
            <tempMaxC>23</tempMaxC>
            ...
        </weather>
        <weather>
            <date>2010-10-25</date>
            ...
        </weather>
        ...
    </data>
    <data>
        <request>
            <type>City</type>
            <query>Montevideo, Uruguay</query>
        </request>
        ...
    </data>
    <data>
    ...
    </data>
    ...
</wound>
```

This structure contains the weather forecast for a group of cities. For each city, you have the current weather and the forecast for the next three days.

> The sample XML was obtained by using a free local weather API. To learn how to use that API, visit www.worldweatheronline.com. Note that the sample is a slightly modified version of the original result.

Now, you want to specify the Path for the following data (highlighted in the sample structure):

- ▶ City
- ▶ Observation time
- ▶ Temperature (scale and degrees)
- ▶ Weather description

Getting ready

This recipe is theoretical and has the purpose of helping you when it's time to enter a Path notation. You will not develop a transformation here. However, for a better understanding of what's being explained, you can do the following:

1. Download the sample XML file.
2. Read it by using the **Get data from XML** step.
3. Try introducing the different Path notations in the **Fields** grid, as they are explained.
4. To check if you are entering the correct notations, do a preview and check it for yourself.

How to do it...

Perform the following steps:

1. Pick the node that will be the base for specifying your fields. In the sample data, the node will be `/wound/data`.

   For each desired element, repeat steps 2 and 3.

2. Look at the XML structure to see if it is a node or an attribute. In the sample data, the temperature scale and the units for the wind speed are attributes. The rest of the fields are nodes.

3. Identify the absolute location of the element, that is, the complete path from the root element to the desired element. For example, for `city` the absolute location would be `/wound/data/request/query`. If the element is an attribute, prepend @ to the name.

4. Identify the location relative to the base node identified in step 1. For example, for the city the relative location would be `request/query`. If the element is an attribute, prepend @ to the name.

The following table shows the absolute and relative locations for the sample data:

Data	Absolute Location	Relative Location
City	`/wound/data/request/query`	`request/query`
Observation time	`/wound/data/current_cond/` `observation_time`	`current_cond/` `observation_time`
Temperature(degrees)	`/wound/data/current_cond/temp`	`current_cond/temp`
Temperature(scale)	`/wound/data/current_cond/` `temp/@scale`	`current_cond/` `temp/@scale`
Weather description	`/wound/data/current_cond/` `weatherDesc`	`current_cond/` `weatherDesc`

The preceding locations are the Path notations for the selected data in the sample XML structure.

How it works...

Path is a set of rules used for getting information from an XML document. Path treats an XML structure as a tree of nodes. The tree can be compared to a directory tree in your system. The way you specify relative or absolute locations in that tree is much the same in both cases.

In Kettle, you use Path both for getting data from XML structures and for generating XML structures.

The reason for specifying both absolute and relative locations in the recipe is that in Kettle you need one or the other depending on what you are doing. For example, when you read an XML structure, you have to select a node and define the fields as locations relative to that node. When you join two XML structures, the Path statement that you need to specify is an absolute location.

There's more...

The Path notations in the recipe are the simplest Path notations you will find, but Path allows you to write really complex expressions. The next sections provide you with more detail about specifying nodes with Path notation. For more information on Path, you can follow this link: `http://www.w3schools.com/Path/` or see the W3C recommendation: `http://www.w3.org/TR/xpath`.

Getting data from a different path

When you read an XML structure, you don't specify absolute paths, but paths relative to a node selected as the current node. In the sample recipe, the current node was `/wound/data`. If the fields are inside that node, you get the relative location just by cutting the root part from the absolute location. For example, the absolute path for the weather description is `/wound/data/current_cond/weatherDesc`.

Then, for getting the location relative to the current node, just cut `/wound/data/` and you get `current_cond/weatherDesc`.

If the data you need is not in the tree below the selected node, you have to use the `..` notation, which is used to specify the parent of the current node. For example, suppose that the current node is `/wound/data/current_cond` and you want to know the name of the city to which this condition belongs. The `city` element is not inside the selected node. To reach it, you have to type `../request/city`.

Getting data selectively

If you are reading a structure where there might be more than one element with the same Path notation, you have the option to select just the one that interests you. Look for example at the temperature elements in the sample structure:

```
<temp scale="C">19</temp>
<temp scale="F">66</temp>
```

These lines belong to the Celsius and the Fahrenheit scales respectively. Both lines share the same Path notation. Suppose that you are interested in the Celsius line. To get that element, you have to use a **predicate**. A predicate is an expression used to find a specific node or a node that contains a specific value. In this case, you need a predicate to find a node that contains an attribute named `scale` with value `C`. The notation for getting that node is `temp[@scale='C']`. In general, for getting a node that contains a specific value, the notation is `Path[condition]`, that is, the Path expression followed by the condition within brackets.

Now, let's make it a bit more complicated. Suppose that you don't even know which scale to return because the scale is part of the XML structure, as shown in the following example:

```
<request>
    <type>City</type>
    <query>Buenos Aires, Argentina</query>
    <preferredScale>C</preferredScale>
</request>
```

Each city will have its own preferred scale and you should return the temperature in Celsius or Fahrenheit depending on the city's preferred scale. What you need is a dynamic predicate. The way to implement this is through the use of a non-standard extension named **tokens**. Let's explain it based on our example:

1. The first thing you have to do is to add the field in which the token is based: `preferredScale`. So, add a field named `preferredScale` and for Path, type `../request/preferred_scale`.

2. Then, add a new field for the temperature in the desired scale. For **Name**, type `temperature` and as **Path** type `../temp[@scale =@_preferredScale-]/text()`.

3. Finally, under the **Content** tab, check **Use tokens**. If you don't, this will not work!

Assuming that you defined the fields: `city`, `preferredScale`, `temperature_C`, and `temperature_F` for the temperature in Celsius and Fahrenheit degrees respectively, and `temperature`, if you do a preview you should see something like the following:

#	city	preferredScale	observa∧	temperature_C	temperature_F	temperature
1	Buenos aires, Argentina	C	08:12	19	66	19
2	Montevideo, Uruguay	C	08:12	16	61	16
3	Santiago, Chile	C	08:12	25	77	25
4	Brasilia, Brazil	C	08:12	23	73	23
5	Rio de janeiro, Brazil	C	08:12	25	77	25
6	New york, United States of America	F	08:12	19	67	67
7	Washington, United States of America	F	08:12	22	71	71
8	Barcelona, Spain	C	08:12	18	64	18

In general, the expression for a token is `@_<tokenized_field>-`, where `<tokenized_field>` is the field in which the token is based and has to be previously defined.

PEDI will build a dynamic predicate by replacing each `<tokenized_field>` by its current value and then returning the proper node value.

Getting more than one node when the nodes share their Path notation

Look at the `weather` nodes in the sample XML structure:

```
<weather>
  <date>2010-10-24</date>
  <tempMaxC>23</tempMaxC>
  ...
</weather>
<weather>
  <date>2010-10-25</date>
  <tempMaxC>23</tempMaxC>
  ...
</weather>
<weather>
  <date>2010-10-26</date>
  <tempMaxC>24</tempMaxC>
```

For each node `/wound/data` (the current node in the example), there are three different `weather` nodes.

Suppose that you want to read all of them. In this case, you have to use a predicate just as explained in the previous section. In this case the predicate is not used to find a node that contains a specific value, but to find the nodes by position, you need the first, second, and third `weather` nodes. The notation that you have to use is `Path[position]`, that is, the Path expression followed by the position of the desired element within brackets.

In the example, the notation for the first, second, and third `weather` nodes would be `weather[1]`, `weather[2]`, and `weather[3]` respectively. For getting nodes inside those, the notation is as usual. For example, for getting the date of the second node, you should write `weather[2]/date`.

Note that if you are reading an XML structure, each element that you get by using this notation may be used as a new column in the dataset. Instead of that, if you want to generate a different row for each `weather` node, then you should take another approach: instead of using this notation, simply change the current node (**Loop Path** element) from `/wound/data` to `/wound/data/weather`.

Saving time when specifying Path

In most of the Kettle steps where you have to provide a Path, you must type it manually. That's why you need to understand this notation. However, when you read an XML structure by using the **Get Data from XML** step, you have the option to use the **Get Fields** button to get the nodes and attributes automatically. Note that Kettle will get only the trivial elements:

 ▸ It will get only the fields that are below the node you typed as **Loop Path**.

 ▸ It will bring all the elements. For getting elements selectively, as in the temperature example above, you'll have to modify the grid manually.

 ▸ If there is more than one element with the same Path notation, as in the weather example above, it will bring only the first element.

To summarize, if you fill the grid with the **Get Fields** button you will save time, but on most occasions, you will still have to adjust the data in the grid manually.

Validating well-formed XML files

PEDI offers different options for validating XML documents, including the validation of a well-formed document. The structure of an XML document is formed by tags that begin with the character < and end with the character >. In an XML document, you can find start tags `<example tag>`, end tags `</example tag>`, or empty element tags `<example tag/>`, and these tags can be nested. An XML document is called well-formed when it follows the following set of rules:

 ▸ They must contain at least one element.

 ▸ They must contain a unique root element—this means a single opening and closing tag for the whole document.

- The tags are case sensitive—this means that beginning and ending tags match (for instance, `<example Tag></example Tag>` versus `<example Tag> </Example Tag>`). The second tag set will throw an error.

- All of the tags must be nested properly, without overlapping.

> There is a lot more that goes into consideration around what a well-formed XML file is. Wikipedia has an overview of what it means to have a well-formed document. Check out the article at `http://en.wikipedia.org/wiki/Well- formed_document`.

In this recipe you will learn to validate whether a document is well-formed, which is the simplest kind of XML validation. Assume that you want to extract data from several XML documents with museum's information, but only want to process those files that are well-formed.

Getting ready

To use this recipe, you need a set of XML files in a directory named `museums`. This recipe reads a directory containing three files, where the first one has an intentional tag mistake. You can download the sample files from Packt's site.

How to do it...

Perform the following steps:

1. Create a new job and add a **Start** entry.

2. Drop a **Check if XML is well formed** entry from the **XML** category into the canvas.

3. Under the **General** tab, you must type the path to the `museum` directory in the **File/Folder source** textbox, and type `.+\.xml` in the **wildcard** textbox, in order to use only the files with the `.xml` extension.

4. Click on the **Add** button to populate the **File/Folder** grid.

5. Under the **Advanced** tab, choose the following configuration:

6. Then, create a new transformation in order to process the well-formed XML files obtained from the previous job entry. Add this transformation as the last step in the job.

7. In the transformation, drop a **GET files from result** step from the **Job** category.

8. Add the **Get data from XML** step.

9. Under the **File** tab, set the following screenshot:

10. Under the **Content** tab, type /museums/museum in the **Loop Path** textbox.

11. Finally, the grid under the **Fields** tab must be completed manually, as shown in the following screenshot:

#	Name	XPath	Element	Result type	Type
1	name	name	Node	Value of	String
2	city	city	Node	Value of	String
3	country	country	Node	Value of	String
4	id_museum	@id_museum	Node	Value of	Integer

12. When you run the job, you will obtain the `museums` dataset with data coming only from the well-formed XML files. You can take a look at the **Logging** window to verify this. You will see something like the following:

```
2010/11/01 11:56:43 - Check if XML file is well formed - ERROR
(version 4.1.0, build 13820 from 2010-08-25 07.22.27 by tomcat) :
Error while checking file [file:///C:/museums1.xml].
Exception :
2010/11/01 11:56:43 - Check if XML file is well formed - ERROR
(version 4.1.0, build 13820 from 2010-08-25 07.22.27 by tomcat) :
org.xml.sax.SAXParseException:
```

Element type museum must be followed by either attribute specifications, > or />.

13. Further, you can see in the **Logging** window that only two files out of three were read:

```
2010/11/01 11:56:43 - Get XMLs well-formed.0 - Finished
   processing (I=0, O=0, R=2, W=2, U=0, E=0)
```

How it works...

You can use the **Check if XML is well-formed** job entry to check if one or more XML files are well-formed.

In the recipe the job validates the XML files from the source directory and creates a list with only the valid XML files.

As you saw in the logging window, only two files were added to the list and used later in the transformation. The first file (`C:/museums1.xml`) had an error; it was not well-formed and because of that it was not added to the list of files.

The **Get files from result** step in the transformation gets the list of well-formed XML documents created in the job. Then, a **Get data from XML** step read the files for further processing. Note that in this case, you didn't set the names of the files explicitly, but used the field `path` coming from the previous step.

See also

▸ *Specifying fields by using the Path notation*

▸ *Validating an XML file against DTD definitions*

▸ *Validating an XML file against an XSD schema*

Validating an XML file against DTD definitions

A **Document Type Definition** (**DTD**) defines the document structure of an XML document with a list of elements and attributes. Kettle provides the *DTD validator* entry job to do a validation against a DTD definition file.

For example, suppose you have an XML file with museum's information, as follows:

```
<museums>
    <museum>
        <name>Fundacion Federico Klemm</name>
        <city>Buenos Aires</city>
        <country>Argentina</country>
    </museum>
    <museum id_museum= '2'>
        <name>Fundacion Proa</name>
        <city>Buenos Aires</city>
        <country>Argentina</country>
    </museum>
    <museum id_museum= '9'>
        <name>Museu Nacional de Belas Artes</name>
```

```
            <country>Brazil</country>
      </museum>
      <museum id_museum= '19'>
          <name>Biblioteca Luis Angel Arango</name>
            <city>Bogota</city>
            <country>Colombia</country>
      </museum>
</museums>
```

You want to validate it against the following DTD definition file:

```
<!DOCTYPE museums [
<!ELEMENT museums (museum+)>
<!ELEMENT museum (name+, city, country)>
<!ELEMENT name (#PCDATA)>
<!ELEMENT city (#PCDATA)>
<!ELEMENT country (#PCDATA)>
<!ATTLIST museum id_museum CDATA #REQUIRED >
  ]>
```

With this definition, you are declaring the museum structure elements: `name`, `city`, and `country`, and defining the attribute `id_museum` as required.

Getting ready

For this recipe, you need a `museum.xml` document with DTD definition included. You can download it from Packt's website.

You can have the DTD definition as an independent file or inside the XML document. If the DTD is declared inside the XML file, it should be wrapped in a `DOCTYPE` definition with the following syntax: `<!DOCTYPE root-element [element-declarations] >`.

How to do it...

Perform the following steps:

1. Create a new job and add a **Start** entry.
2. Drop a **DTD Validator** job entry from the **XML** category into the canvas.
3. Here, you must point to your XML file in the **XML File name** textbox.
4. Check the **DTD Intern** checkbox.
5. Run this job, so that the XML data gets validated against the DTD definitions, which are inside the XML file.

6. You can see the result of the validation including information about the errors under the **Logging** tab in the **Execution results** window. In this case, the results are as follows:

   ❏ For the first element, the job will detect this error:

   ```
   Attribute "id_museum" is required and must be specified for
      element type "museum"
   ```

   ❏ The second and fourth museum elements are correct

   ❏ For the third element, you will receive the following message:

   ```
   The content of element type "museum" must match
      "(name+,city,country)"
   ```

How it works...

The **DTD Validator** job entry does the entire task of validating an XML file against a DTD definition. In the recipe, you checked the **DTD Intern** checkbox because the DTD definitions were inside the XML file. Otherwise, you must fill the DTD **File name** textbox with the name of the proper DTD file.

There's more...

DTD has a lot of limitations. For example, you cannot define types for the XML elements or attributes. If you need more flexibility, another step that can be used is the **XSD validatior** step.

 You can learn more about DTD definitions at http://www.w3schools.com/dtd/default.asp.

See also

▸ *Validating an XML file against an XSD schema*

▸ *Validating well-formed XML files*

Validating an XML file against an XSD schema

In this recipe, you will learn how to use the **XSD Validator** step, in order to verify a particular XML structure using an **XSD** (**XML Schema Definition**). For example, you will use a database of books (with the structure shown in the *Appendix A, Data Structures*) and an XSD schema file with the books, structure. You want to validate each book element against the XSD schema file.

The XSD file is named `books.xsd` and it looks like following:

```
<xs:schema xmlns:xs="http://www.w3.org/2001/XMLSchema">
  <xs:simpleType name="idTitle">
    <xs:restriction base="xs:string">
      <xs:pattern value="\d{3}\-\d{3}"/>
    </xs:restriction>
  </xs:simpleType>
  <xs:simpleType name="positiveDecimal">
    <xs:restriction base="xs:decimal">
      <xs:minInclusive value="0.0" />
    </xs:restriction>
  </xs:simpleType>
  <xs:element name="book">
    <xs:complexType>
      <xs:sequence>
        <xs:element name="title" type="xs:string"/>
        <xs:element name="genre" type="xs:string"/>
        <xs:element name="price" type="positiveDecimal"/>
        <xs:element name="author" type="xs:string"/>
      </xs:sequence>
      <xs:attribute name="id_title" type="idTitle" />
    </xs:complexType>
  </xs:element>
</xs:schema>
```

This schema file verifies the following features:

▶ Inside a sequence, there are three elements of string type: `title`, `genre`, and `author`.

▶ There is an element named `price` of a `simpleType` named `positiveDecimal`, declared earlier as a decimal type with `0.0` as its minimum value.

▶ There is a `simpleType` named `idTitle` for the `id_Title` attribute. This type is declared as a string with a pattern expression. In this case, you will use `\d{3}\-\d{3}` which means three decimal followed by a hyphen and then three more decimals, for example, `123-456`.

Getting ready

You need a database with books' and authors' information. You will also need the XSD schema as a separate file. You can download the file from Packt's site. Since we are validating the data against an XSD, we need to edit a couple of records in the books table of the books database:

1. Remove the - in id_title for the record containing information on the book titled Star Island.

2. Change the price of the book titled The Girl with the Dragon Tatoo to -5.

How to do it...

Perform the following steps:

1. Create a new transformation.

2. Drop a **Table Input** step and make a selection from the books database with the following statement:

```
SELECT id_title
     , title
     , genre
     , price
     , concat(lastname,", ",firstname) author
FROM books
LEFT JOIN authors
ON authors.id_author=books.id_author
```

3. Use the **Add XML** step from the **Transform** category, in order to create a new column with the data for each book in XML format.

4. Under the **Content** tab, type xmlBook in **Output Value** and book as **Root XML element**.

5. Under the **Fields** tab, use the **Get Fields** button to populate the grid automatically. Modify the **Attribute** field for the id_title row to Y. Then, modify the **Format** and **Decimal** fields for the price row, as shown in the following screenshot:

#	Fieldname	Element name	Type	Format	Le	Pre(	Curl	De	↕	Nu	Attribute
1	title		String								N
2	genre		String								N
3	price		Number	0.00				.			N
4	author		String								N
5	id_title		String								Y

6. If you do a preview on this step, then you will see a new column with an XML structure for each book. The following is a sample XML structure created with this step:

```
<book id_title="423-006">
<title>Harry Potter and the Order of the Phoenix</title>
<genre>Childrens</genre>
<price>32.00</price>
<author>Rowling, Joanne</author>
</book>
```

 The structure is shown in several lines for clarity. In the preview, you will see the structure in a single line.

7. Add an **XSD Validator** step from the **Validation** category.

8. In the **XML field** located under the **Settings** tab, select the column **xmlBook** that you created in the previous step.

9. Under the same tab, complete the **Output Fields** frame, as shown in the following screenshot:

10. In the **XSD Source** listbox inside the **XML Schema Definition** frame, select the option **is a file, let me specify filename**.

11. Then, in the **XSD Filename** textbox, type or select the `books.xsd` file. When you run this transformation, you will obtain the dataset with books along with a field indicating the result of the validation and the validation message in case of failure. Assuming that you have introduced the errors from the *Getting ready* section, your final dataset will look similar to the one shown in the following screenshot:

#	id_title	title	genre	price	author	resultValidation	ValidationMsgField
3	123-348	The Shining	Fiction	31	King, Stephen	OK	
4	123-349	The Dead Zone	Fiction	37	King, Stephen	OK	
5	123-351	Pet Sematary	Fiction	41	King, Stephen	OK	
6	123-352	The Tommyknockers	Fiction	39	King, Stephen	OK	
7	123-353	Bag of Bones	Fiction	40.9	King, Stephen	OK	
8	123-400	The Girl with the Dragon Ta	Fiction	-5	Larsson, Stieg	Fail	cvc-minInclusive-valid: Value '-5.00' is not f
9	123-401	The Girl who Played with Fi	Fiction	35.9	Larsson, Stieg	OK	
10	123-402	The Girl who Kicked the Ho	Fiction	39	Larsson, Stieg	OK	
11	123-506	Basket Case	Fiction	31	Hiaasen, Carl	OK	
12	123505	Star Island	Fiction	36	Hiaasen, Carl	Fail	cvc-pattern-valid: Value '123505' is not face
13	223-200	Chelsea Chelsea Bang Bang	Non-fiction	25	Handler, Chelsea	OK	
14	223-201	My Horizontal Life	Non-fiction	24	Handler, Chelsea	OK	
15	223-202	Are You There, Vodka? It's r	Non-fiction	19.9	Handler, Chelsea	OK	

How it works...

An XSD file defines a set of rules for validating an XML document. An XSD file allows you to verify whether a document, written in XML format, is well-formed and also respects those rules.

In this example, you created a new column with each book in XML format, and then applied the **XSD Validator** step to verify this column against the `books.xsd` schema file.

In the result of your transformation, you could see that one book didn't follow the pattern expected for the `id_title` field, because it didn't contain a hyphen. In that case, you obtained the following message:

```
cvc-pattern-valid: Value '123505' is not facet-valid with respect
    to pattern '\d{3}\-\d{3}' for type 'idTitle'
```

Also, one book had an incorrect price (a negative one). In that case, you got the following error:

```
cvc-minInclusive-valid: Value '-5.00' is not facet-valid with
    respect to minInclusive '0.0' for type 'positiveDecimal'
```

There's more...

In the recipe, you used the **XSD Validation** step to validate an XML structure, which in turn was made from a field in a database. In general, you can use this step to validate any XML structure, both supplied as a field, or saved in a file.

In cases where you want to validate a file, you can also take advantage of the same functionality from a job entry named **XSD Validation** inside the **XML** category. The configuration of that entry is simple—it's just setting the paths to the XML file and the XSD schema file.

You can learn more about XSD from the following URL: `http://www.w3.org/TR/xmlschema-0/`.

See also

- ▸ *Validating well-formed XML files*
- ▸ *Validating an XML file against DTD definitions*

Generating a simple XML document

In order to create a new XML document, you can use the **XML Output** step. In this recipe you will create a new XML file from a database containing information about books.

Getting ready

You will need a `books` database with the structure described in *Appendix A, Data Structures*.

How to do it...

Perform the following steps:

1. Create a new transformation.

2. Drop a **Table Input** step, in order to obtain the book's information and type the following query:

```
SELECT id_title
     , title
     , genre
     , price
     , concat(lastname,", ",firstname) author
FROM books
LEFT JOIN authors
ON authors.id_author=books.id_author
```

3. Add an **XML Output** step.

4. In the **Filename** textbox of the **File** tab, type the destination filename, including its complete path (without extension). In the **Extension** textbox, leave the default value, `xml`.

5. Fill the **Content** tab as **Parent XML element**, type `Books` and as the **Row XML element**, type `Book`.

6. Under the **Fields** tab, use the **Get Fields** button to get the fields. In the `price` field, set the **Format** to `$0.00`.

7. Run the transformation and look at the generated XML file. It should look like the following:

```
<Books>
    <Book>
        <id_title>123-346</id_title>
        <title>Carrie </title>
        <genre>Fiction</genre>
        <price>$41,00</price>
        <author>King, Stephen</author>
    </Book>
    <Book>
        <id_title>123-347</id_title>
        <title>Salem›s Lot </title>
        ...
    </Book>
    ...
</Books>
```

How it works...

The **XML output** step does the entire task. It creates the XML file with rows coming in the stream, using the **Parent XML element** and **Row XML element** values to complete the structure of the XML file. It encloses each row between tags with the name you provided for **Row XML element** (`<Book>` and `</Book>`), and the whole structure between tags with the name provided for **Parent XML element** (`<Books>` and `</Books>`).

The **XML output** step has some properties in common with other output steps. For example, there is the option to add the date and time as part of the name of the file or to split the output into several files using the **Split every ... rows** textbox from the **Content** tab.

There's more...

In the recipe, you wrote the XML information into a file, but you may want to have the information in XML format as a new column of your dataset. The following section explains how to do this.

Generating fields with XML structures

If, rather than generating the XML structure in a file, you want the structure as a new field, you should use the **Add XML** step from the **Transform** category instead of using the **XML output** step.

The **Add XML** step encodes several fields into an XML fragment. In this step, you must set **Root XML element** (for example `Book`) and the name for the new column. The **Fields** tab is quite similar to the same one in the **XML output** step, but here you can also specify if the element is a node or an attribute. In the example, you can set the field `id_title` as an attribute of the element `Book`, set **Attribute** as `Y` and **Attribute parent name** as `Book`, and you will have the following XML structure:

```
<book id_title ="123-346">
    <title>Carrie </title>
    <genre>Fiction</genre>
    <price>41.00</price>
    <author>King, Stephen</author>
</book>
```

This step is particularly useful for generating complex structures, as you will see in the next recipe.

See also

▸ *Generating complex XML structures*

▸ *Validating an XML file against an XSD schema*

Generating complex XML structures

In previous recipes, you learned how to read and write simple XML structures. With Kettle, you can also generate more complex structures with different levels of information, which is more likely to be similar to the structures you find in real case scenarios. Suppose you need to create a complex XML structure with a hierarchy of two levels: the authors in the first level and their books as their children. In this case, you can't use the **XML output** job entry, because it only works with simple structures. For theses cases, you must learn to use the **XML Join** step.

The objective for the recipe is to get the following XML structure:

```
<result>
    <authors>
        <author id_author =...>
            <lastname>...</lastname>
            <firstname>...</firstname>
            <nationality>...</nationality>
            <birthyear>...</birthyear>
            <books>
                <book id_title =...>
                    <title>...</title>
                    <price>...</price>
```

```
              <genre>...</genre>
          </book>
        </books>
      </author>
      <author id_author =...>
      . . .
      </author>
      . . .
    </authors>
  </result>
```

Getting ready

In this recipe you will use a database of books with the structure shown in *Appendix A, Data Structures*.

How to do it...

We can generate complex XML structures by performing the following three steps:

1. First of all, we will create an empty XML root structure.

2. Then we will add the author's information.

3. Finally, we will inject the book's information inside the `authors` tag.

The following steps explain how to create the XML root structure:

1. Create a new transformation.

2. Drop a **Generate Rows** step into the canvas, in order to create the authors tag.

3. In the **Fields** grid, type the **Name** `authors` and select **String** in the **Type** column.

4. For creating the root XML structure, add an **Add XML** step from the **Transform** category. Name this step `Create XML root structure`.

5. Under the **Content** tab of this step, type `xmlResult` in the **Output Value** textbox, and `result` in the **Root XML element** textbox.

6. Under the **Fields** tab, add the only field that you have: **authors**. Don't forget to set the type as **String**. If you do a preview on this step, you will see a new field named `xmlResult` with the following information:

   ```
   <result><authors/></result>
   ```

Now, the following steps explain how to create the authors piece of XML:

1. Drop a **Table Input** step into the canvas, and select the `authors` table using the following SQL statement:

```
SELECT *
FROM authors
```

2. Use the **Add constants** step from the **Transform** folder and create the entry `books` (`String` type). This literal will be replaced later with the books' authors.

3. Add another **Add XML** step. Name this step as `Create Authors XML`.

4. Under the **Content** tab, type `author` for **Root XML element** and `xmlAuthors` for the **Output Value**.

5. Click on the **Get Fields** button to add to the grid all the fields (including the empty `books` field). For the `id_author` field, select **attribute** as `Y`. Doing a preview on this step, for each author you will see something like the following:

```
<author id_author="A00001">
    <lastname>Larsson</lastname>
    <firstname>Stieg</firstname>
    <nationality>Swedish</nationality>
    <birthyear> 000000000001954</birthyear>
    <books/>
</author>
```

In the preview, you will see the XML structure in a single line. In the examples, the structures are shown over several lines and indented just for better understanding.

Now, you need to insert the authors' data inside the XML root structure created previously. The next steps explain how to merge both streams:

1. Add an **XML Join** step from the **Join** category and use it to link the streams, as shown in the following screenshot:

2. Name this step as `Merge Authors and root XML`.

3. Double-click on the step and fill the **Target stream properties**, **Source stream properties**, and **Join condition properties** frames, as shown in the following screenshot:

4. In the **Result XML field** inside the **Result Stream properties** frame, type `xmlauthors2`.

5. Do a preview of this step. You will see that there is a new field named `xmlauthors2` containing the XML structure for the root XML and the authors. Also note that there is an empty tag named `books` for each author's node:

```
<result>
    <authors>
        <author id_author ="A00001">
            <lastname>Larsson</lastname>
            <firstname>Stieg</firstname>
            <nationality>Swedish</nationality>
            <birthyear>1954</birthyear>
            <books/>
        </author>
        <author id_author ="A00002">
            <lastname>King</lastname>
            <firstname>Stephen</firstname>
            <nationality>American</nationality>
        ...
        </author>
    ...
    </authors>
</result>
```

Finally, it's time to create the XML structure for the books and merge them with the main structure:

1. Drop a **Table input** step into the canvas, in order to select all the books. Use the following SQL statement:

```
SELECT *
FROM books
ORDER BY title
```

2. Add an **Add XML** step. Name this step as `Create Books XML`.

3. Under the **Content** tab, type `book` in the **XML root element** textbox and `xmlBooks` in the **Output Value** textbox.

4. Under the **Fields** tab, use the **Get Field** button to obtain all the fields. Select **attribute** as `Y` for the `id_title` field. Also, for the `price` field, set **Format** to `$0.00`.

5. Do a preview on this step. You will see a new XML field named `xmlBooks` with the book's data. For example:

```
<book id_title ="123-346">
    <title>Carrie </title>
    <price>$41,00</price>
    <genre>Fiction</genre>
</book>
```

6. Finally, you must do the last merge; this time between the output of the **Merge Authors and root XML** step and the output of the recently created **Create Books XML** step. Add one more **XML Join** step and link these two steps. The transformation should look similar to the following:

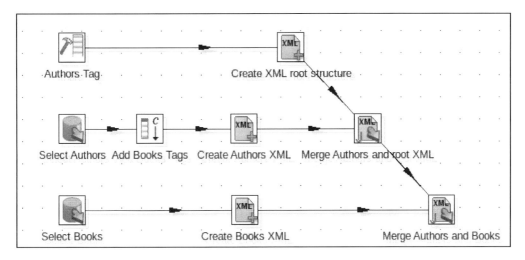

7. In this last step, set the following properties:

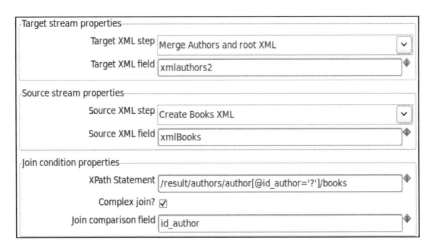

8. In the **Result XML field** inside the **Result Stream properties frame**, type `xmlfinalresult`. This field will contain the final result.

9. You can do a preview on this last step and you will obtain something like the following:

```
<result>
  <authors>
...
      <author id_author ="A00002">
        <lastname>King</lastname>
        <firstname>Stephen</firstname>
        <nationality>American</nationality>
        <birthyear>1947</birthyear>
        <books>
          <book id_title ="123-353">
            <title>Bag of Bones</title>
            <price>$40,90</price>
            <genre>Fiction</genre>
          </book>
          <book id_title=" 123-346">
            <title>Carrie</title>
            ...
          </book>
          ...
        </books>
      </author>
      <author id_author=" A00007">
        <lastname>Kiyosaki</lastname>
        ...
      </author>
  </authors>
</result>
```

How it works...

The basic idea when you have to generate a complex XML structure is to create partial XML outputs in different steps and then use the **XML Join** step to create the merged structure.

The **XML Join** step allows you to incorporate one XML structure (with one or multiple rows) inside another leading XML structure that must have only one row.

In the first join step of the sample transformation, you combined the XML that contains the empty root structure with the author's XML structure. This is a simple join—the step replaces the tag `<authors/>` of the root XML structure (the target stream) with all of the authors coming from the author XML structure (the source stream). The Path expression, `/result/authors`, tells Kettle which node in the root structure is to be filled with the author's structure.

The second **XML Join** step is a little more complex. It combines the result from the first **XML Join** step and the selection of books. In this case, you have a complex join because you need to join each group of books with their corresponding author. To do this, you must type the condition of the join with the following Path expression: `/result/authors/author[@ id_author='?']/books`. The `?` character is used as a placeholder. During execution, this character will be replaced with the **Join Comparison Field** value (in this case, the `id_author` field value). So, all books in XML format with a particular `id_author` will replace the tag `<books/>` inside the tag `<author>` who have the same `id_author`. For example, the following book by Stieg Larsson (already converted to the XML format) is in a row where `id_author` is equal to `A00001`:

```
<book id_title="123-401">
<title>The Girl who Played with Fire</title>
<price>$35,90</price>
<genre>Fiction</genre>
</book>
```

Therefore, this structure will be inserted in the main XML structure in the following path: `/result/authors/author[@id_author='A00001']/books`.

This is the path belonging to that author.

See also

- ▸ *Generating a simple XML document*
- ▸ *Generating complex XML structures*
- ▸ *Specifying fields by using the Path notation*

Generating an HTML page using XML and XSL transformations

Sometimes, you don't have access to the source database from the web server, or you just want static pages in your site. Under this scenario, you can create a web page through **XSLT** (**Extensible Stylesheet Language Transformations**) and then publish it. In this recipe you will take advantage of the **XSL Transformation** job entry features to do just that: taking an XML file and transforming it into HTML.

XSLT is for more than just building HTML files from XML! It acts as a translator, allowing for creating pretty much any kind of text output desired. While this recipe focuses on the ability to build HTML, don't forget that it can also build CSV and other delimited files, semi-structured files, and yes, even other XML files! To learn more about XSLT, check out the great introduction tutorials over at `http://www.w3schools.com/xsl`.

Suppose you want to publish a books catalog on a website. In this recipe, you will generate an HTML page, taking as its source, data that you have in a database.

Getting ready

You must have a database of books with the structure shown in *Appendix A, Data Structures*.

How to do it...

The first group of steps is meant for exporting the book's information from the database to an XML file. if you already have the information in this format, then you can skip to step 7.

1. Create a new transformation.

2. Drop a **Table Input** step into the canvas and select the book's information. Use the following SQL statement:
   ```
   SELECT *
   FROM books
   LEFT JOIN authors
   ON books.id_author = authors.id_author
   ```

3. Add an **XML Output** step from the **Output** category.

4. Fill in the **File** tab giving the file the name `books` and leaving the default `xml` as the proposed extension.

5. Under the **Content** tab, type `Books` in **Parent XML element** and `Book` in **Row XML element**.

6. Under the **Fields** tab, press the **Get Fields** button, in order to retrieve the entire field's information. Modify the **Price** field giving it the **Format** $0.00. The result from these steps will be a file named books.xml with the book's structure. It must look like the following:

```
<Books>
   <Book>
       <title>Carrie</title>
       <price>$41,00</price>
       <genre>Fiction</genre>
       <lastname>King</lastname>
       <firstname>Stephen</firstname>
   </Book>
   <Book>
       <title>Salem>s lot</title>
          ...
   </Book>
</Books>
```

7. Now, you must create the XSL file (booksFormat.xsl), based on the books.xml structure. Create a new file with your preferred text editor and type the following:

```
<?xml version="1.0" encoding="UTF-8"?>
<xsl:stylesheet    version="1.0"
  xmlns:xsl="http://www.w3.org/1999/XSL/Transform"
  xmlns="http://www.w3.org/1999/xhtml">
  <xsl:output method="xml" indent="yes" encoding="UTF-8"/>
  <xsl:template match="/Books">
    <html>
      <head> <title>Books</title> </head>
      <body>
        <h1>Books</h1>
        <table border="1">
        <!-- grid header -->
        <tr bgcolor="lightblue"><td>Title</td><td>Author</td>
          <td>Price</td><td>Genre</td></tr>
          <xsl:apply-templates select="Book">
            <xsl:sort select="title" />
          </xsl:apply-templates>
        </table>
      </body>
    </html>
  </xsl:template>
  <xsl:template match="Book">
    <!-- grid value fields -->
    <tr>
```

```
        <td><xsl:value-of select="title"/></td>
        <td><xsl:value-of select="lastname"/>, <xsl:value-of
          select="firstname"/></td>
        <td><xsl:value-of select="price"/></td>
        <td><xsl:value-of select="genre"/></td>
      </tr>
    </xsl:template>
  </xsl:stylesheet>
```

> You can save a lot of time by downloading the sample XSL file from Packt's website!

1. Create a new job and add a **Start** entry.

2. Add a **Transformation** entry to execute the preceding transformation. Add an **XSL Transformation** job entry from the **XML** category. Set the **Files** frame to the following:

Files

Get filenames from previous result ☐

XML File name: `${Internal.Job.Filename.Directory}\books.xml` Browse...

XSL File name: `${Internal.Job.Filename.Directory}\BooksFormat.xsl` Browse...

Output Filename: `${Internal.Job.Filename.Directory}\Books.htm` Browse...

3. Run the job. A file named `Books.htm` will be created, having the following layout:

Books

Title	Author	Price	Genre
Are You There, Vodka? It's me, Chelsea	Handler, Chelsea	$19.90	Non-fiction
Bag of Bones	King, Stephen	$40.90	Fiction
Basket Case	Hiaasen, Carl	$31.00	Fiction
Carrie	King, Stephen	$41.00	Fiction
Cashflow Quadrant	Kiyosaki, Robert	$25.00	Business
Chelsea Chelsea Bang Bang	Handler, Chelsea	$25.00	Non-fiction
Harry Potter and the Chamber of Secrets	Rowling, Joanne	$32.00	Childrens
Harry Potter and the Deathly Hallows	Rowling, Joanne	$38.00	Childrens
Harry Potter and the Goblet of Fire	Rowling, Joanne	$33.00	Childrens
Harry Potter and the Half-Blood Prince	Rowling, Joanne	$31.00	Childrens
Harry Potter and the Order of the Phoenix	Rowling, Joanne	$32.00	Childrens
Harry Potter and the Philosopher's Stone	Rowling, Joanne	$31.00	Childrens
Harry Potter and the Prisoner of Azkaban	Rowling, Joanne	$29.00	Childrens

How it works...

XSL is used to transform and render XML documents. In this recipe, you generated an XML file with book's information and then used an XSL file to transform that XML file into an HTML page.

Looking at the XSL file, you can see how it transforms the fields from the source into an HTML code. The file has different sections, which are as follows:

▶ One section for the header: a `<table>` tag with a row containing the field's headers

▶ The tag `<xsl:apply-templates select="Book">` indicating a loop over the template `Book` for each book

▶ The template `Book`, that creates a new row with the field's values

In order to apply the transformation defined in the XSL file effectively, you used the **XSL Transformation** job entry. The configuration of the entry is straightforward; you simply provide names of the XML file, the XSL file, and the resulting file, and you're done.

There's more...

As an option, right after creating the page, you may publish it automatically on the website. For doing that, simply extend the job with a file transfer entry.

You will find more information about XSL at `http://en.wikipedia.org/wiki/XSLT`.

You can also follow the following tutorial: `http://www.w3schools.com/xsl/`.

See also

▶ The *Putting files on a remote server* recipe in *Chapter 5, File Management*

Reading an RSS Feed

RSS (Really Simple Syndication) feeds allow websites to provide a structured listing of content that can be parsed out across various tools such as news aggregators, social sites, and so on. RSS feeds are created using a specialized XML format that makes it easy to parse through.

Getting ready

For this recipe, we will be using an RSS feed from Packt Publication's website which shows the latest news and releases. The feed is available at `https://www.packtpub.com/rss.xml`.

Take a moment and look through the feed by opening the link in a browser to get familiar with the data before going through the recipe. You can also save a copy of the page and view the XML structure.

How to do it...

Perform the following steps:

1. Create a new transformation.

2. From the **Input** section, select an **RSS Input** step and add it to the canvas.

3. Open the RSS Input step. In the URL List section, add the following URL: `https://www.packtpub.com/rss.xml`.

4. Switch to the **Fields** tab and click on the **Get Fields** button. This will parse the RSS feed for all the fields available.

5. Add a **Filter Rows** step. In the condition, select **Title** as the field, **CONTAINS** as the evaluation, and **SQL** as the value. This will filter out all records that do not have SQL in the **Title** field. Your filter rows condition should look like the following:

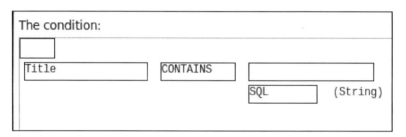

6. Now right-click on the **Filter rows** step and select preview. You should now see only the entries that contain SQL in their titles.

 If no results return back, change the value to something that matches in the current RSS feed.

How it works...

Since an RSS feed is a standardized XML format, Kettle can parse the dataset and provide all the fields that are made available within it. As long as the feed is properly formatted, the data can be fed into Kettle and parsed just like any other data stream. To find out more about RSS, check out the tutorials that are available via `http://www.w3schools.com/rss/`.

See also

▶ *Generating an RSS Feed*

Generating an RSS Feed

RSS feeds allow for a quick means of staying current on many different media types (blogs, news sites, alert notifications, and so on). By utilizing the data integration capabilities of Kettle, we can create our own customized RSS feeds that can then be consumed by any tool that can read the specialized RSS feed format, such as Feedly (`http://www.feedly.com`) or NewsBlur (`http://www.newsblur.com`).

Getting ready

You must have a database of books with the structure shown in *Appendix A, Data Structures*.

How to do it...

Perform the following steps:

1. Create a new transformation.
2. Under the **Input** section, bring over a **Table Input** step.
3. Open the **Table Input** step and select the `books` database connection. For the SQL statement, add the following:

```
SELECT
  id_title
, title
, price
, genre
, CONCAT(firstname, ' ', lastname) AS author_name
, b.create_date AS publish_date
FROM books b
JOIN authors a ON b.id_author = a.id_author
```

4. Click on **OK** and exit the **Table Input** step.
5. From the **Transformation** category, select an **Add constants** step. Add the following details to the **Fields** data grid:

Fields :

#	Name	Type	Fc	Le	P	C	D	Gr	Value
1	website	String							https://www.google.com/search?q=
2	channel_title	String							Latest Book List
3	channel_description	String							List of all the cool books
4	channel_link	String							testing

6. From the **Transformation** category, select a **Calculator** step. We need to define a new field called `link_detail`, which will add the website field and the title field together to create a valid link. The field's details will look like the following screenshot:

^	#	New field	Calculation	Field A	Field B	Fi	Value type	Le	Pro	Remove
	1	link_detail	A + B	website	title		String			N

Fields:

7. From the **Output** category, select an **RSS Output** step. On the **Channel** tab, fill in the **Channel title** field with `channel_title`, the **Channel description** field with `channel_description`, and the **Channel link** field with `channel_link`.

8. On the **Item** tab, we want to include the book details that match the stream values. Fill in the fields as in the following screenshot:

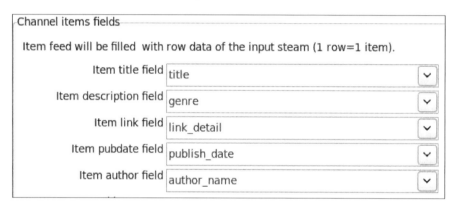

Channel items fields

Item feed will be filled with row data of the input steam (1 row=1 item).

Item title field	title
Item description field	genre
Item link field	link_detail
Item pubdate field	publish_date
Item author field	author_name

9. On the **Output File** tab, enter `${Internal.Transformation.Filename.Directory}/book_rss` as the value for the **Filename** field and click on **OK**.

10. Run the transformation. Open the `book_rss.xml` file that was created and look over the RSS feed that was created.

How it works

While RSS feeds are a standardized XML format, it can be more complicated than the typical data stream output from Kettle. RSS requires some static values for the file to be created appropriately which we added to the stream via the **Add constants** step. We also wanted our links to be uniform, so we created the link stub (called `website`) in the stream, so that we could create custom links for each book title.

Each book is added as an individual item to the RSS feed where the book's title, genre, publish date (which is not the book's publish date, but when the record was created), and the author are all added as elements. In a typical feed, these details would describe the items in the list and provide a link to read the rest of the blog post or news item.

There's more...

The **RSS Output** step also provides a way to generate custom fields in the RSS feed. Open the **RSS Output** step and select the **Custom Output** tab. Here you can add custom tags and their corresponding fields to each channel and item in the feed.

See also

- ▸   *Reading an RSS Feed*

5
File Management

In this chapter, we will cover the following topics:

- ▸ Copying or moving one or more files
- ▸ Deleting one or more files
- ▸ Getting files from a remote server
- ▸ Putting files on a remote server
- ▸ Copying or moving a custom list of files
- ▸ Deleting a custom list of files
- ▸ Comparing files and folders
- ▸ Working with ZIP files
- ▸ Encrypting and decrypting files

Introduction

On many occasions, the development of Kettle jobs and transformations involves manipulation of files, such as reading or writing a file along with other manipulations. Look at the following sample scenario, where you have to:

- ▸ Get a file with orders from a remote server
- ▸ Validate and load the orders into a database
- ▸ Move the processed file to a designated folder
- ▸ Rename the older version if a file with that name already exists
- ▸ Generate a logfile with details of the errors and put that logfile back on to the server for further review if the orders in the file are not valid

In this situation, besides reading and writing files, you also have to transfer, rename, and move them.

Copying, moving, deleting, and transferring files, and listing of files or directories, are tasks not only needed for these situations, but in everyday life. It's common to have lot of files that need to be organized in several ways, and for different purposes.

Kettle has a rich set of steps and job entries for doing this. However, you might get lost or frustrated trying to pick and then configure the option that suits your needs. The recipes in this chapter should help you with that task.

Copying or moving one or more files

The **Copy Files** job entry allows you to copy one or more files or folders. Let's see this step in action. Assume that you have a folder with a set of files, and you want to copy them to three folders depending on their extensions: you have one folder for text files, another for Excel files, and the last one for the rest of the files.

Getting ready

You will need a directory named `sampleFiles` containing a set of files with different extensions, including `.txt` and `.xls`. You will also need three destination directories, named `txtFiles`, `xlsFiles`, and `OtherFiles`.

How to do it...

Perform the following steps:

1. Create a new job and drop a **Start job** entry into the canvas.

2. Add a **Copy Files** job entry. In this entry, you will add the directions for copying the files into the three available destination folders. Double-click on the entry to open it.

3. In the **File/Folder source** textbox, type or browse for the `sampleFiles` folder. In the **File/Folder destination** textbox, type or browse for the `txtFiles` folder. Also, type `.*\.txt` in the **Wildcard (regExp)** textbox. Click on the **Add** button.

4. In the **File/Folder source** textbox, type or browse for the `sampleFiles` folder. In the **File/Folder destination**, type or browse for the `xlsFiles` folder. Also, type `.*\.xls` in the **Wildcard (regExp)** textbox. Click on the **Add** button.

5. In the **File/Folder source** textbox, type or browse for the `sampleFiles` folder. In the **File/Folder destination**, type or browse for the `OtherFiles` folder. Also, type `.+(?<!(txt|xls))$` in the **Wildcard (regExp)** textbox. Click on the **Add** button.

Assuming that all folders are inside the directory where you have your job, the **Files/Folders** grid will look like the following screenshot:

Files/Folders:			
^ #	File/Folder source	File/Folder destination	Wildcard (RegExp)
1	${Internal.Job.Filename.Directory}\sampleFiles	${Internal.Job.Filename.Directory}\txtFiles	.*\.txt
2	${Internal.Job.Filename.Directory}\sampleFiles	${Internal.Job.Filename.Directory}\xlsFiles	.*\.xls
3	${Internal.Job.Filename.Directory}\sampleFiles	${Internal.Job.Filename.Directory}\OtherFiles	.+(?<!(txt|xls))$

Kettle uses Java's **Regular Expressions** (**RegExp**) syntax wherever it can be used. Also, note that `Internal.Job.Filename.Directory` is a predefined Kettle variable whose value is the full directory where the job is saved.

When you run the job, each file from the `sampleFiles` folder will be copied into the folder associated in the settings window, depending on its extension.

How it works...

You use the **Copy Files** job entry to perform the task of copying files. As you can see in the recipe, you can execute several copy instructions with a single job entry by entering different lines in the **Files/Folders** section from the **General** tab.

In the sample grid, you have three lines. For each line, the objective is to copy all the files from the source folder (first column) to the destination folder (second column) that match the regular expression (third column).

The first and second lines copy the `.txt` and `.xls` files by using the regular expressions `.*\.txt` and `.*\.xls` respectively.

The third line copies the rest of the files. The regular expression that matches those files is a little more complex; the characters `?<!` represent a negation over the rest of the expression, so the expression `.+(?<!(txt|xls))$` means all files whose extension is neither `.txt` nor `.xls`.

There's more...

The recipe showed you the basics of copying files with Kettle. The following sections explain how to add more functionality, for example, validating the existence of files or folders before copying. You will also see the extra settings available for the **Copy Files** job entry.

Moving files

You can move the file (instead of copying) by checking the **Remove source files** checkbox in the **Settings** section under the **General** tab in the **Copy Files** job entry. If you check it, Kettle will delete the files after a successful copy. This is analogous to using a **Delete file** job entry right after the **Copy Files** entry.

Detecting the existence of the files before copying them

In the recipe, you simply wanted to organize some files in folders, and you didn't care if the files existed or not. However, the most common scenario is the one in which it's assumed that the files to copy or move already exist. You cannot perform that verification with the **Copy Files** entry, but there are other means.

Suppose that you want the files to be copied only if there is a mixture of file extensions. If there are only Excel files, or text files, they will not be copied and the situation will be recorded in a log.

In order to do that, you can create a transformation that succeeds if there is a mixture of files, or fails if you have only Excel files or only text files.

 The transformation should start with a **Get File Names** step to get the list of files in the folder, and proceed differently according to the validations you want to do.

Then, in your job, you call the transformation before copying the files. The copy will be done only after the success of the transformation, as shown in the following figure:

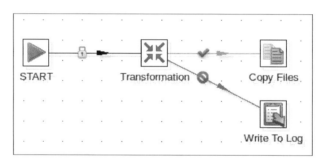

In the simplest case where you have to copy files specified by their exact name—that is, not expressed with regular expressions—you can verify their existence simply with a **File Exists** (for a single file) or a **Checks if files exist** (for multiple files) entry.

Creating folders

You can create the destination directory automatically by selecting the **Create destination folder** checkbox in the **Settings** section under the **General** tab in the **Copy Files** job entry. You could also create those directories by using a **Create a folder** job entry from the **File management** category. The difference is that, with the **Create a folder** entry, you can detect if the directory already exists; if you didn't expect that situation, you can act accordingly by, for example, aborting the job.

See also

▶ *Copying or moving a custom list of files*

Deleting one or more files

Kettle provides two job entries for deleting files: **Delete file** and **Delete files**. You can find both in the **File management** category of entries.

In this recipe, you will see an example of how to delete a file. You will delete a file that includes the current date as part of its name, for example `test_20101020.txt`.

Getting ready

You must create a sample file; for example, `test_20101020.txt`. Make sure to use your current date instead of `20101020`. Use the same format (`yyyyMMdd`).

How to do it...

Perform the following steps to learn how to delete one or more files:

1. Create a new transformation.

2. Drop a **Get System Info** step from the **Input** category into the work area.

3. Double-click on the step and add a field named `date`. In the **Type** column, select **system date(fixed)**.

4. Add a **Select values** step from the **Transform** category. Open it, and under the **Meta-data** tab, add `date` as **Fieldname**, set the type to **String**, and type or select **yyyyMMdd** in the **Format** column.

5. From the **Job** category, add a **Set Variables** step. Double-click on it and fill in the grid, as shown in the following screenshot:

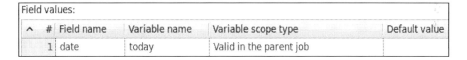

	#	Field name	Variable name	Variable scope type	Default value
^	1	date	today	Valid in the parent job	

6. The transformation is ready. Save it. Now, create a new job and drop a **Start** entry.

7. Add a **Transformation** job entry and configure it to run the transformation created previously. In the **Transformation Filename:** textbox type the complete path to the transformation file.

8. Add a **Delete file** entry from the **File management** category.

9. Double-click on this step. In the **File name** textbox, type the location of the file to be deleted and concatenate it with `test_` and the `today` variable, for example, `${Internal.Job.Filename.Directory}\test_${today}.txt`.

10. Run the job and the file will be deleted.

How it works...

The **Delete file** job entry simply deletes a file. In the recipe, you used it to delete a file whose name was not fixed, but depended on the current date.

The transformation has the purpose of building the last part of the name of the file. It gets the present date with a **Get System Info** step, converts the date to a `String` by using a **Select values** step, and sets a variable named `today` with this information. As the scope, you specified **Valid in the parent job**.

> In general, if you are unsure of the scope to set, you should choose **Valid in the root job**. That is usually the best choice. A variable with that scope will be valid in the root job and all sub jobs and transformations.

In this case, **Valid in the parent job** will suffice because you will use the variable in the job that calls this transformation.

The main job runs the transformation and then uses the variable `${today}` to build the name of the file to delete. Assuming that your transformation is located in `/home/my_work/`, when you execute the job, the text `${Internal.Job.Filename.Directory}\test_${today}.txt` will be replaced by `/home/my_work/test_20101020.txt`, and the **Delete file** step will remove that file if it exists.

There's more...

If you need to delete a set of files instead of just one, you can use the **Delete files** job entry from the **File Management** category. With this entry, you can delete several files or folders, including subfolders and can also use wildcards for the selection.

If you just want to delete folders instead of files, you can use the **Delete folders** job entry, whose configuration is quite straightforward.

Whichever is your use case, deleting one or more files, with or without folders, take a look at the following subsection. It gives you more tricks to use when deleting files.

Figuring out which files have been deleted

When you delete a single file by using the **Delete File** job entry, you can easily detect if the file was deleted or not, and act accordingly. Let's summarize how:

Result of the job	Method for detecting the result
File was deleted	The **Delete File** job entry succeeds
File wasn't deleted because of an error	The **Delete File** job entry fails
File wasn't deleted because it didn't exist	If you checked **Fail if the file doesn't exist:**, the **Delete File** job entry fails

The problem arises when you try to delete several files with the **Delete Files** entry. How can you be sure whether your job is behaving correctly and deleting the expected files? How can you know the exact names of the files that were deleted?

There is no direct way of determining that, but there are some interesting solutions.

When you run a job that deletes files, the names of the files being deleted are written into the log. If you are developing the job, just take a look at the **Logging** tab of the **Execution results** pane in Spoon. If you want to have the list of files for further processing, save the log into a file; then you can open that file and look for the lines containing the text `Deleting file`. To be more precise, you will find a bunch of lines with the details, as in the following example:

```
... - Delete some files - Processing folder [file:///C:/test]
... - Delete some files - Deleting file [file:///C:/test/
test_20101020.txt] ...
... - Delete some files - Deleting file [file:///C:/test/
test_20101021.txt] ...
...
... - Delete some files - Total deleted files = 5
```

Another way of getting the list of deleted files would be as follows: create a transformation that lists the existing files with the same directory/file specifications as those in the **Delete Files** entry.

You should run the transformation with a **Transformation** entry just before the **Delete Files** entry. If the **Delete Files** entry succeeds, you know that the deleted files are the ones in the list you created. This method is easy, but you have to be careful. If more than one process or person is accessing the folder or files at the same time, there is a risk that the built list and the real names of the deleted files don't coincide.

See also

▸ *Deleting a custom list of files*

Getting files from a remote server

When you need to copy files from or to remote machines, you can use the standard network protocol **File Transfer Protocol** (**FTP**) built on client-server architecture.

Kettle provides the **Get a file with FTP** job entry to get files from an FTP server. In the example, you will connect to a remote directory named remoteDir on an FTP server and copy some text files from that server to a local folder named destinationDir.

How to do it...

You need access to an FTP server to be able to continue with this recipe.

Perform the following steps:

1. Create a new job and drop a **Start** entry into the canvas.

2. Add a **Get a file with FTP** job entry from the **File transfer** category.

3. Under the **General** tab, type the server name or its IP address in the **FTP server name / IP address** textbox.

4. Type the port number in the **Server port** textbox. Usually, it is port 21.

5. In the **Username** and **Password** textboxes, type the credentials to log in to the FTP server.

> You can verify the connection information by clicking on the **Test connection** button.

6. In the **Remote directory** textbox under the **Files** tab, you must type the name of the remote directory on the FTP server from where the source files will be retrieved.

> You can check if the folder exists by clicking on the **Check folder** button.

7. Type .*\.txt as the **Wildcard**.

8. In the **Target directory** textbox inside the **Local** frame, type the destination directory on the local machine. Under the **Files** tab, you have various fields, as shown in the following screenshot:

9. Run the job. The files with the `.txt` extension will be copied from `remoteDir` on the FTP server to `destinationDir` on the local machine.

How it works...

The **Get a file with FTP** job entry performs the copy task, it uses the configuration set under the **General** tab to connect to the remote FTP server.

Under the **Files** tab, you defined the source directory (in the example, the remote folder `remoteDir`) and target directory (in the example, the local folder `destinationDir`).

Try to avoid the use of directories with special characters, such as spaces. Some FTP servers don't allow these special characters.

You also provided a regular expression for the files to get. In this case, you typed `.*\.txt` which is a regular expression representing all `.txt` files.

There's more...

The following sections give you some additional information and useful tips to transfer files from a remote server.

Specifying files to transfer

In the recipe, you copied all files with a given extension; you did it by providing a regular expression that all those files matched. As another possibility, you may need to transfer a single file.

 Note that even if you have the exact name of the file, you still have to provide a regular expression.

For example, if the name of the file is `my_file.txt` you have to type `my_file\.txt`.

As a last possibility, instead of typing a wildcard, you may provide a Kettle variable name. Using a variable is particularly useful if you don't know the name of the file beforehand. Suppose that you have to get a file named `daily_update_yyyyMMdd.csv` where `yyyyMMdd` represents year, month, and day. In that case, you can create a transformation that builds a regular expression representing that filename (for example, `daily_update_20101215\.csv`) and sets a variable with that value. In the job, you should execute that transformation before the **Get a file with FTP** job entry.

Your job would look like the one shown in the following screenshot:

Finally, in the **Get a file with FTP** entry, you should type that variable (for example, `${DAILY_FILENAME}`) as the wildcard.

Some considerations about connecting to an FTP server

In order to be able to connect to an FTP server, you must complete the connection settings for the FTP server under the **General** tab of the **Get a file with FTP** job entry. If you are working with an anonymous FTP server, you can use **anonymous** as the username and the password can remain blank. This means that you can access the machine without having to have an account on that machine.

If you need to provide authentication credentials for access via a proxy, you must also complete the following textboxes: `Proxy host`, `Proxy port`, `Proxy username`, and `Proxy password`.

Access via SFTP

SSH File Transfer Protocol (**SFTP**) is a network protocol used to secure the file transfer capability. With Kettle, you can get files from an SFTP server by using the **Get a file with SFTP** job entry. To configure this entry, you have to enter the name or IP of the SFTP server in the **SFTP server name / IP** textbox. The rest of the configuration of the **General** and **Files** tabs is pretty similar to the **Get a file with FTP** entry.

More information on SFTP, can be found at `http://en.wikipedia.org/wiki/` `SSH_file_transfer_protocol.`

Access via FTPS

A **File Transfer Protocol Secure** (**FTPS**) server extends the standard FTP protocol, adding cryptographic protocols, such as the **Transport Layer Security** (**TLS**) and the **Secure Sockets Layer** (**SSL**). You can use the **Get a file with FTPS** job entry to get files from an FTPS server. To configure this entry, you have to enter the name or IP address of the FTPS server in the **FTPS server name / IP address:** textbox. The rest of the configuration of the **General** and **Files** tabs is pretty similar to the **Get a file with FTP** entry.

More information about FTPS can be found at `http://en.wikipedia.org/wiki/Ftps.`

Getting information about the files being transferred

A drawback when accessing an FTP server is that, from the job, you can only know if the entry succeeded or failed; you don't have control over how files behave, for example, how many files were transferred. To overcome this situation, it is recommended that you keep the log generated by the job, which is the only source of information about what happened. To see the details, you can simply take a look at the log, or parse it in a subsequent Kettle transformation.

See also

> ▶ *Putting files on a remote server*

> ▶ *Deleting one or more files*

Putting files on a remote server

This recipe is similar to the previous one, *Getting files from a remote server*, but in this case, you want to copy the text files from a local machine to a remote machine using the FTP network protocol and the **Put a file with FTP** job entry.

Getting ready

You need write access to an FTP server.

How to do it...

Perform the following steps:

1. Create a new job. Drop a **Start** entry into the canvas.

2. Add a **Put a file with FTP** job entry from the **File transfer** category.

3. Under the **General** tab, type the server name (or its IP address) in the **FTP server name / IP address:** textbox.

4. Type the port number in the **Port** textbox. Usually, it is port 21.

5. In the **Username:** and **Password:** textboxes, type the credentials to log in to the FTP server.

 You can verify if the connection settings are valid by clicking on the **Test connection** button.

6. Type the source folder in the **Local directory** textbox inside the **Source (local) files** frame located under the **Files** tab. In this example: c:\sourceDir.

7. Type .*\.txt as the **Wildcard**.

8. In the **Remote directory** textbox, type the destination directory on the remote machine, for example, remoteDir.

 You can check for the existence of the folder by clicking on the **Test folder** button.

9. The **Files** tab will look like the one shown in the following screenshot:

10. Run the job. The files with a .txt extension will be copied from the sourceDir local folder to the destinationDir on the FTP Server.

How it works...

The **Put a file with FTP** job entry uses the configuration set under the **General** tab to connect to the remote FTP server. The entry copies the files from the local machine to the remote server by using the configuration typed under the **Files** tab. In the recipe, you set the source directory as `c:\sourceDir` and the destination directory as `remoteDir` and as the list of files to transfer you typed a regular expression representing all `.txt` files. You could also have typed a regular expression representing the exact name of the file to transfer, as well as Kettle variables, both for the files and for the directories.

There's more...

In the recipe, you put some files on an FTP server. Kettle also provides job entries for putting files on SFTP and FTPS servers. They are the **Put a file with SFTP** and the **Upload files to FTPS** entries respectively. The configuration for these entries is quite similar to the one you used earlier.

See also

 ▶ *Getting files from a remote server*

Copying or moving a custom list of files

Sometimes, you don't have the names of files to move or copy beforehand. In these cases, you can take advantage of the **Add filename to result** prompt existing in several Kettle steps and job entries.

Let's see an example. Suppose that you receive Excel files daily, with book orders from different branches, and you need to process these files creating a new Excel file with all the incoming orders. Then, finally, you want to move the source files to a destination folder.

Getting ready

In order to do this exercise, you need a directory named `booksOrders` with several Excel files. Each file should have two columns: one for the `id_title` and another for the `Quantity`. Also, it is necessary to have a destination folder named `processedOrders`.

How to do it...

Perform the following steps:

1. Create a new transformation. This transformation will take all Excel files from the source directory and write them into a single Excel file.

2. Drop an **Excel Input** step into the canvas.

3. Under the **Files** tab, fill in the grid in order to read all Excel files in the source directory. Under **File/Directory**, type `${Internal.Transformation.Filename.Directory}\booksOrders` and under **Wildcard (RegExp)**, type `.*\.xls`.

4. Under the **Content** tab, make sure that the **Add filenames to result** prompt is checked.

5. Under the **Fields** tab, add to the grid a `String` field named `id_title` and a `Number` field named `Quantity`.

6. Add an **Excel Output** step after the **Excel Input** step.

7. Under the **File** tab, type the destination Excel file (for example, `allBookOrders`) including the path, and leave `.xls` as the **Extension**. Also, check the **Include date in filename?** prompt. With these settings, your final file will have a name such as `allBookOrders_101011.xls`.

> Note that `yyMMdd` is the default format for the appended date. If you want to append the date with a different format, check the **Specify Date time format** option and select or type the desired format in the **Date time format** option.

8. Under the same tab, uncheck the **Add filename to result** prompt.

9. Under the **Fields** tab, click on the **Get Fields** button to fill in the grid.

10. Save the transformation.

Now, let's see how to move the source files between the folders.

1. Create a new job and add a **Start** entry.

2. Add a **Transformation** entry and configure it to run the transformation created previously.

3. Add a **Copy or Move result filenames** entry from the **File management** category.

4. Open the step. In the **Destination folder** textbox, browse or type the target directory (for example, `${Internal.Job.Filename.Directory}\processedOrders`).

5. Change the value in the **Action** field from `Copy` to `Move`. Click on **OK** to close the step.

6. Run the job. It will execute the transformation and will move the source files from the `booksOrders` folder to the `processedOrders` folder.

How it works...

In the recipe, you used the Kettle **result filelist** feature to automatically build a list of files to copy.

In the transformation, you used an **Excel input** step to read all the files with the `.xls` extension from a source directory and an **Excel output** step to write this information to a new file.

The important setting here is the **Add filename to result** prompt in the **Excel input** step. When this option is checked (which is the default setting), the names of the files read in the step are saved to the result filelist, which is no more than a list of files in memory.

Back in the job, the **Copy or Move result filenames** entry reads the names saved in memory and moves the files in that list to the destination folder.

Note that in the **Excel output** step, you unchecked the **Add filename to result** prompt. If you had left this prompt checked, the job would have moved the `completeBookOrders_101011.xls` file too.

See also

▸ The following recipes in *Chapter 2, Reading and Writing Files*:
  ❑ *Reading an Excel file*
  ❑ *Writing an Excel file with several sheets*

Deleting a custom list of files

Consider a scenario where you have to delete some files but you don't have the names of the files to delete beforehand. If you can specify that list with regular expressions, it wouldn't be a problem, but sometimes that is not possible. In such cases you should use a helper transformation that builds the list of files to delete. This recipe shows you how to do that.

For this recipe, assume that you want to delete from a source directory all the temporary files that meet two conditions: the files have a `.tmp` extension and a size of `0` bytes.

Getting ready

In order to create and test this recipe, you need a directory with a set of sample files; some of them should have the `.tmp` extension and zero size. Some example files are shown in the following screenshot:

Name	Size
sample1.txt	25 bytes
sample2.tmp	25 bytes
sample3.tmp	0 bytes
sample4.log	8 bytes
sample5.tmp	0 bytes
sample6.tmp	24 bytes
sample7.tmp	0 bytes
sample8.txt	0 bytes
sample9.tmp	106 bytes

In the preceding screenshot, the files that must be deleted are **sample3.tmp**, **sample5.tmp**, and **sample7.tmp** because they match the requirements of having `.tmp` as their file type and they do not contain anything (being 0 bytes in size).

How to do it...

Perform the following steps:

1. Create the transformation that will build the list of files to delete.

2. Drop a **Get File Names** step into the canvas.

3. Under the **File** tab, fill the **Selected files:** grid. Under **File/Directory**, type `${Internal.Transformation.Filename.Directory}\sample_directory` and under **Wildcard (RegExp)**, type `.*\.tmp`.

4. From the **Flow** category, add a **Filter rows** step.

5. Use this step to filter the files with a size equal to 0. In order to do that, add the condition `size = 0`.

6. After the **Filter rows** step, add the **Select values** step. When asked for the kind of hop to create, select **Main output of step**. This will cause only those rows that meet the condition to pass the filter.

7. Use the **Select values** step to select the field's `path` and `short_filename` in that order.

8. From the **Job** category of **Steps**, add a **Copy rows to result** step.

9. Save the transformation.

10. Create a new job and add a **Start** entry.

11. Add a **Transformation** entry and configure it to run the transformation previously created.

12. Add a **Delete files** entry from the **File management** category.

13. Double-click on it and check the **Copy previous Results to args?** prompt.

14. Save the job and run it. The files with a `.tmp` extension and a size of `0` bytes will be deleted.

How it works...

In this recipe, you deleted a list of files by using the **Delete files** job entry. In the **Selected files:** grid of that entry, you have to provide the complete name of the files or the directory to delete and a regular expression. Instead of typing that information directly, here you built the rows for the grid in a separate transformation.

The first step used in the transformation is **Get File Names**. This step allows you to get information about a file or a set of files or folders. In this example, the step gets the list of `.tmp` files from the `sample_directory` folder.

The following screenshot shows all of the information that you obtain with this step:

^	#	Fieldname	Type	Length	Precision	Step origin	Storage	Mask	Decimal	Group	Trim	Comments
	1	filename	String	500	-	dir tmp files	normal		.	,	none	
	2	short_filename	String	500	-	dir tmp files	normal		.	,	none	
	3	path	String	500	-	dir tmp files	normal		.	,	none	
	4	type	String	500	-	dir tmp files	normal		.	,	none	
	5	exists	Boolean	-	-	dir tmp files	normal		.	,	none	
	6	ishidden	Boolean	-	-	dir tmp files	normal		.	,	none	
	7	isreadable	Boolean	-	-	dir tmp files	normal		.	,	none	
	8	iswriteable	Boolean	-	-	dir tmp files	normal		.	,	none	
	9	lastmodifiedtime	Date	-	-	dir tmp files	normal		.	,	none	
	10	size	Integer	-	0	dir tmp files	normal	#;-#	.	,	none	
	11	extension	String	-	-	dir tmp files	normal		.	,	none	
	12	uri	String	-	-	dir tmp files	normal		.	,	none	
	13	rooturi	String	-	-	dir tmp files	normal		.	,	none	

You can see these field names by pressing the Space bar while having the focus on the **Get File Names** step.

After that step, you used a **Filter rows** step to keep just the files with a size of 0 bytes.

If you do a preview on this step, you will see a dataset with the list of the desired files, that is, those that meet the two conditions: having the `.tmp` extension and a size equal to 0 bytes.

After that, you selected just the fields holding the `path` and the `short_filename` and copied these rows to memory. You did that with the **Copy rows to result** step.

Now, let's go back to the job. The **Copy previous result to args?** prompt selected in the **Delete files** entry causes the job to read the rows coming from the transformation, and copy them to the grid. In other words, each row coming out of the transformation (a data pair: `path`, `short_filename`) becomes a row in the **Files/Folders:** grid.

With that information, the job is finally able to delete the specified files.

See also

> ▸ *Deleting one or more files*

Comparing files and folders

Kettle allows you to compare files and folders through the following job entries: **File Compare** and **Compare folder**. In this recipe, you will use the first of those entries, which is used for comparing the content of two files. Assume that periodically you receive a file with new museums data to incorporate into your database. You will compare the new and the previous version of the file. If the files are equal, you do nothing, but if they are different, you will read the new file.

Getting ready

To create and test this recipe, you will need two files: the older version of the museum file (`LastMuseumsFileReceived.xml`), and the new file (`NewMuseumsFileReceived.xml`).

On the book's website, you will find sample files to play with. In particular, `NewMuseumsFileReceived(equal).xml` is equal to the `LastMuseumsFileReceived.xml` file, and `NewMuseumsFileReceived(different).xml`, as implied by its name, is different. With these files, you will be able to test the different situations in the recipe.

How to do it...

Perform the following steps:

1. Create a new job, and drop a **Start** entry into the work area.

2. Add a **File Compare** job entry from the **File management** category. Here you must type or browse to the two files that must be compared, as shown in the following screenshot:

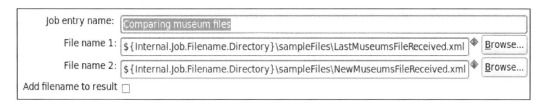

Job entry name: Comparing museum files

File name 1: ${Internal.Job.Filename.Directory}\sampleFiles\LastMuseumsFileReceived.xml — Browse...

File name 2: ${Internal.Job.Filename.Directory}\sampleFiles\NewMuseumsFileReceived.xml — Browse...

Add filename to result ☐

3. Add a **Transformation** job entry and a **DUMMY** job entry, both from the **General** category. Create a hop from the **File Compare** job entry to each of these entries.

4. Right-click on the hop between the **File Compare** job entry and the **Transformation** job entry to show the options, choose the **Evaluation** item and then select the **Follow when result is false** item.

5. Right-click on the hop between the **File Compare** job entry and the **DUMMY** job entry, choose the **Evaluation** item, and this time select the **Follow when result is true** item.

6. The job should look like the one shown in the following diagram:

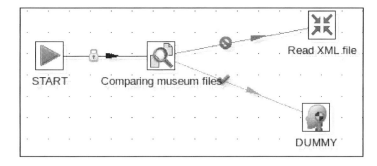

7. Then, create a new transformation in order to read the XML file. Drop a **Get data from XML** step from the **Input** category into the canvas and type the complete path for the XML file in the **File or directory** textbox under the **File** tab. In this case, it is `${Internal.Transformation.Filename.Directory}\sampleFiles\NewMuseumsFileReceived.xml`. Use `/museums/museum` in the **Loop XPath** textbox under the **Content** tab and use the **Get fields** button under the **Fields** tab to populate the list of fields automatically.

8. Save the transformation.

9. Configure the **Transformation** job entry for the main job to run the transformation you just created.

10. When you run the job, the two files are compared.

11. Assuming that your files are equal, in the **Logging** window you will see a line similar to the following:

```
2010/11/05 10:08:46 - fileCompare - Finished job entry [DUMMY]
(result=[true])
```

This line means that the flow went toward the **DUMMY** entry.

12. If your files are different, in the **Job metrics** window you will see that the **fileCompare** entry fails, and under the **Logging** tab, you will see something similar to the following:

```
. . .
... - Read XML file - Loading transformation from XML file
[file:///C:/readXMLFile.ktr]
... - readXMLFile - Dispatching started for transformation
[readXMLFile]
... - readXMLFile - This transformation can be replayed with
replay date: 2010/11/05 10:14:10
... - Read museum data.0 - Finished processing (I=4, O=0, R=0,
W=4, U=0, E=0)
... - fileCompare - Finished job entry [Read XML file]
(result=[true])
. . .
```

13. This means that the transformation was executed.

How it works...

The **File Compare** job entry performs the comparison task. It verifies whether the two files have the same content. If they are different, the job entry fails. Then, the job proceeds with the execution of the transformation that reads the new file. However, if the files are the same, the job entry succeeds and the flows continue to the **DUMMY** entry.

In other words, the new file is processed if and only if the **File Compare** fails, that is, if the two files are different.

There's more...

Besides comparing files with Kettle, you can also compare directories; let's see how it works.

Comparing folders

If you want to compare the content of two folders, you can use the **Compare folder** job entry from the **File management** category.

In this job entry, you must browse to or type the complete paths of the two folders in the **File / Folder name 1** and **File / Folder name 2** textboxes respectively and configure the comparison to be done. You can see the possible settings in the following screenshot:

The **Compare** option, set to **All** by default, can be changed to compare just files, just folders, or just the files indicated by a regular expression. The usual requirement would be to compare the list of files and then their sizes.

 Note that you can even compare the content of the files, but that will affect performance considerably.

Working with ZIP files

Compressed files are a convenient storage method. If you have many files or your files are very large, compressing them makes it easier to store them and transfer them through e-mails or between different media (PC, USB devices, and so on).

For example, consider managing the log information from a web server, which generates a new text file every day with data about the web traffic (pages, IPs, operations, status codes, and so on). After several months, you have a lot of files with a substantial amount of information.

Now, suppose that you want to create a local copy of those files. You don't have access to the server from your computer, so you have to copy the files onto some media and then onto your computer. As the size of these files can be huge, instead of directly copying the files, you will compress them first.

Once you have the ZIP file on your computer, you want to unzip it and create one separate `.zip` file per month. Assuming that the files are named `exYYMMDD.log` you will create `.zip` files named `YYMM.zip`. For example, a file named `ex101115.log` will be zipped along with all other logs from November 2010 as `1011.zip`.

Getting ready

You will need access to a directory containing logfiles.

How to do it...

You will create this recipe in two different steps. In the first step, you will compress the logfiles, and in the second step, you will uncompress them and organize them in monthly ZIP files.

So, let's compress the weblog files, by carrying out the following steps:

1. Create a new job and drop a **Start** job entry into the canvas.

2. Add a **Zip file** job entry from the **File management** category.

3. Under the **General** tab, select the source directory by clicking on the **Folder...** button. The example points to a web server log directory, such as `C:\WINDOWS\system32\Logfiles\W3SVC1\test_files`.

4. Type `.+\.log` in the **Include wildcard (RegExp):** textbox in order to read all the files with the `.log` extension.

5. In the **Zip File name:** textbox, type the path and name for the destination ZIP file. For example, `C:\WINDOWS\system32\Logfiles\W3SVC1\test_files\web logs.zip`.

6. You have several additional options for including date and time to the ZIP filename. You don't need to set those options for this recipe.

7. Under the **Advanced** tab, choose **Delete files** in the **After Zipping** drop-down list.

8. When running this job, a new file named `web logs.zip` will be created containing the log information from the web server and the logfiles will be deleted.

Now assuming that you have copied the generated ZIP file to your computer, you want to unzip the weblogs and generate small ZIP files grouping them by month:

1. Create a new job and drop a **Start** job entry into the canvas.

2. Add an **Unzip file** job entry and open it.

3. In the **Zip File name** textbox, you must browse for the ZIP file you created previously (`web logs.zip`).

4. Choose a **Target Directory**, for example, `${Internal.Job.Filename.Directory}\logs` and check the **Create folder** checkbox to create that folder, if it doesn't exist.

5. Type `.+\.log` in the **Include wildcard** textbox.

6. In the **After extraction** drop-down box select **Delete files**.

7. Under the **Advanced** tab, set the **Success on** condition to **At least we successfully unzipped x files**, and set the value of **Limit files** textbox to 1.

8. The next step for the job will be calling a transformation that creates the groups of logs for the smaller ZIP files. Add a **Transformation** job entry.

9. Double-click on the new entry. As **Transformation filename:** type `${Internal.Job.Filename.Directory}/read_log_list.ktr`. Click on the squared icon to the right of the name of the transformation, and a dialog window will appear asking if you want to create the transformation. Answer **Yes**.

10. In the transformation, add the following steps and link them one after the other:

    ❑ **Get File Names** (**Input**)

    ❑ **Strings cut** (**Transform**)

    ❑ **User Defined Java Expression** or **UDJE** for short (**Scripting**)

    ❑ **Select values** (**Transform**)

    ❑ **Sort rows** (**Transform**)

    ❑ **Copy rows to result** (**Job**)

    When asked about the kind of hop to create, always choose the **Main output of step** option. The transformation should look like the one shown in the following screenshot:

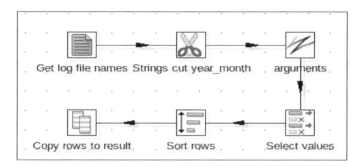

11. Double-click on the first step. With this step, you will get the complete list of logfiles.

 In order to test this transformation, copy some logfiles to the `logs` folder. This way, you will be able to preview each step.

12. Fill the grid by typing `${Internal.Transformation.Filename.Directory}\logs` under **File/directory** and `.+\.log` under **Wildcard (RegExp)**. Close the window.

13. Double-click on the **Strings cut** step. This step will generate a `String` with the year and month part of the filenames. Then, fill the following fields:

    ❑ Under **In stream field**, type `short_filename`

    ❑ Under **Out stream field**, type `year_month`

    ❑ Under **Cut from** type 2. This will remove the `ex` from `exYYMMDD.log`

    ❑ Under **Cut to** type 6 and close the window. This will remove everything after the sixth character, which would be `DD.log`. This leaves us with `YYMM`.

14. Double-click on the **UDJE** step. With this step, you will create the fields for the .zip grid. Add three String fields named wildcard, wildcardexc, and destination. As **Java expression**, type ex+year_month+[0-9]\\.log, and path+\\zip_files\\+year_month+.zip respectively. Don't forget to set the **Value type** to String.

15. Double-click on the **Select values** step. Use it to select the field's path, wildcard, wildcardexc, and destination. Close the window.

16. Double-click on the **Sort rows** step. Use it to sort by destination. Check the **Only pass unique rows? (verifies keys only)** option. With this, you generate a single row by month.

17. Save the transformation.

18. Go back to the job, and add a **Zip file** job entry.

19. Double-click on the entry, check the **Get arguments from previous** option and close the window.

20. Save the job, and run it.

21. Browse the log folder. You will see all logfiles that were compressed in the web logs.zip file along with a subfolder named zip.

22. Browse the ZIP folder. You will see one ZIP file for each month for which you had logfiles.

How it works...

In this recipe, you saw the functionality of the **Zip File** and **Unzip File** job entries.

First, you zipped all logfiles in a folder. You specified the files to zip and the name and location of the ZIP file to generate. This is quite simple and doesn't require further explanation.

In the second part of the recipe, you performed two different tasks:

The first was to unzip a file. You specified the ZIP file, the regular expression that indicates which files to extract from the ZIP file, and the destination of the files. This is also a simple and intuitive operation.

The last part, the most elaborate task of the recipe, was compressing the logfiles grouped by month. In order to do this, you couldn't fill the grid in the **Zip file** job entry manually because you didn't know in advance the names of the logfiles. Therefore, instead of filling the grid you checked the **Get arguments from previous** option. The transformation was responsible for generating the values for the grid in the **Zip file** entry setting window. The columns generated by the transformation were as follows:

 ▶ Folder of the files to zip

 ▶ Regular expression for the files to zip

- ▶ Regular expression for the files to exclude (in this case, you set a null value)
- ▶ Destination ZIP filename

These are the four fields that the **Zip file** entry needs in order to zip the files. For each row generated in the transformation, a new ZIP file was created based on these values.

There's more...

Look at some notes about zipping and unzipping files:

Avoiding zipping files

If you need to zip some files for attaching to an e-mail, you don't have to use the **Zip file** entry. The **Mail** job entry does the task of zipping for you.

Avoiding unzipping files

In the recipe you unzipped a file because you had to manipulate the files. If, instead of manipulating the files as you did, you need to read them, you don't have to use the Unzip file entry. Kettle is capable of reading those files as they are. For a complete reference on this subject, you can take a look at the following entry in *Slawomir Chodnicki's* blog at `http://type-exit.org/adventures-with-open-source-bi/2010/11/directly-accessing-remote-andor-compressed-files-in-kettle/`.

See also

- ▶ The *Sending e-mails with attached files* recipe of *Chapter 10, Getting the Most Out of Kettle*

Encrypting and decrypting files

Moving files around sometimes requires sensitive data to be exposed in ways that require more secure measures to be taken than simply pushing or pulling the data without encrypting it first. Fortunately, Kettle provides steps that interface with a common security application (GnuPG) and will encrypt, decrypt, and verify that files are secure.

Gnu Privacy Guard (**GnuPG**) is an implementation of the OpenPGP standard. **Open Pretty Good Privacy** (**OpenPGP**) is one of the most used encryption systems in technology and is widely used due to it's ability to digitally sign files to ensure they have not been tampered with. The use of public and private keys allows for files to be encrypted until the right key can be used to decrypt the file and make it accessible again.

To learn more about OpenPGP, check out their official site at `http://www.openpgp.org`.

Getting ready

This recipe requires GnuPG to be installed on the system running Kettle. It can be found over at the GnuPG website at `http://www.gnupg.org`.

How to do it...

Perform the following steps:

1. Create a new job.

2. Bring a **Start** step from the **General** section over to the canvas.

3. Under the **File Encryption** section, find the **Encrypt files with PGP** step and add it to the canvas.

4. Create a hop from the **Start** step to the **Encrypt files with PGP** step.

5. Open the **Encrypt files with PGP** step. For the **GPG location** field, enter the path where GnuPG is installed.

6. For the **File/Folder source**, enter the location where the files to be encrypted are located (`${Internal.Transformation.Filename.Directory}/test_files`).

7. For the **File/Folder destination**, enter the location where the encrypted files will be placed (`${Internal.Transformation.Filename.Directory}/encrypted_files`).

8. Click on the **Add** button next to the **File/Folder source** field for the record to be added to the **Files/Folders** data grid.

9. Click on **OK** and run the job. The encrypted files should now be in the `encrypted_files` folder.

A similar setup can be done with the **Decrypt files with PGP** step:

1. In the same job, add a **Decrypt files with PGP** step, which can be found in the **File Encryption** section.

2. Open the step and, in the **GPG location** field, enter the path where GnuPG is installed.

3. For the **File/Folder source**, we will be using the encrypted file location (`${Internal.Transformation.Filename.Directory}/encrypted_files`).

4. For the **File/Folder destination**, enter the location where the decrypted files will be stored (`${Internal.Transformation.Filename.Directory}/decrypted_files`)

5. Click on the **Add** button next to the **File/Folder source** field for the record to be added to the **Files/Folders** data grid.

6. Add a hop between the **Encrypt files with PGP** and **Decrypt files with PGP** steps.

7. Run the job and view the files in the encrypted and decrypted folders. The encrypted files are secured and can not be viewed as easily as if no encryption had been added.

How it works...

The **Encrypt/Decrypt files with PGP** steps utilize a standard application that handles encryption and digital signing of files. By telling the steps where GnuPG is located, the steps are able to execute the commands needed to process any files given and secure them as needed.

There's more...

We only used the basic encryption capabilities of these steps. In **the Encrypt files with PGP** step, each **File/Folder** source and destination combination can actually be **Encrypted**, **Signed**, or **Encrypted and Signed** depending on how secured the files need to be. This can be switched in the **Action** column in the **Files/Folders** data grid as shown:

Files/Folders:

∧	#	Action	File/Folder source
	1	Encrypt	${Internal.Transformation.Filename.Directory}/test_files

See also

▶ *Copying or moving one or more files*

6
Looking for Data

In this chapter, we will cover the following topics:

- ▸ Looking for values in a database table
- ▸ Looking for values in a database with complex conditions
- ▸ Looking for values in a database with dynamic queries
- ▸ Looking for values in a variety of sources
- ▸ Looking for values by proximity
- ▸ Looking for values by using a web service
- ▸ Looking for values over intranet or the Internet
- ▸ Validating data at runtime

Introduction

With transformations, you manipulate data in many ways—doing mathematical or logical operations, applying string functions, grouping by one or more columns, sorting, and much more. Besides transforming the data you already have, you may need to search and bring data from other sources. Let us look at the following examples:

- ▸ You have some product codes and you want to look for their descriptions in an Excel file
- ▸ You have a value and want to get all products whose price is below that value from a database
- ▸ You have some addresses and want to get the coordinates (latitude and longitude) for those locations from a web service

Searching for information in databases, text files, web services, and so on, is a very common task, and Kettle has several steps for doing it. In this chapter, you will learn about the different options.

Looking for values in a database table

In order to search for data in a database, Kettle offers several ways of accessing the data. The simplest situation is the one in which you need to get one or more columns from a single database table. In this recipe, you will learn how to do this by using the **Database lookup** step. We will work with the **Steel Wheels** sample data. If you wish to become more familiar with the sample dataset or need to learn how to configure database access, refer to *Chapter 1, Working with Databases*. Suppose that you want to look for products that match a given search term, and whose prices are below a given value, this recipe shows you how to do this.

Getting ready

In order to follow this recipe, you need the Steel Wheels database.

How to do it...

Perform the following steps:

1. Create a new transformation.
2. Bring over a **Data Grid** step from the **Input** category. Open the step. Under the **Meta** tab, add two string items `prod` and `max_price`. Then, complete the **Data** tab, as shown in the following screenshot:

Meta	Data	
#	prod	max_price
1	Aston Martin	90
2	Ford Falcon	70
3	Corvette	70

3. Add a **User Defined Java Expression** step.
4. Use that step to add a string named `like_statement`. In **Java expression**, type `%+%+prod+%.+%`.
5. Add a **Database lookup** step. You will find it in the **Lookup** category of steps.
6. Double-click on the step. As **Connection**, select (or create if it does not exist) the connection to the `sampledata` database. As **Lookup table** type or browse for PRODUCTS.

7. Fill the upper and lower grid, as shown in the following screenshot:

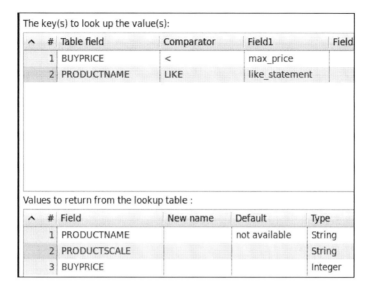

8. Close the **Database lookup** configuration window and do a preview on this step. You will see something like the following screenshot:

#	prod	max_price	like_statement	PRODUCTNAME	PRODUCTSCALE
1	Aston Martin	90	%Aston Martin%	1965 Aston Martin DB5	1:18
2	Ford Falcon	70	%Ford Falcon%	not available	
3	Corvette	70	%Corvette%	1958 Chevy Corvette Limited Edition	1:24

Rows of step: Database lookup (simple) (3 rows)

How it works...

The **Database lookup** step allows you to look for values in a database table. To perform that search, you need to specify at least the following things:

- The database connection and the database table you want to search
- The conditions for the search
- The fields to retrieve from the table

The upper grid is where you specify the conditions. Each row in the grid represents a comparison between a column in the table, and a field in your stream, by using one of the provided comparators.

Take a look at the upper grid in the recipe. The conditions you entered were:

BUYPRICE < max_price and PRODUCTNAME LIKE like_statement

If we take, for example, the first row in the dataset, the condition can be restated as:

`BUYPRICE < 90` and `PRODUCTNAME LIKE %Aston Martin%`

That's exactly the search you wanted to perform for that row—look for the records where the column `BUYPRICE` was less than `90`, and the column `PRODUCTNAME` contained `Aston Martin`.

The **Database lookup** step allow us to retrieve any number of columns based on the search criteria. Each database column you enter in the lower grid will become a new field in your dataset. You can rename them (this is particularly useful if you already have a field with the same name) and supply a default value if no record is found in the search.

In the recipe, you added three fields: `PRODUCTNAME`, `PRODUCTSCALE`, and `BUYPRICE`. By default, for `PRODUCTNAME` you typed `not available`. In the final preview, you can see that description in the second row. This means that there were no products with `Ford Falcon` as part of their description and a price lower than `70`.

There's more...

The recipe showed the minimal setting of the **Database lookup** step. The step has more options that can be useful, as explained in the following subsections.

Taking some action when the lookup fails

When you perform a search with the **Database lookup** step, you expect that the search returns a row. If the data you are looking for doesn't exist in the table, then the lookup fails. If this happens, the fields you added in the lower grid are added to the dataset anyway, with null values or with the default values, if you provided them. That is the default behavior. However, you have two more options if you don't like that, which are as follows:

1. If the data should be present, then the failure of the lookup is considered an error. In that case, you can handle the error. You can, for example, send the rows that cause the failure to a different stream , as shown in the following screenshot

Remember that you can capture errors by right-clicking on the **Database lookup** step, selecting the **Define error handling...** option and configuring the **Step error handling settings** window properly. At least, you have to check the **Enable the error handling?** option and select the **Write to log step** as the **Target step**.

If you do this, the rows for which the lookup fails, go directly to the stream that captures the error, in this case, the **Write to log** step.

2. If the rows are useless without the fields that you are looking for, then you can discard them. You do that by checking the **Do not pass the row if the lookup fails** option. This way, only the rows for which the lookup succeeds will pass to the next step.

Taking some action when there are too many results

The **Database lookup** step is meant to retrieve just one row of the table for each row in your dataset. If the search finds more than one row, the following two things may happen:

1. If you check the **Fail on multiple results?** option, the rows for which the lookup retrieves more than one row will cause the step to fail. In that case, in the **Logging** tab window, you will see an error similar to the following:

```
... - Database lookup (fail on multiple res.).0 - ERROR... Because
of an error, this step can't continue:
... - Database lookup (fail on multiple res.).0 - ERROR... :
Only 1 row was expected as a result of a lookup, and at least 2
were found!
```

Then you can decide whether you want to leave the transformation or capture the error.

2. If you don't check the **Fail on multiple results?** option, the step will return the first row it encounters. You can decide which one to return by specifying the order. You do that by typing an order clause in the **Order by** textbox. In the `sampledata` database, there are three products that meet the conditions for the `Corvette` row. If, for **Order by**, you type `PRODUCTSCALE DESC, PRODUCTNAME`, then you will get `1958 Chevy Corvette Limited Edition`, which is the first product after ordering the three found products by the specified criterion.

If, instead of taking some of those actions, you realize that you need all the resulting rows, you should take another approach—replace the **Database lookup** step with a **Database join** or a **Dynamic SQL row** step. For recipes explaining these steps, see the following *See also* section.

Looking for non-existent data

If, instead of looking for a row, you want to determine if the row doesn't exist, the procedure is much the same. You configure the **Database lookup** step to look for those rows. Then you capture the error, as depicted in the following screenshot:

In this case, the stream that you use for capturing the error becomes your main stream. The rows that didn't fail will be discarded, and the rows for which the lookup failed go directly to the main stream for further treatment.

See also

 ▶ *Looking for values in a database with complex conditions*
 ▶ *Looking for values in a database with dynamic queries*

Looking for values in a database with complex conditions

In the previous recipe, you saw how to search for columns in a database table based on simple conditions. With Kettle, you can also search by providing complex conditions or involving more than one table. In this recipe, you will learn how to perform that kind of search by using the **Database join** step. To let you compare the different options for searching data in a database with ease, we will work with the same example that you saw in the preceding recipe—the Steel Wheels sample data. You want to look for products that match a given search term and whose prices are below a given value.

Getting ready

In order to follow this recipe, you need the Steel Wheels database. The code to generate this database is available from several locations, as mentioned in *Chapter 1, Working with Databases*.

How to do it...

Perform the following steps:

1. Create a new transformation.

2. Add a **Data Grid** step that generates a dataset like the one shown in the following screenshot:

#	prod	max_price
1	Aston Martin	90
2	Ford Falcon	70
3	Corvette	70

Meta (Data)

 You can type the data into a file and read the file, or use a Data Grid.

3. Add a **Database join** step. You will find it in the **Lookup** category of steps.

4. Double-click on the step. As **Connection**, select (or create if it doesn't exist) the connection to the `sampledata` database.

5. In the SQL frame, type the following statement:

```
SELECT  PRODUCTNAME
      , PRODUCTSCALE
      , BUYPRICE
FROM    PRODUCTS
WHERE   PRODUCTNAME LIKE concat(<%>,?,>%>)
AND     BUYPRICE < ?
```

6. Check the **Outer join?** option.

7. Click on **Get Fields** to fill the grid with two parameters—`prod` and `max_price`.

8. Close the **Database join** configuration window and do a preview on this step. You will see something like the following screenshot:

Rows of step: Database join (4 rows)

^	#	prod	max_price	PRODUCTNAME	PRODUCTSCALE
	1	Aston Martin	90	1965 Aston Martin DB5	1:18
	2	Ford Falcon	70		
	3	Corvette	70	1958 Chevy Corvette Limited Edition	1:24
	4	Corvette	70	2002 Chevy Corvette	1:24

How it works...

The **Database join** step is a powerful step for looking for data in a database, based on given conditions. The conditions usually involve comparisons between columns in tables and fields in your stream; therefore it's called a join.

 This is not really a database join. Instead of joining tables in a database, you are joining the result of a database query with a Kettle dataset.

The question marks you type in the SQL statement (those in the highlighted lines in the recipe) represent parameters. The purpose of these parameters is to be replaced with the fields you provide in the lower grid. For each row in your stream the **Database join** step replaces the parameters in the same order as they are in the grid, and executes the SQL statement.

If we take as an example the first row in the dataset, the SQL statement after the replacement of the parameters would look like the following query:

```
SELECT  PRODUCTNAME
      , PRODUCTSCALE
      , BUYPRICE
FROM    PRODUCTS
WHERE   PRODUCTNAME LIKE concat('%','Aston Martin','%')
AND     BUYPRICE < 90
```

And that's exactly the search you wanted to do for that row: look for the records where the column BUYPRICE was less than 90 and the column PRODUCTNAME contained Aston Martin. As a result of the database join, you can retrieve any number of columns. Each database column that you type in the SELECT clause will become a new field in your dataset. In the recipe, those fields were PRODUCTNAME, PRODUCTSCALE, and BUYPRICE. In particular, if you had typed SELECT *, you would have retrieved all columns in the tables involved in the statement.

In the recipe, you checked the **Outer join?** option. The effect of this is as follows: For the rows where the lookup fails, the new fields are retrieved with null values. That was the case for the second row. There were no products with Ford Falcon as part of its description and a price lower than 70. Therefore, that row shows empty values for the PRODUCTNAME, PRODUCTSCALE, and BUYPRICE fields.

Note that in the recipe, you filled the grid with two fields. That is exactly the same number of question marks in the statement.

 The number of fields in the grid must be exactly the same as the number of question marks in the query.

Also, note that in the grid the `prod` field was in the first place and the `max_price` in the second place. If you look at the highlighted lines in the recipe, you will see that the statement expected the parameters in exactly that order.

 The replacement of the markers respects the order of the fields in the grid.

So far, the results are quite similar to those you got with a database lookup. There is a significant difference, however. For the third row, the `Corvette` product, you can see two results. This means that the **Database join** found two matching rows in the database, and retrieved them both. This is not possible with a **Database lookup** step.

There's more...

The **Database join** step can be a little complicated to use, or to understand, compared to the **Database lookup** step. While the **Database lookup** step has a UI that makes the configuration of the step easy, in the **Database join** step, you have to write an SQL statement. That implies that you need a good knowledge of SQL. However, the **Database join** step has several advantages over the **Database lookup** one:

- It allows you to look up from a combination of tables.
- It allows you to retrieve fields from more than one table at a time.
- It allows you to retrieve aggregate results, fragments of a field (for example, a substring of a field), or a combination of fields (for example, two strings concatenated).
- It allows you to retrieve more than one row from the database for each incoming row in the Kettle dataset. This is by far the most important advantage. By default, all matching rows are retrieved. If you want to limit the number of rows to retrieve for each row in your stream, just change the **Number of rows** to return value.

See also

- *Looking for values in a database table*
- *Looking for values in a database with dynamic queries*

Looking for values in a database with dynamic queries

The **Database join** step that you learned to use in the previous recipe is quite powerful and has several advantages over the simple **Database lookup** step. There is a still more powerful step for searching in a database; The **Dynamic SQL row** step. This recipe explains to you its capabilities and shows you how to use it.

In order to let you compare the different options for searching in a database with ease, we will work with an example similar to that you saw in the previous two recipes—we will work with the Steel Wheels sample data. You want to look for the following products:

▶ Products that contain `Aston Martin` in their description

▶ Products that contain `Ford Falcon` in their name and with a scale of `1:18`

▶ Products that contain `Corvette` in their name and with a scale of `1:24`

Getting ready

In order to follow this recipe, you need the Steel Wheels database.

How to do it...

Perform the following steps:

1. Create a new transformation.

2. Create a stream that generates a dataset like the one shown in the following screenshot.

#	prod	column_name	cond
1	Aston Martin	PRODUCTDESCRIPTION	
2	Ford Falcon	PRODUCTNAME	PRODUCTSCALE="1:18"
3	Corvette	PRODUCTNAME	PRODUCTSCALE="1:24"

(Meta / Data)

 You can type the data into a file and read the file, or use a Data Grid.

3. At the end of your stream, add a **User Defined Java Expression** step.

4. Use that step to add a **String** named `statement`. As **Java expression**, type the following query:

```
SELECT PRODUCTNAME, PRODUCTSCALE, BUYPRICE FROM PRODUCTS WHERE
PRODUCTNAME LIKE '%"+prod+"%'"+(cond!=null?" AND "+cond:").
```

5. Do a preview on this step. You will see a new column named `statement` with a complete SQL statement, for example:

```
SELECT PRODUCTNAME, PRODUCTSCALE, BUYPRICE FROM PRODUCTS WHERE
PRODUCTDESCRIPTIONPRODUCTDESCRIPTION LIKE '%Aston Martin%'
```

6. Add a **Dynamic SQL row** step. You will find it in the **Lookup** category of steps.

7. Double-click on the step. As **Connection**, select (or create if it doesn't exist) the connection to the `sampledata` database.

8. As the SQL field name, type or select `statement`.

9. Check the **Outer join?** option.

10. In the **Template SQL (to retrieve Meta data)** frame, type the following query:

```
SELECT 'NAME', 'SCALE', 1 as BUYPRICE
```

11. Close the **Dynamic SQL row** configuration window and do a preview on this step. You will see something like the following screenshot (note that the `statement` field is hidden):

Rows of step: Dynamic SQL row (4 rows)

#	prod	column_name	cond	statement	NAME	SCALE	BUYPRICE
1	Aston Martin	PRODUCTDESCRIPTION		SELECT PRODUCTNAME, PRODU	1965 Aston Martin DB5	1:18	66
2	Ford Falcon	PRODUCTNAME	PRODUCTSCALE="1:18"	SELECT PRODUCTNAME, PRODU			
3	Corvette	PRODUCTNAME	PRODUCTSCALE="1:24"	SELECT PRODUCTNAME, PRODU	1958 Chevy Corvette Limited Edition	1:24	16
4	Corvette	PRODUCTNAME	PRODUCTSCALE="1:24"	SELECT PRODUCTNAME, PRODU	2002 Chevy Corvette	1:24	62

How it works...

The **Dynamic SQL row** step is a very powerful step for looking for data in a database.

If we take, for example, the first row in the dataset, the SQL statement (the one that you build with the Java expression) is similar to the following query:

```
SELECT PRODUCTNAME, PRODUCTSCALE, BUYPRICE FROM PRODUCTS WHERE
PRODUCTDESCRIPTION LIKE '%Aston Martin%'
```

That's exactly the search you wanted to perform for that row—look for the records where the column `PRODUCTDESCRIPTION` contained `Aston Martin`.

Now look at the following SQL statement for the last row:

```
SELECT PRODUCTNAME, PRODUCTSCALE, BUYPRICE FROM PRODUCTS WHERE
PRODUCTNAME LIKE '%Corvette%' AND PRODUCTSCALE="1:24"
```

In this case, you are filtering both by the name and by the scale.

As you see, what you are doing is dynamically creating an SQL statement. Then, in the **Dynamic SQL row** configuration window, you just use the **SQL field name** to indicate which field contains the SQL statement to execute.

As the output of the **Dynamic SQL row** step, you can retrieve any number of columns. Each database column in the `SELECT` statement will become a new field in your dataset.

In order to tell Kettle the metadata of the new fields being added with this dynamic statement, you must fill in the **Template SQL (to retrieve Meta data)** frame. Here, you have to type any statement that returns the same structure as the new fields. Kettle will take from here both the names and the types for the new fields.

In the recipe, you typed `SELECT 'NAME', 'SCALE', 1 as BUYPRICE`. With this statement, you are telling Kettle that you are adding three fields—two strings named `NAME` and `SCALE` and an integer field named `BUYPRICE`.

> Both the statement and this template are written using MySQL syntax. It's mandatory that you restate them to match the syntax of the database engine you are using.

In the recipe, you checked the **Outer join?** option. The effect of this is the same as in the **Database join** step—for the rows where the lookup fails, the new fields are retrieved with null values. That was the case for the second row. There were no products with `Ford Falcon` as part of its name and a scale of `1:18`. Therefore, that row shows empty values for the `PRODUCTNAME`, `PRODUCTSCALE`, and `BUYPRICE` fields. For the third row, the `Corvette` product, you can see two results. This means that the **Dynamic SQL row** step found two matching rows in the database and retrieved them both. This also resembles the behavior of the **Database join** step.

Finally, note that in the recipe, the statement was different for each row. It may happen however, that your statements do not change a lot. If this is the case, you can reduce the number of physical database queries by checking the **Query only on parameters change** option.

There's more...

The **Dynamic SQL row** step is the most flexible step for looking up data in a database. As you saw, there are a couple of similarities between this and the **Database join** step. What really makes a difference between them is that with the **Dynamic SQL row** step, any part of the statement can be built dynamically based on the fields in your stream. For example, the columns used for comparison in the recipe were the product description in the first row and the product name in the others. What you did in the recipe is not possible to achieve by using the **Database join**, at least in a simple fashion.

Note that you could also have had the statement already built, for example, in a property file or saved in a column in a database table. In that case, you also could have used the **Dynamic SQL row** step to execute the statement and that is definitely impossible to do with any other step.

See also

▸ *Looking for values in a database*

Looking for values in a variety of sources

The first recipes in the chapter showed you how to look for additional information in a database. There are still many other sources of information. You may need to look in property files, in Excel files, in text files, and so on. Kettle allows you to look for data coming from all those sources with the **Stream lookup** step. In this example, you have information about books coming from an Excel file, and you need to complete this dataset by looking up the author's data and genre description, which are in external sources. In this case, the author's information is inside a text file and the genres are in a fixed predefined list.

Getting ready

For doing this recipe, you will need the following:

> ► A CSV file (`authors.txt`) with the authors' data. The file should have the following columns: `lastname`, `firstname`, `nationality`, and `id_author`. The following are sample lines of this file:

```
"lastname","firstname","nationality","id_author"
"Larsson","Stieg","Swedish","A00001"
"King","Stephen","American","A00002"
"Hiaasen","Carl ","American","A00003"
"Handler","Chelsea ","American","A00004"
"Ingraham","Laura ","American","A00005"
```

> ► An Excel file with the books' information (`books.xls`). The sheet should have the following columns: `title`, `id_author`, `price`, `id_title`, and `id_genre` as shown in the following screenshot:

	A	B	C	D	E
1	title	id_author	price	id_title	id_genre
2	Carrie	A00002	41	123-346	F
3	Salem's Lot	A00002	33	123-347	F
4	The Shining	A00002	31	123-348	F
5	The Dead Zone	A00002	37	123-349	F
6	Pet Sematary	A00002	41	123-351	F
7	The Tommyknockers	A00002	39	123-352	F
8	Bag of Bones	A00002	40.9	123-353	F
9	The Girl with the Dragon Tatoo	A00001	35	123-400	F
10	The Girl who Played with Fire	A00001	35.9	123-401	F

Books

You can also download sample files from Packt's website.

How to do it...

Perform the following steps:

1. Create a new transformation.

2. Drop an **Microsoft Excel input** step and a **Text file input** step into the canvas.

3. In the **Microsoft Excel input** step, browse for the `books.xls` file under the **Files** tab and click on the **Add** button. Populate the grid under the **Fields** tab by clicking on the **Get fields from header row** button.

4. In the **Text file** input step, browse for the `authors.txt` file and click on the **Add** button. Type , as the **Separator** under the **Content** tab and finally, populate the **Fields** tab grid by clicking on the **Get Fields** button.

5. Add a **Stream lookup** step from the **Lookup** category.

6. Create a hop from the **Microsoft Excel input** step to the **Stream lookup** step and another from the **Text file input,** also to the **Stream lookup** step.

7. Double-click on the **Stream lookup** step and in the **Lookup step** listbox select the name of the **Text file input** step previously created.

8. Complete the grids with the following information:

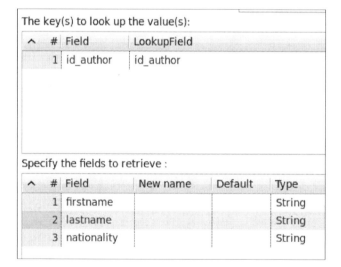

The key(s) to look up the value(s):

#	Field	LookupField
1	id_author	id_author

Specify the fields to retrieve :

#	Field	New name	Default	Type
1	firstname			String
2	lastname			String
3	nationality			String

> To save time, you can click on the **Get Fields** button to automatically load the fields in the upper grid, and the **Get lookup fields** button to populate the lower grid.

9. Previewing this step, you can verify that the dataset includes, for each book, the information for its author. Now, let's add the genre description.

10. Drop a **Data Grid** step from the **Input** category. Under its **Meta** tab, add two String items `id_genre` and `genre`. Then, complete the **Data** tab as shown in the following screenshot:

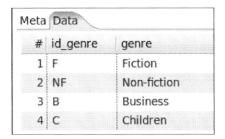

11. Add a new **Stream lookup** step and create a hop from the **Data grid** step toward this new step.

12. Also, create a hop between both **Stream Lookup** steps. The transformation should look like the one shown in the following screenshot:

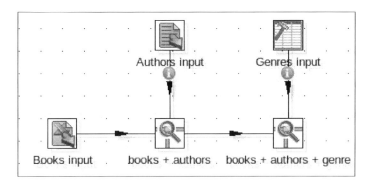

13. Double-click on the last **Stream lookup** step. In the **Lookup step** listbox, type or select the name of the **Data grid** step created earlier.

14. In the upper grid, add a row typing `id_genre` under the **Field** column and `id` under **LookupField**.

15. In the lower grid, add a genre `Field`, of `String` Type. Add `Unknown` as the **Default** value.

16. Doing a preview of this step, you will obtain a dataset of the books, their authors, and also the description of their genres. An example is shown in the following screenshot:

Rows of step: books + authors + genre (34 rows)

^	#	title	id_author	price	id_title	id_genre	firstname	lastname	nationality	genre
	1	Carrie	A00002	41.0	123-346	F	Stephen	King	American	Fiction
	2	Salem's Lot	A00002	33.0	123-347	F	Stephen	King	American	Fiction
	3	The Shining	A00002	31.0	123-348	F	Stephen	King	American	Fiction
	4	The Dead Zone	A00002	37.0	123-349	F	Stephen	King	American	Fiction
	5	Pet Sematary	A00002	41.0	123-351	F	Stephen	King	American	Fiction
	6	The Tommyknockers	A00002	39.0	123-352	F	Stephen	King	American	Fiction
	7	Bag of Bones	A00002	40.9	123-353	F	Stephen	King	American	Fiction
	8	The Girl with the Dragon Tatoo	A00001	35.0	123-400	F	Stieg	Larsson	Swedish	Fiction
	9	The Girl who Played with Fire	A00001	35.9	123-401	F	Stieg	Larsson	Swedish	Fiction
	10	The Girl who Kicked the Hornett's Nest	A00001	39.0	123-402	F	Stieg	Larsson	Swedish	Fiction
	11	Star Island	A00003	36.0	123-505	F	Carl	Hiaasen	American	Fiction
	12	Basket Case	A00003	31.0	123-506	F	Carl	Hiaasen	American	Fiction
	13	Chelsea Chelsea Bang Bang	A00004	25.0	223-200	NF	Chelsea	Handler	American	Non-fiction
	14	My Horizontal Life	A00004	24.0	223-201	BG	Chelsea	Handler	American	Unknown
	15	Are You There, Vodka? It's me, Chelsea	A00004	19.9	223-202	NF	Chelsea	Handler	American	Non-fiction

How it works...

The **Stream Lookup** step is the step that you should use to look for additional information in other sources. In this recipe, the main data comes from an Excel file with book titles and also, the identification for their authors and genres. You used two **Stream Lookup** steps to look up for each title, the author's information, and the genre description respectively.

In the first **Stream Lookup** step, the purpose is to look for the author's data; in this step, you configure the **Lookup step** listbox pointing to the **Text file input** step, which is where the author's data is coming from.

In the upper grid named **The key(s) to lookup the values(s)**, you have to specify the fields used to join both data sources. In this case, those fields are `id_author` and `id`.

The second grid titled **Specify the fields to retrieve** is to declare the fields to add to the main dataset. You have typed the fields—`firstname`, `lastname`, and `nationality`. The last **Stream Lookup** step was created in order to retrieve the genre description that matches the genre identification in the main dataset. Here the key values are the fields `id_genre` and `id` and the only data to retrieve is the field `genre`. Here you entered `Unknown` as the **Default** value. This means that if the **Stream Lookup** step doesn't find a matching genre for a row, the genre description will be set to `Unknown`.

There's more...

The following sections provide you with some alternatives to the use of the **Stream Lookup** step.

Looking for alternatives when the Stream Lookup step doesn't meet your needs

The **Stream Lookup** step compares the fields with an equal operator. There are a couple of situations where this may not be what you need.

If you are not sure about the similarity of the values between the fields that you are comparing, a comparison by equal may fail. In that case, you could use the **Fuzzy match** step, which allows you to search for similar values. For instance, if you are comparing a dataset of first names, Bob would match to Bob. Sometimes data entry errors can occur, and you may have to compare Bob to Lob or any other misspelling. **Fuzzy match** would provide the probability that Lob really should have been Bob. This could become problematic if there was also a Rob in the dataset; but **Fuzzy match** provides a way to at least call out potential issues.

If you need to compare using other operators, for example, <=, then you should also look for an alternative step. One possible approach would be to use the **Join Rows (artesian product)** to retrieve all the data, and filter the rows from that step with a **Filter rows** or a **Java Filter** step afterwards.

Keep in mind that **Join Rows (cartesian product)** might increase the number of records you are processing, slowing down your process significantly. Cartesian products provide all the pairings of the two datasets, For example, if we were joining a dataset with ten records and another dataset with thirty records, we would end up with 300 records.

Another option would be to transfer the source data to a database table and then lookup in the database. This approach takes a little more effort, but it has its advantages. You have more flexible ways for looking up data in a database compared with looking up in a stream. Besides, for big datasets, you can also gain performance as explained in the next subsection.

Speeding up your transformation

For big datasets, looking up in plain files with a **Stream Lookup** step can start becoming cumbersome to work with. As a workaround to speed things up, you should consider moving the data to a database table before looking up in it. The main advantages of this approach is that you can cache and index data, which makes the lookup task faster.

What if your project doesn't involve database tasks? For these temporary lookup tables, you may want to use an in-memory database such as HSQLDB or H2. In-memory databases provide all the benefits of traditional databases for situations where the data does not have to be constantly persisted.

For a practical example of this, take a look at the blog post by *Slawomir Chodnicki* at `http://type-exit.org/adventures-with-open-source-bi/2011/01/using-an-on-demand-in-memory-sql-database-in-pdi/`.

Using the Value Mapper step for looking up from a short list of values

The second **Stream Lookup** step in the recipe only returns a simple description and has a short list of possible values. In these cases, you can replace this step with a **Value Mapper** from the **Transform** category.

You should complete the step, as shown in the following screenshot:

In the **Source value** column, you define the possible values for the `id_genre` field, and in the **Target value** column, you define their descriptions. Also, in the **Default upon non-matching** textbox, you can enter a default value to be returned for the rows with invalid genre identification.

See also

- ▶ *Looking for values by proximity*
- ▶ The recipe *Generating all possible pairs formed from two datasets* in *Chapter 7, Understanding and Optimizing Data Flows*

Looking for values by proximity

This chapter is about looking for values in different sources based on given conditions. Those conditions are a comparison between fields in your stream and fields in the source that you are looking into. As you know, or could see in the rest of the recipes, you usually compare by equality and sometimes you do it by using different operators such as LIKE, NOT EQUAL, <, and so on. What if you need to look for a value that is more or less equal to a field in your stream? None of the options you saw in the other recipes will give you the solution to this problem. In these situations, you need to perform a fuzzy search, that is, a search that looks for similar values. Kettle allows you to perform such a search by providing you the **Fuzzy match** step. In this recipe, you will learn how to use this step.

Suppose that you receive an external text file with book orders and you need to find the prices for these books. The problem is that you don't have the identification for that book, you only have the title, and you are not sure if the spelling is correct.

Getting ready

You must have a books database with the structure shown in the *Appendix A, Data Structures*.

The recipe uses a file named `booksOrder.txt` with the following book titles, which deliberately includes some typos:

```
Carry
Slem's Lot
TheShining
The Ded sone
Pet Cemetary
The Tomyknockers
Bag of Bones
Star Island
Harry Potter
```

How to do it...

Perform the following steps:

1. Create a new transformation.

2. Drop a **Text file input** step into the work area, in order to retrieve the book order.

3. In the **File or directory** textbox under the **File** tab, browse to the `booksOrder.txt` file and then click on the **Add** button.

4. Under the **Content** tab, uncheck the **Header** checkbox.

5. Under the **Fields** tab, add a new `String` field named `TitleApprox`.

6. Drop another step in order to read the books database. Use a **Table input** step and type the following SQL statement:

```
SELECT title
     , price
FROM Books
```

7. Add a **Fuzzy match** step from the **Lookup** category. Add a hop from the **Table input** step toward this step. Add another hop from the **Text file input** step created before, also toward the **Fuzzy match** step.

8. Double-click on the **Fuzzy match** step. Under the **General** tab, go to the **Lookup stream (source)** frame and as **Lookup step**, select the **Table input** step created before. In the **Lookup field**, select **title**.

9. In the **Main stream field**, select the **TitleApprox** field.

10. Now, you must select the fuzzy match algorithm to be used. In this case, you will use **Levenshtein**. Select it from the **Algorithm** drop-down list. Set the **minimal value** to **0** and the **Maximal value** to **3**. Also, uncheck the **Case sensitive** checkbox.

11. Select the **Fields** tab and type **match** in **Match field** and **measure_value** in **Value field**.

12. Under the same tab, add the `price` field to the grid.

13. After this, the transformation should look like the one shown in the following screenshot:

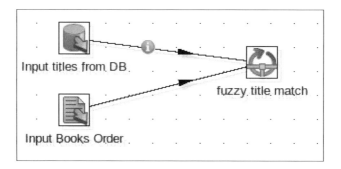

14. If you select the **Fuzzy match** step and preview the transformation, the result will look like the following screenshot:

^	#	TitleApprox	match	measure_value	price
	1	Carry	Carrie	3	41
	2	Slem's Lot	Salem's Lot	2	33
	3	TheShining	The Shining	2	31
	4	The Ded sone	The Dead Zone	2	37
	5	Pet Cemetary	Pet Sematary	2	41
	6	The Tomyknockers	The Tommyknockers	1	39
	7	Bag of Bones	Bag of Bones	1	40.9
	8	Star Island	Star Island	0	36
	9	Harry Potter			

How it works...

The **Fuzzy match** step is used to look in another stream for values that are similar to the value of a field in your stream. For each row in your dataset, a comparison is made between the main stream field (`TitleApprox` in this case) and each lookup field in the secondary stream (`title`). In other words, for each book in the list, a comparison is made between the provided title and the real titles coming from the database.

The comparison consists of applying a given fuzzy match algorithm. A **fuzzy match algorithm** compares two strings and calculates a similarity index. The row with the lowest index is returned, as long as it is between the **Minimum value** and the **Maximum value**.

In this recipe, we used the Levenshtein match algorithm that calculates a metric distance. The similarity index for this algorithm represents the number of edits needed to transform one field into the other. These edits can be character insertion, deletion, or substitution of a single character.

As minimum and maximum values, you specified 0 (meaning that the exact title was found) and 3 (meaning that you will accept as valid a title with a maximum of three edits). For example, when you preview the result of this step, you can see a title named `The Ded sone` which matches the real title `The Dead Zone` with a distance of 2. For the `Star Island` title the distance is 0 because the spelling was correct and a book with exactly the same title was found. Finally, for the `Harry Potter` row, there are no matching rows because you need too many editions to transform the provided title into one of the Harry Potter titles in the database.

There's more...

The **Fuzzy match** step allows you to choose among several matching algorithms, which are classified in the following two groups:

▶ **Algorithms based on a metric distance**: The comparison is based on how the compared terms are spelled

▶ **Phonetic algorithms**: The comparison is based on how the compared terms sound, as read in English

The following is a brief comparative table for the implemented algorithms:

Algorithm	Classification	Explanation	Example
Levenshtein	Metric distance	The distance is calculated as the minimum edit distance that transforms one string into the other. These edits can be character insertion or deletion, or substitution of a single character.	The transformation of "pciking" into "picking" requires two changes (the c and i need to be replaced), which would be a distance of 2.
Damerau-Levenshtein	Metric distance	Similar to Levenshtein, but adds the transposition operation.	The transformation of "pciking" into "picking" requires one change (the i and c are transposed), which would be a distance of 1.
Needleman-Wunsch	Metric distance	A variant of the Levenshtein algorithm. It adds a gap cost, which is a penalty for the insertions and deletions.	The transformation of "pciking" into "picking" still requires two changes (the c and i need to be replaced), but a distance of 1 is returned due to the gap cost.
Jaro	Metric distance	Based on typical spelling deviations. The index goes from 0 to 1, with 0 as no similarity, and 1 as the identical value.	The transformation of "pciking" into "picking" requires one change (the i and c are transposed). Since this is a common spelling issue, the return value is 1 (they are identical).
Jaro-Winkler	Metric distance	A variant of the Jaro algorithm, appropriate for short strings such as names.	The transformation of "pciking" into "picking" requires one change (the i and c are transposed). Since this is a common spelling issue, the return value is 1 (they are identical).

Algorithm	Classification	Explanation	Example
Pair letters Similarity	Metric distance	The strings are divided into pairs, and then the algorithm calculates an index based on the comparison of the lists of pairs of both strings.	The pairing of 'pciking' to 'picking' provides 3 common pairs (ki, in, ng) of a total 6 pairs. The returned value is 0.5.
SoundEx	Phonetic	It consists of indexing terms by sound. It only encodes consonants. Each term is given a **soundex** code. Each soundex code consists of a letter and three numbers. Similar sounding consonants share the same digit (for example, b, f, p, v are equal to 1).	
Refined SoundEx	Phonetic	A variant of the SoundEx algorithm optimized for spell checking.	
Metaphone	Phonetic	The algorithm is similar to the SoundEx algorithm, but produces variable length keys. Similar sounding words share the same keys.	
Double Metaphone	Phonetic	An extension of the Metaphone algorithm where a primary and a secondary code are returned for a string.	

The decision of which algorithm to choose depends on your problem and the kind of data you have or you expect to receive. You can even combine a fuzzy search with a regular search. For example, in the recipe, you didn't find a match for the `Harry Potter` row. Note that increasing the maximum value wouldn't have found the proper title. Try raising the maximum value to `10`, and you will see that the algorithm brings `Carrie` as the result, which clearly has nothing to do with the wizard. However, if you look for this value with a **Database join** step by comparing with the `LIKE` operator, you could retrieve not just one, but all the Harry Potter titles.

Further details on the individual similarity metrics can be found at `http://en.wikipedia.org/wiki/String_metrics`.

Wikipedia also has articles for the algorithms that go into more detail on how they work.

Looking for values by using a web service

Web services are interfaces that are accessed through HTTP and executed on a remote hosting system. They use XML messages that follow the **Simple Object Access Protocol** (**SOAP**) standard. Some examples of web services that use SOAP are Salesforce, Amazon Web Services, and eBay. With Kettle, you can look for values in available web services by using the **Web service lookup** step. In this recipe, you will see an example that shows the use of this step.

Suppose that you have a dataset of museums and you want to know about their opening and closing hours. That information is available as an external web service. The web service has a web method named GetMuseumHour that receives the id_museum as a parameter, and returns the museum schedule as a String. The request and response elements for the GetMuseumHour web method used in this recipe look like the following:

▶ Request:

```
<soap:Envelope xmlns:xsi="http://www.w3.org/2001/XMLSchema-
instance" xmlns:xsd="http://www.w3.org/2001/XMLSchema"
xmlns:soap="http://schemas.xmlsoap.org/soap/envelope/">
  <soap:Body>
    <GetMuseumHour xmlns="http://tempuri.org/">
      <idMuseum>int</idMuseum>
    </GetMuseumHour>
  </soap:Body>
</soap:Envelope>
```

▶ Response:

```
<soap:Envelope xmlns:xsi="http://www.w3.org/2001/XMLSchema-
instance" xmlns:xsd="http://www.w3.org/2001/XMLSchema"
xmlns:soap="http://schemas.xmlsoap.org/soap/envelope/">
  <soap:Body>
    <GetMuseumHourResponse xmlns="http://tempuri.org/">
      <GetMuseumHourResult>string</GetMuseumHourResult>
    </GetMuseumHourResponse>
  </soap:Body>
</soap:Envelope>
```

As with any XML, the structure of both the request and response are important. The request is asking for the hours of the provided museum. The response will return the hours in the GetMuseumHourResponse as a string.

Getting ready

You must have a database with the museum structure shown in *Appendix A, Data Structures* and access to a web service similar to the one detailed earlier. On Packt's website, there is sample code for those services. The services run with a server that supports ASP.NET, such as Microsoft's **Internet Information Services (IIS)** or using Apache's web server with mono, a cross platform, open source .NET development framework.

How to do it...

Perform the following steps:

1. Create a new transformation.

2. Drop a **Table input** step into the work area in order to obtain the data with the list of museums. Type the following SQL statement:

```
SELECT id_museum
     , name
     , city
     , country
FROM museums
JOIN cities
ON museums.id_city=cities.id_city
```

3. Add a **Web service lookup** step from the **Lookup** category.

4. Double-click on the step. In the **Web Services** tab, type the URL address for the web service. It is important to point to the **Web Service Definition Language (WSDL)** declaration path, for example, `http://localhost/museumHours/Service.asmx?wsdl`.

5. Click on the **Load** button in order to refresh the web methods for the **Operation** prompt.

6. In the **Operation** listbox, select the web method named **GetMuseumHour**. This generates the necessary inputs and outputs tabs; you can also generate them by clicking on the **Add Input** and **Add Output** buttons.

> Additionally, you can also include authentication credentials for the web service and proxy information, if needed.

7. Select the **In** tab. Click on the **Get Fields** button and you will obtain the parameter name and type for the web service. Type **id_museum** in the **Name** column.

8. Under the output tab named **GetMuseumHourResult**, you must set the field where the result will be written. Clicking on the **Get Fields** button will obtain the return value name. Change the **Name** column to **Hours**.

9. You could execute the transformation now and examine the results. A better approach would be to check the availability of the web service before execution. So, create a new job and add a **Start** entry.

10. Add a **Check webservice availability** job entry from the **Conditions** category.

11. Double-click on the step. Set the **URL** textbox to the WSDL address, in this case `http://localhost/museumsHours/Service.asmx?wsdl`.

12. After that entry, add a **Transformation** entry to run the transformation created earlier. Make sure that the transformation runs only if the previous entry succeeds. That is, right-click on the hop and check the **Follow when result is true** evaluation option.

13. Running the job will return the list of museums, their geographic location, and their hours of operation.

How it works...

The objective in the example is to look for a value that is hosted on a web server. You do it by consuming a web service.

Note that the URL of the web service in the **Web service lookup** step points to a WSDL address. WSDL is an XML-based language used to describe web services.

When you click on the **Load** button in the **Web service lookup** step, the information retrieved from the WSDL contract is interpreted and used to fill the **Operation** combo with the web methods found in the web service. When you choose a method, it automatically sets the necessary values for the input and the output. You only need to write the local values that will be passed as parameters (**In** tab), and the value for the result (**GetMuseumHourResult** tab).

If the tabs for the input and output are not created automatically, you can write the specifications manually, by clicking on the **Add Input** and **Add Output** buttons. For each museum row, there will be a request to the web service passing the **id_museum** parameter declared in the **In** tab. The result containing the museum opening hours will be saved in the **Hours** field declared under the **GetMuseumHourResult** tab.

There's more...

There is also a step named **Check if webservice is available** from the **Lookup** category. You can use it to verify that the web service is available just before consuming it. In this step, you must have the URL address as a field in each row.

In some cases, the web server could be flooded due to the multiple simultaneous requests, and it could return an error similar to **Too many users are connected**.

In these cases, you can check the configuration of the web server. Alternatively, you can rerun the transformation consuming the web service by groups of rows, forcing a delay to avoid the web server saturation.

For more information about web services, you can visit `http://en.wikipedia.org/wiki/Web_service`.

More information about WSDL can be obtained from `http://www.w3.org/TR/wsdl`.

See also

▸ *Looking for values over intranet or the Internet*

Looking for values over intranet or the Internet

This example is similar to the previous one, with the difference being that you have to lookup the museum opening hours on a website instead of a web server. In this case, you will use the **HTTP Client** step. This step is useful to retrieve information from websites that do not normally provide data through web services, like in the previous recipe. This method is also known as **web scraping**.

Getting ready

You must have a database with the museum structure shown in *Appendix A, Data Structures*, and a web page that provides the museum opening hours. The recipe uses an ASP page named `hours.asp`, but you can use the language of your preference. This recipe will require a server that supports ASP (or the language of your preference), such as Microsoft's IIS, or using Apache's web server with mono, a cross platform, open source .NET development framework. The page receives the museum's identification and returns a string with the schedule. You can download a sample web page from Packt's website.

How to do it...

Perform the following steps:

1. Create a new transformation.
2. Drop a **Table input** step into the canvas, in order to obtain the museum's information. Use the following SQL statement:

```
SELECT id_museum
     , name
     , city
     , country
FROM museums
JOIN cities
ON museums.id_city=cities.id_city
```

3. Add an **HTTP Client** step from the **Lookup** category.

4. Double-click on the step. In the **URL** field under the **General** tab, type the HTTP web address of the webpage that provides the opening hours. For example: `http://localhost/museum/hours.asp`.

5. Set the **Result fieldname** textbox to **Hours**.

6. In the **HTTP status code fieldname**, type `status`.

 Under the **General** tab, you can include authentication credentials for the web service and proxy information, if it is needed.

7. Under the **Fields** tab, set the parameter that will be sent to the page as a `GET` parameter. Type `id_museum` in both, the **Name** and **Parameter** columns.

8. The result for the transformation will be the same as the one obtained in the previous recipe.

9. Take a look at that recipe for a preview of the final results.

How it works...

The **HTTP Client** step looks for the museums' opening hours over the intranet—the step does a request to the web page for each museum in the dataset. One example of this request passing the parameter would be `http://localhost/museum/hours.asp?id_museum=25`.

Then, the response of the page containing the museum opening hours will set the `Hours` field.

The `status` field will hold the status code of the operation. For example, a status code equal to `200` means a successful request, whereas a status code `400` is a bad request. You can check the different status codes at `http://en.wikipedia.org/wiki/List_of_HTTP_status_codes`.

There's more...

Suppose that each museum has a different website (and a different URL address) with a web page that provides its opening hours. In this case, you can store this specific URL as a new field in the museum dataset. Then in the **HTTP Client** step check the **Accept URL from field?** checkbox and select that field from the **URL field name** drop-down list.

One alternative to this step is the **HTTP Post Lookup** step. Using this step, you connect to the website and pass the parameters through a POST method instead of a GET method.

See also

▸ The *Introduction* section of *Chapter 9, Integrating Kettle and the Pentaho Suite*

Validating data at runtime

While processing data there will eventually come a time where it is critical to validate the data while in stream, to ensure it is of enough high quality to continue executing the process. Kettle comes with several built-in steps that provide validation capabilities, including a generic **Data Validator** step which allows for data to be processed with a custom set of rules. For this recipe, we will be building some custom rules to validate author data from the books' database.

Getting ready

You must have a database that matches the books' data structures, as listed in *Appendix A, Data Structures*. The code to build this database is available from Packt's website.

How to do it...

Perform the following steps:

1. Create a new transformation.
2. Add a **Table input** step from the **Input** category.
3. Open the step and configure it to connect to the books' database. For the query, click on **Get SQL select statement...** and select the authors' table.
4. Add all the columns from the authors' table.
5. Click on **OK** and exit the step.
6. Under the **Validation** category, select the **Data Validator** step. Add a hop between the **Table input** step and the **Data Validator** step.
7. Open the **Data Validator** step. Click on **New validation**.
8. Call the new rule birthyear_check and click on **OK**.

9. Click on the **birthyear_check** rule. Notice that the right-hand side of the **Data Validator** window is now filled with many different types of checks. Fill the form out, as shown in the following screenshot:

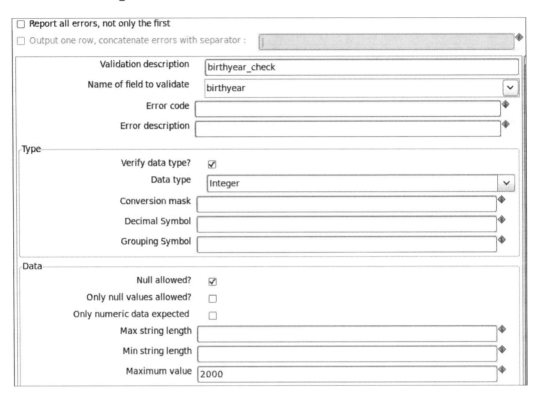

10. Click on **New Validation** again. This time, call the new rule `lastname_check`.

11. Fill out the details like before, with the data type being **String**. In the **Regular expression not allowed to match** field, enter \d+. In the **Name of field to validate** textbox, enter the **last_name** field.

12. Check the option **Report all errors, not only the first**. Click on **OK** to exit the step.

13. Preview the **Data Validator** step, and the author data should process without issue.

    Now, let's introduce an error that would cause the **Data Validator** rules to trigger a failure.

14. From the **Transform** category, select a **Replace in string** step and bring it onto the canvas between the **Table Input** and **Data Validator** steps. Open the step and enter the details, as shown in the following screenshot:

Fields string								
#	In stream field	Out s	use ∧	Search	Replace with	Repl	Whole Word	Case sensitive
1	lastname		N	King	123		Y	N

15. From the **Flow** category, select a **Dummy** step and make it the error handling step of the **Data Validator** step by creating a hop to it and right-clicking on the **Data Validator** step and selecting **Define error handling...**.

16. Preview the **Dummy** step. Every author record with a `lastname` field value of `King` will now error out and appear in the error handling step.

How it works...

The **Data Validator** step takes very basic, to moderately advanced logic to apply to data in stream, and validate if the data at least conforms to those rules. If the data is not clean, it may be possible to apply more transformation logic to clean the data up, otherwise a process can continue to run with the validated data and not fail due to dirty records.

There's more...

There are a few other specialized validation steps that are customized for particular use cases. The following table lists these specialized steps, and when it is appropriate to use them:

Step Name	When to use
Credit card validator	Validating credit card numbers to ensure they are at least formatted appropriately
Mail validator	Validates e-mail addresses, in that they are properly formatted. Can also be verified as a live e-mail address.
XSD Validator	Validates XML based on a schema file.

See also

- ▶ *Looking for values in a database table*
- ▶ The recipe *Validating an XML file against DTD definitions* in *Chapter 4, Manipulating XML Structures*
- ▶ The recipe *Validating an XML file against an XSD schema* in *Chapter 4, Manipulating XML Structures*

7
Understanding and Optimizing Data Flows

In this chapter, we will cover the following topics:

- Splitting a stream into two or more streams based on a condition
- Merging rows of two streams with the same or different structure
- Adding checksums to verify datasets
- Comparing two streams and generating differences
- Generating all possible pairs formed from two datasets
- Joining two or more streams based on given conditions
- Interspersing new rows between existent rows
- Executing steps even when your stream is empty
- Processing rows differently based on the row number
- Processing data into shared transformations via filter criteria and subtransformations
- Altering a data stream with Select values
- Processing multiple jobs or transformations in parallel

Introduction

The main purpose of Kettle transformations is to manipulate data in the form of a dataset—a task done by the steps of the transformation. When a transformation is launched, all its steps are started. During the execution, the steps work simultaneously reading rows from the incoming hops, processing them, and delivering them to the outgoing hops. When there are no more rows left, the execution of the transformation ends.

The dataset that flows from step to step is effectively a set of rows with the same metadata. This means that all rows have the same number of columns, and the columns in all rows have the same type and name.

Suppose that you have a single stream of data and that you apply the same transformations to all rows, that is, you have all steps connected in a row one after the other. In other words, you have the simplest of the transformations from the point of view of its structure. In this case, you don't have to worry much about the structure of your data stream, nor the origin or destination of the rows. The interesting part comes when you face other situations, for example:

▶ You want a step to start processing rows only after another given step has processed all rows.

▶ You have more than one stream and you have to combine them into a single stream. For instance, loading data from multiple sources that will be entered into a single target.

▶ You have to inject rows in the middle of your stream and those rows don't have the same structure as the rows in your dataset. For instance, you have data that is already formatted, but a new set of data (with a different structure) needs to be formatted before both sets are entered into a target.

With Kettle, you can actually do this, but you have to be careful because it's easy to end up doing wrong things and getting unexpected results or even worse; undesirable errors.

With regard to the first example, it doesn't represent a default behavior due to the parallel nature of the transformations as explained earlier. There are two steps however, that might help, which are as follows:

▶ **Blocking step**: This step blocks processing until all incoming rows have been processed

▶ **Block this step until steps finish**: This step blocks processing until the selected steps finish

Both these steps are in the **Flow** category.

You will find examples of the use of the last of these steps in the following recipes:

▶ The *Writing an Excel file with several sheets* recipe in *Chapter 2, Reading and Writing Files*

▶ The *Generating a custom logfile* recipe in *Chapter 10, Getting the Most Out of Kettle*

This chapter focuses on the other two examples and some similar use cases by explaining the different ways for combining, splitting, or manipulating streams of data.

Splitting a stream into two or more streams based on a condition

In this recipe, you will learn to use the **Filter rows** step in order to split a single stream into different smaller streams. In the *There's more...* section, you will also see alternative and more efficient ways for doing the same thing in different scenarios.

Let's assume that you have a set of outdoor products in a text file, and you want to differentiate tents from other kinds of products, and also create a subclassification of the tents depending on their prices.

Let's see a sample of this data:

```
id_product,desc_product,price,category
1,"Swedish Firesteel - Army Model",19,"kitchen"
2,"Mountain House #10 Can Freeze-Dried Food",53,"kitchen"
3,"Lodge Logic L90G3 Pre-Seasoned 10-1/2-Inch Round
Griddle",14,"kitchen"
...
```

Getting ready

To run this recipe, you will need a text file named `outdoorProducts.txt` with information about outdoor products. The file contains information about the category and price of each product.

How to do it...

Perform the following steps:

1. Create a transformation.

2. Drag a **Text file input** step into the canvas and fill in the **File** tab to read the file named `outdoorProducts.txt`. If you are using the sample text file, type `,` as the **Separator**.

3. Under the **Fields** tab, use the **Get Fields** button to populate the grid. Adjust the entries so that the grid looks like the one shown in the following screenshot:

^	#	Name	Type	Format	Pc	Length	Pre	Currency	Decimal	Group	Null if	Default	Trim type	Repeat
	1	id_product	Integer	#		15		$	.	.	-		none	N
	2	desc_product	String			92		$	.	.	-		none	N
	3	price	Integer	0.00		15		$	.	.	-		none	N
	4	category	String			13		$	.	.	-		none	N

File · Content · Error Handling · Filters · Fields · Additional output fields

4. Now, let's add the steps to manage the flow of the rows. To do this, drag two **Filter rows** steps from the **Flow** category. Also, drag three **Dummy** steps that will represent the three resulting streams.

 Dummy steps are used so that we can preview the filtered data. Normally, we would continue working with the data until it was ready to go into an output step.

5. Create the hops, as shown in the following screenshot. When you create the hops, make sure that you choose the options according to the image: **Result is TRUE** for creating a hop with a green icon, and **Result is FALSE** for creating a hop with a red icon in it.

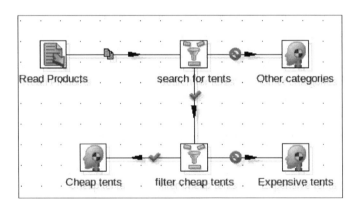

6. Double-click on the first **Filter rows** step and complete the condition, as shown in the following screenshot:

The condition:

category = tents (String)

7. Double-click on the second **Filter rows** step and complete the condition with `price < 100`.

8. You have just split the original dataset into three groups. You can verify it by previewing each **Dummy** step. The first one has products whose category is not tents; the second one, the tents under 100 US$; and the last group, the expensive tents, those whose price is over 100 US$.

9. The preview of the last **Dummy** step is shown in the following screenshot:

Rows of step: Expensive tents (5 rows)

^ #	id_product	desc_product	price	category
1	47	Coleman Instant 14- by 10- Foot 8- Pe	183.00	tents
2	49	Eureka Apex 2XT Adventure 7' 5" by 4	104.00	tents
3	52	Coleman WeatherMaster 8 Tent	206.00	tents
4	56	Eureka Solo Backcountry 1 Tent	122.00	tents
5	57	Kelty Grand Mesa 2-Person Tent (Ruby/	107.00	tents

How it works...

The main objective in the recipe is to split a dataset with products depending on their category and price. To do this, you used the **Filter rows** step.

In the **Filter rows** setting window, you tell Kettle where the data flows to, depending on the result of evaluating a condition for each row. In order to do that, you have two list boxes: **Send 'true' data to step** and **Send 'false' data to step**. The destination steps can be set by using the hop properties, as you did in the recipe. Alternatively, you can set them in the **Filter rows** setting dialog by selecting the name of the destination steps from the available drop-down lists.

You also have to enter the condition. When entering conditions, you will see a condition form similar to the one shown in the following screenshot:

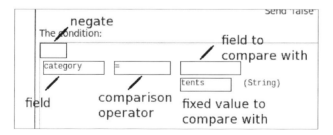

The condition has the following different parts:

▶ The textbox on the top-left corner is meant to negate the condition.

▶ The textbox on the left-hand side is meant to select the field that will be used for comparison.

▶ Then you have a list of possible comparators to choose from.

▶ On the right-hand side you have two textboxes: the upper textbox for comparing against a field and the bottom textbox for comparing against a constant value.

Also, you can include more conditions by clicking on the **Add Condition** button on the right-hand side. If you right-click on a condition, a contextual menu appears to let you delete, edit, or move it. In the first **Filter rows** step of the recipe, you typed a simple condition: you compared a field (`category`) with a fixed value (`tents`) by using an equals to (`=`) operator. You did this to separate the tent products from the others. The second filter had the purpose of differentiating the expensive and the cheap tents.

There's more...

You will find more filter features in the following subsections:

Avoiding the use of Dummy steps

In the recipe, we assumed that you wanted all three groups of products for further processing. Now, suppose that you only want the cheapest tents and you don't care about the rest. You could use just one **Filter rows** step with the condition `category = tents AND price < 100`, and send the "false" data to a **Dummy** step, as shown in the following screenshot:

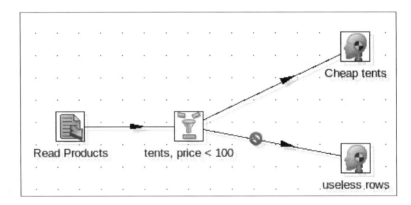

The rows that don't meet the condition will end at the **Dummy** step. Although this is a very commonly used solution for keeping just the rows that meet the conditions, there is a simpler way to implement it. When you create the hop from the **Filter rows** step toward the next step, you are asked for the kind of hop that you plan to use. If you choose **Main output of step**, the two options **Send 'true' data to step** and **Send 'false' data to step** will remain empty. This will cause two things:

▶ Only the rows that meet the condition will pass

▶ The rest will be discarded

Comparing against the value of a Kettle variable

This recipe shows you how to configure the condition in the **Filter rows** step to compare a field against another field or a constant value; but what if you want to compare against the value of a Kettle variable?

Let's assume, for example, you have a named parameter called `categ` with `kitchen` as **Default Value**. As you might know, named parameters are a particular kind of Kettle variable.

 You create the named parameters under the **Parameter** tab from the **Settings** option of the **Edit** menu.

To use this variable in a condition, you must add it to your dataset in advance. You do this as follows:

1. Add a **Get Variables** step from the **Job** category. Put it in the stream after the **Text file input** step and before the **Filter Rows** step; use it to create a new field named `categ` of **String** type with the value `${categ}` in the **Variable** column.

2. Now, the transformation looks like the one shown in the following screenshot:

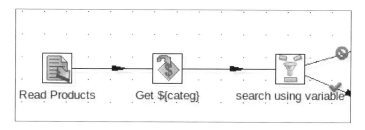

Read Products   Get ${categ}   search using variable

3. After this, you can set the condition of the first **Filter rows** step to `category = categ`, selecting **categ** from the listbox of fields to the right. This way, you will be filtering the `kitchen` products.

4. If you run the transformation and set the parameter to `tents`, you will obtain similar results to those that were obtained in the main recipe.

Avoiding the use of nested Filter rows steps

Suppose that you want to compare a single field against a discrete and short list of possible values and do different things for each value in that list. In this case, you can use the **Switch / Case** step instead of nested **Filter rows** steps. In this recipe, we were filtering on both categories and pricing information. We could easily replace the **Filter rows** steps with a **Switch / Case** step.

Let us assume that you have to send the rows to different steps depending on the category. The best way to do this is with the **Switch / Case** step. This way you avoid adding one **Filter rows** step for each category.

In this step, you have to select the field to be used for comparing. You do it in the **Field name to switch** listbox. In the **Case values** grid, you set the **Value-Target step** pairs. The following screenshot shows how to fill in the grid for our particular problem:

The following are some considerations about this step:

▶ You can have multiple values directed to the same target step.

▶ You can leave the value column blank to specify a target step for empty values.

▶ You have a listbox named **Default target step** to specify the target step for rows that do not match any of the case values.

▶ You can only compare with an equal operator.

▶ If you want to compare against a substring of the field, you could enable the **Use string contains** option and as **Case Value**, type the substring you are interested in. For example, if for **Case Value**, you type `tent_`, all categories containing `tent_` such as `tent_large`, `tent_small`, or `tent_medium` will be redirected to the same target step.

Overcoming the difficulties of complex conditions

There will be situations where the condition is too complex to be expressed in a single **Filter rows** step. You can nest them and create temporary fields in order to solve the problem, but it would be more efficient if you used the **Java Filter** or **User Defined Java Expression** step, as explained next.

You can find the **Java Filter** step in the **Flow** category. The difference compared to the **Filter rows** step is that in this step, you write the condition using a Java expression.

The names of the listboxes—**Destination step for matching rows (optional)** and **Destination step for non-matching rows (optional)**—differ from the names in the **Filter rows** step, but their purpose is the same.

As an example, the following are the conditions you used in the recipe rewritten as Java expressions: `category.equals("tents")` and `price < 100`. These are extremely simple, but you can write any Java expression as long as it evaluates to a Boolean result.

 If you can't guarantee that the category will not be null, it is recommended that you invert the first expression and put `"tents".equals(category)` instead. By doing this, whenever you have to check if a field is equal to a constant, you avoid an unexpected Java error.

Finally, suppose that you have to split the streams simply to set some fields and then join the streams again. For example, assume that you want to change the category as follows:

Condition	New category
Category equal to tents and price below 100	`cheap_tents`
Category equal to tents and price above or equal to 100	`expensive_tents`
Category different from tents	Keep the old category

Doing this with nested **Filter rows** steps leads to a transformation, such as the following:

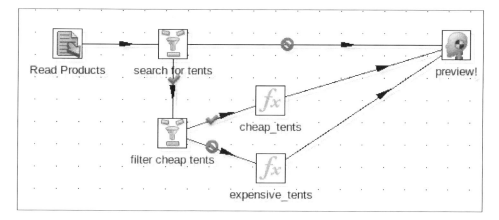

You can do the same thing in a simpler way:

Replace all the steps, but fill the **Text file** input with a **User Defined Java Expression** step located in the **Scripting** category.

1. In the setting window of this step, add a row in order to replace the value of the **category** field: as **New field** and **Replace value** type category. As **Value type** select **String**. As **Java expression**, type the following:

    ```
    (category.equals("tents"))?(price<100?"cheap_tents":"expensive_
    tents"):category
    ```

> The preceding expression uses the Java ternary operator ?:.
> If you're not familiar with the syntax, think of it as shorthand
> for the if-then-else statement. For example, the inner
> expression price<100?"cheap_tents":"expensive_
> tents" means if (price<100) then return
> "cheap_tents" else return "expensive_tents".

2. Do a preview on this step. You will see something similar to the following:

Rows of step: preview! (67 rows)

#	id_product	desc_product	price	category
1	1	Swedish Firesteel - Army Model	19.00	kitchen
2	2	Mountain House #10 Can Freeze-Dried Food	53.00	kitchen
3	3	Lodge Logic L9OG3 Pre-Seasoned 10-1/2-Inch Rou	14.00	kitchen
4	4	Lodge Logic L5SK3 Pre-Seasoned Cast-Iron 8-Inch	12.00	kitchen
5	5	Coleman 70-Quart Xtreme Cooler (Blue)	59.00	kitchen
6	6	Kelsyus Floating Cooler	26.00	kitchen
7	7	Lodge LCC3 Logic Pre-Seasoned Combo Cooker	41.00	kitchen
8	8	Guyot Designs SplashGuard-Universal	7.00	kitchen
9	9	Coleman 62-Quart Xtreme Wheeled Cooler (Blue)	62.00	kitchen
10	10	Coleman RoadTrip Accessory Stove Grate	16.00	kitchen
11	11	Coleman PerfectFlow InstaStart 2-Burner Stove	69.00	kitchen

Merging rows of two streams with the same or different structures

It's a common requirement to combine two or more streams into a single stream that includes the union of all rows. In these cases, the streams come from different sources and don't always have the same structure. Consequently, combining the streams is not as easy as just putting in a step that freely joins the streams. Issues can quickly arise if row formats and column orders are mixed between streams. This recipe gives you the tips to make it easier.

Suppose that you received data about roller coasters from two different sources. The data in one of those sources looks like the following:

```
roller_coaster|speed|park|location|country|Year
Top Thrill Dragster|120 mph|Cedar Point|Sandusky, Ohio||2003
Dodonpa|106.8 mph|Fuji-Q Highland|FujiYoshida-shi|Japan|2001
Steel Dragon 2000|95 mph|Nagashima Spa Land|Mie|Japan|2000
Millennium Force|93 mph|Cedar Point|Sandusky, Ohio||2000
Intimidator 305|90 mph|Kings Dominion|Doswell, Virginia||2010
Titan|85 mph|Six Flags Over Texas|Arlington, Texas||2001
Furious Baco|84 mph|PortAventura|Spain||2007
...
```

The other source data looks like the following:

```
attraction|park_name|top_speed|trains_qt|ride_time
Expedition Everest|Disney's Animal Kingdom|50 mph|6 - 34 passenger|

Goofy'S Barnstormer|Disney's Magic Kingdom|25 mph|2 - 16 passenger|

Gwazi|Busch Gardens Tampa|50 mph|4 - 24 passenger|2 minutes, 30
seconds

Journey To Atlantis|SeaWorld Orlando||8 passenger boats|
Kraken|SeaWorld Orlando|65 mph|3 - 32 passenger|2 minutes, 2 seconds

...
```

You want to merge those rows into a single dataset with the following columns:

- ► `attraction`
- ► `park_name`
- ► `speed`
- ► `trains_qt`
- ► `ride_time`

Getting ready

Download the files `roller_coasters_I.txt` and `roller_coasters_II.txt` from the book's site. These files represent the two sources mentioned in the introduction.

How to do it...

Perform the following steps:

1. Create a transformation and drag two **Text file input** steps into the canvas.

2. Use one of the steps to read the file `roller_coasters_I.txt`. Set the data types as follows: the **speed** as **Number** with **Format #0.### mph**, and the rest of the fields as **String**. Do a preview to make sure that you are reading the file properly.

3. Drag the cursor over the step and press the Space bar to see the output fields:

#	Fieldname	Type	Length	Precision	Step origin	^	Storage	Mask	Decimal	Group	Trim	Comments
1	roller_coaster	String	-	-	roller_coasters_I		normal				none	
2	speed	Number	-	-	roller_coasters_I		normal	#0.### mph	.		none	
3	park	String	-	-	roller_coasters_I		normal				none	
4	location	String	-	-	roller_coasters_I		normal				none	
5	country	String	-	-	roller_coasters_I		normal				none	
6	year	String	-	-	roller_coasters_I		normal				none	

4. Use the other step to read the file `roller_coasters_II.txt`. Set the data type of **top_speed** to **Integer** and the rest of the fields to **String**. Do a preview to make sure that you are reading the file properly.

5. Drag the cursor over the step and press the Space bar to see the output fields:

#	Fieldname	Type	Length	Precision	Step origin	Storage	Ma:	Dec	Gr ^	Trim	Comments
1	attraction	String	-	-	roller_coasters_II	normal				none	
2	park_name	String	-	-	roller_coasters_II	normal				none	
3	top_speed	Integer	-	0	roller_coasters_II	normal				none	
4	trains_qt	String	-	-	roller_coasters_II	normal				none	
5	ride_time	String	-	-	roller_coasters_II	normal				none	

6. As you can see, the outputs of the streams are different. You have to insert the necessary steps to make them alike. That's the purpose of the next steps.

7. After the first **Text file input** step add an **Add constants** step. Use it to add two fields of type **String**. Name the fields `trains_qt` and `ride_time` and as **Value** type `Not available`.

8. After it, add a **Select values** step. Fill in the **Select & Alter** tab, as shown in the following screenshot:

^	#	Fieldname	Rename to
	1	Roller_Coaster	attraction
	2	park	park_name
	3	Speed	
	4	trains_qt	
	5	ride_time	

9. After the second **Text file input** step, add another **Select values** step. Select the **Meta-data** tab and fill it in, as shown in the following screenshot:

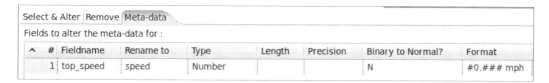

^	#	Fieldname	Rename to	Type	Length	Precision	Binary to Normal?	Format
	1	top_speed	speed	Number			N	#0.### mph

Fields to alter the meta-data for :

10. Repeat the procedure to see the output fields of the streams: drag the cursor over the last step of each stream and press the Space bar. Now, both streams should have the same layout.

You can keep both windows open at the same time: the one showing the output fields of the upper stream, and the one showing the output fields of the lower one. If you put one next to the other, you can immediately see if they are equal or not.

11. Finally, join the streams with a **Dummy** step, as depicted in the following diagram:

12. Do a preview on the **Dummy** step. You will see something similar to the result shown in the following screenshot:

Rows of step: preview! (25 rows)

^	#	attraction	park_name	speed	trains_qt	ride_time
	14	Mean Streak	Cedar Point	65 mph		
	15	T Express	Everland	65 mph		
	16	Expedition Everest	Disney's Animal Kingdom	50 mph	6 - 34 passenger	
	17	Goofy'S Barnstormer	Disney's Magic Kingdom	25 mph	2 - 16 passenger	
	18	Gwazi	Busch Gardens Tampa	50 mph	4 - 24 passenger	2 minutes, 30 seconds
	19	Journey To Atlantis	SeaWorld Orlando		8 passenger boats	
	20	Kraken	SeaWorld Orlando	65 mph	3 - 32 passenger	2 minutes, 2 seconds
	21	Kumba	Busch Gardens Tampa	60 mph	4 - 32 passenger	2 minutes, 54 seconds
	22	Manta	SeaWorld Orlando	56 mph	3 - 32 passenger	2 minutes, 35 seconds
	23	Montu	Busch Gardens Tampa	60 mph	3 - 32 passenger	3 minutes
	24	Shamu Express	SeaWorld Orlando	28 mph	1 - 28 passenger	
	25	Sheikra	Busch Gardens Tampa	70 mph	5 - 24 passenger	3 minutes

How it works...

When you need to merge the rows of two streams into a single stream, you have to do all you can to make the metadata of the streams alike. That's what you did in this recipe. In the first stream, you added the fields you needed that were absent. You also selected and reordered the desired fields to resemble the second stream. After that, you changed the metadata of the `top_speed` field in the second stream. You converted the field from **Integer** to **Number**, which was the type of the analogous field in the first stream.

When you did the preview, you could see the rows from both incoming steps.

There's more...

In the recipe, you merged two streams with data coming from different sources. However, that is not the only situation in which you may need to merge streams. It is common to split a stream into two or more streams to perform some particular manipulations and then merge them back together, as depicted in the following diagram:

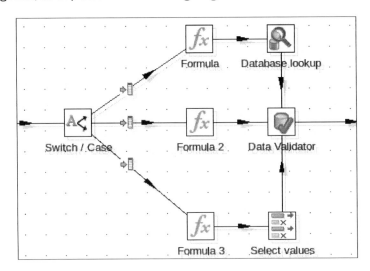

Whichever the case, when you have to merge two or more streams, there are the following two things that you should remember:

- Make sure that the metadata of all streams is exactly the same
- Decide and tell Kettle how you want to merge the streams

The following subsections explain these things in detail.

Making sure that the metadata of the streams is the same

In order to merge two or more streams, their metadata has to coincide. This basically means that all streams have to have the same layout: same number of columns, same names, same types, and the columns must be in the same order.

If you try to merge streams that don't meet that requirement, you will receive a warning. A window will show up with the title **This hop causes the target step to receive rows with mixed layout!** and a text explaining the differences found. That means that you have to find the way to fix that situation. The following is a quick list that will help you make the metadata of several streams alike:

- Identify the fields that you want in the final dataset that are not present in all streams. In the streams that don't have those fields, add them. You can get the value from any source (a text file, the command line, and so on), or simply think of a default value and add the field with an **Add constant** step from the **Transformation** category. This is what you did with the fields `trains_qt` and `ride_time`.

- Identify the fields that you want to keep that are present in all streams, but with a different structure. Change the metadata of those fields in the streams where the metadata is not as desired. You can do this with a **Select values** step by using the **Metadata** tab. This is what you did for the field `top_speed`.

- Verify the layouts of the streams. If they still differ, for each stream that does not have the proper layout, add a **Select values** step at the end. With this step, select the fields you want to keep (implicitly deleting the others), rename and reorder them in order to match the desired layout. This was what you did with the first **Select values** step.

Now, you are free to merge the streams, as explained in the next subsection.

> If you have to merge streams in a subtransformation, it's advisable to read the tip under the *Moving part of a transformation to a subtransformation* recipe in *Chapter 8, Executing and Re-using Jobs and Transformations*.

Telling Kettle how to merge the rows of your streams

Once your streams are ready to be merged, you can then proceed in the following ways:

- Suppose that you want to put all the rows of one of the streams below all the rows of the other. If you don't care about the order of the streams, you can use any step to merge them. This was what you did in the recipe with the **Dummy** step.

- If you care about the order of the streams, you should use the **Append Streams** step from the **Flow** category in order to merge the streams. By selecting a **Head hop** and a **Tail hop**, you can tell Kettle which stream goes first.

This only works for just two streams. If you need to merge several streams, you need to add nested **Append Streams** steps.

▶ Suppose that you really want to merge the rows of the streams and leave them ordered by certain fields. You do it with a **Sorted Merge** step from the **Join** category. The step assumes that each stream in turn is sorted by the same fields. Note that Kettle warns you, but it doesn't prevent you from mixing row layouts when you merge streams. If you see a warning of this kind, refer to the tips in the previous subsection.

 If you want Kettle to prevent you from running a transformation with mixed layout, check the option **Enable safe mode** located in the windows that shows up when you run the transformation. Note that the use of the **Enable safe mode** option will cause a drop in performance and should only be used when you are debugging a transformation.

See also

▶ *Comparing two streams and generating differences*

Adding checksums to verify datasets

While there are many ways to verify that your datasets are valid, a common practice is to create a checksum based on the data to determine if it is different from a reference data set. **Checksums** are a hash of the data provided to the algorithm generating it, making each one nearly unique to the data that built it.

Kettle provides a way to add a checksum to each record in your dataset through the **Add a Checksum** *step*.

For this recipe, we will be comparing data between the roller coaster database and a flat file that may have new roller coasters listed in it.

Getting ready

For this recipe, you will need the the files associated with this recipe, which can be downloaded from the book's site. More details about the files can be found in the recipe *Comparing two streams and generating differences*. There is a SQL file that will create the parks' database and a flat file we will be comparing the data to.

How to do it...

Perform the following steps:

1. Create a new transformation.

2. Drag a **Table input** step onto the canvas. This step will be used to execute the following SQL statement:

```
SELECT    roller_coaster
        , speed
        , park
        , location
        , country
        , year
FROM      rollercoasters
ORDER BY roller_coaster
        , park
```

3. Drag a **Text file** input onto the canvas and use it to read the `top_roller_coasters_updates.txt` file. As a separator, type `|`.

4. On the **Fields** tab, be sure to select **Get Fields** to pull the file's metadata into the step.

5. Click on **OK** and close the step.

6. Drag two **Add a Checksum** steps to the canvas. Create a hop between the **Table input** and one of the **Add a Checksum** steps. Repeat the process between the **Text file input** step and the other **Add a Checksum** step. Your transformation should look like the following:

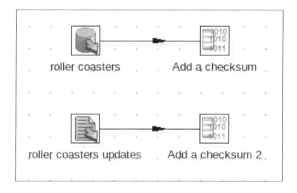

7. Open the **Add a Checksum** step for the **Table Input** step. Fill in the step as follows:

8. Repeat the process for the other **Add a Checksum** step.

9. Add a **Sort rows** step to both streams, sorting on the checksum fields.

10. Merge the two streams using a **Merge Join (diff)** step, comparing on the **db_checksum** and the **file_checksum** fields.

11. Add a **Filter rows** step. For the filtering criteria, make sure that the **flag** field value is equal to **new**.

12. Previewing the **Filter Rows** step shows the records that have been changed since the data was loaded into the database. You should see data similar to the following:

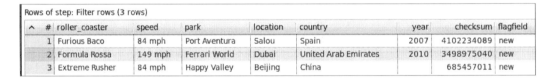

#	roller_coaster	speed	park	location	country	year	checksum	flagfield
1	Furious Baco	84 mph	Port Aventura	Salou	Spain	2007	4102234089	new
2	Formula Rossa	149 mph	Ferrari World	Dubai	United Arab Emirates	2010	3498975040	new
3	Extreme Rusher	84 mph	Happy Valley	Beijing	China		685457011	new

How it works...

Checksums are essentially hashes of the dataset. It provides a very fast and efficient way to compare datasets, albeit with a couple caveats:

▶ Checksums ignore null values, so it may not produce a true hash of a record

▶ No matter what algorithm is chosen, there is always a chance of two different records having the same hash

There is a great article on hash collision probabilities found on the preshing on programming blog: `http://preshing.com/20110504/hash-collision-probabilities`.

Comparing two streams and generating differences

Suppose that you have two streams with the same structure and want to find out the differences in the data. Kettle has a step meant specifically for that purpose: the **Merge Rows (diff)** step. In this recipe, you will see how it works.

Suppose that you have a file with information about the fastest roller coasters around the world. Now, you get an updated file and want to find out the differences between the files: there can be new roller coasters in the list; maybe some roller coasters are no longer among the fastest. Besides, you were told that in the old file, there were some errors about the location, country, and year information, so you are also interested in knowing if some of these have changed.

Getting ready

For this recipe, you will need two files with information about roller coasters. You can download them from the book's site.

Both files have the same structure and look like the following:

```
Roller_Coaster|Speed|park|location|country|Year
Kingda Ka|128 mph|Six Flags Great Adventure|Jackson, New Jersey||2005
Top Thrill Dragster|120 mph|Cedar Point|Sandusky, Ohio||2003
Dodonpa|106.8 mph|Fuji-Q Highland|FujiYoshida-shi|Japan|2001
Steel Dragon 2000|95 mph|Nagashima Spa Land|Mie|Japan|2000
Millennium Force|93 mph|Cedar Point|Sandusky, Ohio||2000
. . .
```

For the *There's more...* section, you will also need a database with the first file already loaded in a table. You will find a script for creating and loading it also available for downloading.

How to do it...

Perform the following steps:

1. Create a transformation.
2. Drag a **Text file input** step into the canvas and use it to read the file `top_roller_coasters.txt`. As a separator, type |.
3. Do a preview to make sure that you are reading the file as expected.
4. Add a **Sort rows** step to sort the rows by `roller_coaster` and `park`.
5. Repeat steps 2 to 4 to read the file named `top_roller_coasters_updates.txt` and sort the rows also by `roller_coaster` and `park`.

6. From the **Join** category, add a **Merge Rows (diff)** step, and use it to join both streams, as depicted in the following diagram:

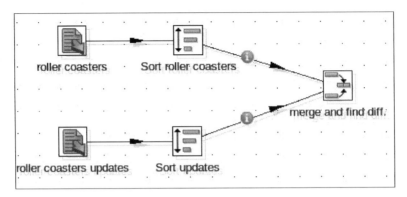

7. Double-click on the step you just added. In the **Reference rows origin:** select the name of the step coming from the stream that reads the `top_roller_coasters.txt` file.

8. In the **Compare rows origin:** select the name of the step coming from the stream that reads the `top_roller_coasters_updates.txt` file.

9. As **Flag fieldname**, type `flag`.

10. Fill the **Keys to match:** and **Values to compare:** grids, as shown in the following screenshot:

Keys to match :			Values to compare :		
∧	#	Key field	∧	#	Value field
	1	roller_coaster		1	location
	2	park		2	country
				3	year

Now that the step has been filled in, we can compare the streams and get the difference between them.

You can save time by clicking on the **Get key** fields and **Get value** fields buttons to fill each grid respectively. Then, just delete the fields that you don't need.

Close the window and do a preview; you should see the following:

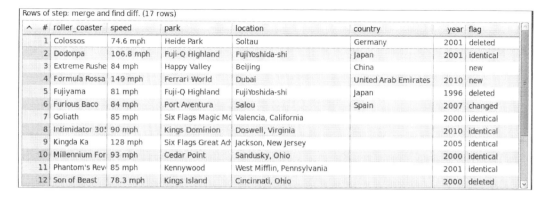

Rows of step: merge and find diff. (17 rows)

^	#	roller_coaster	speed	park	location	country	year	flag
	1	Colossos	74.6 mph	Heide Park	Soltau	Germany	2001	deleted
	2	Dodonpa	106.8 mph	Fuji-Q Highland	FujiYoshida-shi	Japan	2001	identical
	3	Extreme Rushe	84 mph	Happy Valley	Beijing	China		new
	4	Formula Rossa	149 mph	Ferrari World	Dubai	United Arab Emirates	2010	new
	5	Fujiyama	81 mph	Fuji-Q Highland	FujiYoshida-shi	Japan	1996	deleted
	6	Furious Baco	84 mph	Port Aventura	Salou	Spain	2007	changed
	7	Goliath	85 mph	Six Flags Magic Mc	Valencia, California		2000	identical
	8	Intimidator 30!	90 mph	Kings Dominion	Doswell, Virginia		2010	identical
	9	Kingda Ka	128 mph	Six Flags Great Ad	Jackson, New Jersey		2005	identical
	10	Millennium For	93 mph	Cedar Point	Sandusky, Ohio		2000	identical
	11	Phantom's Rev	85 mph	Kennywood	West Mifflin, Pennsylvania		2001	identical
	12	Son of Beast	78.3 mph	Kings Island	Cincinnati, Ohio		2000	deleted

How it works...

The **Merge Rows (diff)** step is used for comparing two streams and finding out the differences between them. The output of the step is a single stream. The output stream contains a new field that acts as a flag indicating the kind of difference found as explained next.

 When you use the **Merge Rows (diff)** step, the two streams you are merging must have the same metadata, that is, the name, order, and type of the fields must be the same.

Let's call the streams being merged **reference stream** and **compare stream**. The first holds the old data while the second holds the new data. In the recipe, the old data is the data coming from the `top_roller_coasters.txt` file and the new data is the data coming from the `top_roller_coasters_update.txt` file.

 Both streams must be sorted on the specified keys.

In order to perform the comparison, you have to tell Kettle how to detect that a row is the same in both streams, that is, you have to specify the key fields. You do it by entering them in the first grid. In the recipe, the key was made up by the roller coaster name and the park name (`roller_coaster` and `park` fields).

 If your data comes from a database instead of using a **Sort rows** step for sorting the rows, you can sort them in the **Table input** step. That will give you better performance.

Given the two streams, Kettle tries to match rows of both streams based on the key fields provided. Depending on the result, it sets a different value for the flag, as explained in the following table:

Result of the comparison	Flag	Example
The key was only found in the reference stream	`new`	`Formula Rossa` roller coaster.
The key was only found in the compared stream	`deleted`	`Colossos` roller coaster.
The key was found in both streams and the fields typed in the **Value to compare** grid are equal	`identical`	`Millennium Force` roller coaster. The `location` (Sandusky, Ohio), `country` (empty), and `year` (2000) were the same in both streams.
The key was found in both streams but at least one of the fields typed in the **Value to compare** grid is different	`changed`	`Furious Baco` roller coaster. The location changed from Spain to Salou and the Country changed from empty to Spain.

Note that if a row is found in both streams with identical key fields and compare fields, it is marked as identical, even if there are differences in other fields. For example, the `Dodonpa` roller coaster has a speed of `106.8` mph in the reference stream, but a speed of `106` mph in the compare stream. As you didn't put the `speed` in the values to compare list, the rows are marked as identical.

As a final remark, note that for the rows marked as `new` or `changed`, and the values that pass to the output stream are those coming from the compare stream.

For the rows marked as `identical` or `deleted`, the values that are passed are those coming from the reference stream.

There's more...

The **Merge Rows (diff)** step is commonly used together with the **Synchronize after merge** step to keep a database table updated. The following section shows an example of how to do this.

Using the differences to keep a table up-to-date

Suppose that you have a table in a database with information about roller coasters, and that you have already inserted the data in the `top_roller_coasters.txt` file in that table.

As new roller coasters are built and old roller coasters are moved or retired, the table will need to be updated. Using the `top_roller_coasters_updates.txt` file, we can use the updated data and update the table based on the differences.

 The table is totally de-normalized on purpose to keep the exercise simple.

Try the following:

1. After running the script mentioned in the introduction, modify the transformation in the recipe by replacing the first stream with a **Table Input** step, in order to read the table `rollercoasters`. Use the following statement:

```
SELECT    roller_coaster
      , speed
      , park
      , location
      , country
      , year
FROM      rollercoasters
ORDER BY roller_coaster
      , park
```

2. You will have something like the following:

Rows of step: roller coasters (15 rows)

#	roller_coaster ∧	speed	park	location	country	year
1	Colossos	74.6 mph	Heide Park	Soltau	Germany	2001
2	Dodonpa	106.8 mph	Fuji-Q Highland	FujiYoshida-shi	Japan	2001
3	Fujiyama	81 mph	Fuji-Q Highland	FujiYoshida-shi	Japan	1996
4	Furious Baco	84 mph	Port Aventura	Spain		2007
5	Goliath	85 mph	Six Flags Magic Mountain	Valencia, California		2000
6	Intimidator 305	90 mph	Kings Dominion	Doswell, Virginia		2010
7	Kingda Ka	128 mph	Six Flags Great Adventure	Jackson, New Jersey		2005
8	Millennium Force	93 mph	Cedar Point	Sandusky, Ohio		2000
9	Phantom's Revenge	85 mph	Kennywood	West Mifflin, Pennsylvania		2001

3. Do a preview on the last step, that is the **Merge Rows (diff)** step. The output should be exactly the same as the output in the recipe.

4. Now, add a **Synchronize after merge** step. Select the connection to the database or create it if it doesn't exist and as **Target table**, type `rollercoasters`. Fill the grids, as shown in the following screenshot:

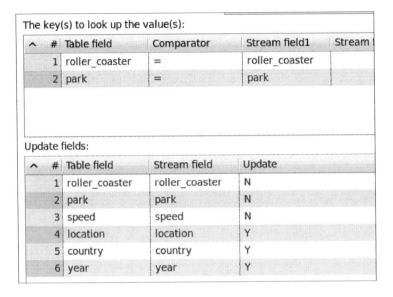

The key(s) to look up the value(s):

^	#	Table field	Comparator	Stream field1	Stream
	1	roller_coaster	=	roller_coaster	
	2	park	=	park	

Update fields:

^	#	Table field	Stream field	Update
	1	roller_coaster	roller_coaster	N
	2	park	park	N
	3	speed	speed	N
	4	location	location	Y
	5	country	country	Y
	6	year	year	Y

5. Select the **Advanced** tab and fill in the **Operation** frame, as shown in the following screenshot:

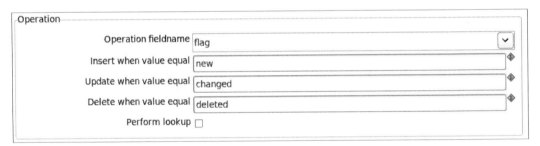

Operation

Operation fieldname	flag
Insert when value equal	new
Update when value equal	changed
Delete when value equal	deleted
Perform lookup	☐

6. Close the window, save the transformation, and run it.

7. Execute a `SELECT` statement to see the data in the `rollercoaster` table. The roller coasters with the flag **deleted** should have been deleted from the table. The rows with the flag **new** should have been inserted in the table, and the rows with the flag **changed** should have been updated.

See also

▶ The *Inserting, deleting, or updating a table depending on a field* recipe in *Chapter 1, Working with Databases*

Generating all possible pairs formed from two datasets

This is a quick recipe that teaches you how to do a Cartesian product between datasets. A Cartesian product is created by taking all rows from one dataset, all rows from another dataset, and generating a new dataset with all the possible combinations of rows.

This particular recipe is, in fact, the implementation of the **Community Acronym Generator** (**CAG**) as proposed by Nicholas Goodman (@nagoodman) on Twitter:

> @webdetails @pmalves @josvandongen How about CAG? Community Acronym Generator? A project to generate new acronyms for community projects?!

There are already several community projects around Pentaho such as CDF (Community Dashboard Framework), CDE (Community Dashboard Editor), or CDA (Community Data Access). Why don't we follow Nicholas's suggestion and develop the CAG as follows?:

Given two lists of words, the Kettle transformation will generate all combinations of words that lead to potential community projects.

How to do it...

Perform the following steps:

1. Create a new transformation and add two **Data Grid** steps from the **Input** category.

2. Use one of the **Data Grid** steps to create a dataset with a single **String** field named middle_word. Under the **Data** tab, enter a set of names for the middle word of the acronym. Here, you have a sample list: Dashboard, Data, Chart, Acronym, Cube, and Report.

3. Use the other **Data Grid** step to create a dataset with a single **String** field named last_word. Under the **Data** tab, enter a set of names for the last word of the acronym. Here, you have a sample list: Framework, Editor, Translator, Access, Generator, Integrator, Component.

4. From the **Join** category, add a **Join Rows (Cartesian product)** step.

5. Create hops from the **Data Grid** steps toward this step. You will have something like the following:

6. From the **Scripting** category, add a **User Defined Java Expression** step (**UDJE** for short).

7. Use the **UDJE** to add two `String` fields. Name the first `new_component` and as **Java Expression** type `"CommunityCommunity "+middle_word+" "+last_word`. Name the second field `acronym` and as **Java Expression** type `"C"+middle_word.substring(0,1)+last_word.substring(0,1)`. Do a preview on this last step. You will see a list of candidate community projects, as shown in the following screenshot:

Rows of step: join version (34 rows)

^	#	middle_word	last_word	new_component	acronym	version
	1	Dashboard	Translator	Community Dashboard Translator	CDT	CE
	2	Dashboard	Generator	Community Dashboard Generator	CDG	CE
	3	Dashboard	Integrator	Community Dashboard Integrator	CDI	CE
	4	Dashboard	Component	Community Dashboard Component	CDC	CE
	5	Data	Translator	Community Data Translator	CDT	CE
	6	Data	Generator	Community Data Generator	CDG	CE
	7	Data	Integrator	Community Data Integrator	CDI	CE
	8	Data	Component	Community Data Component	CDC	CE
	9	Chart	Framework	Community Chart Framework	CCF	CE
	10	Chart	Editor	Community Chart Editor	CCE	CE
	11	Chart	Translator	Community Chart Translator	CCT	CE
	12	Chart	Access	Community Chart Access	CCA	CE

How it works...

The **Join Rows (Cartesian product)** step has the task of performing the Cartesian product of all streams coming to it. In this case, you had two streams but you could have had more. The step received those two streams and created all combinations of rows. Then, with the UDJE, you simply build the strings with the name of the candidate community projects and their acronyms, as for example, **Community Chart Framework** (**CCF**). While we had a bit of fun generating different names for community projects, it is up to you to adopt a generated name and build the project behind it!

There's more...

In the recipe, you used the **Join Rows (Cartesian product)** step for joining two datasets. You could join more datasets if you want to; however that is not a common requirement.

There are a couple of settings in the step that you didn't use in the recipe. They are explained in the following subsections.

Getting variables in the middle of the stream

This section describes one of the most common situations in which you may see the **Join Rows (Cartesian product)** step in action. Back to the recipe. Suppose that you have a named parameter named VERSION, which can be CE (representing Community Edition) or EE (representing Enterprise Edition). After generating the names of the candidate projects and their acronyms, you want to add the version. You can add the version to your stream by using a **Get Variable** step from the **Job** category. However, instead of getting the variable for each row, it's recommended to get it outside the main stream and then join both streams, as shown in the following screenshot:

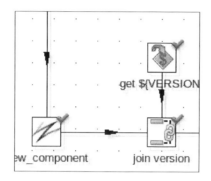

As the stream coming out of the **Get Variable** step has a single row, the Cartesian product will have all the possible combinations of N rows of the main stream with a single row, that is, N rows. In this case, it is important that in the **Main step to read from** option, you select the main stream, the stream coming from the UDJE. Doing so, you tell Kettle that most of the data will come from this step and Kettle will cache or spool to disk the data coming from the **Get Variable** step.

Limiting the number of output rows

With a **Join Rows (Cartesian product)** step, you can limit the number of output rows by entering a simple or complex condition in its setting window. The rows that don't meet the condition are discarded.

Back to the recipe. As you might have noticed, it is possible for the transformation to generate acronyms that already exist, for example, **CDF**. In the previous subsection, you added a second **Join Rows (Cartesian product)** step. In this step, you could add a condition to discard the rows with acronyms that already exist, except when the product is Enterprise Edition. The condition area in the setting window of the step would look like the one shown in the following screenshot (except for the exact list of acronyms, which might have changed by the time you're reading this):

```
                  NOT ( acronym IN LIST [CBF;CCC;CDE;CDF;CDA;CST] )

OR

                       version <> [CE]
```

If you do a preview on this step, you will see something like the following:

#	middle_word	last_word	new_component	acronym	version
1	Dashboard	Translator	Community Dashboard Translator	CDT	CE
2	Dashboard	Generator	Community Dashboard Generator	CDG	CE
3	Dashboard	Integrator	Community Dashboard Integrator	CDI	CE
4	Dashboard	Component	Community Dashboard Component	CDC	CE
5	Data	Translator	Community Data Translator	CDT	CE
6	Data	Generator	Community Data Generator	CDG	CE
7	Data	Integrator	Community Data Integrator	CDI	CE
8	Data	Component	Community Data Component	CDC	CE
9	Chart	Framework	Community Chart Framework	CCF	CE
10	Chart	Editor	Community Chart Editor	CCE	CE
11	Chart	Translator	Community Chart Translator	CCT	CE
12	Chart	Access	Community Chart Access	CCA	CE

Rows of step: join version (34 rows)

If you take a look at the **Step Metrics** tab of the **Execution Results** window, you will notice that the number of written rows is less than the Cartesian product of incoming rows. Note that the GUI for entering the condition is the same as the one in the **Filter rows** step.

 As you may pick fields from more than one stream in the condition of the **Join Rows (Cartesian product)** step, it is therefore required that the picked fields have unique names in the streams.

See also

▶ *Joining two or more streams based on given conditions*

▶ *Splitting a stream into two or more streams based on a condition*

Joining two or more streams based on given conditions

There are occasions where you will need to join two datasets. If you are working with databases, you could use SQL statements to perform this task, but for other kinds of input (XML, text, Excel), you will need another solution.

Kettle provides the **Merge Join** step to join data coming from any kind of source. Let's assume that you are building a house and want to track and manage the costs of building it. Before starting, you prepared an Excel file with the estimated costs for the different parts of your house. Now, you are given a weekly file with the progress and the real costs. So, you want to compare both to see the progress.

Getting ready

To run this recipe, you will need two Excel files, one for the budget and another with the real costs. The `budget.xls` has the estimated starting date, estimated end date, and the cost for the planned tasks. The `costs.xls` has the real starting date, end date, and the cost for tasks that have already started.

You can download the sample files from the book's site.

How to do it...

Perform the following steps:

1. Create a new transformation.

2. Drop two **Excel input** steps into the canvas.

3. Use one step for reading the budget information (`budget.xls` file) and the other for reading the costs information (`costs.xls` file).

4. Under the **Fields** tab of these steps, click on the **Get fields from header row...** button in order to populate the grid automatically. Apply the format `dd/MM/yyyy` to the fields of type **Date** and `$0.00` to the fields with costs.

5. Add a **Merge Join** step from the **Join** category and create a hop from each **Excel input** step toward this step. The following diagram depicts what you have so far:

6. Configure the **Merge Join** step, as shown in the following screenshot:

7. If you do a preview on this step, you will obtain the result of the two Excel files merged. In order to have the columns more organized, add a **Select values** step from the **Transform** category. In this new step, select the fields in the following order: `task, starting date (est.), starting date, end date (est.), end date, cost (est.),` and `cost`.

8. Doing a preview on the last step, you will obtain the merged data with the columns of both Excel files interspersed, as shown in the following screenshot:

Rows of step: Reorder columns (10 rows)

^	#	task	starting date (est.)	starting date	end date (est.)	end date	cost (est.)	cost
	1	foundations	01/12/2010	01/12/2010	31/12/2010	10/01/2011	$45000.00	$52000.00
	2	walls	01/01/2011	11/01/2011	25/01/2011	15/02/2011	$280000.00	$259000.00
	3	roof	26/01/2011		14/02/2011		$150000.00	
	4	swimming pool	01/01/2011	07/01/2011	05/02/2011		$98000.00	$77000.00
	5	electrical work	01/03/2011		10/03/2011		$66500.00	
	6	plumbing	01/03/2011		25/03/2011		$48000.00	
	7	painting	15/04/2011		25/04/2011		$34000.00	
	8	kitchen	01/04/2011		30/04/2011		$124500.00	
	9	bathrooms	01/04/2011		30/04/2011		$92800.00	
	10	laundry	01/04/2011		30/04/2011		$55000.00	

How it works...

In the example, you saw how to use the **Merge Join** step to join data coming from two Excel files. You can use this step to join any other kind of input.

In the **Merge Join** step, you set the name of the incoming steps and the fields to use as the keys for joining them. In the recipe, you joined the streams by just a single field: the **task** field.

 The rows are expected to be sorted in an ascending manner on the specified key fields.

There's more...

In the example, you set the **Join Type** to **LEFT OUTER JOIN**. Let's see explanations of the possible join options:

Join	Description	In the example
INNER	The result contains only the rows with the same key in both sources	You will obtain only the tasks that have estimated and real information.
LEFT OUTER	The result contains all the rows from the first source, and the correspondent values for the second source (or empty values for non-matching keys)	You will obtain all the tasks from the budget, and the real costs related to these tasks (with empty values for the tasks that still haven't any associated costs).
RIGHT OUTER	The result contains all the rows from the second source, and the corresponding values for the first source (or empty values for non-matching keys)	You will obtain all the real tasks' costs and their related information from the budget. If there is a cost for a task that hadn't been estimated, the estimated cost will be empty.
FULL OUTER	The result contains all the rows from both sources (with empty values for non-matching keys)	You will obtain all the tasks from the budget and the real costs. This was the case in the recipe.

See also

▸ The *Reading an Excel file* recipe in *Chapter 2, Reading and Writing Files*

Interspersing new rows between existent rows

In most Kettle datasets, all rows share a common meaning; they represent the same kind of entity, for example:

▸ In a dataset with sold items, each row has data about one item.

▸ In a dataset with the mean temperature for a range of days in five different regions, each row has the mean temperature for a different day in one of those regions.

▸ In a dataset with a list of people ordered by age range (0-10, 11-20, 20-40, and so on), each row has data about one person.

Sometimes, there is a need for interspersing new rows between your current rows. Taking the previous examples, imagine the following situations:

▶ In the sold items dataset, every 10 items, you have to insert a row with the running quantity of items and running sold price from the first line until that line.

▶ In the temperature's dataset, you have to order the data by region and the last row for each region has to have the average temperature for that region.

▶ In the people's dataset, for each age range, you have to insert a header row just before the rows of people in that range.

In general, the rows you need to intersperse can have fixed data, subtotals of the numbers in previous rows, header to the rows coming next, and so on. What they have in common is that they have a different structure or meaning, compared to the rows in your dataset.

Interspersing these rows is not a complicated task, but is a tricky one. In this recipe, you will learn how to do it.

Suppose that you have to create a list of products by category. For each category, you have to insert a header row with the category description and the number of products inside that category.

The final result should be as follows:

#	desc_product	qty_prod	order
1	CATEGORY: KITCHEN	24	1
2	Swedish Firesteel- Scout Model		2
3	Swedish Firesteel - Army Model		2
4	Sigg Classic Bottle - Traveller (1.0-Liters)		2
5	Mountain House #10 Can Freeze-Dried Food		2
6	Lodge Logic L9OG3 Pre-Seasoned 10-1/2-Inch Round		2
7	Lodge Logic L5SK3 Pre-Seasoned Cast-Iron 8-Inch Sk		2
8	Lodge LCC3 Logic Pre-Seasoned Combo Cooker		2
9	Light My Fire Titanium Spork		2
10	Light My Fire Spork 4-Pack		2
11	Kwik Tek Airhead Aqua Oasis		2

Rows of step: Sort rows (60 rows)

Getting ready

This recipe uses an outdoor database with the structure shown in *Appendix A, Data Structures*. As the source, you can use a database like this or any other source, for example, a text file with the same structure.

How to do it...

Perform the following steps:

1. Create a transformation, drag into the canvas a **Table Input** step, select the connection to the outdoor database, or create it if it doesn't exist. Then enter the following statement:

```
SELECT category
     , desc_product
FROM    products p
        ,categories c
WHERE  p.id_category = c.id_category
ORDER by category
```

2. Do a preview of this step. You already have the product list!

3. Now, you have to create and intersperse the header rows. In order to create the headers, do the following: from the **Statistics** category, add a **Group by** step and fill in the grids, as shown in the following screenshot:

The fields that make up the group:		
^ # Group field		
1 category		

Aggregates :		
^ # Name	Subject	Type
1 qty_prod	desc_product	Number of Values (N)

4. From the **Scripting** category, add a **User Defined Java Expression** step, and use it to add two fields: the first will be a **String** named desc_product, with value ("Category: " + category).toUpperCase(). The second will be an **Integer** field named order with value 1.

5. Use a **Select values** step to reorder the fields as category, desc_product, qty_product, and order. Do a preview on this step; you should see the following result:

Rows of step: Select values (5 rows)

^ #	category	desc_product	qty_prod	order
1	kitchen	CATEGORY: KITCHEN	24	1
2	lights	CATEGORY: LIGHTS	15	1
3	sleeping bags	CATEGORY: SLEEPING BAGS	6	1
4	tents	CATEGORY: TENTS	8	1
5	tools	CATEGORY: TOOLS	2	1

6. Those are the headers. The next step is mixing all the rows in the proper order. Drag an **Add constants** step and a **Sort rows** step into the canvas. Link them to the other steps as shown:

7. Use the **Add constants** to add two **Integer** fields: qty_prod and order. As **Value**, leave the first field empty, and type 2 for the second field.

8. Use the **Sort rows** step for sorting by category, order, and desc_product.

9. Select the last step and do a preview. You should see the rows exactly as shown in the introduction.

How it works...

When you have to intersperse rows between existing rows, there are just four main tasks to do, as follows:

1. Create a secondary stream that will be used for creating new rows. In this case, the rows with the headers of the categories.

2. In each stream, add a field that will help you intersperse rows in the proper order. In this case, the key field was named order.

3. Before joining the two streams, add, remove, and reorder the fields in each stream to make sure that the output fields in each stream have the same metadata.

4. Join the streams and sort by the fields that you consider appropriate, including the field created earlier. In this case, you sorted by category, inside each category by the field named order and finally by the products description.

Note that in this case, you created a single secondary stream. You could create more if needed, for example, if you need a header and footer for each category.

See also

▶ *Merging the rows of two streams with the same or different structures*

Executing steps even when your stream is empty

As you must know, a Kettle transformation is a group of linked steps through which data flows. Each step is meant to receive rows of data, process the data somehow, and deliver those rows to the next step or steps. If there are no rows coming to the step, the step will not be executed.

This seems reasonable, but on occasions, it can be a problem. To get an idea of that kind of situation, look at the following scenarios:

▶ You have a very simple transformation that reads a file, does some calculations, and finally updates a table with the system date and the number of processed rows. If the file doesn't exist or if it is empty, then no rows will go out from the file input step. Consequently and contrary to what you need to do, the step that updates the table will never be executed.

▶ You have a file that has the values of some variables that are needed for a process. As long as the file exists and has the correct variables in it, the process will execute. If the process needs to run even without the file, it is recommended that the variables have default values set in the process.

▶ You have a database with products and want to generate a list of products whose descriptions match a given text. For example, if the text is `lamp`, your file will have all products that contain `lamp` in their descriptions. If there are no lamps, you want to generate a file with a single row recording the situation. The problem is that if there are no lamps, no row will come out of the input step. Consequently, the output step, as in the first example, will never be executed.

For situations like these, there is a way to overcome the problem: the use of the **Detect empty stream** step. This recipe shows you how to use it. It implements the last of the examples: the generation of the file with a list of products.

Getting ready

For this recipe, you will need a database with outdoor products with the structure defined in *Appendix A, Data Structures*.

How to do it...

Perform the following steps:

1. Create a transformation and drag a **Table Input** step.

2. Double-click on the step and select the connection to the `outdoors` database or create it if it doesn't exist. Then enter the following statement:

```
SELECT
      category
    , id_product
    , desc_product
    , price
FROM products p
      ,categories c
WHERE p.id_category = c.id_category
AND desc_product like '%${PROD_FILTER}%'
ORDER by category, desc_product
```

3. Check the **Replace variables in script?** option.

4. Add an **Excel output** step. Configure the step to generate a file with all fields coming from the **Table Input** step. From the **Flow** category, add a **Detect empty stream** step. Also, add a **User Defined Java Expression** or **UDJE** step, and link all steps as follows:

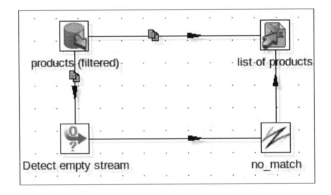

5. Use the **UDJE** step and fill it in, as shown in the following screenshot:

Fields:

^	#	New field	Java expression	Value type	Length	Precision	Replace value
	1	category	"criteria doesn't match any product"	String			category

That's all! Let's test the transformation:

1. Press the *F9* key to run it; give the `PROD_FILTER` variable the value `lamp` (or any value that you know is part of the description of some of your products). You do this by typing the value into the grid named **Variables**. Click on **Launch**.

2. Open the generated file. It should look like the one shown in the following screenshot:

	A	B	C	D
1	category	id_product	desc_product	price
2	lights	34	Petzl E41 PBY Tikkina 2-LED Headlamp, Black and Yellow	19.95
3	lights	36	Petzl E49P TacTikka Plus 4-LED Headlamp, Black	43.95
4	lights	26	Petzl E97 PP Tikka Plus 2 Headlamp, Pistachio	39.94

3. Run the transformation again, but this time, type a value that you know isn't part of the descriptions of your products, for example `motorcycle`.

4. Open the file. This time it should have the content as shown in the following screenshot:

	A	B	C	D
1	category	id_product	desc_product	price
2	criteria doesn't match any product			

How it works...

When a step doesn't return data, the flow ends. None of the steps that follow that step are executed because they don't receive data for processing. The **Detect empty stream** step, as the name suggests, detects that situation. As a consequence, it generates a stream with the same metadata as the expected stream, and a single row with null values. This way, you avoid the stream from dying.

In order to understand what the step does in a better way, try the following:

1. In the transformation that you just created, select the **Detect empty stream** step.

2. Press the *F9* key to do a preview, give to the variable PROD_FILTER the value `lamp`, and click on **Launch**.

3. You will see a message informing you that there are no rows to preview. That's because the main stream had rows and they went toward the Excel step.

4. Try the same procedure again, but this time, enter an invalid value, for example, `motorcycle`. You will see a single row with the columns `category`, `id_product`, `desc_product`, and `price`, all with null values.

In the recipe, in the step that follows the **Detect empty stream** step, you replaced the null value in the **category** column with the message you wanted to write in the file, and sent the data toward the Excel file. The **Excel output** step doesn't care if the data came from the main stream or the alternative one that you created for the empty stream. It simply sends the columns to the Excel file.

Finally, it's worth mentioning why we used the **UDJE** step. The selection of this step is smart because it replaces the value of the **category** field. Most steps add new fields, but are not able to manipulate existing ones.

There's more...

You can use the **Detect empty stream** step in the same way you would implement error handling. The difference is that here there are no errors; you simply have an exceptional situation.

As you would do when handling errors, you can fix or manipulate the stream and send it back to the main stream, as you did in the recipe, or you could completely ignore the metadata generated by the **Detect empty stream** step and simply use that step as the beginning of a new independent stream. For example, instead of generating the Excel file when there are no rows, you could write a message to the log, such as `criteria doesn't match any product`.

Processing rows differently based on the row number

There will be some situations where you will need to process the data differently depending on the position or number of each row.

Let's assume that you have a bookstore and want to know the top five bestsellers books, the following 10 bestsellers, and the rest of the books for different purposes (for example, to do a differentiated marketing promotion for each group). To do this, you will divide the list of books into different groups depending on their sales.

Getting ready

You need an Excel spreadsheet file containing a list of books with the following columns:

- ▶ `title`
- ▶ `id_author`
- ▶ `price`
- ▶ `id_title`
- ▶ `genre`
- ▶ `sales`

This last column represents the quantity of books sold in the last period. You can download a sample file from the book's website.

How to do it...

Perform the following steps:

1. Create a new transformation and drag an **Excel Input** step from the **Input** category.

2. Under the **Files** tab, browse to and select the `sales_books.xls` file.

3. Complete the **Fields** tab with the following values:

#	Name	Type	Format
1	title	String	
2	id_author	String	
3	price	Number	$0.00
4	id_title	String	
5	genre	String	
6	sales	Number	0

4. Add a **Sort rows** step from the **Transform** category. Complete the step grid with the **sales Fieldname**. Type N in the **Ascending** column.

5. Add an **Add sequence** step from the **Transform** category. Type `rank` in the **Name of value** textbox.

6. By previewing this step, you will obtain a list of books ranked by their sales. Add two **Filter rows** steps and three **Dummy** steps (all from the **Flow** category) and create the hops, as depicted in the following diagram:

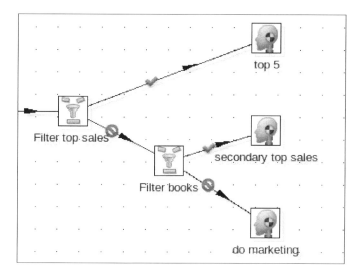

7. In the first **Filter rows**, set the following condition `rank <= 5`.

8. In the last **Filter rows** step add the condition `rank <= 15`.

9. The **Dummy 1** step represents the five best-selling books. For example:

Rows of step: top 5 (5 rows)

#	title	id_author	price	id_title	genre	sales	rank
1	Rich Dad, Poor Dad	A00007	$19.90	323-602	Business	570	1
2	Pet Sematary	A00002	$41.00	123-351	Fiction	478	2
3	Harry Potter and the Deathly	A00008	$38.00	423-007	Children	470	3
4	The Obama Diaries	A00005	$28.90	223-301	Non-fiction	456	4
5	Who Took My Money	A00007	$21.00	323-603	Business	450	5

10. The **Dummy 2** step represents the next 10 best-selling books.

11. The rest of the books can be seen in the **Dummy 3** step.

12. You can do a preview of each of these **Dummy** steps and verify the results.

How it works...

This recipe reads the `sales_books.xls` file to create a dataset of the book titles along with their sales information. The **Sort rows** step is necessary to order the books by sales starting with the best seller.

Then, you dropped an **Add sequence** step to enumerate the rows. In this case, the field you added represents the ranking value. The best selling book will have the number one.

At this moment, you have the list of books ranked by their sales. Now, you only have to filter the books based on their ranks. You do it by using the **Filter rows** step. The first **Filter rows** step uses the condition `rank <= 5` to get the top five best-selling books. The rest of the books will be filtered again, now with the condition `rank <= 15`; this will bring the rows ranked from 6 to 15. The remaining books, those with a rank greater than 15, will go to the last **Dummy** step.

There's more...

In the recipe, you enumerated the rows and then you did different things based on the row number. There are also some specific use cases, which are explained in the following subsections.

Identifying specific rows

Suppose that you only want to keep the books with rank 15 to 20 and discard the rest. In this case, you don't have to add the **Add sequence** step and the **Filter rows** step afterward. There is a simpler way of doing that. There is also a step named **Sample rows** in the **Statistics** category that allows picking specific rows from a dataset. For example, filling the **Lines range** textbox with 1..5,9,15..20, you will get:

- The rows 1 to 5
- The row 9
- The rows 15 to 20

The rest of the lines will be discarded. For the preceding example, you should just type 15..20.

Identifying the last row in the stream

Suppose that you want to know which book sold the least. In this case, you cannot filter by row number because you don't know how many books there are. In this case, instead of enumerating the rows, you can use the **Identify last row in a stream** step from the **Flow** category.

In this step, you only have to type a value for the **Result fieldname** textbox. When you execute the transformation, this new field will return Y for the last row and N otherwise. In the example, you can know which the least sold book was by filtering the row where the field is equal to Y.

Avoiding using an Add sequence step to enumerate the rows

If you need to enumerate the rows just after reading the data, you don't need to add an **Add sequence** step. In several of the input steps, such as **Text file input** or **Get data from XML**, you have a checkbox named **Rownum in output?** under the **Content** tab. This allows you to create a new field with a sequence for the rows. The name of this new field must be typed in the **Rownum fieldname** textbox.

This also applies when you need to rank the rows as in the recipe, and your input data is already ordered.

See also

- *Splitting a stream into two or more streams based on a condition*

Processing data into shared transformations via filter criteria and subtransformations

Processing data is one of the key capabilities of any **Extract, Transform, and Load** (**ETL**) tool and Kettle is no different. Sometimes though, data must be processed differently (usually due to data quality issues or business rules). If this logic is needed in multiple places, it makes sense to break that code out into its own transformation using a **Mapping (sub-transformation)**.

This recipe will be creating a simple usage of the **Mapping (sub-transformation)** step.

Getting ready

For this recipe, we will be building off of the *Splitting a stream in two or more streams based on a condition* recipe, presented earlier in this chapter. It is recommended to follow this recipe and understand how the **Switch/Case** step works before continuing. Alternatively, the code for this recipe is available on the book's website.

How to do it...

Perform the following steps:

1. Open the transformation created from the *Splitting a stream in two or more streams based on a condition* recipe (or from the book's site).

2. Create two new transformations. One will be used to process the kitchen products data stream and the other will be used to process the tents' data stream.

3. From the pallet, bring over two **Mapping (sub-transformation)** steps to put between the kitchen product and tent **Dummy** steps. Your transformation should now look similar to the following:

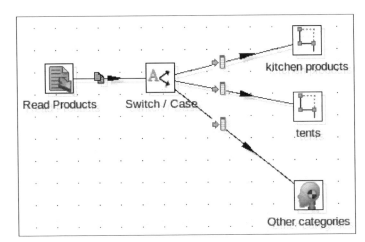

4. Switch to the kitchen products subtransformation. Drag a **Mapping input specification** and a **Mapping output specification** step onto the canvas.

5. Add a **String operations** step and connect it between the input and output specification steps.

6. Open the **Mapping input specification** step. Add **desc_product** as a string to the fields data grid. Be sure to check the **Include unspecified fields**, ordered by name box and click on **OK**.

7. Open the **String operations** step. Change the **desc_product** field to upper and click on **OK**.

8. Repeat steps 4 through 6 on the tents' subtransformation. Instead of upper case, switch the **desc_product** field to lower case.

9. Go back to the parent transformation and open the **Mapping (sub-transformation)** step for the kitchen products. Point the step to the kitchen processing subtransformation. Click on **OK** to exit the step.

10. Repeat step 9 for the tents' **Mapping (sub-transformation)**.

11. Preview the kitchen product output **Dummy** step and you should get output similar to the following:

Rows of step: kitchen product output (24 rows)

#	id_product	desc_product	price	category
1	1	SWEDISH FIRESTEEL - ARMY MODEL	19.00	kitchen
2	2	MOUNTAIN HOUSE #10 CAN FREEZE-DRIE	53.00	kitchen
3	3	LODGE LOGIC L9OG3 PRE-SEASONED 10-1	14.00	kitchen
4	4	LODGE LOGIC L5SK3 PRE-SEASONED CAST	12.00	kitchen
5	5	COLEMAN 70-QUART XTREME COOLER (BL	59.00	kitchen
6	6	KELSYUS FLOATING COOLER	26.00	kitchen
7	7	LODGE LCC3 LOGIC PRE-SEASONED COMB	41.00	kitchen
8	8	GUYOT DESIGNS SPLASHGUARD-UNIVERSA	7.00	kitchen
9	9	COLEMAN 62-QUART XTREME WHEELED C	62.00	kitchen
10	10	COLEMAN ROADTRIP ACCESSORY STOVE (	16.00	kitchen
11	11	COLEMAN PERFECTFLOW INSTASTART 2-B	69.00	kitchen
12	12	COLEMAN HIGH-PRESSURE PROPANE HOS	24.00	kitchen
13	13	COLEMAN SPECKLED ENAMELWARE DININC	38.00	kitchen
14	14	LIGHT MY FIRE TITANIUM SPORK	10.00	kitchen

How it works...

Subtransformations provide the power of transformations, but the flexibility to share transformation logic across many different transformations and jobs. The **Mapping (sub-transformation)** step allows for the data stream of a given transformation to be mapped to the subtransformation flow and be returned back for further processing, if desired.

In this recipe's transformation, we combined the subtransformation feature with the **Switch/Case** step to perform a simple transformation based on the logic in the switch. Normally, we would put such simple steps as a **String** operation inside the actual transformation that was using it. Subtransformations really come in handy when a complex piece of logic is required in many different places and it would be difficult to maintain the code if it were stored as such.

See also

▶   The *Moving part of a transformation into a subtransformation* recipe in *Chapter 8, Executing and Re-using Jobs and Transformations*

Altering a data stream with Select values

While processing data there will come a need to alter field names, their data types or formats, and even removing fields altogether. The **Select values** step allows for all three functions and this recipe will show how to use it. The code for this recipe is available from the book's website.

How to do it...

1.   Create a new transformation. Add a **Generate Rows** step and a **Generate random value** step to the canvas.

2.   Create a hop between the two steps.

3.   Open the **Generate Rows** step. Create a field named `row_test` of type `String` and with a default value of `test`. Click on **OK** to close the step.

4.   Open the **Generate random value** step. Create two fields, one a random string (named `random_num`) and the other a random string (named `random_string`). Click on **OK** to close the step.

5.   Bring over three **Select values** steps onto the canvas. Create hops from the **Generate random value** step to each of the **Select values** steps. When prompted to specify how to handle the stream of data, select **Copy**.

6.   Open one of the **Select values** steps and rename it to `Alter`. On the **Select & Alter** tab, click on **Get fields to select** to bring the fields from the stream into the step.

7. For the row with the field `random_num`, change the name to `random_number` by filling in the **Rename to** column. Click on **OK** to close the step.

8. Open another of the **Select values** steps and rename it to `Remove`. Switch to the **Remove** tab and select the field `row_test`. Click on **OK** to close the step.

9. Open the final **Select values** step and rename it `Metadata`. Switch to the **Meta-data** tab and change the `random_num` field to type **Integer**. Click on **OK** to close the step.

10. Now, preview each of the three **Select values** steps to see how each function alters the stream.

How it works...

The **Select values** step is designed with three types of functions: **Select & Alter**, **Remove**, and **Meta-data**. All three deal with making significant changes to the data stream while processing data. The **Select & Alter** tab provides basic renaming and length/precision altering. The **Remove** tab clears those fields from the data stream. Finally, the **Meta-data** tab also allows for renaming and length/precision altering but will also change field types and formatting.

> Even though the **Select values** step has three tabs, each one is independent of the others. If you want to use more than one of the functions, you have to add additional **Select values** steps to your streams.

This step is especially handy if the data types of source fields do not match the target fields, which will cause type mismatch errors otherwise. If you are using this step to remove fields, please note that it is a resource-intensive process. Sometimes it is better to just leave the fields in place for performance rather than cleaning up. It is typical to remove fields from a stream if they will no longer be needed and the dataset is large enough that memory may be an issue.

Processing multiple jobs or transformations in parallel

Running jobs or transformations serially is fine initially, but as more processes come online, the need for executing more in less time becomes very evident. Kettle has the ability to run multiple jobs and transformations at the same time, and in this recipe, we will be going over how to utilize this functionality for both jobs and transformations. The code for this recipe is available on the book's website.

How to do it...

Perform the following steps to learn how to execute job steps in parallel.

1. Open Spoon and create a new job.

2. Add a **Start** step to the canvas. Also, add three **Transformation** steps.

3. Create a hop between the **Start** step and one of the **Transformation** steps. Repeat the process between the **Transformation** step and the other two **Transformation** steps. Your job should now look similar to the following:

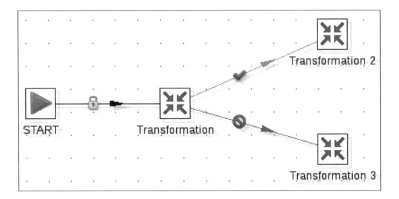

4. Right-click on the first **Transformation** step and select the **Launch next entries in parallel** option. Two parallel lines should now appear over the hops between the first **Transformation** step and the other two.

5. Change the hop between the **Transformation** and **Transformation 3** steps to be for a success (green with a check) instead of a failure. This can be done by either clicking on the hop or right clicking the hop and changing the **Evaluation condition**. The transformation should now look like the following:

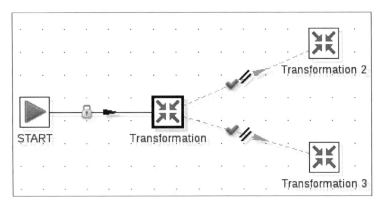

A warning message popped up while enabling the parallel processing of the other **Transformation** steps. As long as the two transformations do not have a dependency on each other (that is working on the same tables or files, one needing to be finished before the other, and so on) the process will execute without a problem. Now, let's look at how parallelization is handled within transformations.

1. Open a new transformation and bring over a **Generate Rows** step, as well as an **Add sequence** step.

2. Create a hop between the **Generate Rows** step and the **Add sequence** step.

3. Add two **Dummy (do nothing)** steps to the canvas. Create a hop from the **Add sequence** step to one of the **Dummy (do nothing)** steps. Repeat the process for the other **Dummy (do nothing)** step. A window pops up asking how the data stream should be handled. Select **Copy**.

4. Run the transformation. Notice that the two **Dummy (do nothing)** steps are receiving the same number of records.

5. Right-click on the **Add sequence** step and select **Data Movement | Distribute data to next steps**.

6. Run the transformation. Notice that the two **Dummy (do nothing)** steps now only receive half the number of records that they originally were receiving.

How it works...

Running processes in parallel allows for more efficient usage of computing resources and time. Kettle's built-in functionality allows for jobs and transformations to take advantage of executing multiple processes simultaneously. There are a few caveats to address if trying to tune your processes to run in parallel:

▸   Streams running in parallel cannot modify the same objects (that is, database tables) without running into potential deadlocks.

▸   Processes tuned for higher memory, CPUs, and so on, will perform slower than if running them separately. Be sure to tune the processes for the new parallel execution.

▸   Transformations running multiple parallel streams that are joining back together require the same layout. Fields that are out of order or removed will cause issues when merging the streams back together.

▸   For transformations, streams that are distributed rather than copied will be randomly split, with no guarantee which records end up in a given stream.

It is also important to note that running processes in parallel will generally utilize more memory and CPU. Also, processes can only be tuned up to the maximum amount allowed by the hardware it is being run on. If you are using a 4 core processor and trying to run 50 processes in parallel, the processes will likely crash!

See also

▸ *Merging rows of two streams with the same or different structures*

▸ *Splitting a stream into two or more streams based on a condition*

8
Executing and Re-using Jobs and Transformations

In this chapter, we will cover the following topics:

- ▶ Launching jobs or transformations
- ▶ Executing a job or a transformation by setting static arguments and parameters
- ▶ Executing a job or a transformation from a job by setting arguments and parameters dynamically
- ▶ Executing a job or a transformation whose name is determined at runtime
- ▶ Executing part of a job once for every row in the dataset
- ▶ Executing part of a job several times until a condition is true
- ▶ Creating a process flow
- ▶ Moving part of a transformation to a subtransformation
- ▶ Using Metadata Injection to re-use transformations

Introduction

A transformation by itself rarely meets all the requirements of a real-world problem. It's common to face some of the following situations:

- You need to execute the same transformation over and over again
- You need to execute a transformation more than once, but with different parameters each time
- You need to decide at runtime which job to run from a group of jobs
- You have to re-use part of a transformation in a different scenario

Kettle is versatile enough to meet those situations. However, it is easy to get confused trying to do some of them without guidance.

This chapter contains quick recipes just meant to teach you the basics. The transformations and jobs used are simple enough to serve as templates for you to modify for your own needs.

Before starting on the recipes, let's take a look at the following subsections:

- **Sample transformations**: As the name suggests, this section explains the sample transformations that will be used throughout the chapter.
- **Launching jobs and transformations**: This section quickly introduces Kitchen and Pan, the tools for launching jobs and transformations from the command line.

Sample transformations

The recipes in this chapter show you different ways of running Kettle transformations and jobs. In order to focus on the specific purposes of the recipes rather than on developing transformations, we've created some sample transformations that will be used throughout the chapter.

 These transformations generate files in a directory pointed to by a variable named ${OUTPUT_FOLDER}. In order to run the transformations, this variable must be predefined.

The transformations are described in the following subsections. You can download them from the book's website.

 Remember that you have several ways of defining variables: as a named parameter in the Kettle properties file, in a previous job, or a transformation (if this transformation is going to be called from a job), or in the **Variables** section of the **Execute a transformation** window (the window that shows up when you run the transformation from **Spoon**).

Sample transformation – hello

This transformation receives the name of a person as the first command-line argument and generates a file saying hello to that person.

The transformation looks like the one shown in the following screenshot:

A sample output file is as follows:

```
Hello, Eva! It's January 09, 09:37.
```

Sample transformation – random list

This transformation generates a file with a list of random integers. The quantity generated is defined as a **named parameter** called QUANTITY, with a default value of 10. The QUANTITY named parameter will produce 10 random integers if no other value for it is passed to the transformation at runtime. The transformation looks like the one depicted in the following screenshot:

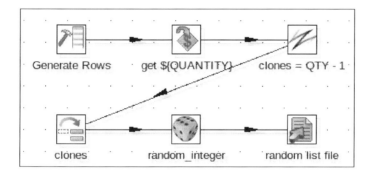

A sample output file is as follows:

```
-982437245
1169516784
318652071
-576481306
1815968887
```

Sample transformation – sequence

This transformation generates a file with a sequence of numbers. The transformation receives two command-line arguments representing FROM and TO values. It also has a named parameter called INCREMENT with a default value of 1. The transformation generates a list of numbers between FROM and TO, with increments of INCREMENT.

The transformation looks like the one shown in the following screenshot:

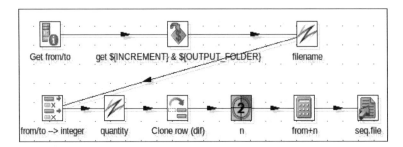

A sample output file using from=0, to=6, and increment=2 is as follows:

```
0
2
4
6
```

Sample transformation – file list

This transformation generates a file containing the names of the files in the current directory, with the current directory being where the transformation is located.

The transformation looks like the one depicted in the following screenshot:

A sample output file is as follows:

```
gen_random.ktr
gen_sequence.ktr
get_file_names.ktr
hello.ktr
```

Launching jobs and transformations

As was mentioned in the *Introduction* section, the recipes in this chapter are focused on different ways of running Kettle transformations and jobs. Ultimately, you will end up with a main job. In order to test your job with different inputs or parameters, you can use Spoon as usual, but it might be useful or even simpler to use **Kitchen**—a command-line program meant to launch Kettle jobs. If you're not familiar with Kitchen, this recipe gives you a quick overview.

How to do it...

In order to run a job with Kitchen, perform the following steps:

1. Open a terminal window by navigating to **Start | All Programs | Accessories | Command Prompt** (Windows) or by going to the desktop **Application** menu and typing `Terminal` (Gnome environment for Linux).

2. Go to the Kettle installation directory.

3. Run `kitchen.bat /file:<kjb file name>` (Windows system) or `kitchen.sh /file:<kjb file name>` (Unix-based system), where `<kjb file name>` is the name of your job, including the complete path. If the name contains spaces, you must surround it with double quotes.

If you want to provide command-line parameters, just type them in order as part of the command. If you want to provide a named parameter, use the following syntax:

```
/param:<parameter name>=<parameter value>
```

For example, `/param:INCREMENT=5`.

Additionally, you can specify the logging level by adding the following option:

```
/level:<logging level>
```

The logging level can be one of the following: `Error`, `Nothing`, `Minimal`, `Basic` (this is the default level), `Detailed`, `Debug`, or `Rowlevel`.

If you intend to run a transformation instead of a job, use **Pan**. Just replace `kitchen.bat/kitchen.sh` with `pan.bat/pan.sh`, and provide the name of the proper `.ktr` file.

While you use Spoon for developing, debugging, and testing transformations and jobs, Kitchen and Pan are most commonly used for running jobs and transformations in production environments. For a complete list of available options and more information on these commands, visit the Pan documentation at `http://wiki.pentaho.com/display/EAI/Pan+User+Documentation`.
For documentation on Kitchen, visit `http://wiki.pentaho.com/display/EAI/Kitchen+User+Documentation`.

How it works...

Kettle has several tools built in to run jobs and transformations in a server environment. Servers do not typically have graphical user interfaces and are connected through tunneling from other computers. Kitchen and Pan are built to run from the command line for that very reason. There are other tools that are part of the Kettle suite. **Carte** is a lightweight server that connects to a master Kettle server to build dynamic server clusters that can handle distributing jobs and transformations. To learn more about Carte, check out the Pentaho community wiki at http://wiki.pentaho.com/display/EAI/Carte+User+Documentation.

Another useful tool is **Encr**, which encrypts database and Carte passwords. Its use is described in the Carte user documentation.

Both Carte (carte.bat/carte.sh) and Encr (encr.bat/encr.sh) can be found in the Kettle installation directory.

Executing a job or a transformation by setting static arguments and parameters

When you develop a transformation that reads command-line arguments or defines named parameters, you usually intend to call it more than once with different values for those parameters or arguments. If you know the values beforehand, there is an easy way to call the transformation, as you will see in this recipe. Suppose that you want to create the following three files:

▶ **First file**: Numbers from 1 to 10, incrementing by 1, as in 0, 1,..., 10

▶ **Second file**: Numbers from 0 to 100, incrementing by 20, as in 0, 20, 40,..., 100

▶ **Third file**: Numbers from 100 to 500, incrementing by 100, as in 100, 200,.., 500

You have a transformation that generates sequences like these. You just have to call it three times with the proper arguments and parameters.

Getting ready

You need the sample transformation that generates a file with a sequence described in the introduction.

Make sure you have defined the variable ${OUTPUT_FOLDER} with the name of the destination folder. Also, make sure that the folder exists.

How to do it...

Perform the following steps:

1. Create a job.

2. Drag a **Start** job entry and three **Transformation** job entries into the canvas. Link all the entries one after the other.

3. Double-click on the first **Transformation** entry.

4. As **Transformation filename**, browse to and select the sample transformation `gen_sequence.ktr`.

5. Select the **Argument** tab and fill the grid with a value of `1` in the first row and `10` in the second row.

6. Double-click on the second **Transformation** entry.

7. For the **Transformation filename**, select the sample transformation `gen_sequence.ktr`.

8. Select the **Argument** tab and fill the grid with `0` in the first row and `100` in the second.

9. Select the **Parameters** tab. In the first row of the grid, type `INCREMENT` under **Parameter** and `20` under **Value**.

10. Double-click on the last **Transformation** entry.

11. For **Transformation filename**, select the sample transformation `gen_sequence.ktr`.

12. Select the **Argument** tab and fill the grid with `100` in the first row and `500` in the second.

13. Select the **Parameters** tab. In the first row of the grid, type `INCREMENT` under **Parameter** and `100` under **Value**.

14. Save and run the job.

15. Check the output folder. You will find the following three files:

    ❏ `sequence_1_10_1.txt`

    ❏ `sequence_0_100_20.txt`

    ❏ `sequence_50_500_50.txt`

16. Edit the files. You will see that they contain the sequences of numbers `0, 1,..., 10` in the first file, `0, 20, 40,..., 100` in the second, and `100, 200,..., 500` in the third, just as expected.

How it works...

When you run a transformation from a job, you have to specify at least the name and location of the transformation. There are however, a couple of extra settings that may be useful. In this recipe, you saw the use of the **Argument** and the **Parameters** tabs. The **Argument** tab is used for sending command-line arguments to the transformation. The grid in the **Argument** tab is equivalent to the **Arguments** grid you see when you run a transformation from Spoon. Each row belongs to a different command-line argument.

In this case, your transformation expected two command-line arguments: the limits `from` and `to` of the sequence. In the recipe, you set values for those arguments in the **Argument** tab of each **Transformation** entry setting window.

The **Parameters** tab is used for setting values for the named parameters defined in the transformation. The grid under the **Parameters** tab is equivalent to the **Parameters** grid you see when you run a transformation from Spoon. Each row belongs to a different named parameter. You only have to provide values if they are different to the default values.

In this case, your transformation defined one named parameter `INCREMENT` with a default value of `1`. Therefore, you skipped the setting of this parameter in the first **Transformation** entry, but set values in the others.

Note that if you set arguments or parameters in the **Transformation** entry setting window, the corresponding argument or parameters sent from the command line will be ignored if you run the job with Kitchen.

There's more...

All that was said for the Transformation job entry is also valid for Job entries. That is, you can use the **Argument** and **Parameters** tabs in a **Job** entry to send fixed values of command-line arguments or named parameters to the job.

See also

▸ *Executing a job or a transformation from a job by setting arguments and parameters dynamically*

Executing a job or a transformation from a job by setting arguments and parameters dynamically

Suppose that you developed a transformation which reads command-line arguments or defines named parameters. Now you want to call that transformation from a job, but you don't know the values for the arguments or the parameters; you have to take them from some media, for example, a file or a table in a database. This recipe shows you how to get those values and pass them to the transformation at runtime.

For this recipe, suppose that you want to create a file with a sequence of numbers. You have a transformation that does it. The problem is that the limits FROM and TO and the INCREMENT value are stored in a `properties` file. This presents an obstacle to calling the transformation directly, but can be done with Kettle in a very simple way.

Getting ready

You need a sample transformation that generates a file with a sequence as described in the introduction. Make sure you have defined the variable `${OUTPUT_FOLDER}` with the name of the destination folder. Also, make sure that the folder exists.

You also need a file named `sequence.properties` with the following content:

```
from=0
to=90
increment=30
```

With these values your transformation should generate the values 0, 30, 60, 90.

How to do it...

Perform the following steps:

1. Create a transformation.
2. From the **Input** category, drag a **Property Input** step into the canvas, and use it to read the `properties` file. Under the **File** tab, enter the name and location of the file. Under the **Fields** tab, click on **Get Fields** to fill the grid with the fields Key and Value.
3. From the **Transform** category, add a **Row denormalizer** step and create a hop from the input step toward this one.

4. Double-click on the step. For **Key field**, select `Key`. Fill the **Target fields:** grid, as shown in the following screenshot:

	#	Target fieldname	Value fieldname	Key value	Type
	1	from_value	Value	from	String
	2	to_value	Value	to	String
	3	increment_value	Value	increment	String

Target fields:

5. After that step, add a **Copy rows to result** step. You will find it under the **Job** category.

6. Do a preview on the last step. You should see the following screen:

Rows of step: Copy rows to result (1 rows)

	#	from_value	to_value	increment_value
	1	0	90	30

7. Save the transformation and create a job.

8. Drag a **Start** job entry and two **Transformation** job entries into the canvas. Link the entries, one after the other.

9. Double-click on the first **Transformation** entry, and for **Transformation filename**, select the transformation you just created.

10. Close the window and double-click on the second **Transformation** entry.

11. For **Transformation filename**, select the sample transformation `gen_sequence.ktr`.

12. Select the **Advanced** tab and check the first three options: **Copy previous results to args?**, **Copy previous results to parameters?**, and **Execute for every input row?**.

13. Select the **Parameters** tab. For the first row in the grid, type `INCREMENT` under **Parameter** and `increment_value` under **Stream column name**.

14. Close the window.

15. Save and run the job.

16. As a result, you will have a new file named `sequence_0_90_30.txt`. The file will contain the sequence of numbers `0`, `30`, `60`, `90`, just as expected.

How it works...

The transformation you ran in the recipe expects two arguments: FROM and TO. It also has a named parameter called INCREMENT. There are a couple of ways to pass those values to the transformation:

- Typing them on the command line when running the transformation with Pan or Kitchen (if the transformation is called by a job)
- Typing them in the transformation or job setting window when running it with Spoon
- In a static way by providing fixed values in the **Transformation** entry setting window, as in the previous recipe
- Dynamically, by taking the values from another source as you did in this recipe

If the values for the arguments or parameters are stored in other media, for example, a table, an Excel sheet, or a `properties` file, you can easily read them and pass the values to the transformation. First, you call a transformation that creates a dataset with a single row with all required values. Then you pass the values to the transformation by configuring the **Advanced** tab properly. Let's see an example.

In the recipe, you created a transformation that generates a single row with the three required values: from_value, to_value, and increment_value. By adding a **Copy rows to result** step, that row became available for later use.

In the main job, you did the trick: by checking the **Copy previous results to args?** and **Execute for every input row?** options, you take that row and pass it to the transformation as if the fields were command-line arguments. That is, the values of the fields from_value, to_value, and increment_value—namely 0, 90, and 30—are seen by the transformation as if they were the command-line arguments 1, 2, and 3 respectively. Note that in this case the transformation only read two of those arguments, the third one was ignored.

With regard to the named parameter, INCREMENT, you passed it to the transformation by checking the **Copy previous results to parameters?** option and adding a row in the **Parameters** tab grid. Here you entered the map between the named parameter INCREMENT and the incoming stream field increment_value.

There's more...

All that was said for the Transformation job entry is also valid for Job entries. That is, you can set the **Advanced** tab in a **Job** entry to copy the previous results as arguments or as parameters to the job that is going to be executed.

See also

- *Executing a job or a transformation by setting static arguments and parameters*
- *Executing part of a job once for every row in a dataset*

Executing a job or a transformation whose name is determined at runtime

Suppose that you have a couple of transformations, but you do not want to run all of them. The transformation to be executed will depend on conditions only known at runtime. If you have just two transformations, you could explicitly call one or the other in a simple fashion. On the other hand, if you have several transformations or if you do not even know the names of the available transformations, you must take another approach. This recipe shows you how.

Suppose that you want to run one of the three sample transformations described in the introduction. The transformation to run will be different depending on the time of day:

► Before 8:00 A.M. in the morning, you will call the `Hello` transformation

► Between 8:00 A.M. and 20:00 P.M., you will call the transformation that generates random numbers

► From 20:00 P.M. to midnight, you will call the transformation that lists files

Here's how to do it.

Getting ready

You will need the transformations described in the introduction. Make sure you have defined the variable ${OUTPUT_FOLDER with the name of the destination folder. Also, make sure that the folder exists.

Also, define a variable named ${COMMON_DIR} with the path to the folder where you have the sample transformations, for example, `c:/my_kettle_work/common`.

How to do it...

Perform the following steps:

1. Create a transformation that will pick the transformation to run.

2. Drag-and-drop a **Get System Info** step and use it to create a field named `now` with the system date.

3. Drag-and-drop a **Select Values** step and use it to get the current hour. Select the **Meta** tab; add the field named `now`, for **Type** select **String**, and for **Format**, type HH. Rename the field as `hour`.

4. Drag another **Select Values** step and use it to change the value of field `hour` to **Integer**.

5. After the last step, add a **Number range** step. You will find it in the **Transformation** category.

6. Double-click on the step. As **Input field:** select the field `hour` and as **Output field:** type `ktr_name`. Fill in the grid, as shown in the following screenshot:

#	Lower Bound	Upper Bound	Value
1		8.0	hello
2	8.0	20.0	gen_random
3	20.0		get_file_names

Ranges (min <= x< max):

7. From the **Job** category, add a **Set Variables** step and use it to create a variable named KTR_NAME with the value of the field `ktr_name`. For **Variable scope type**, leave the default **Valid in the root job**.

8. Save the transformation and do a preview on the last step. Assuming that it is 3:00 P.M., you should see something like the following:

Rows of step: Set Variable ${KTR_NAME} (1 rows)

#	hour	ktr_name
1	15	gen_random

9. Save the transformation and create a job.

10. Drag a **Start** job entry and two **Transformation** job entries into the canvas. Link the entries one after the other.

11. Configure the first **Transformation** entry to run the transformation just created.

12. Double-click on the second **Transformation** entry. For **Transformation filename:** type `${COMMON_DIR}/${KTR_NAME}.ktr` and close the window.

13. Run the job.

14. Supposing that it is 3:00 P.M., the log should look like the following:

```
2010/12/04 15:00:01 - Spoon - Starting job...
...
... - Set Variable ${KTR_NAME}.0 - Set variable KTR_NAME to value
[gen_random]
...
... - run the transformation - Loading transformation from XML
file [C:/my_kettle_work/common/gen_random.ktr]
...
2010/12/04 15:00:02 - Spoon - Job has ended.
```

15. Browse the output folder (the folder defined in the variable `${OUTPUT_FOLDER}`). You should see a new file named `random.txt` with 10 random numbers in it.

Note that this file is generated whenever you run the transformation between 12:00 P.M. and 20:00 P.M. At a different time of the day, you will see a different output.

How it works...

When you execute a transformation from a job, you can either type the exact name of the transformation, or use a combination of text and variables instead.

In this recipe, you implemented the second option. As you did not know which of the three transformations you had to run, you created a transformation that set a variable with the proper name. Then, in the job, instead of typing the name of the transformation, you used that variable in combination with a variable representing the path to the `.ktr` file. When you ran the job, the first transformation set the name of the transformation to run depending on the current time. Finally, that transformation was executed.

There's more...

In the recipe, you were sure that no matter what the value of the variable `${KTR_NAME}` was, the transformation would exist. If you are not sure, it is recommended that you insert a **File exist** entry before the second **Transformation** entry. This step verifies that a given file exists, which is a great way to ensure that a file is in place before running a process that relies on it. This way, you avoid your job crashing.

If, instead of files you are working with a repository, you can also verify the existence of the transformation. Instead of verifying the existence of a file, you have to run a SELECT statement on the repository database to see if the transformation exists or not. If your transformation is in the root directory of the repository, this is quite simple, but it can become a little more complicated if your transformation is deep in the transformations directory tree.

Finally, all said so far about transformations is valid for jobs as well. In order to run a job, you can either type its exact name or use a combination of text and variables, just as you did in the recipe for running a transformation.

See also

▶ The *Getting information about transformations and jobs (repository-based)* recipe in Chapter 10, *Getting the Most Out of Kettle*

Executing part of a job once for every row in a dataset

Assume that you have a list of things or entities such as students, files, dates, products, and so on. Now, suppose that you want to execute a group of job entries once for every entity in that list.

Suppose that you have a file with a list of names, for example:

```
name
Paul
Santiago
Lourdes
Anna
```

For each person, you want to do the following:

▸ Generate a file saying hello to that person

▸ Wait for 2 seconds

▸ Write a message to the log

For a single person, these tasks can be done with a couple of entries. If you have a small known list of entities (persons in this example), you could copy and paste that group of entries, once for each. On the other hand, if the list is long, or you do not know the values in advance, there is another way to achieve this. This recipe shows you how.

Getting ready

For this recipe, we will use the `Hello` transformation described in the introduction.

The destination folder for the file that is generated is in a variable named `${OUTPUT_FOLDER}` that has to be predefined. Make sure that the folder exists.

You will also need a sample file such as the one described. Both the sample file and the transformation are available for download.

How to do it...

This recipe is split into three parts. The first part is the development of a transformation that generates the list of people. To build the first component, perform the following steps:

1. Create a transformation. This transformation will read the list of people and send the rows outside the transformation for further processing.

2. Read the sample file with a **Text file input** step.

3. After reading the file, add a **Copy rows to result** step. You will find it under the **Job** category.

4. Do a preview on this step. You should see the following screen:

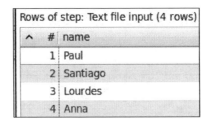

5. Save the transformation.

Now, you will create a job that will generate a file for every person in the list; then deliberately wait for 2 seconds and write a message to the log.

1. Create a job. Add to the job a **START**, a **Transformation**, a **Wait for** (from the **Conditions** category), and a **Write To Log** (from the **Utility** category) entry. Link them one after the other in the same order.

2. Double-click on the **Transformation** entry and configure it to run the `Hello` transformation explained earlier.

3. Double-click on the **Wait for** entry and set the **Maximum timeout** to 2 seconds.

4. Double-click on the **Write To Log** entry. For **Log subject**, type `Information` and for **Log message**, type `A new file has been generated`.

5. The final job should look similar to the following screenshot:

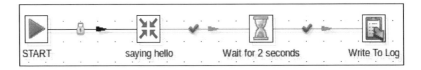

6. Save the job.

Finally, you will create the main job by carrying out the following steps:

1. Create another job. Add to the job a **START**, a **Transformation**, and a **Job** entry. Create a hop from the **START** to the **Transformation** entry, and another hop from this entry toward the **Job** entry.

2. Use the first entry to run the transformation that reads the file and copies the rows to result.

3. Double-click on the second entry. As **Job filename**, select the job that generates a file for a single person, that is, the job created previously.

4. Select the **Advanced** tab and check the **Execute for every input row?** and **Copy previous results to args?** options.

5. Close the setting window and save the job.

6. Run the job. Under the **Job metrics** tab in the **Execution results** window, you will notice that the `saying_hello_to_a_single_person` transformation is firing off for each name.

7. If you explore the output directory, you will find one file for every person in the list. The dates of the files will differ by 2 seconds one from another.

How it works...

You need to execute a couple of entries for every person in the list. The first thing you did was to create a job (let's call it the sub job from now on), encapsulating the functionality you wanted for each person; generate the file, wait for 2 seconds, and write a message to the log.

In order to iterate the execution of the sub job over the list of people, you did the following:

▸ You created a transformation that built the list of people and copied the rows to result.

▸ You created a main job that called that transformation and then executed the sub job once for every person in the list. You did this by clicking on the **Execute for every input row?** option in the **Job** entry. In the **Job Metrics** tab in the **Execution results** pane, you can see it; the execution of the transformation in the first place, followed by four executions of the sub job. Four is the number of people in our example list.

Finally, the **Copy previous results to args?** option that you checked in the **Job** entry caused the copied rows to become available (one at a time) to the sub job and, in particular, to the `Hello` transformation inside the sub job in the form of command-line arguments.

There's more...

When you have a set of entries that you want to execute once for every element in a list, you can do it with the following three steps:

1. Create a transformation that builds the list you need. The stream should end with a **Copy rows to result** step.

2. Create a job with the set of entries that you need to execute for every element in the list.

3. Create a job that first calls the transformation and then calls the job created above. In the **Job** entry settings window, check the **Execute for every input row?** option.

The **Copy rows to result** step causes the rows in the transformation to be copied to the outside.

The **Execute for every input row?** option causes the sub job to be executed as many times as the number of copied rows, unless an error occurs.

If an error occurs while executing the sub job, the iteration is aborted and the main job fails.

 If you want the iteration to continue even if the sub job fails for a single row, modify the sub job by handling the errors properly in order to avoid it failing.

With regard to the copied rows, they will be available one at a time to the sub job. The first execution of the sub job will see the first copied row; the second execution will see the second row, and so on. In the recipe, you accessed the copied rows by checking the **Copy previous results to args?** option, which made the rows available as command-line arguments to the sub job. There are other available options for accessing the copied rows in subsequent job entries, as you will see in the following subsection.

After that, you will see particular use cases for executing entries for every element in a list.

Accessing the copied rows from jobs, transformations, and other entries

When you copy rows by using the **Copy rows to result** step, the copied rows become available to be used by the entries that are executed afterward.

There are four methods for accessing the fields of the copied row in subsequent entries:

Method	How to do it	Entries that support this procedure
Copying them to the arguments of an entry	Checking the **Copy previous results to args?** option	**Transformation, Job, Copy Files, Move Files, Delete files, Delete folders, Zip file, Unzip file, Truncate tables,** and **Add filenames to result.**
Copying them as parameters	Checking the **Copy previous results to parameters?** option	**Transformation, Job**
Getting the rows from result	Using a **Get rows from result** step at the beginning of a transformation	**Transformation**

Method	How to do it	Entries that support this procedure

With JavaScript	Accessing the variable `row`. For example, the following expression gets the value of the field name of the first row:
	
	`rows[0].`
	`getString("name", "")`
		JavaScript

In the recipe, you used the first of these options: you checked the **Copy previous results to args?** option and that caused the rows to become available as the command-line arguments to the `Hello` transformation.

In this particular example, you could also have used the last method. In the `Hello` transformation, instead of reading the name as the command-line parameter `1`, you could have used a **Get rows from result** step obtaining the same results. As implied from the preceding table, you don't have to check the **Copy previous results to args?** option in this case.

Executing a transformation once for every row in a dataset

If, instead of a set of entries you just want to execute a single transformation once for every row in a dataset, you don't have to move it to a sub job. Just leave the Transformation entry in the main job. Double-click on the entry, select the **Advanced** tab, and check the **Execute for every input row?** option. This will cause the transformation to be executed once for every row coming from a previous result.

Executing a transformation or part of a job once for every file in a list of files

If you want to execute part of a job (as a sub job) or a transformation once for every file in a list of files, the procedure is much the same. In the transformation that builds the list, use a **Get File Names** step from the **Input** category in order to create the list of files. After modifying the dataset with the list of files as needed, add a **Copy rows to result** step just as you did in the recipe. The list of files will be sent outside for further processing.

Some novice users are tempted to use the **Set files in result** step instead.

 Do not use the **Set files in result** step for copying to result a row with a list of files. The **Set files in result** step has a completely different purpose compared to the **Copy rows to result** step—it adds files to a **result filelist**. Check the following *See also* section for further information about this.

See also

▶ *Executing a job or a transformation from a job by setting arguments and parameters dynamically*

▶ *Executing part of a job several times until a condition is true*

▶ The *Working with ZIP files* recipe in *Chapter 5, File Management*

▶ The *Copying or moving a custom list of files* recipe in *Chapter 5, File Management*

▶ The *Sending e-mails with attached files* recipe in *Chapter 10, Getting the Most Out of Kettle*

Executing part of a job several times until a condition is true

Suppose that you have a list of tasks that have to be repeated while or until a condition is true (or false). If you know about programming languages, think of this as an analogy of a `while` or `repeat until` loop. Kettle allows you to implement these kinds of iterations and this recipe explains how to do it.

For the recipe, you will use one of the transformations described in the introduction of this chapter—the transformation that generates random numbers and writes them to a file. You will execute the transformation repeatedly and keep track of the number of lines written to those files. You will continue executing the transformation as long as the total number of written lines is less than 25.

Getting ready

You will need the transformation that generates random numbers described in the introduction. If, instead of downloading the transformation you created it yourself, you will have to do a quick fix in order to make Kettle save the number of written lines to the log (this has already been done in the transformation available on the book's site):

1. Edit the transformation.
2. Press *Ctrl + T* to bring up the transformation's setting window.
3. Select the **Logging** tab and click on the **Transformation** heading.

4. In the **Fields to log:** grid, search for the entry named **LINES_OUTPUT**. Under **Step name**, select the name of the step that generates the file of random numbers. The result is shown in the following screenshot:

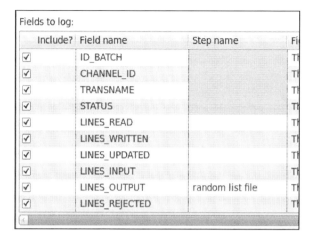

5. Save the transformation.

How to do it...

Perform the following steps:

1. Create a job.

2. From the **General** category, drag the **START**, **Set variables**, and **Transformation** entries. Create a hop from the **START** entry toward the **Set variables** entry, and another from this entry toward the **Transformation** entry.

3. Double-click on the **Set variables** entry. Add a row in order to define the variable that will keep track of the number of lines written. Under **Variable name**, type total_lines, for **Value** type 0, and for **Variable scope type** select **Valid in the current job**.

4. Configure the **Transformation** entry to run the transformation that generates the random numbers.

5. From the **Scripting** category, add a **JavaScript** entry.

6. From the **Utility** category, drag two **Write To Log** entries.

7. Link the entries as shown in the following screenshot:

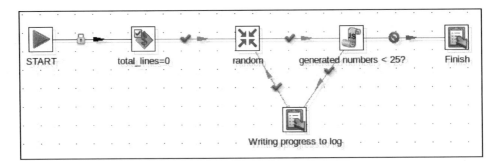

8. Double-click on the **JavaScript** entry. In the **JavaScript:** area, type the following code:

```
var total_lines = parseInt(parent_job.getVariable("total_lines"));
var new_total_lines = total_lines + previous_result.
getNrLinesOutput();
parent_job.setVariable("total_lines", new_total_lines);
new_total_lines < 25;
```

9. Double-click on the **Write To Log** entry that is executed after the success of the **JavaScript** entry (the entry at the end of the green hop). For **Log level**, select **Minimal logging**. For **Log subject**, type `lines written=${total_lines}`. For **Log message** type `Ready to run again`.

10. Double-click on the other **Write To Log** entry, the one that is executed after the failure of the **JavaScript** entry (the entry at the end of the red hop). For **Log level**, select **Minimal logging**. For **Log subject** type `${total_lines} lines have been written`. For **Log message**, type `The generation of random numbers has succeeded`.

11. Save the job.

12. Press *F9* to run the job. For **Log level**, select **Minimal logging** and click on **Launch**.

13. In the **Logging** tab of the **Execution results** pane, you will see the following:

```
2011/01/11 22:43:50 - Spoon - Starting job...
2011/01/11 22:43:50 - main - Start of job execution
2011/01/11 22:43:50 - lines written=10 - Ready to run again ...
2011/01/11 22:43:50 - lines written=20 - Ready to run again ...
2011/01/11 22:43:51 - 30 lines have been written. - The generation
of random numbers has been successful.
2011/01/11 22:43:51 - main - Job execution finished
2011/01/11 22:43:51 - Spoon - Job has ended.
```

14. In order to confirm that 30 lines have actually been written, open the generated files.

How it works...

In order to run the transformation that generates a file with random numbers until the number of written lines is greater than 25, you implemented a loop. The following flowchart shows you the logic of this process:

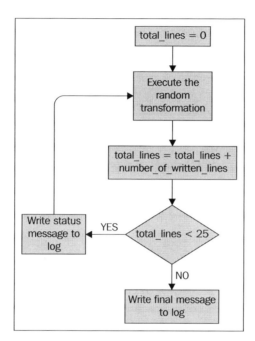

To control the execution of the transformation, you created a variable named total_lines and initialized this variable with the value 0. After executing the transformation, you incremented the value of the variable using JavaScript code. If the value was less than 25, you wrote a message to the log and reran the transformation. If not, you wrote a final message to the log.

The JavaScript code deserves a separate explanation:

previous_result.getNrLinesOutput() is the function that returns the number of lines that were written by the previous job entry. That is the value that you have to add to the total_lines variable in order to keep the variable updated.

The functions parent_job.getVariable() and parent_job.setVariable are meant to get and set the value of the Kettle variable named total_lines. By default, the type of the Kettle variables is String. Therefore, in order to do the math, you had to use the parseInt() JavaScript function.

The fourth line in the JavaScript code evaluates to `True` or `False`. If it evaluates to `True`, the **JavaScript** entry follows the success path (identified with a green arrow in the transformation). If it evaluates to `False`, the **JavaScript** entry follows the failure path (identified with a red arrow in the transformation).

There's more...

In this recipe, you built a loop and controlled the execution with the help of a **JavaScript** entry. The following subsections give you more information about these topics.

Implementing loops in a job

Suppose that you need to build a job in which one or more entries have to be executed repeatedly until a condition is met. People refer to these repetitive tasks as a **loop**. The first thing you have to have in mind is a clear understanding of the logic of this loop, that is, the condition that will cause the exit from the loop. You may want to exit the loop when:

- There are no more files for processing
- The number of errors exceeds a predefined threshold
- The job is taking more time than expected—maybe due to an unavailable service
- The number of records inserted into a table exceeded the expected value and so on

Once you understand this, you have to implement the logic. In the recipe, you implemented the logic with a **JavaScript** job entry. There are other entries that you can use for deciding whether to exit a loop or not. You will find useful entries for this purpose in the **Conditions** category: **Simple evaluation**, **Evaluate file metrics**, **Check webservice availability**, and so on. You can even implement the logic with an extra transformation that will succeed or fail according to your rules.

 Make sure that the number of iterations is small. If you build an endless loop or a loop with many iterations, you risk running out of heap space.

If your loop is causing you problems—for instance, you run out of memory—try to rethink the solution. The following are some alternatives you can think of:

- Solve the same problem by creating a list of elements and iterating over that list
- Consider limiting the number of iterations to a maximum value *n*
- In the logic that determines whether to exit the loop or not, add a condition for ensuring that the number of iterations remains below *n*

Using the JavaScript step to control the execution of the entries in your job

The **JavaScript** entry is a useful step for controlling whether a job entry or a group of job entries should be executed or not. In particular, you used it in the recipe for deciding if the loop should end or not.

This entry works as follows: in its setting window, you should type JavaScript code that ends with an expression that evaluates to a `Boolean`. As with any job entry, the **JavaScript** entry either succeeds or fails. Success or failure is decided by the result of evaluating that expression. Then, based on that value, Kettle knows which entry to execute next.

Within the code, you are free to use the `previous_result` element. The `previous_result` element is the representation of the **result object**—an object that contains the result of the execution of the previous job entry. In the recipe, you used the `previous_result` element to ask for the number of written lines, but you can ask for the number of read lines, the number of errors, the number of executed job entries, and so on. You can find a complete description of the available `previous_result` options at `http://wiki.pentaho.com/display/EAI/Evaluating+conditions+in+The+JavaScript+job+entry`.

See also

► *Executing part of a job once for every row in a dataset*

Creating a process flow

Suppose that you have a dataset with a list of entities such as people, addresses, products, or names of files, just to give some examples. You need to take that data and perform some further processing such as cleaning the data, discarding the useless rows, or calculating some extra fields. Finally, you have to insert the data into a database and build an Excel sheet containing statistics about the just processed information. All of this can be seen as a simple task flow or a **process flow**. With Kettle, you can easily implement a process flow like this.

Suppose that you have a file with a list of names and dates of birth, for example:

```
name,birthdate
Paul,31/12/1969
Santiago,15/02/2004
Santiago,15/02/2004
Lourdes,05/08/1994
Isabella
Anna,08/10/1978
Zoe, 15/01/1975
```

The file may have some duplicates (identical consecutive rows) and some birth dates may be absent. You want to keep only the unique rows and discard the entries of people whose date of birth is missing. Finally, you want to generate a file with the list of people you kept, along with their age sorted by date of birth.

Getting ready

You will need a sample file such as the one shown earlier in this recipe.

How to do it...

You will implement the task flow with two transformations. The first will read the data and clean it according to the earlier requirements and the second will calculate the age and generate the file. So perform the following steps:

1. Create a transformation.

2. With a **Text file input**, read the sample file. Do a preview to make sure you are reading it properly.

3. After that step, add a **Filter rows** step (**Flow** category) and enter the condition `birthdate IS NOT NULL`.

4. Add **Unique rows** (**Transform** category).

5. Finally, add a **Copy rows to result** step. You will find it in the **Job** category. Your final transformation should look like the one in the following screenshot:

6. Do a preview on the last step; you should see the following result:

Rows of step: Copy rows to result (5 rows)		
^ #	name	birthdate
1	Paul	31/12/1969
2	Santiago	15/02/2004
3	Lourdes	05/08/1994
4	Anna	08/10/1978
5	Zoe	15/01/1975

7. Now create the second transformation.

8. From the **Job** category, add a **Get rows from result** step.

Open the **Get rows from result** step and add two fields: a field named `name (String)` and a field named `birthdate (Date)`. The following steps are meant to calculate the age of a person at the present day, given the date of birth:

1. From the **Transform** category, add a **Calculator** step. Open the **Calculator** step and fill in the settings window as shown in the following screenshot:

Fields:

#	New field	Calculation	Field A	Fie	Fie	Value type ^	Lei	Pre	Remove
1	b_year	Year of date A	birthdate			Integer			N
2	b_month	Month of date A	birthdate			Integer			N
3	b_day	Day of month of date A	birthdate			Integer			N

2. From the **Scripting** category, add a **User Defined Java Expression** step (**UDJE** for short). Double-click on it and fill in the grid as shown in the following screenshot:

Fields:

^	#	New field	Java expression	Value type
	1	t_day	java.util.Calendar.getInstance().get(java.util.Calendar.DATE)	Integer
	2	t_month	java.util.Calendar.getInstance().get(java.util.Calendar.MONTH) + 1	Integer
	3	t_year	java.util.Calendar.getInstance().get(java.util.Calendar.YEAR)	Integer

3. Add a fourth field named `calculated_age`. For **Value type**, select **Integer**. For **Java expression** type the following:

```
((b_month > t_month) ||
(b_month == t_month && b_day > t_day))?
(t_year - b_year - 1):(t_year - b_year)
```

4. This expression is written over three lines for clarity. You should type the whole expression on a single line. From the **Transform** category, add a **Sort rows** step. Use it to sort the rows by `birthdate`.

5. Finally, add a **Text file output** step and use it to generate the desired file. Provide a name for the file. For **Separator**, leave the default (;). Fill in the **Fields** grid as shown in the following screenshot:

File	Content	Fields								

^	#	Name	Type	Format	Len	P	Cu	D	G	Trim Type
	1	name	String							both
	2	birthdate	Date	dd/MM/yyyy						both
	3	age	Integer	0						both

6. Save the transformation.

Now you will create a job that will execute the transformations in order:

1. Create a job and add a **START** and two **Transformation** entries and link them one after the other.

2. Configure the entries to run the transformations you just created in the same order. First the transformation that gets the list of people and cleans the data, then the transformation that calculates the age and generates the file.

3. Save the job and run it.

4. Look at the output file. Assuming that today is January 18, 2011, the file should look like the following:

```
name;birthdate;age
Santiago;15/02/2004;6
Lourdes;05/08/1994;16
Anna;08/10/1978;32
Zoe;15/01/1975;36
Paul;31/12/1969;41
```

How it works...

You needed to perform a task defined by the following two subtasks:

1. Read and clean some data about people

2. Calculate their age and generate a sorted file

You implemented the task as a mini process flow made up of two transformations, one for each subtask, and then you embedded the transformations into a job that executed them one after the other. The flow of data between the first and the second transformation was determined by using the **copy/get rows mechanism**. With a **Copy rows to result** step, you sent the flow of data outside the first transformation, and with a **Get rows from result** step in the second transformation, you picked up that data to continue the process flow.

In the recipe, you did a preview on the **Copy rows to result** step and you were able to see the final data that would be sent outside the transformation. Normally you cannot preview the second transformation as is. The **Get rows from result** step is just a definition of the data that will be provided; it has no data for previewing.

While you are designing a transformation starting with a **Get rows from result** step, you can provisionally replace that step with a step that provides some fictional data, for example, a **Text file input**, a **Generate rows**, a **Get System Info**, or a **Data Grid** step.

This fictional data has to have the same metadata as defined in the **Get rows from result** step. This will allow you to preview and test your transformation before using it as part of your process flow.

Note that the tasks performed in this recipe could easily be done in a single transformation. We split it into two for demonstration purposes only.

The next section explains in detail when and why you should consider splitting a process into several transformations.

There's more...

There is no limit to the number of transformations that can be chained using this mechanism. You may have a transformation that copies the rows, followed by another that gets the rows and copies again, followed by a third transformation that gets the rows, and so on.

In most cases, it is possible to put them all into a single transformation. Despite this, there are still some reasons for splitting the tasks up and creating a process flow. Look at some examples:

- The transformation is so big that it's worthwhile splitting it into smaller transformations for simplicity.

- You want to separate different parts of the transformation for re-use. In the example, you might want to use the cleaned list of people for a purpose beyond that of generating a file with their ages. You can re-use the first transformation on another process without modifying it.

- You want to separate different parts of the transformation for maintainability. In the example, if you know new rules for cleansing the data (suppose that now you have to remove special characters such as quotes or brackets from the name field), you just have to modify the first transformation leaving the second untouched.

The copy of the rows is made in memory. While this is useful when you have small datasets, for larger ones you should choose one of the following alternatives:

Serializing/De-serializing data

For transferring a dataset between transformations, there is an alternative approach—the **serialize/de-serialize mechanism**. There are two main differences between this and the copy/get rows mechanism, which are as follows:

- ▶ With the serialize/de-serialize mechanism, the copy of the rows is made in files (where performance is based on hard disk speeds) rather than in memory

- ▶ The serialize/de-serialize mechanism copies not only the data but the metadata as well

Let's see it applied to our recipe.

To change the method from copy/rows to serialize/de-serialize, perform the following steps:

1. In the first transformation, replace the **Copy rows to result** step with a **Serialize to file** step from the **Output** category.

2. Double-click on the step and provide a name for the file in the **Filename** text box.

3. In the second transformation, replace the **Get rows from result** step with a **De-serialize from file** step, found in the **Output** category.

4. Double-click on the step and in the **Filename** textbox and type the same filename you typed in the **Serialize to file** step.

5. Execute the first transformation; a file with the given name should have been generated.

6. Do a preview in the **De-serialize from file** step; you will see the data copied from the first transformation.

If you run the job, you should obtain the same results as you obtained using the main recipe. For large datasets this method is recommended over the previous one. This method is also practical for datasets that have many columns or where the number or order of columns changes over time. As the metadata is saved in the file along with the data, you are not required to specify the details in the second transformation.

 Note that the file generated with a **Serialize to file** step has a binary format and cannot be read with a text editor.

Other means for transferring or sharing data between transformations

As mentioned earlier, a simple way for transferring or sharing data between transformations is by the use of the copy/get rows mechanism. A step further is the use of the serialize/de-serialize method. Now, suppose that you need the data for some extra purpose besides transferring it between these two transformations. For example, suppose that you need to send it to someone by e-mail. Neither of those methods will work in this case. As said, the first copies the data via memory and the second saves the data to an unreadable file. In this case, you have other alternatives, such as saving the data in a text file or to a database table in the first transformation, and then creating the dataset from the file or table in the second transformation.

The database method is also the preferred method in the case where you are dealing with large datasets. Staging large quantities of data on disk should be avoided if possible.

Moving part of a transformation to a subtransformation

Suppose that you have a part of a transformation that you would like to use in another transformation. A quick way to do that would be to copy the set of steps and paste them into the other transformation, and then perform some modifications, for example, changing the names of the fields accordingly. Now you realize that you need it in a third place. You do that again: copy, paste, and modify.

What if you notice that there was a bug in that part of the transformation? Or maybe you'd like to optimize something there? You would need to do that in three different places! This inconvenience is one of the reasons why you might like to move those steps to a common place—a **subtransformation**.

In this recipe, you will develop a subtransformation that receives the following two dates:

▶ A date of birth

▶ A reference date

The subtransformation will calculate how old a person was (or will be) at the reference date if the date of birth provided was theirs.

For example, if the date of birth is December 30, 1979 and the reference date is December 19, 2010, the age would be calculated as 30 years.

Then, you will call that subtransformation from a main transformation.

Getting ready

You will need a file containing a list of names and dates of birth, for example:

```
name,birthdate
Paul,31/12/1969
Santiago,15/02/2004
Lourdes,05/08/1994
Anna,08/10/1978
```

How to do it...

This recipe is split into two parts. First, you will create the subtransformation by carrying out the following steps:

1. Create a transformation.

2. From the **Mapping** category, add two **Mapping input specification steps** and one **Mapping output specification** step. Rename this step `output`.

3. Also, add a **Join Rows (Cartesian product)** (**Join** category), a **Calculator** (**Transform** category), and a **User Defined Java Expression** or **UDJE** for short (**Scripting** category) step. Link the steps as shown in the following screenshot:

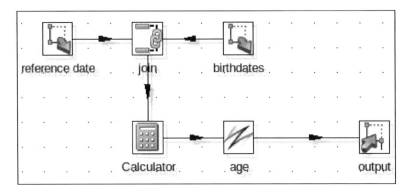

4. Double-click on one of the **Mapping input specification** steps. Add a field named `birth_field`. For **Type**, select **Date**. Name the step `birthdates`.

5. Double-click on the other **Mapping input specification** step. Add a field named `reference_field`. For **Type**, select **Date**. Name the step `reference date`.

6. Double-click the **Join** step. For **Main step to read from**, select **birthdates**.

The following two steps perform the main task—the calculation of the age:

 Note that these steps are a slightly modified version of the steps you used for calculating the age in the previous recipe.

1. Double-click on the **Calculator** step and fill in the settings window, as shown in the following screenshot:

Fields:

^	#	New field	Calculation	Field A	Fie	Fi	Value type	Le	P	Remove
	1	b_year	Year of date A	birth_field			Integer			N
	2	b_month	Month of date A	birth_field			Integer			N
	3	b_day	Day of month of date A	birth_field			Integer			N
	4	t_year	Year of date A	reference_field			Integer			N
	5	t_month	Month of date A	reference_field			Integer			N
	6	t_day	Day of month of date A	reference_field			Integer			N

2. Double-click on the **UDJE** step. Add a field named `calculated_age`. As **Value type**, select **Integer**. For **Java expression** type:

```
((b_month > t_month) ||
(b_month - t_month ==0  && b_day > t_day))?
(t_year - b_year - 1):(t_year - b_year)
```

 The expression is written over three lines for clarity. You should type the whole expression on a single line.

3. Save the transformation.

Now you will create the main transformation. It will read the sample file and calculate the age of the people in the file as at the present day.

1. Create another transformation.

2. Use a **Text file input** step to read the sample file. Name the step `people`.

3. Use a **Get System Info** step to get the present day and add a field named `today`. For **Type**, select **Today 00:00:00**. Name the step `today`.

4. From the **Mapping** category, add a **Mapping (sub-transformation)** step. Link the steps as shown in the following screenshot:

5. Double-click on the **Mapping** step. The following are the most important steps in this recipe!

6. In the first textbox, under the text **Use a file for the mapping transformation,** select the transformation created earlier.

7. Click on the **Add Input** button. A new **Input** tab will be added to the window. Under this tab, you will define a correspondence between the incoming step people and the subtransformation step birthdates.

8. In the **Input source step name**, type people, the name of the step that reads the file.

9. Alternatively, you can select it by clicking on the **Choose...** button. In the **Mapping target step name**, type birthdates—the name of the subtransformation step that expects the dates of birth.

10. Click on **Ask these values to be renamed back on output?**.

11. Under the same tab, fill in the grid as follows: under **Fieldname from source step** type birthdate, the name of the field coming out of the **people** step containing the date of birth. Under **Fieldname to mapping input step**, type birth_field—the name of the field in the subtransformation step **birthdates** that will contain the date of birth needed for calculating the age.

[Alternatively, you can add the whole line by clicking on **Mapping...** and selecting the matching fields in the window that is displayed.]

12. Add another **Input** tab. Under this tab, you will define a correspondence between the incoming step today and the subtransformation step reference date. Fill in the tab as follows:

13. Finally, click on **Add Output** to add an **Output** tab. Under this tab, click on **Is this the main data path?**

14. Under the same tab, fill in the grid as follows: under **Fieldname from mapping step**, type `calculated_age`. Under **Fieldname to target step**, type `age`. Close the mapping settings window and save the transformation.

15. Do a preview on the last step; you should see the following screen:

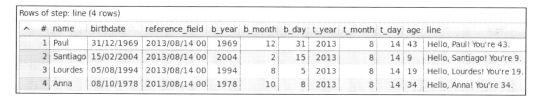

How it works...

The subtransformation (the first transformation you created) has the purpose of calculating the age of a person at a given reference date. In order to do that, it defines two entry points through the use of the **Mapping input specification** steps. These steps are meant to specify the fields needed by the subtransformation. In this case, you defined the date of birth in one entry point and the reference date in the other. Then it calculates the age in the same way you would do with any regular transformation. Finally, it defines an output point through the **Mapping output specification** step.

Note that we developed the subtransformation blindly, without testing or previewing. This was because you cannot preview a subtransformation. The **Mapping input specification** steps are just a definition of the data that will be provided; they have no data to preview.

> While you are designing a subtransformation, you can provisionally substitute each **Mapping input specification** step with a step that provides some fictional data, for example, a **Text file input**, a **Generate rows**, a **Get System Info**, or a **Data Grid** step.

This fictional data for each of these steps has to have the same metadata as the corresponding **Mapping input specification** step. This will allow you to preview and test your subtransformation before calling it from another transformation.

Now, let's explain the main transformation, the one that calls the subtransformation. You added as many input tabs as entry points to the subtransformation. The input tabs are meant to map the steps and fields in your transformation to the corresponding steps and fields in the subtransformation. For example, the field that you called `today` in your main transformation became `reference_field` in the subtransformation.

On the other side, in the subtransformation, you defined just one output point. Therefore, under the **Output** tab, you clicked on **Is this the main data path?**. Selecting it means that you don't need to specify the correspondence between steps. What you did under this tab was fill in the grid to ask the field `calculated_age` be renamed to `age`.

In the final preview, you can see all the fields you had before the subtransformation, plus the fields added by it. Among these fields, there is the `age` field which was the main field you expected to be added.

As you can see in the final dataset, the field `birthdates` kept its name, while the field `today` was renamed to `reference_field`. The field `birthdates` kept its name because you checked the **Ask these values to be renamed back on output?** option under the **people** input tab. On the other hand, the field `today` was renamed because you didn't check that option under the **today** input tab.

There's more...

Kettle sub-transformations are a practical way to centralize some functionality so that it may be used in more than one place. Another use of sub-transformations is to isolate a part of a transformation that meets some specific purpose as a whole, in order to keep the main transformation simple, no matter whether you will re-use that part or not.

Let's look at some examples of what you might like to implement via a subtransformation:

- Take some free text representing an address, parse it, and return the street name, street number, city, zip code, and state.
- Take some text, validate it according to a set of rules, clean it, for example by removing some unwanted characters and return the validated clean text along with a flag indicating whether the original text was valid or not.
- Take an error code and write a customized line to the Kettle log.
- Take the date of birth of a person and a reference date and calculate how old that person was at the reference date.

If you then wish to implement any of the following enhancements, you will need to do it in one place:

- ▸ Enhance the process for parsing the parts of an address
- ▸ Change the rules for validating the text
- ▸ Internationalize the text you write to the Kettle log
- ▸ Change the method or algorithm for calculating the age

From the development point of view, a subtransformation is just a regular transformation with some input and output steps connecting it to the transformations that use it.

Back in *Chapter 7, Understanding and Optimizing Data Flows*, it was explained that when a transformation is launched, each step starts a new thread, that is, all steps work simultaneously. The fact that we are using a subtransformation does not change that. When you run a transformation that calls a subtransformation, both the steps in the transformation and those in the subtransformation start at the same time, and run in parallel. The subtransformation is not an isolated process; the data in the main transformation just flows through the subtransformation. Imagine this flow as if the steps in the subtransformation were part of the main transformation. In this sense, it is worth noting that a common cause of error in the development of subtransformations is the wrong use of the **Select values** step. For instance, selecting some values with a **Select values** step by using the **Select & Alter** tab in a subtransformation will implicitly remove not only the rest of the fields in the subtransformation, but also all of the fields in the transformation that calls it.

 If you need to rename or reorder some fields in a subtransformation, make sure you check the **Include unspecified** fields and the **ordered by name** option in order to keep not only the rest of the fields in the subtransformation but also the fields coming from the calling transformation.

If what you need is to remove some fields, do not use the **Select & Alter** tab; use the **Remove** tab instead. If needed, use another **Select values** step to reorder or rename the fields afterward.

Using Metadata Injection to re-use transformations

Earlier in this chapter, we covered how to re-use transformations and jobs that utilize the same data structures and allowed for smaller portions of transformations to be broken out and used by several different transformations. Another common pattern is repeating a given process, but having a very different dataset flow. For instance, suppose we wanted to pull data from multiple tables and perform the same kind of logic on the data stream without having to write the transformation over for the different data stream. While some of that functionality could be done with Mappings and parameterization of jobs or transformations, Metadata Injection will allow for a transformation to be reused against different data streams based on the metadata of the stream.

Getting ready

For this recipe, we will be reusing the book_news dataset used in earlier chapters. You can find the files used to create this dataset on the book's website.

How to do it...

This recipe will be utilizing two transformations. One will provide the metadata details of a data stream while the other will take the metadata and inject it into a process to output the data from the book's database into a flat file.

The first file we will create is the transformation that will have metadata injected into it to function.

1. Create a new transformation.

2. Bring over a **CSV File Input** step from the pallet. Do not fill in any of the details of the step other than changing the delimiter to |. The other details will be passed in through the **Metadata Injection** step of the other transformation.

3. Add a **Select Values** step from the pallet and add a hop from the **CSV File Input** step to the **Select Values** step. As with the **CSV File Input** step, do not fill in any of the details of the step.

4. Finally, add a **Table Output** step from the pallet. Add a hop from the **Select Values** step to the **Table Output** step. Select the following for the options of the **Table Output** step:

   ❏ **Connection**: books

   ❏ **Target table**: book_stats

5. We need to make sure that the `book_stats` table exists. Run the following script to do so:

```
delimiter $$

CREATE TABLE `book_stats` (
  `book_stats_id` int(11) NOT NULL AUTO_INCREMENT,
  `title` varchar(400) DEFAULT NULL,
  `price` decimal(10,0) DEFAULT NULL,
  PRIMARY KEY (`book_stats_id`)
) ENGINE=InnoDB DEFAULT CHARSET=latin1$$
```

Now that we're ready to process data, let's go ahead and build the transformation that will inject metadata into the transformation we just created.

1. Create a new transformation.

2. Add a **Data Grid** step from the pallet onto the canvas.

3. Fill in the **Meta** tab as follows:

4. On the **Data** tab, add the `${Internal.Transformation.Filename.Directory}/book_news.txt` filename to the grid.

5. Click on **OK** to close the step.

6. Add a second **Data Grid** step from the pallet onto the canvas. This data grid will handle the field names and data types of the data in our `book_news.txt` file.

7. Fill in the **Meta** tab as follows:

8. Fill in the **Data** tab as follows:

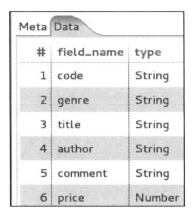

9. Add a third **Data Grid** step. This will list the fields we wish to remove from the stream.
10. Fill in the **Meta** tab with a single field named `field_name`.
11. Fill in the **Data** tab as follows:

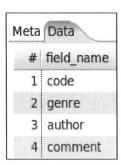

12. Now, add an **ETL Metadata Injection** step from the pallet. Add hops from the three data grid steps to the **ETL Metadata Injection** step.
13. Open the **ETL Metadata Injection** step. Select the first transformation we created for the recipe as the input for the **Use a file for the transformation template** field. Click on **OK** to close the step.
14. Open the **ETL Metadata Injection** step again. The fields that can interface with the **ETL Metadata Injection** step are now filled in and we can fill in the details from our **Data Grid** steps.

15. For the **CSV file input** step, fill in the following details:

16. For the **Select Values** step, fill in the following details:

17. Click on **OK** to exit the **ETL Metadata Injection** step. Save and run the transformation. Reading the data in the `book_stats` table, we see that the empty transformation successfully loaded the book data:

#	book_stats_id	title	price
1	10	The Girl with the Dragon Tattoo	35
2	11	The Girl Who Played with Fire	36
3	12	The Girl Who Kicked the Hornet's Nest	38
4	13	Freedom: A Novel	28
5	14	Eat, Pray, Love: One Woman's Search for Everything Across Italy, India and Indonesia	36
6	15	A Journey: My Political Life	35
7	16	The Business of the 21st Century	24
8	17	Mockingjay	38
9	18	Catching Fire	38
10	19	The Hunger Games	38

How it works...

The **Data Grid** steps provided a static place to store the metadata about both the file that we wanted to load as well as list the functionality that we wanted to perform on the data in the file. By listing what we wanted to do with the data, we were able to apply the various streams to different parts of a generic transformation, building a custom version of the transformation on the fly.

There's more...

While we used Data Grid steps to load stream metadata into the ETL Metadata Injection step, we could also have utilized another step from the Utility section of the pallet called the Metadata structure of stream, which will read the live data stream and return the metadata for it. Metadata can essentially come from any source. As long as it is fed into the ETL Metadata Injection step, transformation logic that has dynamic requirements but similar functionality can re-use the same transformation and load the proper metadata into the steps that support it.

Metadata Injection is able to interact with a growing number of steps. The best place to view what steps can be interacted with (as well as the version of Kettle they were enabled) is on the Pentaho wiki page at `http://wiki.pentaho.com/display/EAI/ETL+Metadata+Injection`.

9
Integrating Kettle and the Pentaho Suite

In this chapter, we will cover:

- ▶ Creating a Pentaho report with data coming from PDI
- ▶ Creating a Pentaho report directly from PDI
- ▶ Configuring the Pentaho BI Server for running PDI jobs and transformations
- ▶ Executing a PDI transformation as part of a Pentaho process
- ▶ Executing a PDI job from the Pentaho User Console
- ▶ Populating a CDF dashboard with data coming from a PDI transformation

Introduction

Kettle, also known as PDI, is mostly used as a standalone application. However, it is not an isolated tool, but part of the **Pentaho Business Intelligence Suite**. As such, it can also interact with other components of the suite, For example, having Kettle act as the data source for a report or a dashboard, or even interfacing with the Pentaho User Console, so that users can run Kettle jobs that clean up their data as needed. This chapter shows you how to run Kettle jobs and transformations in that context.

This chapter assumes a basic knowledge of the **Pentaho Business Intelligence platform** and the tools that make up the Pentaho Suite. If you are not familiar with these tools, it is recommended that you visit the wiki page (`wiki.pentaho.com`) or the **Pentaho BI Suite Community Edition** (**CE**) site: `http://community.pentaho.com/`.

As another option, there is a general reference to the suite called Pentaho Solutions (Wiley) by Roland Bouman and Jos van Dongen that provides a good introduction to the whole suite as well as to data warehousing and business intelligence principles.

A sample transformation

The different recipes in this chapter show you how to run Kettle transformations and jobs, integrated with several components of the Pentaho BI suite. In order to focus on the integration itself, rather than on Kettle development, we have created a sample transformation file named `weather.ktr` that will be used through the different recipes.

The transformation receives the name of a city as the first parameter from the command line, for example `Madrid` and `Spain`. Then, it consumes a web service to get the current weather conditions and the forecast for the next five days for that city. The transformation has a couple of named parameters:

Name	Purpose	Default
TEMP	Scale for the temperature to be returned; it can be C (Celsius) or F (Farenheit)	

The following diagram shows what the transformation looks like:

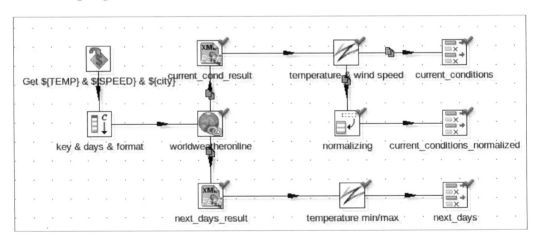

It receives the command-line argument and the named parameters, consumes the service, and retrieves the information in the desired scales for temperature and wind speed.

You can download the transformation from Packt's site and test it. Do a preview on the **next_days**, **current_conditions**, and **current_conditions_normalized** steps to see what the results look like. The following is a sample preview of the **next_days** step:

Rows of step: next_days (5 rows)

∧	#	city	date	temperatureMin	temperatureMax
	1	Orlando, FL	2013-08-26	24	32
	2	Orlando, FL	2013-08-27	23	32
	3	Orlando, FL	2013-08-28	24	32
	4	Orlando, FL	2013-08-29	24	33
	5	Orlando, FL	2013-08-30	25	32

Finally, the following screenshot shows you a sample preview of the **current_conditions_normalized** step:

Rows of step: current_conditions_normalized (11 rows)

∧	#	FEATURE	VALUE
	1	City	Orlando, United States Of America
	2	Observation time	12:45 AM
	3	Weather description	Clear
	4	Temperature	27
	5	Wind speed	17
	6	Wind direction	E
	7	Precipitation	0.8
	8	Humidity	77
	9	Visibility	16
	10	Pressure	1018
	11	Cloud Cover	0

> For details about the web service and understanding the results, you can take a look at the *Specifying fields by using Path notation* recipe in *Chapter 4, Manipulating XML Structures*.

There is also another transformation file named `weather_np.ktr`. This transformation does exactly the same, but it reads the city as a named parameter instead of reading it from the command line. The *Getting ready* sections of each recipe will tell you which of these transformations will be used.

If you are unable to consume the weather web service, it may happen that you do not want to consume the web service (for example, for delay reasons), or you cannot do it (for example, if you do not have Internet access). Besides, if you call a free web service like this too often, then your IP might be banned from the service. Don't worry. Along with the sample transformations on Packt's site, you will find another version of the transformations that, instead of using the web service, reads sample fictional data from a file containing the forecast for over 250 cities. The transformations are `weather (file version).ktr` and `weather_np (file version).ktr`. Feel free to use these transformations instead. You should not have any trouble as the parameters and the metadata of the data retrieved are exactly the same as in the transformations explained earlier.

If you use transformations that do not call the web service, remember that they rely on the file with the fictional data (`weatheroffline.txt`). Wherever you copy the transformations from, do not forget to copy that file as well.

Creating a Pentaho report with data coming from PDI

The **Pentaho Reporting Engine** allows designing, creating, and distributing reports in various popular formats (HTML, PDF, and so on) from different kinds of sources (JDBC, **OLAP (On-line Analytical Processing databases)**, XML, and so on).

There are occasions where you need other kinds of sources such as text files or Excel files, or situations where you must process the information before using it in a report. In those cases, you can use the output of a Kettle transformation as the source of your report. This recipe shows you this capability of the Pentaho Reporting Engine.

For this recipe, you will develop a very simple report. The report will ask for a city and a temperature scale and will report the current conditions in that city. The temperature will be expressed in the selected scale.

Getting ready

A basic understanding of the Pentaho Report Designer tool is required in order to follow this recipe. You should be able to create a report, add parameters, build a simple report, and preview the final result.

Regarding the software, you will need the Pentaho Report Designer. You can download the latest version from the following URL: `http://sourceforge.net/projects/pentaho/files/Report%20Designer/`.

You will also need the sample transformation file, `weather.ktr`.

The sample transformation has a couple of **UDJE** steps. These steps rely on the **Janino** library. In order to be able to run the transformation from Report Designer, you will have to copy the `janino.jar` file from the Kettle `libext` directory into the Report Designer `lib` directory. If Pentaho Report Designer was open when installing the Janino library, it will need to be closed and reopened.

How to do it...

In the first part of the recipe, you will create the report and define the parameters for the report: the city and the temperature scale.

1. Launch Pentaho Report Designer and create a new blank report.

2. Add two mandatory parameters. A parameter named `city_param`, with `Orlando, FL` as **Default Value** and a parameter named `scale_param` which accepts two possible values: `C` meaning Celsius or `F` meaning Fahrenheit.

3. Now, you will define the data source for the report:

4. In the **Data** menu, select **Add Data Source** and then **Pentaho Data Integration**.

5. Click on the **Add a new query** button. A new query named `Query 1` will be added. Give the query a proper name, for example, `forecast`.

6. Click on the **Browse** button. Browse to the sample transformation and select it. The **Steps** listbox will be populated with the names of the steps in the transformation.

7. Select the step `current_conditions`. So far, you have the following:

> The specification of the transformation filename with the complete path will work only inside Report Designer. Before publishing the report, you should edit the filename (<book code location>\weather.ktr in the preceding example) and leave just a path relative to the directory where the report is to be published (for example, reports\weather.ktr).

8. Click on **Preview**; you will see an empty result set. The important thing here is that the headers should be the same as the output fields of the **current_conditions** step: city, observation_time, weatherDesc, and so on.

9. Now, close that window and click on **Edit Parameters**.

10. You will see two grids: **Transformation Parameter** and **Transformation Arguments**. Fill in the grids as shown in the following screenshot. You can type the values or select them from the available dropdown lists:

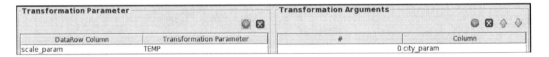

11. Close the **Pentaho Data Integration Data Source** window. You should have the following screenshot:

The data coming from Kettle is ready to be used in your report.

12. Build the report layout. Drag-and-drop some fields into the canvas and arrange them as you please. Provide a title as well. The following screenshot is a sample report you can design:

13. Now, you select **Print Preview**. The sample report above will look like the one shown in the following screenshot:

The output of the **current_condition** step has just one row.

If, for data source, you choose the **next_days** or the **current_condition_normalized** step instead, then the result will have several rows. In that case, you could design a report by columns: one column for each field.

How it works...

Using the output of a Kettle transformation as the data source of a report is useful because you can take advantage of all the functionality of the PDI tool. For instance, in this case, you built a report based on the result of consuming a web service. You could not have done this with Pentaho Report Designer alone.

In order to use the output of your Kettle transformation, you just added a **Pentaho Data Integration** data source. You selected the transformation to run and the step that would deliver your data.

In order to be executed, your transformation needs a command-line parameter: the name of the city. The transformation also defines two named parameters: the temperature scale and the wind scale. From the Pentaho Report Designer you provided both—a value for the city and a value for the temperature scale. You did it by filling in the **Edit Parameter** settings window inside the **Pentaho Data Integration Data Source** window.

You did not supply a value for the SPEED parameter, but that is not necessary because Kettle uses the default value.

As you can see in the recipe, the data source created by the report engine has the same structure as the data coming from the selected step: the same fields with the same names, same data types, and in the same order.

Once you configured this data source, you were able to design your report as you would have done with any other kind of data source.

Finally, when you are done and want to publish your report on the server, do not forget to fix the path as explained in the recipe—the **File** menu should be specified with a path relative to the solution folder. For example, suppose that your report will be published in my_solution/ reports, and you put the transformation file in my_solution/reports/resources. In that case, for **File**, you should type resources/ plus the name of the transformation.

There's more...

Pentaho Reporting is a suite of Java projects built for report generation.
The suite is made up of the Pentaho Reporting Engine and a set of tools such as the Report Designer (the tool used in this recipe), Report Design Wizard, and Pentaho's web-based ad hoc Reporting user interface.

In order to be able to run transformations, the Pentaho Reporting software includes the Kettle libraries. To avoid any inconvenience, be sure that the versions of the libraries included are the same or newer than the version of Kettle you are using. For instance, Pentaho Reporting 3.8 includes Kettle 4.1.2 libraries. If you are using a different version of Pentaho Reporting, then you can verify the Kettle version by looking in the `lib` folder inside the reporting installation folder. You should look for files named `kettle-core-<version>.jar`, `kettle-db-<version>.jar`, and `kettle-engine-<version>.jar`. Besides, if the transformations you want to use as data sources rely on external libraries, you have to copy the proper jar files from the Kettle `libext` directory into the Report Designer `lib` folder, just as you did with the `janino.jar` file in the recipe.

For more information about Pentaho Reporting, just visit the following wiki website:
`http://wiki.pentaho.com/display/Reporting/Pentaho+Reporting+Community+Documentation`.

Alternatively, you can get the book, *Pentaho Reporting 3.5 for Java Developers, Packt Publishing* by Will Gorman.

Creating a Pentaho report directly from PDI

Reports are usually very useful when they are processed as needed for given parameters. Sometimes those parameters are dynamically generated at runtime and are not necessarily known to a user. For this recipe, we will be using the built-in functionality of PDI to process the report created in the previous recipe to find the current weather for a given set of cities.

Getting ready

Before continuing this exercise, you will need the `forecast.prpt` report created in the last recipe. This can be obtained either through Packt's website or by creating the report as per the previous recipe in this chapter.

How to do it...

Follow the steps to generate reports within PDI:

1. Create a new transformation.

2. Add **Data Grid** to the canvas from the pallet. Add two fields:

   - city, type: String
   - scale, type: String

3. On the **Data** tab, add a few cities and a scale of either C or F.

4. Add an **Add constants** step to the canvas. There will be one field in this step:

   - **Name**: report_file
   - **Type**: String
   - **Value**: forecast.prpt

5. Add a **Calculator** step and fill it in with the following details:

^	#	New field	Calculation	Field A	Field B	Field C	Value type
	1	report_tmp	Set field to constant value /	weather for			String
	2	report_type	Set field to constant value /	.csv			String
	3	report_name	A + B + C	report_tmp	city	report_type	String

6. Add **Modified Java Script Value** to the canvas. Enter the following code (courtesy: the sample for Pentaho Report Generation):

```
var Report_Template;
var Report_Output;


// Create full path combining transformation directory + filename
Report_Template = getVariable("Internal.Transformation.Filename.
Directory"," ")+"/"+ report_file;
Report_Output = getVariable("Internal.Transformation.Filename.
Directory"," ")+"/"+ report_name;

// Trim the leading 'file:C///' characters from the full path
Report_Template = substr(Report_Template,6);
Report_Output = substr(Report_Output,6);
```

7. Two fields should be generated from the script: **Report_Template** and **Report_Output**.

8. Finally, add a **Pentaho Reporting Output** step to the canvas. Your transformation should now look similar to the following screenshot:

9. Open the **Pentaho Reporting Output** step. Click on the **Get Report Parameters** button and find the `forecast.prpt` file. The report's parameters will be filled into the parameter data grid. Fill in the step's options as shown:

10. Click on **OK**, save, and run the transformation. A CSV file for each city entered in the data grid should now be generated.

How it works...

A Pentaho reporting file stores all the details about the report (including how to get it's data) which makes it easy to use with the **Pentaho Reporting file output** step. In the transformation we created a list of cities, what scale we wanted the temperature to return as, where the report file lives, and how we wanted the name of the output to be formatted.

We can pass pretty much any variables we want to a report and get the desired output.

There's more...

To make this transformation even more interesting, we can perform more complicated actions such as e-mailing the report files out to desired recipients or move them to another server for further processing. The flexible capabilities of Pentaho allow for almost any use case.

See also

▸ *Creating a Pentaho report with data coming from PDI*

▸ The *Sending e-mails with attached files* recipe in *Chapter 10, Getting the Most Out of Kettle*

▸ The *Putting files on a remote server* recipe, in *Chapter 5, File Management*

Configuring the Pentaho BI Server for running PDI jobs and transformations

The Pentaho BI Server is a collection of software components that provide the architecture and infrastructure required to build business intelligence solutions. With the Pentaho BI Server, you are able to run reports, visualize dashboards, schedule tasks, and more. Among these tasks, there is the ability to run Kettle jobs and transformations. This recipe shows you the minor changes you might have to make in order to be able to run Kettle jobs and transformations.

Getting ready

In order to follow this recipe, you will need some experience with the Pentaho BI Server.

For configuring the Pentaho BI server, you obviously need the software. You can download the latest version of the Pentaho BI Server from the following URL: `http://sourceforge.net/projects/pentaho/files/Business%20Intelligence%20Server/`.

 Make sure you download the distribution that matches your platform.

If you intend to run jobs and transformations from a Kettle repository, make sure you have the name of the repository and proper credentials (username and password).

How to do it...

Perform the following steps:

1. If you intend to run a transformation or a job from a file, skip to the *How it works...* section.

2. Edit the `settings.xml` file located in the `\biserver-ce\pentaho-solutions\ system\kettle` folder inside the Pentaho BI Server installation folder.

3. In the `repository.type` tag, replace the default value `files` with `rdbms`. Provide the name of your Kettle repository and the username and password, as shown in the following example:

```
<kettle-repository>

   <!-- The values within <properties> are passed directly to the
Kettle Pentaho components. -->

   <!-- This is the location of the Kettle repositories.xml file,
leave empty if the default is used: $HOME/.kettle/repositories.xml
-->
   <repositories.xml.file></repositories.xml.file>

   <repository.type>rdbms</repository.type>

   <!--  The name of the repository to use -->
   <repository.name>pdirepo</repository.name>

   <!--  The name of the repository user -->
   <repository.userid>dev</repository.userid>

   <!--  The password -->
   <repository.password>1234</repository.password>

</kettle-repository>
```

4. Start the server. It will be ready to run jobs and transformations from your Kettle repository.

How it works...

If you want to run Kettle transformations and jobs, then the Pentaho BI server already includes the Kettle libraries. The server is ready to run both jobs and transformations from files. If you intend to use a repository, you have to provide the repository settings. In order to do this, you just have to edit the `settings.xml` file, as you did in the recipe.

There's more...

To avoid any inconvenience, be sure that the version of the libraries included are the same or newer than the version of Kettle you are using. For instance, Pentaho BI Server 4.8 includes Kettle 4.4 libraries. If you are using a different version of the server, then you can verify the Kettle version by looking in the following folder: `\biserver-ce\tomcat\webapps\pentaho\WEB-INF\lib`.

This folder is inside the server installation folder. You should look for files named `kettle-core-<version>.jar`, `kettle-db-<version>.jar`, and `kettle-engine-<version>.jar`. The Version will be the actual version of the files (for instance, `kettle-core-4.4.1-GA.jar`).

There is even an easier way: in the **Pentaho User Console** (**PUC**), go into the `BI Developer Examples` folder under the `Samples` folder and look for the `Data Integration with Kettle` folder. Within the `Data Integration with Kettle` folder, look for option 2, **Get Environment Information**. Run it and you will get detailed information about the Kettle environment.

> For your information, the transformation that is run behind the scenes is `GetPDIEnvironment.ktr` located in the `biserver-ce\pentaho-solutions\bi-developers\etl` folder.

See also

- ▸ *Executing a PDI transformation as part of a Pentaho process*
- ▸ *Executing a PDI job from the Pentaho User Console*

Executing a PDI transformation as part of a Pentaho process

Everything in the Pentaho platform is made of action sequences. An **action sequence** is, as its name suggests, a sequence of atomic actions that together accomplish small processes. Those atomic actions cover a broad spectrum of tasks, for example, getting data from a table in a database, running a piece of JavaScript code, launching a report, sending e-mails, or running a Kettle transformation. For this recipe, suppose that you want to run the sample transformation to get the current weather conditions for some cities. Instead of running this from the command line, you want to interact with this service from the PUC. You will do it with an action sequence.

Getting ready

In order to follow this recipe, you will need a basic understanding of action sequences and at least some experience with the Pentaho BI Server and **Pentaho Design Studio**, the action sequences editor.

Before proceeding, make sure that you have a Pentaho BI Server running. You will also need Pentaho Design Studio. You can download the latest version from the following URL: `http://sourceforge.net/projects/pentaho/files/Design%20Studio/`.

Finally, you will need the sample transformation `weather.ktr`.

How to do it...

This recipe is split into two parts: first, you will create the action sequence, and then you will test it from the PUC. So perform the following steps:

1. Launch Design Studio. If this is your first use, then create the solution project where you will save your work.
2. Copy the sample transformation to the solution folder.
3. Create a new action sequence and save it in your solution project with the name `weather.xaction`.
4. Define two inputs that will be used as the parameters for your transformation: `city_name` and `temperature_scale`.
5. Add two **Prompt/Secure Filter** actions and configure them to prompt for the name of the city and the temperature scale.
6. Add a new process action by selecting **Get Data From | Pentaho Data Integration**.
7. Now, you will fill in the **Input Section** of the process action configuration. Give the process action a name.
8. For **Transformation File**, type `solution:weather.ktr`. For **Transformation Step**, type `current_conditions_normalized` and for **Kettle Logging Level**, type or select **basic**.
9. In **Transformation Inputs**, add the inputs `city_name` and `temperature_scale`.
10. Select the **XML source** tab.
11. Search for the `<action-definition>` tag that contains the following line:

    `<component-name>KettleComponent</component-name>`

12. You will find something like this:

    ```
    <action-definition>
    <component-name>KettleComponent</component-name>
      <action-type>looking for the current weather</action-type>
    ```

```
<action-inputs>
  <city_name type="string"/>
  <temperature_scale type="string"/>
</action-inputs>
<action-resources>
  <transformation-file type="resource"/>
</action-resources>
<action-outputs/>
<component-definition>
  <monitor-step><![CDATA[current_conditions]]></monitor-step>
  <kettle-logging-level><![CDATA[basic]]></kettle-logging-
    level>
</component-definition>
</action-definition>Below <component-definition>, type the
following:
<set-parameter>
    <name>TEMP</name>
    <mapping>temperature_scale</mapping>
</set-parameter>

<set-argument>
    <name>1</name>
    <mapping>city_name</mapping>
</set-argument>
```

In fact, you can type this anywhere between `<component-definition>` and `</component-definition>`. The order of the internal tags is not important.

13. Go back to the tab named **2. Define Process**.

14. Now, fill in **Output Section** of the **Process Data Integration** process action. For **Output Rows Name**, type `weather_result` and for **Output Rows Count Name**, type `number_of_rows`.

15. Below the **Process Data Integration** process action, add **If Statement**. As the condition, type `number_of_rows==0`.

16. Within **If Statement**, add a **Message Template** process action.

17. In the **Text** frame, type `No results for the city {city_name}`. For **Output Name**, type `weather_result`.

18. Finally, in the **Process Outputs** section of the action sequence, add **weather_result** as the only output.

19. Your final action sequence should look like the one shown in the following screenshot:

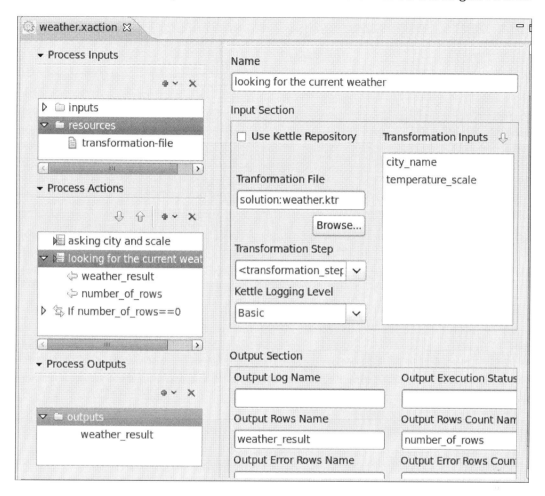

20. Save the file.

Now, it is time to test the action sequence that you just created:

1. Log in to the PUC and refresh the repository, so that `weather.xaction` that you just created shows up.

2. Browse the solution folders and look for **xaction** and double-click on it.

3. Provide the name of a city and change the temperature scale, if you wish.

4. Click on **Run**; you will see a page generate with the names and values of the weather data.

5. You can take a look at the Pentaho console to see the log of the transformation running behind the scenes.

6. Run the action sequence again. This time, type the name of a fictional city, for example, `my_invented_city`. This time, you will see the following message:

```
Action Successful
weather_result=No results for the city my_invented_city
```

How it works...

You can run Kettle transformations as part of an action sequence by using the **Pentaho Data Integration process action** located within the **Get Data From** category of process actions.

The main task of a PDI process action is to run a Kettle transformation. In order to do that, it has a list of checks and textboxes where you specify everything you need to run the transformation and everything you want to receive back after having run it.

The most important setting in the PDI process action is the name and location of the transformation to be executed. In this example, you had a `.ktr` file in the same location as the action sequence, so you simply typed `solution:` followed by the name of the file.

Then, in the **Transformation Step** textbox, you specified the name of the step in the transformation that would give you the results you needed. The PDI process action (just as any regular process action) is capable of receiving input from the action sequence and returning data to be used later in the sequence. Therefore, in the dropdown list in the **Transformation Step** textbox, you could see the list of available action sequence inputs. In this case, you just typed the name of the step.

If you are not familiar with action sequences, note that the dropdown list in the **Transformation Step** textbox is not the list of available steps. It is the list of available action sequence inputs.

You have the option of specifying the Kettle log level. In this case, you selected **Basic**. This was the level of log that Kettle wrote to the Pentaho console. Note that, in this case, you also have the option of selecting an action sequence input instead of one of the log levels in the list.

As said earlier, the process action can use any inputs from the action sequence. In this case, you used two inputs: `city_name` and `temperature_scale`. Then you passed them to the transformation in the XML code:

▶ By putting `city_name` between `<set-parameter></set-parameter>`, you passed the `city_name` input as the first command-line argument.

▶ By putting `temperature_scale` between `<set-argument></set-argument>`, you passed `temperature_scale` to the transformation as the value for the named parameter `TEMP`.

As mentioned, the process can return data to be used later in the sequence. The textboxes in the **Output Section** are meant to do that. Each textbox you fill in will be a new data field to be sent to the next process action. In this case, you defined two outputs: `weather_result` and `number_of_rows`. The first contains the dataset that comes out of the step you defined in **Transformation Step**, in this case, `current_conditions_normalized`. The second has the number of rows in that dataset.

You used those outputs in the next process action. If `number_of_rows` was equal to zero, then you would overwrite the `weather_result` data with a message to be displayed to the user. Finally, you added `weather_result` as the output of the action sequence, so that the user either sees the current conditions for the required city, or the custom message indicating that the city was not found.

There's more...

The following are some variants in the use of the Pentaho Data Integration process action.

Specifying the location of the transformation

When your transformation is in a file, you specify the location by typing or browsing for the name of the file. You have to provide the name relative to the solution folder. In the recipe, the transformation was in the same folder as the action sequence, so you simply typed `solution:` followed by the name of the transformation including the extension `ktr`.

If instead of having the transformation in a file, it is located in a repository, you should check the **Use Kettle Repository** option. The **Transformation File** textbox will be replaced with two textboxes named **Directory** and **Transformation File**. In these textboxes, you should type the name of the folder and the transformation exactly as they are in the repository. Alternatively, you can select the names from the available dropdown lists.

> In these dropdown lists, you will not see the available directories and transformations in the repository. The lists are populated with the available action sequence inputs. This also applies to specifying the location of a job in an action sequence.

Supplying values for named parameters, variables and arguments

If your transformation defines or needs named parameters, Kettle variables or command-line arguments, you can pass them from the action sequence by mapping **KettleComponent** inputs.

First of all, you need to include them in the **Transformation Inputs** section. This is equivalent to typing them inside the KettleComponent action-definition XML element.

Then, depending on the kind of data to pass, you have to define a different element:

Element in the transformation	Element in the action sequence	Description
Command line parameter	`<set-argument></set-argument>`	Values that normally get passed via `kitchen.sh` or `pan.sh` (that is, log level, logfile location, and so on)
Variable	`<set-variable></set-variable>`	Values that normally are passed via `kettle.properties`
Named parameter	`<set-parameter></set-parameter>`	Values that are passed as part of a job or transformation

In the recipe you mapped one command- line argument and one named parameter.

With the following lines, you mapped the input named `temperature_scale` with the named parameter `TEMP`:

```
<set-parameter>
    <name>TEMP</name>
    <mapping>temperature_scale</mapping>
</set-parameter>
```

In the case of a variable, the syntax is exactly the same.

In the case of arguments instead of a name, you have to provide the position of the parameter: `1`, `2`, and so on.

Design Studio does not implement the capability of mapping inputs with variables or named parameters. Therefore, you have to type the mappings in the XML code. If you just want to pass command-line arguments, you can skip this task. Because, by default, it is assumed that the inputs you enter are command-line arguments.

This way of providing values for named parameters, variables, and command-line arguments also applies to jobs executed from an action sequence.

Keeping things simple when it's time to deliver a plain file

Reporting is a classic way of delivering data. In the PUC, you can publish not only Pentaho reports, but also third-party ones, such as Jasper reports, for example. However, what if the final user simply wants a plain file with some numbers in it? You can avoid the effort of creating it with a reporting tool. Just create a Kettle transformation that does it and call it from an action, in the same way you did in the recipe. This practical example is clearly explained by *Nicholas Goodman* in his blog post, *Self Service Data Export using Pentaho*. The following is the link to that post, which also includes sample code for downloading: `http://www.nicholasgoodman.com/bt/blog/2009/02/09/self-service-data-export-using-pentaho/`.

See also

▸ *Configuring the Pentaho BI Server for running PDI jobs and transformations*

▸ *Executing a PDI job from the Pentaho User Console*

Executing a PDI job from the Pentaho User Console

Pentaho User Console (**PUC**) is a web application included with the Pentaho Server, conveniently built for you to generate reports, browse cubes, explore dashboards, and more. Among the list of tasks, is the ability to run Kettle jobs. As mentioned in the previous recipe, everything in the Pentaho platform is made up of action sequences. Therefore, if you intend to run a job from the PUC, you have to create an action sequence that does it.

For this recipe, you will use a job that simply deletes all files with extension .tmp found in a given folder. The objective is to run the job from PUC through an action sequence.

Getting ready

In order to follow this recipe, you will need a basic understanding of action sequences and at least some experience with the Pentaho BI Server and **Pentaho Design Studio**, the action sequences editor.

Before proceeding, make sure you have a Pentaho BI Server running. You will also need Pentaho Design Studio; you can download the latest version from the following URL: `http://sourceforge.net/projects/pentaho/files/Design%20Studio/`.

you will also need a job like the one described in the introduction to the recipe. The job should have a named parameter called `TMP_FOLDER`; simply delete all files with extension .tmp found in that folder.

You can develop the job before proceeding (call it `delete_files.kjb`), or download it from Packt's site. Finally, pick a directory on your computer (or create one) with some .tmp files for deleting.

How to do it...

This recipe is split into two parts: First, you will create the action sequence and then you will test the action sequence from the PUC.

1. Launch Design Studio. If it is the first time you have launched, create the solution project where you will save your work.

2. Copy the sample job to the solution folder.

3. Create a new action sequence and save it in your solution project with the name `delete_files.xaction`.

4. Define an input that will be used as the parameter for your job: `folder`. As **Default Value**, type the name of the folder with the `.tmp` files, for example, `c:\myfolder`.

5. Add a process action by selecting **Execute | Pentaho Data Integration Job**.

6. Now, you will fill in **Input Section** of the process action configuration. Give the process action a name.

7. As **Job File**, type `solution:delete_files.kjb`.

8. In the **Job Inputs**, add the only input you have: `folder`.

9. Select the **XML source** tab.

10. Search for the `<action-definition>` tag that contains the following line:

    ```
    <component-name>KettleComponent</component-name>
    ```

11. You will find something similar to the following:

    ```
    <action-definition>
          <component-name>KettleComponent</component-name>
          <action-type>Pentaho Data Integration Job</action-type>
          <action-inputs>
            <folder type="string"/>
          </action-inputs>
          <action-resources>
            <job-file type="resource"/>
          </action-resources>
          <action-outputs/>
          <component-definition/>
    </action-definition>
    ```

12. Replace the `<component-definition/>` tag with the following:

    ```
    <component-definition>
      <set-parameter>
        <name>TMP_FOLDER</name>
        <mapping>folder</mapping>
      </set-parameter>
    </component-definition>
    ```

13. Save the file.

Now, it is time to test the action sequence that you just created:

1. Log in to the Pentaho BI Server and refresh the repository.

2. Browse the solution folders and look for the `delete_files` action you just created. Double-click on it.

3. You should see a window with the legend **Action Successful**.

4. You can take a look at the Pentaho console to see the log of the job.

5. Take a look at the folder defined in the input of your action sequence. There should be no `.tmp` files.

How it works...

You can run Kettle jobs as part of an action sequence by using **Pentaho Data Integration Job process action** located within the **Execute** category of process actions.

The main task of a **PDI Job** process action is to run a Kettle job. In order to do that, it has a series of checks and textboxes where you specify everything you need to run the job, and everything you want to receive back after having run it.

The most important setting in the PDI process action is the name and location of the job to be executed. In this example, you had a `.kjb` file in the same location as the action sequence, so you simply typed `solution:` followed by the name of the file.

You can specify the Kettle log level, but it is not mandatory. In this case, you left the log level empty. The log level you select here (`Basic`, by default) is the level of log that Kettle writes to the Pentaho console when the job runs.

Besides the name and location of the job, you had to provide the name of the folder needed by the job. In order to do that, you created an input named `folder` and then you passed it to the job. You did it in the XML code by putting the name of the input enclosed between `<set-parameter>` and `</set-parameter>`.

When you ran the action sequence, the job was executed deleting all `.tmp` files in the given folder.

 The action sequence in this recipe has just one process action (the PDI Job). This was made on purpose to keep the recipe simple, but it could have had other actions as well, just like any action sequence.

There's more...

The main reason for embedding a job in an action sequence is for scheduling its execution with the Pentaho scheduling services. This is an alternative approach to the use of a system utility such as cron in Unix-based operating systems or the **Task Scheduler** in Windows.

See also

▸ *Configuring the Pentaho BI Server for running PDI jobs and transformations*

▸ *Executing a PDI transformation as part of a Pentaho process*

Generating files from the PUC with PDI and the CDA plugin

As you know, PDI allows you to generate Excel, CSV, and XML files and, starting with the latest version, also JSON files. You do it with a transformation that has to be executed from Spoon or the command line. There is a quicker way to generate those kinds of files in an interactive fashion from PUC. This recipe teaches you how to do it by using the **Community Data Access (CDA)** plugin.

You will experiment with the **CDA Editor** and the **CDA Previewer** for querying the current weather conditions in a given city. Then, you will learn how to export the results to different formats. You will do that from PUC.

Getting ready

In order to follow this recipe, you will need some experience with the Pentaho BI Server.

Regarding the software, you will need a Pentaho BI Server running. You will also need the CDA plugin. You can download the installer from `http://cda.webdetails.org` or the source code from `http://code.google.com/p/pentaho-cda/`.

> The **Community Dashboard Editor** (**CDE**) includes CDA. Therefore, if you have CDE installed, just skip the CDA installation. You can also install CDA from the BI Server Marketplace (found under **Tools | Marketplace**).

Finally, you will need the sample transformation `weather_np.ktr`.

How to do it...

This recipe is split in two parts. In the first part, you will create a CDA file for getting the data you need. In the second part, you will export the results.

So, perform the following steps in order to complete the first part:

1. Create the solution project where you will save your work.

2. Inside the folder of your project, copy the `weather_np.ktr` transformation into your project directory.

3. Also inside that folder, create an empty file with a `.cda` extension. Name it `weather.cda`.

4. Log in to the Pentaho User Console and refresh the repository. You should see the solution folder with the file that you just created.

5. Right-click on the file and select **Edit**. A new tab window should appear with the CDA Editor ready to edit your CDA file, as shown in the following screenshot:

6. The white area is where you will type the CDA file content. Type the skeleton of the file:

```xml
<?xml version="1.0" encoding="UTF-8"?>
<CDADescriptor>
    <data sources>
    </data sources>
```

7. `</CDADescriptor>`Inside the `<data sources>` tag, type the connection to the Kettle transformation:

```xml
<Connection id="weather" type="kettle.TransFromFile">
<KtrFile>weather_np.ktr</KtrFile>
   <variables datarow-name="CITY"/>
   <variables datarow-name="Scale" variable-name="TEMP"/>
</Connection>
```

8. Now you will define a data access to that data source. In CDA terminology, this is a query over the preceding connection. Below the closing tag `</data sources>`, type the following:

```
<DataAccess access="public"
             cache="true"
             cacheDuration="3600"
             connection="weather"
             id="current"
             type="kettle">
  <Columns/>
  <Parameters>
    <Parameter default="Orlando, FL"
               name="CITY"
               type="String"/>
    <Parameter default="C"
               name="Scale"
               type="String"/>
  </Parameters>
  <Query>current_conditions_normalized</Query>
  <Output indexes="0,1"/>
</DataAccess>
```

9. Click on the **Save** button located at the top of the editor window.

10. Click on **Preview** and a new window is displayed with the CDA Previewer.

11. In the dropdown list, select the data access that you just defined.

12. Take a look at the Pentaho server console. You should see how the `weather_np` transformation is being executed. The following is an excerpt of that log:

```
... - weather_np - Dispatching started for transformation
[weather_np]
... - Get ${TEMP}, ${SPEED} and ${CITY} - Finished processing
(I=0, O=0, R=1, W=1, U=0, E=0)
... - key & days & format - Finished processing (I=0, O=0, R=1,
W=1, U=0, E=0)
... - worldweatheronline - Finished processing (I=0, O=0, R=1,
W=2, U=0, E=0)
... - ...
... - current_conditions_normalized - Finished processing (I=0,
O=0, R=11, W=11, U=0, E=0)
```

13. In the previewer, you will see the results of the CDA query.

14. Try changing the values for the parameters: `city` and `temperature` scale.

15. Click on **Refresh** and the data should be refreshed accordingly.

16. Now that you have a CDA file with a connection and a data access, let's export some results to `.csv` format.

17. Copy the URL of the previewer and paste it into a new tab window of your browser. Assuming that you are running the server on localhost, and your solution is in the folder `pdi_cookbook/CDA`, the complete URL should look like the following URL: `http://localhost:8080/pentaho/content/cda/previewQuery?path=pdi_cookbook/CDA/weather.cda`.

> By double-clicking on the CDA file, the editor opens in a tab inside the PUC. This prevents you from copying the URL.
>
> In order to be able to copy the URL, double-click on the tab that contains the CDA Editor. Alternatively, you can right-click on the CDA file and select **Open in New Window**.

18. In the URL, replace `previewQuery` with `doQuery`.

19. At the end of the URL, add the following:

```
&dataAccessId=current
&paramCITY=›Buenos Aires, Argentina›
&paramScale=F
&outputType=csv
```

> These parameters are written in four lines for simplicity. You should type all in a single line one next to the other.

20. Press **Enter**. A `csv` will be generated that should look like the following:

```
FEATURE;VALUE
City;Buenos Aires, Argentina
Observation time;06:25 PM
Weather description;Moderate or heavy rain in area
Temperature;91
Wind speed;24
Wind direction;W
Precipitation;0.2
Humidity;53
Visibility;3
Pressure;9982
Cloud Cover;100
```

How it works...

In this recipe, you exported the results of a Kettle transformation to a `.csv` file from the PUC. In order to do that, you used CDA.

First, you created a CDA file. You edited it with the CDA Editor. The purpose of this file was to firstly define a connection to the Kettle transformation and then a query over that connection. Let's explain them in detail.

The connection or CDA data source is the definition of the source of your data, in this case, a Kettle transformation. The following is the definition of your connection:

```
<Connection id="weather" type="kettle.TransFromFile">
  <KtrFile>weather_np.ktr</KtrFile>
  <variables datarow-name="CITY"/>
  <variables datarow-name="Scale" variable-name="TEMP"/>
</Connection>
```

The `id` element must be unique in the CDA file. The `type="kettle.TransFromFile"` portion identifies this as a connection to a Kettle transformation. You provide the name of the Kettle transformation inside the tags `<KtrFile></KtrFile>`.

Then you have the variables. The variables are the means for passing parameters from CDA to Kettle; `datarow-name` is the name you use in the CDA file, while `variable-name` is the name of the Kettle named parameter. For example, the named variable `TEMP` defined in the transformation is referred to as `Scale` inside the CDA file.

> If both names coincide, you can just put `datarow-name` and omit `variable-name`, as in the case of the `CITY` variable.
>
> Each variable you define in a CDA connection of type `kettle`, `TransFromFile` must be defined as a named parameter in the transformation. That was the reason for using the transformation `weather_np.ktr` instead of `weather.ktr`.

Now, let's have a look at the CDA query. A CDA `DataAccess` is a query over a CDA data source. In the case of Kettle, a CDA `DataAccess` has the details of a Kettle transformation execution. A CDA query is enclosed inside a tag named `DataAccess`:

```
<DataAccess access="public"
    cache="true"
    cacheDuration="3600"
    connection="weather"
    id="current"
    type="kettle">
</DataAccess>
```

Here you define a unique data access ID (`id="current"`), the data access type (`type="kettle"`), and the connection (`connection="weather"`). The connection must be declared earlier in the same file.

The `<columns></columns>` tag is useful if you want to rename the columns or perform operations between them, which was not the case here. Therefore, you left it empty.

Then you have a parameters section:

```
<Parameters>
  <Parameter default="Orlando, FL"
              name="CITY"
              type="String"/>
  <Parameter default="C"
              name="Scale"
              type="String"/>

</Parameters>
```

Here you define one `<Parameter>` tag for each parameter you want to pass to the transformation. The parameters you type here will be available in the CDA Previewer for you to change.

> In order to be able to pass the parameters, they have to be defined in the data source as explained earlier.

Inside the `<Query></Query>` tag, you type the name of the transformation step that returns the data you need. The sample transformation has three steps that return data: `current_conditions`, `current_conditions_normalized`, and `forecast`. You typed the second of these steps.

Finally, the `<Output>` tag is meant to indicate which columns you want and in which order. The output fields of the `current_conditions_normalized` step are `FEATURE` and `VALUE`. You wanted both fields and in the same order, therefore, you typed `indexes="0,1"`.

> You can edit the CDA files in any text editor. Just remember that if you do not use the CDA Editor, you should periodically refresh the solution repository in order to be able to preview them.

Once you created the contents of the file, you saved it, and previewed the results with the CDA Previewer. This previewer shows the results as a table.

After previewing the results, you experimented with the **doQuery** feature of the **CDA API**.

> The Community Data Access API documentation provides more details on all the functions of CDA and how it can interact with other Pentaho components. It is available from Web Details at http://www.webdetails.pt/ctools/cda.html.

The `doQuery` function allows you to export the results of a data access to different formats. In order to run a `doQuery`, you have to provide the following parameters:

Parameter	Description	Example
`dataAccessId`	ID of the DataAccess to run	`dataAccessId=current`
`param + <name of param.>`	One of this for each parameter you want to pass to the transformation	`paramCITY='Buenos Aires, Argentina'`
`outputType`	Desired output type. Available output types: `Json` (default if the parameter is omitted), `csv`, `Excel`, and `XML`	`outputType=csv`

The parameters you provided in the recipe (shown in the preceding table) meant: run the DataAccess with ID `current`, supplying the parameter `CITY` with values `Buenos Aires, Argentina` and `Scale` with value `F`, and give me a `.csv` file with the results.

There's more...

CDA is a plugin for the Pentaho BI Suite developed by **Webdetails**, one of the main Pentaho Community Contributors and now a member of the Pentaho family.

CDA was designed as an abstraction tool between sources of information, for example, Kettle transformations, databases, or **Mondrian** cubes, and the CDF. As such, it is mainly used in the context of Pentaho Dashboards.

However, it also serves for exporting data to different formats from the PUC. That was exactly what you did in the recipe.

If you are interested in knowing more about CDA, then you will find the complete documentation at the following URL: `http://cda.webdetails.org`.

Populating a CDF dashboard with data coming from a PDI transformation

A dashboard, in its broad sense, is an application that shows you visual indicators, for example, bar charts, traffic lights, or dials. A **CDF** dashboard is a dashboard created with the **Community Dashboard Framework**. CDF accepts many kinds of data sources, the output of a Kettle transformation being one of them.

In this recipe you will create a very simple dashboard that shows this capability. You will type the name of a city and the dashboard will display graphically the 5-days forecast for that city. The forecast information will be obtained with the sample transformation explained in the introduction.

Getting ready

In order to follow this recipe, you will need minimal experience with the Pentaho BI Server. Some experience with the CDE is also desirable.

Before proceeding, make sure you have a Pentaho BI Server running. You will also need the CDE. You can download it from `http://cde.webdetails.org`. To install it, simply unzip the downloaded material and follow the instructions in the `INSTALL.txt` file. Alternatively, you can download CDE through the Marketplace found under `Tools > Marketplace`.

Finally, you will need the sample transformation `weather_np.ktr`.

How to do it...

Perform the following steps:

1. Log in to the Pentaho User Console.

2. Create the solution folder where you will save your work.

3. Copy the sample transformation to the solution folder and refresh the repository.

4. From the **File** menu, select **New | CDE Dashboard** or click on the CDE icon in the toolbar.

5. Save the dashboard in the solution folder that you just created, close the dashboard window, and refresh the repository. A new file with extension `wcdf` will appear in the solution folder.

6. Go to the solution folder, right-click on the dashboard file and select **Edit**. The dashboard editor will appear. Maximize the window, so that you can work more comfortably.

7. Define the dashboard layout by adding rows and columns from the layout toolbar, until you get the following screen:

8. Now, let's add the visual elements of the dashboard: click on **Components** from the menu at the top-right area of the editor.

9. From the **Generic** category, add **Simple parameter**. Name it `city_param` and type `Orlando, FL` for **Property value**.

10. From the **Selects** category, add a **TextInput Component**. Name it `city_text box`. For **Parameter**, select **city_param** and for **HtmlObject**, select **filter_panel**.

11. Click on **Save** on the menu at the top of the editor.

12. Click on **Preview**; you will see the dashboard with a textbox prompting for the `city_name` parameter, showing the default value `Orlando, FL`.

13. Close the preview window.

14. Now, you will add the chart that will display the forecast. From the **Charts** category, add **CCC Bar Chart**.

15. Fill in the properties as follows:

    - For **Name**, type `forecast_bars`
    - For **Width**, type `350`
    - For **Height**, type `250`
    - For **data source**, type `forecast`
    - For **Crosstab mode**, select **True**
    - For **Title**, type `5-days forecast`
    - For **HtmlObject**, select `chart_panel`
    - For **Listeners**, select `city_param`

16. Click on the **Parameters** property and, in the window that displays, add one parameter. For **Arg0**, type `CITY` and for **Val0**, type `city_param`, and then click on **Ok**.

Finally, you have to create the data source for that chart: `forecast`. The following steps will do it:

1. Click on **Data Sources** from the menu at the top-right area of the editor. In the list of available data sources, click on **KETTLE Queries** and select **kettle over kettleTransFromFile**. A new data source will be added.

2. Fill in the list of properties as explained in the following steps.

3. For **Name**, type `forecast`.

4. For **Kettle Transformation File**, type `weather_np.ktr`.

5. Click on **Variables** and in the window that displays, click on **Add**. For **Arg0**, type `CITY` and click on **Ok**.

6. Click on **Parameters** and in the window that displays, click on **Add**.

    - For **Arg0**, type `CITY`
    - For **Val0** type `Orlando, FL`
    - For **Type0** leave the default **String** and click on **Ok**.

7. Click on **Output Options** and in the window that shows up, click on **Add** three times. For **Arg0**, **Arg1**, and **Arg2**, type 1, 2, and 3 respectively and click on **Ok**. Click on **Column Configurations** and, in the window that displays, click on **Add** twice. In the first row, type 2 for **Arg0** and MIN for **Val0**. In the second row, type 3 for **Arg1** and MAX for **Val1**.

8. Click on the little square to the side of the **Query** property. The **Sql Wizard** shows up. In the editing area, type next_days and click on **Ok**.

9. Save the dashboard by clicking on **Save** and click on **Preview** to see the dashboard. You should see a result similar to that shown in the following screenshot:

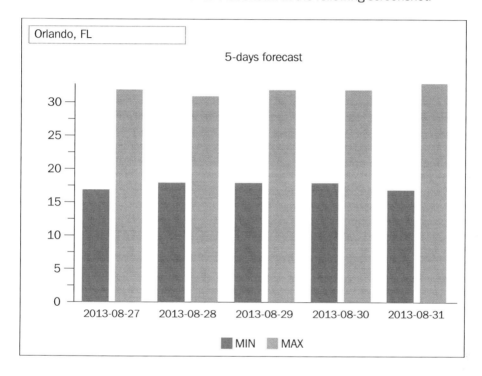

10. If you take a look at the Pentaho console, then you will see the log of the Kettle transformation that is executed.

11. Try changing the value for the city and press *Enter.* The chart should be refreshed accordingly.

How it works...

In this recipe, you created a very simple dashboard. The dashboard allows you to enter the name of a city and then refreshes a bar chart displaying the 5-days forecast for that city. The special feature of this dashboard is that it gets data from a web service through the execution of a Kettle transformation.

In order to use the output of your Kettle transformation the as data source, you just have to add a new data source from **KETTLE Queries | kettle over kettleTransFromFile** and configure it properly. This configuration involves providing the following properties:

Property	Meaning / Purpose	Example
Name	Unique data source name inside the dashboard.	`forecast`
Kettle Transformation File	Name of the transformation file.	`weather_np.ktr`
Variables	Name of variables that are passed to the transformation. You have to provide it in pairs (`<CDE parameter>`,`<Kettle named parameter>`) or (`<CDE parameter>`,`""`) if both coincide.	`"CITY",""`
Access Level	`Public` (available from outside) / `Private` (available only from other data sources)	`Public`
Parameters	Name, default value, and type for each parameter to be passed to the transformation.	`"CITY", "Orlando, FL", "String"`
Output Options (opt)	Indexes of the columns to pick among the fields coming out from the transformation.	`1,2,3`
Column Configurations (opt)	Renaming the columns coming out from the transformation.	`2,"MIN"`
Column Configurations II (opt)	Calculating new columns based on other columns.	`AVG, (MAX + MIN)/2`
Query	Name of the step that delivers the data.	`next_days`
Cache	Keep results in cache (True/False).	`TRUE`
Cache Duration	Time to keep the results in cache in seconds.	`3600`

Once you configured your Kettle transformation as a data source, it was ready to be used in the components of your dashboard.

There's more...

CDF is a community project whose objective is mainly to integrate dashboards in the Pentaho's solution repository structure. In the recipe, you used the CDE, which is a graphical editor that complements the power of the CDF engine. With CDE, you can create dashboards without having to get involved in the low-level details of the CDF files, thus focusing on the business requirements.

Kettle is just one of several kinds of data sources accepted by CDF. Behind the scenes, most of the data sources definitions are saved in a CDA file.

> If you already have a CDA file that has a data access for your transformation, you can avoid configuring the data source twice and use the **Community Data Access | CDA data source** instead.

CDF is bundled with the Pentaho BI Suite, but maintained by Webdetails with the help of the community. For more information about CDF, see the full documentation in the following website: `http://cdf.webdetails.org`. For more on CDE visit `http://cde.webdetails.org`.

10
Getting the Most Out of Kettle

In this chapter, we will cover:

- ▶ Sending e-mails with attached files
- ▶ Generating a custom logfile
- ▶ Running commands on another server
- ▶ Programming custom functionality
- ▶ Generating sample data for testing purposes
- ▶ Working with JSON files
- ▶ Getting information about transformations and jobs (file-based)
- ▶ Getting information about transformations and jobs (repository-based)
- ▶ Using Spoon's built in optimization tools

Introduction

The recipes in this chapter cover a variety of topics that don't fit into any of the previous categories. The topics range from customizing a Kettle log to understanding the structure of a Kettle database repository. Feel free to browse the pages and see if there is a recipe that fits your needs.

Sending e-mails with attached files

Nowadays, it is very common to use e-mails to exchange digital messages from one author to several recipients. These e-mails can also have a list of files attached that will be sent along with the message. Kettle offers job entries and transformation steps that allow the sending of e-mails with attached files. In this recipe, you will use the **Email job** entry to send an e-mail with a set of files attached with a particular condition: the files must have been modified after a given date.

Getting ready

You need a directory named `filesToAttach` containing sample files. You will also need access to an SMTP server. You can use the `smtp.gmail.com` server. You also need at least one valid account to play with.

How to do it...

Carry out the following steps:

1. Create a new transformation.

2. Drop **Get Files Names** from the **Input** category.

3. Under the **File** tab, type or browse for the `filesToAttach` folder in the **File or directory** textbox. Type `.*` in the **Regular Expression** textbox and click on the **Add** button to populate the **Selected files** grid.

4. Under the **Filter** tab, uncheck the **Add filename to result** checkbox.

5. Add a **Filter rows** step from the **Flow** category. Here, add a new condition, select the field `lastmodifiedtime`, the operator `'`, and enter a constant value date to compare with, for example, `2010/11/01`. Don't forget to select the **Conversion format** expression to match the date format.

6. Add a **Set files in result** step (**Job** category).

7. Create a hop from the **Filter rows** step towards this step. When asked for the kind of hop, select **Main output of step**. The transformation will look similar to the one shown in the following screenshot:

8. Double-click on the **Set file in result** step. Select **filename** in the **Filename** field, and **General** in the **Type of file** to prompt.

9. Create a new job, and drop a **START** job entry into the canvas.

10. Add a **Transformation** job entry from the **General** category.

11. Double-click on this job entry and type the complete path of the previously created transformation (or browse for it) in the **Transformation filename** textbox.

12. Add a **Mail validator** job entry from the **email** category. In this step, type the destination account in the **Email address** textbox.

13. Add a **Mail** job from the **Mail** category.

14. Under the **Addresses** tab, fill in the **Destination address** textbox and the **Sender address** textbox with two valid e-mail addresses (they can be the same if you only have one account to play with). In addition, you need to complete the **Sender name** textbox. For example, you can type your name.

 You can specify more than one account, using a space as a separator in the **destination address** of the **email** and **Mail validator** job entries.

15. Complete the **Server** tab as shown in the following screenshot:

 You need to fill the **Authentication user** and **Authentication** textboxes with a valid user and password. If your account is user@gmail.com, you have to type user in the **Authentication user** textbox, and your e-mail password in the **Authentication** textbox.

The default **port** for the **SMTP Server** is 465, but if you use a secure connection through TLS, then the default is 587.

16. Under the **Email Message** tab, complete the **Subject** textbox and the **Comment** area with sample text. Also, check the **Only send comment in the mail body?** checkbox.

17. Select the **Attached Files** tab and check the option **Attach file(s) to message?**.

18. Select the option **General** in the **Select file type** listbox.

19. Check the **Zip files to single archive?** checkbox. Type a filename in the **Name of zip archive** textbox (for example, `files.zip`).

20. Running the job, an e-mail will be sent to the destination address (if it is valid). It will include an attached ZIP file with all of the files from the `filesToAttach` folder that fulfill the date condition.

How it works...

The first task in the example was to create a transformation that gets the files that will be sent as an attachment with the e-mail. For this, you used the **Get Files Names** step to get the files inside the `filesToAttach` folder, and then the **Filter rows** step to filter the files with `lastmodifiedtime` greater than a specific date, in this case, `2010/11/01`. Only the files that pass this condition will be set in the result. Remember to uncheck the **Add filename to result** checkbox in the **Get Files Names** step, because you don't want all the files, only the result after the row filtering.

The job runs this transformation, and then executes the **Email** job entry. This job is quite self-explanatory. Under the **Addresses** tab, you must complete the destination and sender e-mails addresses, and the e-mail content under the **Email Message** tab. The example uses Gmail's SMTP server (`smtp.gmail.com`), but you can use any e-mail server as long as you have access to the information required in the **Server** tab. Take a look at the firewall configuration if you have problems reaching the specified address.

Under the **Attached Files** tab, you selected the file type option named `General`; this indicates that all the files included in the result list will be attached to the e-mail. In addition, you configured the entry to zip all files into a single file.

If the previous jobs or transformations also added files to results, then those files will be attached as well. Therefore, a **Delete filenames from result** job entry might be required at the beginning of this job. You used the **Mail validator** job entry to verify the e-mail address structure. If the structure is not correct, then the **Email** job entry will not run. You could use the **SMTP check?** checkbox here, if you want to validate the existence of the accounts.

There's more...

You will find more features about sending e-mails in the following subsections:

Sending logs through an e-mail

Let's assume that you want to include the log of the transformation inside the attached ZIP file. This is very simple; just double-click on the **Transformation** entry job and set the logfile under the **Logging settings** tab, as shown in the following screenshot:

You can specify a more detailed level of log in the **Loglevel** listbox if you want.

Then, you need to include this file as an attached file. Double-click on the **email** job entry, select the **Attached Files** tab, and select the **Log** item in the **Select file type** list box. As you need to select both **General** and **Log** items, you have to do it by pressing the *Ctrl* key:

After running the job, an e-mail will still be sent, but this time, the ZIP file attached will also contain a new file named `logFile.log` with the log information.

Sending e-mails in a transformation

There is a transformation step named **Mail**, in the **Utility** category, which is very similar to the **Mail** job entry. The main difference is that the **Mail** step sends one e-mail for each existent row.

Its configuration has listboxes instead of textboxes to refer to different settings (addresses, server configuration, subject, body, and so on). Here you should refer to existing fields instead of typing them.

In some cases, you could use either the step or the job entry with similar results, but there are particular scenarios where one approach is better than the other. For example:

> ► If you need to send several e-mails to different destination addresses and/or with different content, and/or with different attached files, it is better to use the **Mail** transformation step.

> ► If you need to send an e-mail with some information about the executed process—for example, the time that it took to execute it—you must use the **Mail** job entry.

> ► If you need to send only one e-mail with attached files coming from different jobs or transformations, you should use the **Mail** job entry.

> ► For an advanced example of using the **Mail** step for mailing, you can follow the given link: `http://kjube.blogspot.com/2011/01/mailing-new-years-cards.html`. The blog post by **KJube** explains a transformation that sends best wishes for New Year to a list of people. The following two considerations arise about the example provided: the transformation uses the **Excel Writer** plugin step. If you are working with Kettle 4.1, you should install the plugin in order to open the transformation. That's not the case for Kettle 4.2, in which the plugin is already included as an **Experimental** step.

> ► The values for the **Server** configuration and **Sender name** and **Sender address** are stored in Kettle variables; they don't change from row to row. However, as explained earlier, you cannot type the values directly in the step configuration window. You should refer to existing fields instead. Therefore, it is necessary to get those variables in a previous step.

Generating a custom logfile

When you run a transformation or a job, all of what is happening in the process is shown in the **Execution Results** window, which has a tab named **Logging** where you can check the execution of your transformation step by step. By default, the level of the logging detail is **Basic**, but you can change it to show different levels of detail.

Under the **Logging** tab, you can see information about how the step is performing, for example, the number of rows coming from previous steps, the number of rows read, the number of rows written, errors in execution, and so on. All this data is provided by the steps automatically, but what if you want to write your custom messages to the **Logging** information? To do this, there is a step and an entry named **Write to log**, in the **Utility** folder.

To put them into practice, let's take a simple transformation that reads a text file with book novelties and splits them into two Excel files depending on their price. The objective here is to include, in the **Logging** window, custom messages about the incoming number of books and also how many of these books are cheap or expensive.

Getting ready

For checking this recipe, you will need a text file that includes information about book title's novelties. For example:

```
title;author_id;price;title_id;genre
Bag of Bones;A00002;51,99;123-353;Fiction
Basket Case;A00003;31,00;123-506;Fiction
Carrie;A00002;41,00;123-346;Fiction
Cashflow Quadrant;A00007;55,00;323-604;Business
Harry Potter and the Half-Blood Prince;A00008;61,00;423-005;Childrens
Harry Potter and the Prisoner of Azkaban;A00008;29,00;423-
003;Childrens
Power to the People;A00005;33,00;223-302;Non-fiction
Who Took My Money;A00007;21,00;323-603;Business
```

You can download the sample file from Packt's website.

How to do it...

Carry out the following steps:

1. Create a new transformation.

2. Drop a **Text file input** step into the canvas. Set the file to read under the **File** tab, and type ; as the character **Separator** under the **Content** tab. Finally, use the **Get Fields** button under the **Fields** tab to populate the grid automatically. Previewing this step, you will obtain the data of the books from the text file. Now, let's add the steps for counting the books and writing the information.

3. Add a **Group by** step from the **Statistics** folder. Create a hop from the text file to this step. In the **Aggregates** grid at the bottom, add a new field named `qty`, choose a field (for example, `title_id`) in the **Subject** column, and select the **Number of Values (N)** option in the **Type** column.

4. Add a **User Defined Java Expression** from the **Scripting** category and link it to the previous step. Create a new field named `line` of `String` type with the following Java expression:

```
"Book news = " + Java.lang.Long.toString(qty)
```

5. From the **Utility** folder, add a **Write to log** step and create a hop from the previous step towards this one; name it `Write books counting`. Add the **line** field to the **Fields** grid. Choose **Basic logging** in the **Log level** listbox.

6. Run the transformation using **Basic logging** and check the **Logging** tab for the results.

7. You can verify the basic logging information where you should see the following line:

```
2011/01/25 10:40:40 - Write books counting.0 - Book news = 8
```

Now, you will generate two Excel files and write the information about cheap and expensive books to the log:

1. Drop one **Filter rows**, two **Excel output**, two **Group by**, two **UDJE**, two **Block this step until steps finish** (from **Flow** category), and two **Write to log** steps into the canvas. Link the steps, as shown in the following screenshot:

2. Create a hop from the **Text file input** step to the **Filter rows** step. Here, set the condition `price <= 50`. We will use an arbitrary price of $50 to determine if a book is cheap or expensive.

3. Point one **Excel Output** step filename to `cheapBooks.xls`, and use the **Get Fields** button to populate the grid under the **Fields** tab.

4. In the **Group by** step, add a new field named `qty` in the **Aggregates** grid, choose the field `title_id` in the **Subject** column, and select the **Number of Values (N)** option in the **Type** column.

5. Add a field named `line` of `String` type in the **UDJE** step with the following Java expression:

```
"Cheap books = " + Java.lang.Long.toString(qty)
```

6. In the **Block this step until steps finish** steps, select the step named **Write books counting** in the **step name** column of the grid.

7. Finally, in the **Write to log** step, add the **line** field to the **Fields** grid and choose **Basic logging** in the **Log level** listbox.

8. Now, repeat the last five steps in order to configure the lower stream. This time, use the **Excel Output** step (named `Excel Output 2`) to generate the `expensiveBooks.xls` file and replace the text `Cheap` for `Expensive` in the other **UDJE** step.

Running the transformation using **Basic logging**, you can verify that your custom messages have been written to the log under the **Logging** tab. Here's an example:

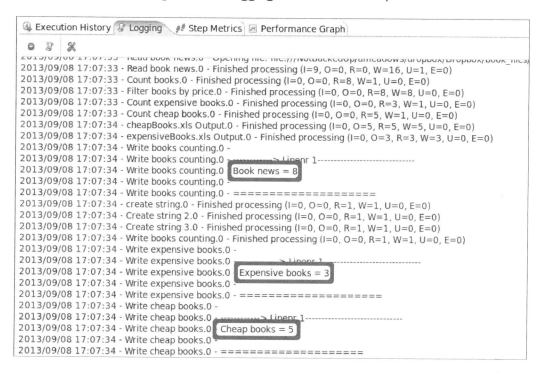

How it works...

The main objective in this recipe is to explain how you can write personalized messages to the logging windows. The task of the transformation is simple—it reads a text file at the beginning, uses a **Filter rows** step to split the list of books into cheap and expensive ones, and then writes two Excel spreadsheets with these details.

Now, let's analyze the task of customizing the log. In the first part of the recipe you wrote into the log the number of books:

▸ The **Group by** step does the counting

▸ The **UDJE** step creates the personalized string in a new field

▸ Finally, the **Write to log** step writes this string to the log

After each of the **Excel output** steps, there is the same sequence of steps (**Group by**, **UDJE**, and **Write to log**), in order to write a message with the number of cheap books and the number of expensive books into the log. There is also a **Block this step until steps finish** step in this sequence before the **Write to log** step; this is because you want to be sure that the total number of books will be written first.

There's more...

This recipe showed you the classic way for adding messages to the log. The following subsections show you some variants or alternative approaches.

Filtering the logfile

Instead of adding text to the log, you may want to filter text in the existing log.

If you select the **Logging** tab in the **Execution Results** window, you will see a toolbar. Under that toolbar, there is a button named **Log settings** that allows you to apply a filter. If you type some text into the **Select filter** textbox, the log of the subsequent executions of the transformation will only show the lines that contain that text. For example, you could use the same text prefix in all of your custom messages, and then apply a filter using this fixed text to see only those messages.

This also works if you run the transformation from a job, and even if you restart Spoon because the filter is saved in a Kettle configuration file.

This is valid only in Spoon. If you intend to run a job or a transformation with Pan or Kitchen and you need to filter a log, for example, by keeping only the lines that contain certain words, then you have to take another approach. One way for performing that would be to save the job or transformation log in a file and then run another transformation that parses and filters that logfile.

Creating a clean logfile

The **Logging** window shows not only your messages, but also all of the information processed by the steps. Sometimes you need a clean logfile showing only your custom messages and discarding the rest.

There is another problem related to that—when you configure the **Write to log** step, you need to specify a level for your log. (in the recipe, you used `Basic logging`.) If you run your transformation using a different log level, you will not see any of your personalized messages. One alternative would be using a **Text file output** instead of the **Write to log** step. With this, you will produce a new text file with only your desired messages. Be sure to point all of the **Text file output** steps to the same filename under the **File** tab, and use the **Append** checkbox under the **Content** tab, in order to avoid overwriting the file with each run.

Isolating logfiles for different jobs or transformations

It is possible that you want to see different log levels depending on the job or transformation, or that you simply want to isolate the log for a particular job or transformation. This is a simple task to accomplish. In the main job, right-click on the **Job** or **Transformation** entry of interest; under the **Logging settings** tab check the **Specify logfile?** option and you will be able to specify a name for the logfile as well as the log level desired. In this way, you can create different logfiles with different log levels for each of the **jobs** and **transformations** that are part of your main job.

See also

▸ _Sending e-mails with attached files_
▸ _Programming custom functionality_

Running commands on another server

There are many times in which data integration code needs to be augmented by other processes, or perhaps trigger other processes after a job or transformation finishes. Kettle has built-in steps that can execute scripts on local and remote servers and make it part of a normal job process.

For this recipe, we will execute some basic shell commands on another server and return the results. There are two ways to execute commands, one via the job and another via the transformation. This recipe will show an example of both.

Getting ready

While we are showing steps that can connect to other servers with this recipe, we will be running commands locally. The process is virtually identical, with the exception that the connection parameters will be different. As long as you can connect to the box and have permissions to run the script written into the step, the process should execute.

> The steps mentioned in this recipe are not limited to running just Linux commands. Check out the wiki for more details: http://wiki.pentaho.com/display/EAI/Shell and http://wiki.pentaho.com/display/EAI/Run+SSH+commands.

How to do it...

Follow the steps to execute a script from a job:

1. Create a new job and add a **Start** step from the pallet onto the canvas.

2. Add a **Shell** step from the pallet onto the canvas.

3. Create a hop from the **Start** step to the **Shell** step.

4. Open the **Shell** step and check the **Insert script** tickbox.

5. Switch to the **Script** tab and enter the following code:

    ```
    export TEST_VAR="Hello world!"
    echo $TEST_VAR
    ```

6. Click on **OK** and close the step.

7. Save and execute the job. Checking out the logging output you should see the output of the echo, which should look similar to the following:

```
/09/09 20:29:14 - Spoon - Starting job...|
/09/09 20:29:14 - running shell script via job - S
/09/09 20:29:14 - running shell script via job - S
/09/09 20:29:14 - Shell - Running on platform : L
/09/09 20:29:14 - Shell - Executing command... : /
/09/09 20:29:14 - Shell - (stdout) Hello world
/09/09 20:29:14 - running shell script via job - S
/09/09 20:29:14 - running shell script via job - F
/09/09 20:29:14 - running shell script via job - F
/09/09 20:29:14 - running shell script via job - Jc
/09/09 20:29:14 - Spoon - Job has ended.
```

Now we will utilize the transformation step to execute a script via SSH:

1. Create a new transformation.

2. From the **Utility** folder of the pallet, bring a **Run SSH commands** step and a **Write to log** step onto the canvas.

3. Create a hop from the **Run SSH commands** step to the **Write to log** step.

4. Open the **Run SSH commands** step. Enter the following details:

    1. **Server name/IP address**: `localhost`

    2. **Server port**: `22`

    3. **Timeout**: `0`

    4. **Username**: This is the account that has access to `localhost`

    5. **Password**: This is the password for the account

5. Uncheck the **Use key** checkbox.

6. Switch to the **Settings** tab. Enter the following commands into the **Commands** textbox:

```
export TEST_VAR="Hello world again!"
echo $TEST_VAR
```

7. Click on **OK**. Open the **Write to log** step and add the stdOut field to the **Fields** grid.

8. Click on **OK**. Save and execute your transformation. Your log should output the value of the TEST_VAR parameter:

```
09/09 20:41:49 - Write to log.0 -
09/09 20:41:49 - Write to log.0 ---------------> Linehr 1---------------
09/09 20:41:49 - Write to log.0   stdOut = Hello world again!
09/09 20:41:49 - Write to log.0
09/09 20:41:49 - Write to log.0 - ====================
09/09 20:41:49 - Write to log.0 - Finished processing (I=0, O=0, R=1, W=1
```

How it works...

While the scripts run for this recipe are rather simple, there is nothing preventing more complicated scripts or programs being executed through these steps. The transformation run SSH commands step also allows for parameters or a script created within the stream to be executed. This will allow for dynamic shell scripts to be run based on the data being output through the normal data integration process.

See also

▸ The *Executing a job or a transformation from a job by setting arguments and parameters dynamically* recipe in *Chapter 8, Executing and Re-using Jobs and Transformations*

Programming custom functionality

In Kettle, you have a lot of functionality provided by the built-in steps, but if that is not enough for you, there is a step named **User Defined Java Class** where you can program custom functionality with Java code. In this way, you can accomplish complex tasks, access Java libraries, and even access the Kettle API. The code you type into this step is compiled once and executed at runtime for each passing row.

Let's create a simple example of the use of the **UDJC** step. Assume that you have a text file containing sentences; you want to count the words in each row and split the flow of data into two streams depending on the number of words per sentence.

Note that, in order to develop a more interesting exercise, we added some extra considerations, as follows:

- There are several characters as separators, not only the blank spaces
- Sometimes, you can have a sequence of separators together
- Some sentences have a special character at the end, and some don't

Getting ready

You need a text file containing sentences, for example:

```
This is a sample text.
Another text with special characters, , ,   END OF FILE
hello,man
I wish you a happy new year:2011
The,last.but,not;the.least
```

You can download the sample file from Packt's website.

How to do it...

Carry out the following steps:

1. Create a new transformation.
2. Drop a **Text file input** step from the **Input** category. Browse to your file under the **Files** tab, and click on the **Add** button to populate the selected files grid. For example:

   `${Internal.Transformation.Filename.Directory}\samplefile.txt`

3. Under the **Content** tab, uncheck the **Header** checkbox, and type ##### in the **Separator** textbox.
4. Under the **Fields** tab, add a field named `line` of `String` type.
5. Add a **UDJC** step from the **Scripting** category. Also, drop two **Dummy** steps from the **Flow** category and name them: `short sentences` step and `long sentences` step.
6. Create the hops between the steps as per the ones shown in the following screenshot:

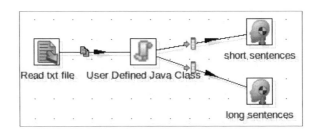

7. Double-click on the **UDJC** step.

8. Under the **Fields** tab of the bottom grid, add a new field named `qty`. Select **Integer** in the **Type** listbox.

9. Under the **Target** steps tab, create two tags and name them: `shortOnes` and `longOnes`. Then, select the steps as shown in the following screenshot:

^	#	Tag	Step	Description
	1	shortOnes	short sentences	
	2	longOnes	long sentences	

Fields | Parameters | Info steps | Target steps

Target steps:

10. In the **Classes and code fragments** section on the left, open the **Code Snippets** folder. Expand the **Common use** option and drop the **Main** item to the editing area on the right. A fragment of Java code will be written for the function `processRow()`.

11. Replace or complete this fragment with the following code:

```java
private RowSet shortSentences = null;
private RowSet longSentences = null;

public boolean processRow(StepMetaInterface smi,
   StepDataInterface sdi) throws KettleException
{
   Object[] r = getRow();
   if (r == null) {
      setOutputDone();
      return false;
   }

   if (first)  {
       first = false;
       shortSentences = findTargetRowSet("shortOnes");
       longSentences = findTargetRowSet("longOnes");
   }
   r = createOutputRow(r, data.outputRowMeta.size());
   String linein;
   linein = get(Fields.In, "line").getString(r);
   long len = linein.length();
   long qty = 0;
   boolean currentSpecialChar = false;

   for (int i=0;i<len;i++) {
      char ch = linein.charAt(i);
      switch(ch) {
```

```
        case ',':
        case '.':
        case ' ':
        case ';':
        case ':':
            if (!currentSpecialChar) qty++;
            currentSpecialChar = true;
            break;
        default:
            currentSpecialChar = false;
            break;
    }
}

if (!currentSpecialChar) qty++;
get(Fields.Out, "qty").setValue(r, qty);
if (qty < 7) {
   putRowTo(data.outputRowMeta, r, shortSentences);
   }
else {
 putRowTo(data.outputRowMeta, r, longSentences);
}

return true;
}
```

> The code snippet added with the **Main** item generates a row with this line:
>
> r = createOutputRow(r, outputRowSize);
>
> This line must be replaced with the following code to compile correctly:
>
> r = createOutputRow(r, data.outputRowMeta.size());

12. This code adds the desired functionality. If you preview this step, you will obtain a new field named `qty` with the number of words in each sentence. The results for the file used as an example would be:

^	#	line	qty
	1	This is a sample text.	5
	2	Another text with special characters, , , END OF FILE	8
	3	hello,man	2
	4	I whish you a happy new year:2011	8
	5	The,last.but,not;the.least	6

Rows of step: User Defined Java Class (5 rows)

13. This **UDJC** step also redirects the rows to the **short sentences** step or the **long sentences** step depending on the field `qty`. You can preview both steps and verify that the sentences with exactly seven or more than seven words flow to the **long sentences** step, and those with fewer words flow to the **short sentences** step.

How it works...

The first step in the recipe has the task of reading the text file. You have used ##### as separator characters because that string is not present in the file. This assures you that the field `line` will contain the entire line of your file.

Now, you need to develop some custom code that counts the words in the `line` field. This task can't be accomplished using standard Kettle steps, so you have programmed the necessary functionality in Java code inside a **UDJC** step. Let's explore the dialog for the **UDJC** step, which is shown in the following screenshot:

Most of the window is occupied by the editing area. Here you write the Java code using the standard syntax of that language. On the left, there is a panel with many code fragments ready to use (**Code Snippets**), and a section with sets and gets for the input and output fields. To add a code fragment to your script either double-click on it, drag it to the location in your script where you wish to use it, or just type it in the editing area.

The **Input** and **Outputs** fields appear automatically in the tree when the Java code compiles correctly; you can use the **Test class** button to verify that the code is properly written. If an error occurs, you will see an error window; otherwise, you will be able to preview the results of the transformation step.

The **Fields** tab on the bottom is to declare the new fields added by the step. In this case, you declared the field `qty` of `Integer` type. This field will be the output variable that will return the word count.

Under the **Target steps** tab, you can declare the steps where the rows will be redirected. In the recipe, you pointed to the two target **Dummy** steps; one for the short sentences, and the other for the long ones.

Let's see the Java code in detail.

At the beginning, there is a section with the variable declarations:

```
private RowSet shortSentences = null;
private RowSet longSentences = null;
```

These variables will represent the two possible target steps. They are declared at the beginning because, in this way, they keep their values between the row processing.

Then, you have the main function:

```
public boolean processRow(StepMetaInterface smi, StepDataInterface
    sdi) throws KettleException
{
    Object[] r = getRow();
    if (r == null) {
        setOutputDone();
        return false;
    }
}
```

The `processRow()` function processes a new row. The `getRow()` function gets the next row from the input steps. It returns an object array with the incoming row. A `null` value means that there are no more rows for processing.

The following code only executes for the first row:

```
if (first)  {
        first = false;
        shortSentences = findTargetRowSet("shortOnes");
        longSentences = findTargetRowSet("longOnes");
    }
```

You can use the flag `first` to prepare a proper environment before processing the rows. In this case, you set the target steps into two variables for further use.

The next code uses the `get()` method to set the internal variable `linein` with the value of the `line` field.

```
r = createOutputRow(r, data.outputRowMeta.size());
String linein;
linein = get(Fields.In, "line").getString(r);
```

Here is the main cycle:

```
long len = linein.length();
long qty = 0;
boolean currentSpecialChar = false;

for (int i=0;i<'len;i++) {
    char ch = linein.charAt(i);
    switch(ch) {
        case ',':
        case '.':
        case ' ':
        case ';':
        case ':':
            if (!currentSpecialChar) qty++;
            currentSpecialChar = true;
            break;
        default:
            currentSpecialChar = false;
            break;
    }
}
```

It parses the entire sentence looking for characters used as separators. If one of these separators is found, then it will increment the qty variable by one and set the flag currentSpecialChar to true, in order to not increment the value if the next character is also a separator.

The next line is to count the last word of the sentence only if it wasn't counted in the main cycle:

```
if (!currentSpecialChar) qty++;
```

Here we set the new field named qty with the value of the internal variable qty, which has the word count:

```
get(Fields.Out, "qty").setValue(r, qty);
```

Finally, if the word count is lower than 7 (an arbitrary value), then the row will be passed to the **short sentences** step; otherwise the target will be the **long sentences** step:

```
if (qty < 7) {
    putRowTo(data.outputRowMeta, r, shortSentences);
    }
else {
 putRowTo(data.outputRowMeta, r, longSentences);
}

return true;
}
```

If you only have one target step, then you can use the simpler putRow() method.

There's more...

To learn about the syntax of the Java language, visit the following URL: http://download.oracle.com/javase/tutorial/.

As mentioned earlier, you can access the Kettle API from inside the UDJC code. To learn the details of the API, you should check the source. For instructions on getting the code, follow the link: http://community.pentaho.com/getthecode/.

To learn more about the UDJC step, visit the Pentaho Community Wiki at http://wiki.pentaho.com/display/EAI/User+Defined+Java+Class.

Let us see some more information to take advantage of this very useful step.

Data type's equivalence

The code you type inside the UDJC step is pure Java. Therefore, the fields of your transformation will be seen as Java objects according to the following equivalence table:

Data type in Kettle	Java Class
String	Java.lang.String
Integer	Java.lang.Long
Number	Java.lang.Double
Date	Java.util.Date
BigNumer	BigDecimal
Binary	byte[]

The opposite occurs when you create an object inside the Java code and want to expose it as a new field to your transformation. For example, in the Java code, you defined the variable qty as long but under the **Fields** tab, you defined the new output field as Integer.

Generalizing your UDJC code

You can generalize your UDJC code by using parameters. You can add parameters and their values using the grid located under the **Parameters** tab at the bottom of the **UDJC** window.

In our example, you could have defined a parameter named qtyParameter with the value 7. Then, in the Java code, you would have obtained this value with the following line of code:

```
long qty = getParameter("qtyParameter");
```

Looking up information with additional steps

You can also have additional steps that provide information to be read inside your Java code. They are called **Info steps**. You declare them in the grid located under the **Info step** tab at the bottom of the **UDJC** window.

In our recipe, suppose that you have the list of separators defined in a **Data Grid** step. In order to pick the separators from that list, you have to create a hop from the **Data Grid** towards the **UDJC** step and fill the **Info step** grid. You must provide a **Tag** name (for example, charsList) and select the name of the incoming step. Then, in the Java code, you can use the findInfoRowSet() method to reference the info step, and the getRowFrom() method to read the rows in a cycle. Check the code:

```
RowSet data = findInfoRowSet("charsList");
Object[] dataRow = null;
while((dataRow = getRowFrom(data)) != null){
//Do something
}
```

Customizing logs

You can add your custom messages for different levels of logging very easily. You can select the fragment of necessary code from the **Step logging** node in the **Code Snippets** folder, or just type the method in the edit area. For example:

```
if (qty <' 10) logBasic("Long sentence found!");
```

Scripting alternatives to the UDJC step

As an alternative to the **UDJC** step, there is another step named **User Defined Java Expression**, also in the **Scripting** category. This step allows you to create new fields in an easy way by typing Java expressions. This step doesn't replace the functionality of that one, but it is more practical when the task you have to accomplish is simple.

 For examples on how to use this step, browse the different recipes in the book. There are several examples that use the **UDJE** step.

If you are more familiar with JavaScript language, instead of **UDJC** you could use the **Modified Java Script Value** (**MJSV**) step. Take into account that the code in the **JavaScript** step is interpreted, against **UDJC** that is compiled; this means that a transformation that uses the **UDJC** step will have much better performance. The UI for the **MJSV** step is very similar to the UI for the **UDJC** step; there is a main area to write the JavaScript code, a left panel with many functions as snippets, the input fields coming from the previous step, and the output fields. You can learn more about JavaScript in the following link: http://www.w3schools.com/js. As an additional resource, you can get *Pentaho 3.2 Data Integration: Beginner's Guide, Packt Publishing* by *María Carina Roldán*. There is a complete chapter devoted to the use of the **Modified Java Script Value** step.

Finally, if you prefer scripting to Java programming, there is a Kettle plugin named **Ruby Scripting** developed by Slawomir Chodnicki, one of the most active Kettle contributors. As the name suggests, the step allows you to develop custom functionality by scripting Ruby code. The UI for the Ruby plugin is very similar to the UI for the **UDJC** step. In this case, you don't have snippets but you have many sample transformations that demonstrate the capabilities of the plugin. Along with the samples, you have a couple of links to Ruby resources on the web. The plugin is available at the following URL: `https://github.com/type-exit/Ruby-Scripting-for-Kettle`.

Generating sample data for testing purposes

Having sample data to test your transformations is very useful and allows you to move faster through your development and testing process. There are several cases where you will want to generate sample data, for example:

- To quickly populate datasets with random data
- Manually generate specific information
- Generate large volumes of custom data

Take a subset from a large volume of data. In this recipe you will learn how to generate a dataset with 100 random rows in different formats (integer, string, and dates). Then, in the *There's more* section, you will find alternative solutions for generating data for testing.

How to do it...

Carry out the following steps:

1. Create a new transformation.

2. Drop a **Generate rows** step from the **Input** category. Here, set the **Limit** textbox to `100`.

3. Add a **Generate random value** step from the **Input** category. Add two elements to the grid: `randomInteger` of `random integer` type, and `randomString` of `random string` type.

4. Doing a preview on this last step, you will obtain a list of 100 random strings and integers. One example of these values would be: `1925608989` (integer) and `1jhn0udelvmpe` (string)

All the integer values have a large number of digits. What if, for some particular purpose, you want an integer with few digits or an integer in a specific range of values? Let's create a random integer in another way:

1. Drop a **User Defined Java Expression** from the **Scripting** category. Add a new field named short Integer and type the following text in the **Java expression** column: (int)Math.floor(Math.random()*3650). Also, select **Integer** in the **Value type** column.

2. Do a preview and check the new short Integer field; it will have values between 0 and 3649.

Now, let's do a simple trick to create a random date:

1. In its **Field**'s grid of the **Generate rows** step, create a new field named aDate, select Date in the **Type** listbox, use MM/dd/yyyy as the **Format**, and type 01/01/2000 in the **Value** column.

2. Add a **Calculator** step from the **Transform** category and complete the grid, as shown in the following screenshot:

Fields:

#	New field	Calculation	Field A	Field B	Fi	Value type	Le	Pr	Remove	Conversion mask
1	randomDate	Date A + B Days	aDate	shortInteger		Date			N	MM/dd/yyyy

3. Finally, if you run a preview on this last step, you will have your desired random values in different formats. See the following screenshot, as an example:

Rows of step: randomDate (100 rows)

#	aDate	randomInteger	randomString	shortInteger	randomDate
1	01/01/2000	-2095151826	i0ledguhb4gq	3526	08/27/2009
2	01/01/2000	-446583077	7gntura0j1aib	632	09/24/2001
3	01/01/2000	1885138640	22p1it5usptvl	1179	03/25/2003
4	01/01/2000	1674733876	6v7ftr7l49civ	2503	11/08/2006
5	01/01/2000	-170182461	qch2mrbs34fg	1781	11/16/2004
6	01/01/2000	-1111778199	6gfdcteuil37b	401	02/05/2001
7	01/01/2000	447270157	66rvhhu033n95	3461	06/23/2009
8	01/01/2000	-1542422017	3vs9l2j2rviel	1552	04/01/2004
9	01/01/2000	-1466719006	1vd8h2bddl2dg	2190	12/30/2005
10	01/01/2000	67344405	2tqfnvf9njbbh	1281	07/05/2003
11	01/01/2000	932885678	42iprju4cfnkd	2904	12/14/2007
12	01/01/2000	-1562683730	3bj457daki71o	797	03/08/2002
13	01/01/2000	870763294	15ptnevdoitkk	2959	02/07/2008

How it works...

In this recipe you have learnt the use of the **Generate random value** step in order to generate random integer and string values. The **Generate rows** step at the beginning has the purpose of generating 100 blank rows, which will be filled later with random values. You can vary the **Limit** textbox if you desire a different number of rows.

Also, you have used the random function inside a Java expression, in order to generate a short integer by taking advantage of the **User Defined Java Expression** step. In this way you can also set the range for your random numbers.

Notice that, in the **Generate rows** step, you have declared a new field named aDate with the value 01/01/2000. This date will then be used in the **Calculator** step. You generated a random date using a calculation that adds a random integer to the original date 01/01/2000. The integer has a value between 0 and 3649, which represents about 10 years, so the random date will be between 01/01/2000 and 28/12/2010.

There's more...

From the **Generate random value** step, you can also generate the following:

- **Random numbers**: This consists of float values between 0 and 1
- **Universally Unique Identifier** (**UUID**): This involves identifier standards such as b8f395d5-1344-11e0-af0b-6319f7359ecb
- Random message authentication code (**HMAC**): This is typically used in cryptography, for example, d59ee7a0e026aa1edc5c3398531d4452

In the following subsections you will find more ways to generate data for testing in other scenarios.

Using a Data grid step to generate specific data

The **Data grid** step allows you to create a dataset including both metadata and values inside the transformation. The step has the following two tabs:

- **Meta**: Under this tab, you add the fields and define their type and format. You can define fields using any of the Kettle data types.
- **Data**: Under this tab, you can enter the values for the fields defined previously.

This step is very useful when you need to populate a short list of rows with particular fields and/or values, thus avoiding creating a text file for that purpose.

Let's look at a practical example of the use of **Data Grid**. Suppose that you have created a regular expression and want to be sure that it is properly written, you can populate a data grid with a single `String` field. As values, you can type the list of values against which you want to test the regular expression, including values that should match the expression and values that shouldn't. After the **Data Grid**, just add a **Regexp Evaluation** step, enter your regular expression, and do a preview on this step. That is a very easy and quick way of testing with the help of a **Data Grid**.

Working with subsets of your data

On many occasions, you have to develop transformations that will process huge volumes of information. However, working with that volume during the development process is not a good idea, it slows down your development process, and makes testing what you are doing difficult. It's better to work with a small sample of that information.

There is a step named **Reservoir Sampling** in the **Statistic** folder that allows you to return a subset of your incoming stream. In this step, you must set the number of rows to get in the **Sample size** textbox, and also set the **Random seed**, used internally in the step to produce a random sample of your data.

In the same category you can find the **Sample rows** step. This step also generates a subset of your incoming stream but, in this case, the rows are not chosen in a random way, you must specify the range as explained in *Chapter 7, Understanding and Optimizing Data Flows*.

See also

▸ The *Processing rows differently based on the row number* recipe in *Chapter 7, Understanding and Optimizing Data Flows*

Working with JSON files

JavaScript Object Notation (**JSON**) is a lightweight language-independent data interchange format. It uses conventions similar to the C or JavaScript languages, with some rules for the representation of structured data. The object is represented as a collection of the `name_of_field:value_of_field` pairs and you can have an array of these elements using the `[]` characters.

PDI allows reading and writing these kinds of files using the **JSON input** and **JSON output** steps from the **Input** category. Let's see an example of reading a JSON file. Let's assume that you have a file named `museums.js` that you want to read for further processing. The file has the following information:

```
{"data": {
   "museum": [
    {
```

```
        "country": "Italy",
        "city": "Venice",
        "id_museum": "109"
        "name": "Palazzo Ducale"},
        {
        "country": "Mexico",
        "city": "Mexico City",
        "id_museum": "36"
        "name": "Museo de Arte Contemporaneo de Monterrey"},
        {
        "country": "Italy",
        "city": "Florence",
        "id_museum": "47"
        "name": "Museo di San Marco"}
        ]
      }
    }
```

In addition, you want to read it for further processing.

Getting ready

To run this recipe, you need the `museums.js` file with the museum information shown earlier. You can also download the file from Packt's site.

How to do it...

Carry out the following steps:

1. Create a new transformation.

2. Drop a **JSON input** step from the **Input** category.

3. Type the name of the file with its complete path in the **File or directory** textbox located under the **File** tab, for example, `${Internal.Transformation. Filename.Directory}\museums.js`. Click on the **Add** button.

4. Complete the **Fields** tab, as shown in the following screenshot:

File	Content	Fields	Additional output fields									
∧	#	Name	Path	Type	Fori	Le	Pr	Cu	De	G	Trim type	Repeat
	1	country	$...country	String							none	N
	2	city	$...city	String							none	N
	3	id_museum	$...id_museum	String							none	N
	4	name	$...name	String							none	N

5. Previewing the transformation, you will obtain a dataset with the museum information from the `museums.js` JSON source file.

How it works...

The **JSON input** step reads and interprets the `museum.js` JSON data using the **Path** column under the **Files** tab. Here, you must use a JSONPath expression, in a similar way to how the XPath expressions are used in XML files. A basic overview of the JSONPath syntax elements is shown in the following table:

JSONPath	Description
$	Root object
.	Child operator
[]	Array operator
[,]	Union operator in XPath

The child operator is used to access different levels inside the JSON structure, for example, `$...city` means the `city` element inside the `museum` element inside the `data` element from the root.

If you want to access a particular element, you should use `$.data.museum[1].city`, that means the `city` of the second `museum` element inside the `data` element from the root.

 In JSON, the lists are zero-based.

There's more...

You can find more information about the JSON language at the following URL: `http://www.json.org/`.

In the following subsections you will find some considerations about reading and writing JSON files.

Reading JSON files dynamically

In this recipe, you used the **JSON input** step to read the `museum.js` JSON file, but you can also read the JSON data from a field by checking the **Source is defined in a field?** checkbox and selecting the field in the **Get source from field** listbox.

Another option is when the name of the JSON file is in a field. In this case, instead of typing the name of the file, you must check both the **Source is defined in a field?** and **Source is a filename?** checkboxes and select the field that contains the name of the JSON file in the **Get source from field** listbox.

Writing JSON files

If you need to create a file or a field in JSON format, you can use the **JSON output** step from the **Output** category. Under the **General** tab of this step, there is a listbox named **Operation** where you can choose either a file or field destination.

If you choose a file destination, you need to fill the **Output File** section with information about the file to be generated. If you choose the **Output value** operation, you must type the name of the new field in the **Output Value** textbox.

Then, under the **Fields** tab, you need to populate the grid with the source fields coming from the data source, and the element name for the JSON structure.

For example, assume that you are using a data source with authors' information like the following:

```
"lastname","firstname","country","birthyear"
"Larsson","Stieg","Swedish",1954
"King","Stephen","American",1947
"Hiaasen","Carl ","American",1953
"Handler","Chelsea ","American",1975
"Ingraham","Laura ","American",1964
"Ramsey","Dave ","American",1960
"Kiyosaki","Robert ","American",1947,"A00007"
"Rowling","Joanne ","English",1965
```

"Riordan", "Rick", "American", 1964. If you add a **JSON output** step and an **Output value** operation, you will obtain a new field with each row in JSON format, with a value, as follows:

```
{"data":[{"lastname":"Larsson"},{"firstname":"Stieg"},{"country":"
    Swedish"},{"birthyear":1954}]}
```

Previewing the step, the result should be similar to the following:

^	#	lastname	firstname	country	birthyear	outputValue
	1	Larsson	Stieg	Swedish	1954	{"data":[{"birthyear":1954,"lastname":"Larsson","firstname":"Stieç
	2	King	Stephen	American	1947	{"data":[{"birthyear":1947,"lastname":"King","firstname":"Stephen
	3	Hiaasen	Carl	American	1953	{"data":[{"birthyear":1953,"lastname":"Hiaasen","firstname":"Carl
	4	Handler	Chelsea	American	1975	{"data":[{"birthyear":1975,"lastname":"Handler","firstname":"Chel
	5	Ingraham	Laura	American	1964	{"data":[{"birthyear":1964,"lastname":"Ingraham","firstname":"Lau
	6	Ramsey	Dave	American	1960	{"data":[{"birthyear":1960,"lastname":"Ramsey","firstname":"Dave
	7	Kiyosaki	Robert	American	1947	{"data":[{"birthyear":1947,"lastname":"Kiyosaki","firstname":"Rob
	8	Rowling	Joanne	English	1965	{"data":[{"birthyear":1965,"lastname":"Rowling","firstname":"Joani
	9	Riordan	Rick	American	1964	{"data":[{"birthyear":1964,"lastname":"Riordan","firstname":"Rick

Rows of step: Json output (9 rows)

Getting information about transformations and jobs (file-based)

The transformations and jobs are files with `.ktr` and `.kjb` extensions, but are, in fact, well-formed XML documents. You can open these files with a text editor to see their structures. You could take advantage of this feature to process some information within these files. Let's look at an example: assume that you want to lookup the **Modified Java Script Value** steps. You want to know where and how many of these steps are there because you want to replace them with a **User defined Java Class** step, which provides better performance.

Getting ready

In order to use this recipe, you need a directory with a set of transformations, some of them including the **Modified Java Script Value** steps. The example points to the Kettle sample transformation directory.

How to do it...

Carry out the following steps:

1. Create a new transformation.

2. Drop a **Get data from XML** step from the **Input** category into the canvas.

3. Type or browse for the source transformations directory under the **File** tab, for example, `C:\Pentaho\pdi-ce-4.1\samples\transformations`. Type `.*\.ktr` in the **Regular Expression** textbox. Click on the **Add** button to populate the **Selected files** grid.

4. Select the **Content** tab and type `/transformation/step` in the **Loop XPath** textbox as shown in the following screenshot.

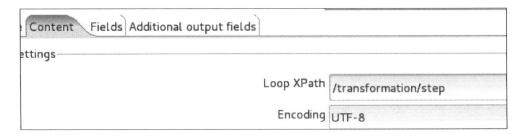

5. Complete the **Fields** tab, as shown in the following screenshot:

#	Name	XPath	Element	Result type	Type
1	name	name	Node	Value of	String
2	type	type	Node	Value of	String

6. Under the **Additional output fields** tab, type `filename` in the **Short filename** field.

7. If you preview this step, you will obtain a list of all the steps from the transformations source directory, including information about what kind of step is it. Here's an example:

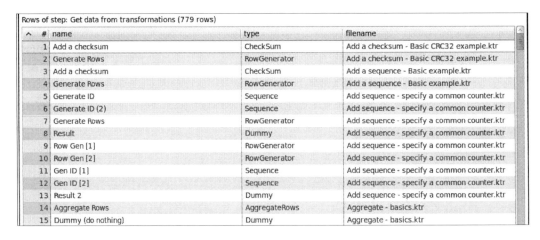

#	name	type	filename
1	Add a checksum	CheckSum	Add a checksum - Basic CRC32 example.ktr
2	Generate Rows	RowGenerator	Add a checksum - Basic CRC32 example.ktr
3	Add a checksum	CheckSum	Add a sequence - Basic example.ktr
4	Generate Rows	RowGenerator	Add a sequence - Basic example.ktr
5	Generate ID	Sequence	Add sequence - specify a common counter.ktr
6	Generate ID (2)	Sequence	Add sequence - specify a common counter.ktr
7	Generate Rows	RowGenerator	Add sequence - specify a common counter.ktr
8	Result	Dummy	Add sequence - specify a common counter.ktr
9	Row Gen [1]	RowGenerator	Add sequence - specify a common counter.ktr
10	Row Gen [2]	RowGenerator	Add sequence - specify a common counter.ktr
11	Gen ID [1]	Sequence	Add sequence - specify a common counter.ktr
12	Gen ID [2]	Sequence	Add sequence - specify a common counter.ktr
13	Result 2	Dummy	Add sequence - specify a common counter.ktr
14	Aggregate Rows	AggregateRows	Aggregate - basics.ktr
15	Dummy (do nothing)	Dummy	Aggregate - basics.ktr

8. Add a **Filter rows step** from the **Flow** category. Add the following condition: `Type = ScriptValueMod`.

9. Now, previewing the step, you will obtain only the name of the **Modified Java Script Value** steps included in the transformations, as well as the transformation filenames where these steps were found.

Rows of step: Filter rows Script Value (31 rows)

#	name	type	filename
1	Modified Java Script Value	ScriptValueMod	Automatic Documentatio
2	encrypt	ScriptValueMod	Encrypt Password.ktr
3	Generate SOAP request	ScriptValueMod	General - Annotated SOA
4	Parse SOAP Response	ScriptValueMod	General - Annotated SOA
5	Java Script Value	ScriptValueMod	General - Load images ar
6	Replace codes	ScriptValueMod	General - replace a serie
7	Java Script Value	ScriptValueMod	JavaScript - Access envir
8	Java Script Value	ScriptValueMod	JavaScript - Base64 Deco
9	E4X	ScriptValueMod	JavaScript - Parse XML.kt
10	Modified Java Script Value	ScriptValueMod	JavaScript - Skip rows aft
11	Java Script Value	ScriptValueMod	JavaScript - create new r
12	Java Script Value	ScriptValueMod	JavaScript - date to string
13	Java-Script with dialog	ScriptValueMod	JavaScript - dialog.ktr
14	Modified Java Script Value	ScriptValueMod	JavaScript - process all fi
15	Java Script Value	ScriptValueMod	JavaScript - replace value

How it works...

In this recipe, you used the **Get data from XML** step to read the transformation files located in the directory `C:\Pentaho\pdi-ce-4.1\samples\transformations`. By using the `/transformation/step` XPath node, you are getting a new row for each step in the transformations. As fields, you picked from that node the name of the step and its type.

Then, you used a **Filter rows** step to keep only the rows where the type of the step was equal to `ScriptValueMod`. This means, the **Modified Java Script Value** steps.

In the **Get data from XML** step, you also included the short filename of the transformation because you wanted to identify the source file of the transformations that had those steps.

There's more...

The following are some of the most important nodes in the transformation and job XML files. With these nodes, you can loop through the jobs and transformations you have created to get specific details about the entire repository of processes (like what data sources are used, what steps are used in which processes, and so on).The following table lists the common XML nodes for transformations.

LoopXPath	Information
/transformation	Root node for each transformation.
/transformation/info	One node for each transformation file. Here, you have the name and description of the transformation, its parameters, and the creation dates among others.
/transformation/notepads	From here you can get the notepads.
/transformation/info/log	You can get information about the transformation logging configuration.
/transformation/connection	One node for each database connection used in the transformation (or one for each database connection defined, if you didn't check the **Only save used connections to XML?** option)
/transformation/step	One node for each step of the transformation. You have the entire configuration of the step in this node; the most important elements here are the name of the step and its type.
/transformation/step/file	One node for each file or folder pointed to from a step. It includes data about the name of the file or folder, the mask typed, subfolders, and so on.
/transformation/step/field	One node for each field declared under the **Fields** tab of a step. You can get all the information about the fields, such as the name, its type, or the format configuration.
/transformation/order/hop	One node for each hop. Here you have the links between the steps.

Job XML nodes

The following table lists the common XML nodes for Jobs.

LoopXPath	Information
`/job`	One node for each job. From here, you can get the name of the job and the parameters among other things.
`/job/notepads`	From here you can get the notepads.
`/job/connection`	One node for each database connection used in the job (or one for each database connection defined if you didn't check the **Only save used connections to XML?** option)
`/job/job-log-table` `/job/jobentry-log-table` `/job/channel-log-table`	These nodes have the job logging configuration.
`/job/entries/entry`	One node for each job entry. You can look here for the name of the entries, their type, and the entire configuration fields for the entries.
`/job/hops/hop`	One entry for each link between job entries.

Steps and entries information

You can check the name and the type of all steps in the **Step Information...** option from the **Help** menu of Spoon, as shown in the following screenshot:

The available steps and step-plugins: (215 rows)

^	#	Plugir	ID	Name	Description	Image file	Main class	Category
	1	org.pe	Abort	Abort	Abort a transfor	ui/images/AB	[org.pentaho.di.!	Flow
	2	org.pe	CheckSum	Add a checksum	Add a checksun	ui/images/CS	[org.pentaho.di.!	Transform
	3	org.pe	Constant	Add constants	Add one or mor	ui/images/CS	[org.pentaho.di.!	Transform
	4	org.pe	Sequence	Add sequence	Get the next val	ui/images/SE	[org.pentaho.di.!	Transform
	5	org.pe	FieldsChange!	Add value fields (	Add sequence d Each time value	ui/images/CS	[org.pentaho.di.!	Transform
	6	org.pe	AddXML	Add XML	Encode several	ui/images/ad	[org.pentaho.di.!	Transform
	7	org.pe	AggregateRov	Aggregate Rows	This step type a It can't do grou	ui/images/AG	[org.pentaho.di.!	Deprecated
	8	org.pe	AnalyticQuery	Analytic Query	Execute analyti	ui/images/AQ	[org.pentaho.di.!	Statistics
	9	org.pe	Append	Append streams	Append 2 strear	ui/images/AP	[org.pentaho.di.!	Flow
	10	org.pe	ArffOutput	ARFF Output	Outputs rows tc	/home/amead	[org.pentaho.di..	Output
	11	org.pe	AutoDoc	Automatic Docun	This step autom	ui/images/aut	[org.pentaho.di.!	Output
	12	org.pe	AvroInput	Avro Input	Reads data fron	Avro.png	[org.pentaho.di.!	Big Data
	13	org.pe	BlockUntilSte!	Block this step ur	Block this step (	ui/images/WF	[org.pentaho.di.!	Flow
	14	org.pe	BlockingStep	Blocking Step	This step blocks	ui/images/BLI	[org.pentaho.di.!	Flow
	15	org.pe	Calculator	Calculator	Create new fielc	ui/images/CLI	[org.pentaho.di.!	Transform

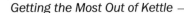

The **ID** column represents the steps identification, the **Name** column is how it appears in **Spoon**, and the **Description** column is the tooltip. You also can see the category of the step in the category column.

In the recipe, you compared the **type** field in the transformation against the **ID** column in this list.

The **Job Entry Information...** option shows similar information, but for the job entries.

See also

▶ *Getting information about transformations and jobs (file-based)*

▶ *Getting information about transformations and jobs (repository-based)*

▶ The *Reading simple XML files* recipe in *Chapter 4, Manipulating XML Structures*

▶ The *Specifying fields by using the XPath notation* recipe in *Chapter 4, Manipulating XML Structures*

Getting information about transformations and jobs (repository-based)

In the previous recipe, you learned to read the .ktr and .kjb files to get information from the transformation and job files respectively. Spoon also allows for storing this data in tables in a relational database when using a repository-based configuration. So, let's do the same task that we did in the previous recipe, but this time connect to a Kettle repository. The objective is to search for the **Modified Java Script Value** steps inside a set of transformations.

Getting ready

For running this recipe, you must have a Kettle repository and a set of transformations stored in it. If you don't have a list of sample transformations to play with, then you can connect to the repository and import them from the PDI samples directory.

How to do it...

Carry out the following steps:

1. Create a new transformation.

2. Drop a **Table input** step from the **Input** category into the canvas.

3. Create a connection to your repository database.

4. Type the following **SQL** statement:

```
SELECT  R_TRANSFORMATION.NAME AS transformation_name,
        R_STEP.NAME AS step_name,
        R_STEP_TYPE.CODE as step_type
FROM    R_STEP
INNER JOIN R_STEP_TYPE ON R_STEP.ID_STEP_TYPE =
        R_STEP_TYPE.ID_STEP_TYPE
INNER JOIN R_TRANSFORMATION ON R_STEP.ID_TRANSFORMATION =
        R_TRANSFORMATION.ID_TRANSFORMATION
WHERE       R_STEP_TYPE.CODE = 'ScriptValueMod'
```

5. Previewing this step, you will obtain a dataset with one row for each **Modified Java Script Value** step. In this dataset, you have the name of the transformation (in the **transformation_name** field) and the name of the Java script step (in the **step_name** field). This list will vary depending on the transformations stored in the repository.

How it works...

This recipe shows you how to read the transformation tables when you are working with a repository-based configuration.

The only thing to do here is to create a connection to the database where you have the repository and write the correct SQL Statement. In this case, you must read the table that contains the steps (R_STEP) and filter those which match a **Modified Java Script Value** step (R_STEP_TYPE.CODE = 'ScriptValueMod'). If you open the R_STEP_TYPE table, then you can see the list of steps and verify that the ScriptValueMod code corresponds to a **Modified Java Script Value** step.

The SQL statement also includes a join with the R_TRANSFORMATION table in order to get the name of the transformation.

There's more...

A Kettle repository is made up of several tables where Kettle stores all the information related to transformations and jobs. The next subsections explain the most significant tables found in a repository.

Transformation tables

These tables store the information regarding Kettle transformation files from the steps and hops that make the transformation up, to the notes that developers have added for future reference.

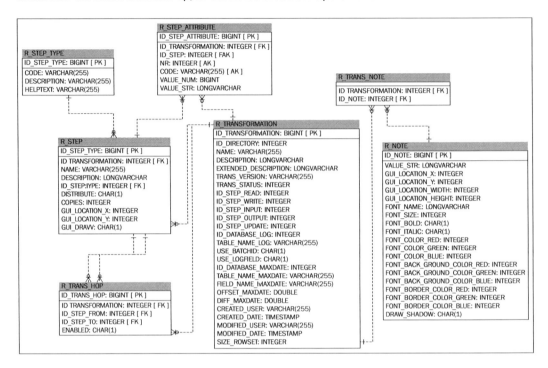

Table	Information
R_TRANSFORMATION	Here we have the basic information for the transformation, such as the transformation name or its creation date.
R_STEP	One record for each step. You can get the name of the step and the identification of its type.
R_STEP_TYPE	The list of step types. Here you can get the name, the description, and the tooltip for each kind of step
R_TRANS_HOP	One record for each hop. It provides the information related to the link between steps.
R_STEP_ATTRIBUTE	Settings for the step. Each feature you define in a step is saved in the columns CODE and VALUE_NUM if the feature is a number, or CODE and VALUE_STR otherwise. For example, if the step represents the name of a file, then you will have CODE=filename and VALUE_STR=c:/files/sample.xls
R_TRANS_NOTE	Here are the notes from the transformation. There is a note identification field linked to the table R_NOTE, where you have the description of the note.

Job tables

As with the transformation tables listed in the previous section, the job tables list the details of the jobs created within Kettle.

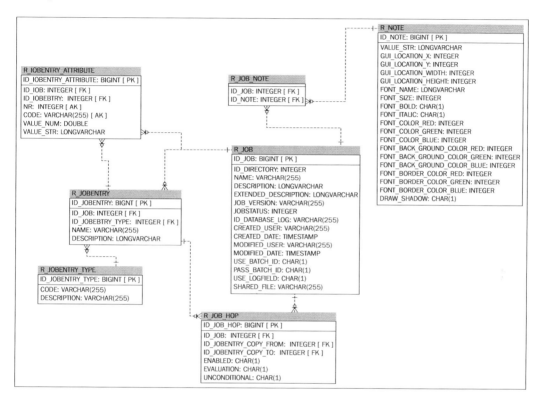

Table	Information
R_JOB	Basic information on the job. For example, its name or creation date.
R_JOBENTRY	One record for each job entry. Here you get the name and the type of the job entries.
R_JOBENTRY_TYPE	The list of the job entries (identification, name, and description).
R_JOB_HOP	One record for each hop. With this information, you know how the job entries are linked.
R_JOBENTRY_ATTRIBUTE	Settings for the step. Each feature you define in a step is saved in the columns CODE and VALUE_NUM if the feature is a number, or CODE, and VALUE_STR otherwise. See R_STEP_ATTRIBUTE in the previous table for an example.
R_JOB_NOTE	Here are the notes from the job. There is a note identification field linked to the table R_NOTE, where you have the description of the note.

Database connections tables

Database connection details are also stored within the Kettle repository. The associated tables are shown in the following screenshot:

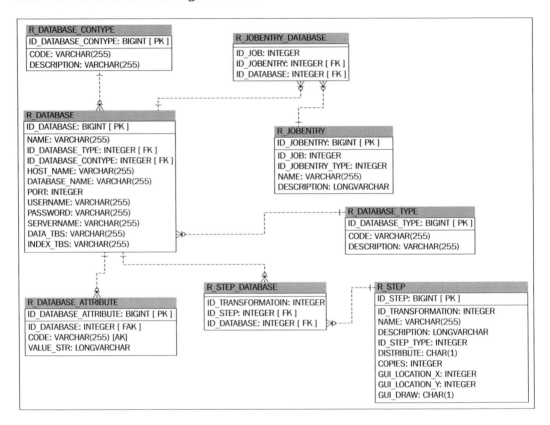

Table	Information
R_DATABASE	Here we have the settings for the database connections used in the steps or entries
R_STEP_DATABASE	One record for each step that uses a database connection. It links the step with the database identification.
R_JOBENTRY_DATABASE	One record for each entry job that uses a database connection. It links the entry job with the database identification.
R_DATABASE_TYPE	List of database engines. For example, MYSQL, ORACLE, DB2, MSSQL, among others.
R_DATABASE_CONTYPE	Type of access to the database: Native, ODBC, OCI, Plugin, and JNDI.

Table	Information
R_DATABASE_ATTRIBUTE	Here, you have the settings for each database connection. In the CODE column, you have the name of the variable whereas in the VALUE_STR column, you have the value.

Using Spoon's built-in optimization tools

Spoon being the developer's tool box, many of the tools used to fine tune and optimize transformations and jobs can be found within the interface. Developers should strive to tune their processes to match the load that it will be processing. Performance is normally measured in a few ways: CPU, RAM, and bandwidth usage, as well as the number of records that can be processed within a given timeframe. With this recipe, we'll dive into the different tools and some of the common techniques that can be used to improve performance.

Getting ready

The transformation and job used in this recipe are available via Packt's website. The example job executes the transformation, which in turn processes some randomly generated values and inserts them into a database table. The transformation is built to not run properly and have issues on execution. The recipe will walk through how to identify those issues using Spoon's built in tools.

How to do it...

Follow the steps to optimize the job and transformation:

1. Open Spoon and the example job.

2. Run the job. Notice that the **Execution Results** pane opens and starts showing stats on the job.

Execution results

History | Logging | Job metrics

Job / Job Entry	Comment	Result	Reason
optimization_job			
Job: optimization_job	Start of job execution		start
START	Start of job execution		start
START	Job execution finished	Success	
optimization_transform	Start of job execution		Followed uncondit

3. Right-click on the transformation and select **Open transformation**. The transformation will open and you can now see the metrics for it.

#	Stepname	Copynr	Read	Written	Input	Output
1	Generate random value	0	70254	70254	0	(
2	Under 100000	0	60253	60253	0	(
3	Generate Rows	0	0	90256	0	(
4	Add sequence	0	80255	80255	0	(
5	Under 100K Group	0	20263	20263	0	(
6	Insert / Update	0	10262	10261	10262	5:

4. While the transformation is running, it will come to the point where it can no longer process data and fail. As shown in the previous screenshot, the failure occurred on the **Insert/Update** step (it will be highlighted in red on the **Step Metrics** tab). We need to further identify why the transformation failed. Click on the **Logging** tab under **Execution Results** and click on the red error icon to show the lines of the logfile that are associated with the error.

5. The error lines that pop up show that the issue is a lock wait timeout. Look at the three **Insert/Update** steps in the transformation. It appears that we are trying to enter data into the same table, which would explain the timeout. Remove the two **Insert/Update** steps from the Over 100K Group **Add Constants** step and the Over 10M Group **Add Constants** step as shown in the following screenshot:

6. Connect the Over 100K Group and Over 10M Group **Add Constants** steps to the remaining **Insert/Update** step as shown in the following screenshot.

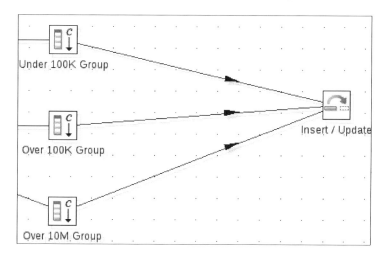

7. Run the transformation again to verify that the lock wait timeout has been resolved.

 Another way to resolve the lock wait timeout would be to add **Block this step until steps finish** steps that wait on the **Insert/ Update** steps to finish before it executes. A word of warning, if using the blocking steps, be aware that a deadlock can be created if multiple are used and they are dependent on each other.

Another common problem is around data streams. Validating stream metadata, ensuring that fields are in the stream, and field placements are all common problems that can impact not only whether a process will execute successfully, but also performance. The next part of the recipe will show how to view data stream metadata, both during development and while testing the process.

8. Right-click on the **Generate random value** step and select the **Show Input fields** option. The stream at that point with its given metadata will appear:

Step name: Generate random value

Fields:

∧	#	Fieldname	Type	Length	Precision	Step origin	Storage	Mask
	1	testing	String	-	-	Generate Rows	normal	
	2	record_sequence	Integer	-	0	Add sequence	normal	#;-#

9. Close the window and then right-click on the **Generate random value** step again, this time selecting the **Show Output fields** option. A similar window will pop up with the added field from the **Generate random value** step now appearing in the stream.

Step name: Generate random value

Fields:

∧	#	Fieldname	Type	Length	Precision	Step origin	Storage	Masl
	1	testing	String	-	-	Generate Rows	normal	
	2	record_sequence	Integer	-	0	Add sequence	normal	#;-#
	3	random_value	Integer	10	0	Generate random value	normal	#;-#

10. Close the window and then run the transformation again. Right-click on the **Generate random value** step one more time and select **Show sniff test during execution** for either input or output. A window appears showing the runtime data stream.

How it works...

Spoon takes a lot of what goes on during the processing of transformations and jobs and exposes it to developers so they can troubleshoot and build better processes. Metadata and live data stream analysis can help correct problems with breaking processes. While the techniques shown in this recipe won't make processes work perfectly overnight, they can help guide you to best practices to identify bottlenecks that would normally not be discovered until the process is closer to production.

There's more...

There are other tools available for monitoring performance. In the **Execution Results** pane, there is a **Performance Graph** that can be enabled and shows various stats for a given process. While the metrics gathering is not CPU intensive running in kitchen or pan, there are some resources used to update the screenshot:

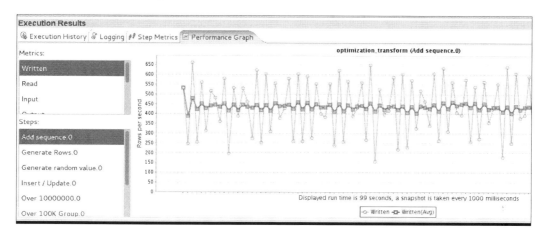

Metrics are collected from every step, matching the categories that are found on the **Step Metrics** tab. This data can also be stored within a database for longer term trending. More details can be found at the Pentaho wiki: `http://wiki.pentaho.com/display/EAI/Step+performance+monitoring`.

The wiki also has a great article on some common performance tuning tips that can boost throughput significantly. Check it out at `http://wiki.pentaho.com/display/COM/PDI+Performance+tuning+check-list`.

11
Utilizing Visualization Tools in Kettle

In this chapter, we will cover:

- ▶ Managing plugins with the Marketplace
- ▶ Data profiling with DataCleaner
- ▶ Visualizing data with AgileBI
- ▶ Using Instaview to analyze and visualize data

Introduction

As we have seen in earlier chapters, Kettle provides a lot of functionality out of the box, but there are a lot of great feedback mechanisms that have been added that can help make developing and working with data even easier. Being able to profile and visualize data streams allows for developers to gather feedback from customers to determine if they have met customer requirements. Some of these features are not provided directly in the tool, but are available as plugins. One of Kettle's most distinguishing features is the ability to create and add plugins directly into the tool.

In this chapter you will learn to work with plugins as well as work with some of the advanced capabilities that they provide.

 The plugin ecosystem is a vibrant and growing component of the Pentaho community. Plugins are sometimes picked up and made part of the core Kettle project. If you find that one of the plugins mentioned in the following recipes is already in your version of Kettle, don't be surprised!

In order to follow these recipes, you will need to have an Internet connection that will allow you to access Pentaho's web resources. The Pentaho wiki has a page dedicated to all of the publicly known available plugins, which can be found at `http://wiki.pentaho.com/display/EAI/List+of+Available+Pentaho+Data+Integration+Plug-Ins`. Many of the plugins listed have made their way into the newer versions of Kettle.

Another way to access plugins is through the new Marketplace feature, which provides a simpler way of managing plugins than the manual process older versions used.

Managing plugins with the Marketplace

Before you can work with all the nifty new features and capabilities that plugins can provide, you have to be able to manage them! In this recipe we will cover how to install and remove plugins through the Marketplace.

 The Marketplace is a new feature to Kettle 5. Earlier versions of Kettle require the manual addition and removal of plugins. All plugins can be found in the plugins directory where Kettle is installed.

Getting ready

For this recipe we will require an Internet connection so that Kettle can connect to the Marketplace and retrieve the plugin we are installing.

How to do it...

Follow the given steps to install a plugin:

1. Open Spoon and click on the **Help** menu and select **Marketplace**.

2. The Marketplace menu will open. Select the **DataCleaner Data Profiling for Kettle version 5 or higher** plugin.

3. Read through the package details. Each plugin should provide details of the author, the location of the plugin, and so on.

4. Click on the **Install this Plugin** button to install DataCleaner. The files will be downloaded and then a dialog will pop up asking you to restart Spoon.

5. Go back into the **Marketplace** and look for the DataCleaner plugin. You will notice that it has been successfully installed.

To remove a plugin, follow the given steps:

1. Enter the **Marketplace** and select the plugin you wish to uninstall.

2. In the package details section, you will notice the **Install this plugin** button has switched to an **Uninstall this plugin** button.

3. Click on the **Uninstall this plugin** button to remove the plugin.

How it works...

The Marketplace utilizes a Git repository to manage what plugins are available to download. This way, plugin developers have an easy way to manage their plugins and provide Pentaho with the details required to streamline the plugin management process. More details can be found on the Pentaho wiki at `http://wiki.pentaho.com/display/EAI/Marketplace`.

There's more...

While the Marketplace does provide a cleaner interface to work with, it is still possible to install plugins manually. All installed plugins can be found in the plugins directory where Kettle is installed. The plugins should provide details on where they should be placed within this directory.

If you are using the 4.x branch of Kettle, details on how to install the DataCleaner plugin are provided on the Pentaho wiki at `http://wiki.pentaho.com/display/EAI/Human+Inference`.

See also

> ▸ *Data profiling with DataCleaner*

Data profiling with DataCleaner

Data profiling is an often overlooked process due to time or resource constraints on projects that, in reality, can save time and catch issues before they occur in your data integration code. For instance, finding data that doesn't match expected formats or fit within ranges, misspellings, improperly formatted dates, or discovering strings in an expected numerical field can all break a transformation.

DataCleaner is an open source data profiling tool that integrates with Kettle and can profile data while code is in the process of being developed. Additionally, DataCleaner jobs can be integrated into Kettle jobs and run as part of larger processes.

Profiling data shows the meta-information about the data being processed—from how many values fit into ranges to how many values fit a given format. This can help data integration developers write more optimized processes and determine if the quality of the source is capable of meeting the requirements of the project it is being used in.

For this recipe we will be working with DataCleaner in two ways. The first will be profiling data while within Spoon. The other will be executing a DataCleaner job as part of a Kettle job.

Getting ready

This recipe assumes that the DataCleaner plugin has been installed into Spoon. The process for installing the plugin is discussed in the earlier *Managing plugins with the Marketplace* recipe. While the recipe will not require any previous experience with DataCleaner, it may be beneficial to work with the tool before diving in to working with it within Kettle. The DataCleaner website provides some really good documentation and can be accessed from `http://datacleaner.org/`.

We will be using the `books` database. The scripts to create the database can be found on Packt's website. This database has been used in other chapters, so it is likely that you have already created and populated the database. Additionally, the code from Packt's website also includes a simple DataCleaner job for the second part of the recipe. If you already know how to create data profiling jobs, feel free to substitute one you have already built with the sample one.

How to do it...

This part of the recipe will show you how to profile data while developing a transformation:

1. Open Spoon and create a new transformation.

2. From the pallet's **Input** folder, bring a **Table input** step to the canvas.

3. Open the **Table input** step and connect to the `books` database.

4. Pull all of the data from the authors table:

   ```
   SELECT
      `lastname`
   , `firstname`
   , `nationality`
   , `birthyear`
   , `id_author`
   FROM `authors`
   ```

5. Click the **OK** button to exit the step.

6. Right click on the **Table input** step and select the **Profile** option.

7. The Kettle **Launch** window will open. Click on **Launch**.

8. DataCleaner will then open and read the metadata information about the data stream in Kettle. Notice that some analyzer defaults have already been selected based on the data types of the data.

9. Click on the **Execute** button in the top-right corner. The data will be processed in the transformation and profiled by DataCleaner. The results will be returned as in the following screenshot:

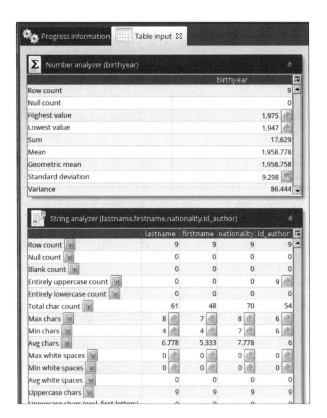

10. We can also customize the profiling job with other analyzers. Let's add a value distribution analyzer by clicking on the **Analyze** menu and selecting **Value Distribution**.

11. Rerun the profiling job by selecting the **Execute** button. The output will now have value distribution entries:

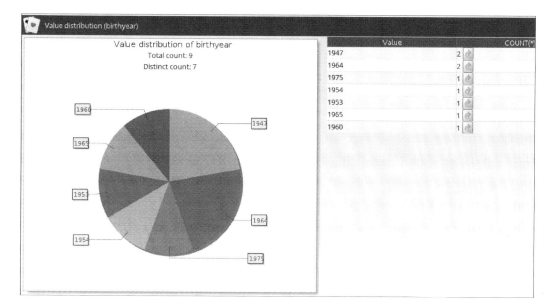

12. Close the results window.

13. Close DataCleaner and return to Spoon.

Now that we have seen how to run DataCleaner to profile data during development, let's now execute a DataCleaner job at runtime:

1. Open Spoon and create a new job.

2. Add a **Start** step from the pallet onto the canvas.

3. Under the **Utility** folder in the pallet, select the **Execute DataCleaner** step and bring it to the canvas. Create a hop between the **Start** and **Execute DataCleaner** steps.

4. Open the **Execute DataCleaner** step. This step will require some configuration to work appropriately. Specifically, we must identify the following:

    ❑ **DataCleaner installation location**: This can be the version included with Kettle, or a version that you have downloaded. It should point to the `datacleaner.sh` or `datacleaner.exe` file, depending on which operating system you are running on.

    ❑ **Job file location**: This is the path to the file from the book's code set, or a profile job that you have created.

- **Output file location**: The location that the output of the profiling job should be stored in.

- **Output type**: For this example, we will be using the HTML output format.

5. Click on **OK** to exit the step.

6. Save and run the job. The output file should be created and can be opened with any browser. Notice that we receive similar output when we run the profiling job directly from within DataCleaner earlier.

Σ Number analyzer · String analyzer · Value distribution

String analyzer (lastname,firstname,nationality,id_author)

	lastname	firstname	nationality	id_author
Row count	9	9	9	9
Null count	0	0	0	0
Blank count	0	0	0	0
Entirely uppercase count	0	0	0	9
Entirely lowercase count	0	0	0	0
Total char count	61	48	70	54
Max chars	8	7	8	6
Min chars	4	4	7	6
Avg chars	6	5	7	6
Max white spaces	0	0	0	0
Min white spaces	0	0	0	0
Avg white spaces	0	0	0	0

How it works...

DataCleaner and Kettle are both Java applications that provide interfaces that allow for the integration of the two tools. By leveraging an existing technology, Kettle gets the benefit of a full-fledged data profiling tool and DataCleaner gets the benefit of interfacing with a very flexible data integration tool. In any case, developers using either tool benefit.

There's more...

While this recipe only covered the basics of using DataCleaner as part of a Kettle process or while developing some new code, the plugin actually provides access to the more advanced features of the DataCleaner API. For instance, with the **Job** step, there is the option to add additional arguments to the DataCleaner job which can change how DataCleaner behaves when running and building the profile output. To learn more about these options, check out the DataCleaner documentation at `http://datacleaner.org/resources/docs/3.5.3/html/pt07.html`.

See also

▸ *Managing plugins with the Marketplace*

Visualizing data with AgileBI

In today's world, where customers demand faster responses and the amount of data needed to be processed has increased dramatically, traditional Business Intelligence shops have experienced pains due to the cadence at which they can deliver value. One of the largest challenges is taking those sometimes vague or misleading requirements around the transformation of source data and then conforming to the new or changing business logic.

Kettle has some built-in tools that allow for developers to work with their customers to work through the data cleansing and transforming process to determine if they are on the right track. In this recipe we will walk through how to use the **Visualize** perspective.

The **Visualize** perspective is part of the AgileBI component of Kettle. The primary tool in the perspective is called Analyzer. Note that Analyzer is available in both the Community and Enterprise editions of Kettle. It is also available as part of the Enterprise edition of the Business Analytics Server.

Getting ready

For this recipe we will be using the `books` database. The scripts for building this database are available on Packt's website.

How to do it...

Follow the given steps to visualize data:

1. Create a new transformation.
2. From the pallet's **Input** folder, bring over a **Table input** step onto the canvas.
3. Open the **Table input** step. Connect the step to the `books` database. For the SQL statement, enter the following:

```sql
SELECT
  firstname
, lastname
, nationality
, birthyear
, title
, price
FROM authors a
LEFT JOIN books b ON a.id_author = b.id_author
```

4. From the pallet's **Output** folder, bring over a **Table output** step onto the canvas. Create a hop between the **Table input** and **Table output** steps.

5. Open the **Table output** step. Connect the step to the `books` database.

6. Enter `authors_books_data` for the **Target table** field.

7. Check the **Truncate table** checkbox.

8. Click on the **SQL** button and view the CREATE statement written for the `authors_books_data` table. Execute the CREATE statement and click on **OK** to exit the SQL window. Then click **OK** to exit the step.

9. Run the transformation. Right-click on the **Table output** step and select the **Visualize | Analyzer** option. Notice that the fields from the table are on the left in two groups: **measure** and **level**.

10. Select the **Price** measure and add it the **Measures** field in the **Layout** section.

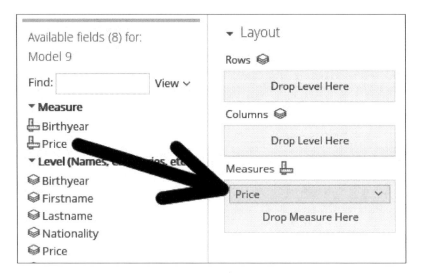

11. Select the **Nationality** level and add it to the **Columns** field in the **Layout** section.

12. Now add the **Lastname** level to the **Rows** field in the **Layout** section. We can now see the sum of prices by the author's last name, which is not necessarily useful. Let's assume that we have been given the requirement for finding the average price of books per author.

13. Right-click on **Price Measure** and select the **Subtotals** option. Uncheck the **Sum** checkbox and select the **Average** checkbox. Click on **OK**.

14. Right-click on the **Price Measure** again and select the **Column Name and Format** option. Change the format to `Currency` and the **Decimal Places** to 2.

15. Click on the **More actions and options** button (it looks like a gear) and select **Report** options:

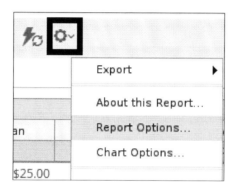

16. Check the options for **Show Grand Totals for Rows** and **Show Grand Totals for Columns**. Click on **OK**.

17. Now you should have a view that shows the average price per nationality as well as per author, similar to the following:

	Nationality			
	American	English	Swedish	**Grand Average**
Lastname	Price	Price	Price	Price
Handler	$25.00	-	-	**$25.00**
Hiaasen	-	$17.95	-	**$17.95**
King	-	-	$15.00	**$15.00**
Kiyosaki	$40.00	-	-	**$40.00**
Grand Average	**$32.50**	**$17.95**	**$15.00**	**$24.49**

18. On the top-right side of Analyzer are the **View As:** options. Click on the small bar graph icon to view the different types of visualizations available. Try a few of them out to get a sense of the different visualization types:

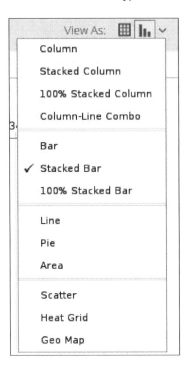

How it works...

The **Visualize** perspective takes advantage of some of the other tools in the Pentaho suite to allow developers to show their data faster and get a sense of whether or not they are meeting the requirements they are developing for. The visualization tool is actually an Enterprise edition tool called Analyzer, which is a front-end tool for the open source **ROLAP (relational OLAP)** database Mondrian. The built-in version of Analyzer requires a dataset provided by Kettle through Mondrian. Mondrian is able to work with most relational databases to build OLAP data sources. While we kept things simple and created a table within the books database, we could have just as easily used an in-memory database such as MonetDB or any other relational data source.

There's more...

While the dataset used in this recipe was extremely simplistic, Mondrian and Analyzer can easily scale to larger and more complex data. As with other tools such as DataCleaner, the reports and visualizations created in this tool can be utilized outside of Kettle as part of the larger Pentaho tool suite.

To learn more about Mondrian, check out *Mondrian In Action*, *Manning Publications* by William Back, Nick Goodman, and Julian Hyde. The Mondrian website also provides some good documentation and can be found at `http://mondrian.pentaho.com/documentation`.

See also

▶ The *Getting data from a database* recipe in *Chapter 1, Working with Databases*

Using Instaview to analyze and visualize data

Instaview is the latest tool to allow for fast insights into data before more intensive work is performed. With it, data from effectively any type of data source can be queried and visualized.

 Instaview is currently an Enterprise edition exclusive. If you do not have an Enterprise license but wish to follow along, download a 30-day trial from `http://www.pentaho.com/download`.

Getting ready

To be able to follow the recipe, access to the Enterprise edition of Pentaho Data Integration is required. For data, we will be using baseball player salary details that were created in *Chapter 2, Reading and Writing Files*. This data is provided in the code for this chapter on Packt's website.

For Instaview to work appropriately, the internal MonetDB database must be turned on. This can be done by going to the PDI installation directory and going to the `/plugins/spoon/agile-bi/platform/pentaho-solutions/system/instaview/scripts` directory. The standard command to activate MonetDB on Linux is as follows:

```
./startMonetDb.sh pentaho-instaview /<home_directory>/.kettle/instaview/
dbfarm/ /usr/bin/monetdb /usr/bin/monetdbd 50006 monetdb
```

For other operating systems, check the documentation page on the Pentaho Infocenter:

```
http://infocenter.pentaho.com/help/topic/troubleshooting_guide/
concept_troubleshooting_monetdb_instaview_config.html.
```

How to do it...

Follow the given steps to run the baseball player salary details through Instaview.

1. Open Spoon and switch to the **Instaview** perspective.

2. Click on the **Create New** button to create a new visualization/analysis.

3. Select the **Local File** option in the **New Data Source** dialog that pops up and choose the **CSV** data type. Click on **OK** to enter the CSV file details.

4. In the **CSV input** step, enter the following details:

   ❑ **Filename**: This gives the location to the file being analyzed

   ❑ **Delimiter**: For the `player_salaries` file, the delimiter is `;`

5. Click on the **Get Fields** button. The step will query the file and make a best guess at the format of the fields. Click on **Close** on the analysis results and click on **OK** to close the step.

Instaview will attempt to configure the analysis file by building a transformation to load the data into the AgileBI MonetDB database, build a Mondrian model, and cache the data into MonetDB to work with the data in Pentaho Analyzer. If everything worked, Instaview will switch to the **View** tab, which is Pentaho Analyzer. Let's play around with some of the capabilities to get a better idea of how Analyzer can work with data:

1. Select **Namelast Level** and add it to the **Rows Layout** section.

2. Select **Salarysum Measure** and add it to the **Measures Layout** section.

3. Now right-click on **Salarysum Measure** in the **Layout** section and navigate to **Conditional Formatting | Color Scale: Green-Yellow-Red**.

4. Right-click on **Salarysum Measure** again in the **Layout** section and select **Column Name and Format**. Change the format to **Currency**.

5. Finally, right-click on **Salarysum Measure** in the **Layout** section once again and select **Sort Values High->Low**.

How it works...

Instaview automates as much of the data integration and model construction as possible, allowing users to start playing with the data and potentially gain new insights that would have normally taken a lot longer and involve more developers. To see what Instaview did behind the scenes, let's return back to the **Configure** tab and view the code created by each of the subprocesses.

There should be a section on the **Configure** tab that shows the status of each process, as shown in the following screenshot:

Click on the **Edit** link for the Data Integration section. A warning about the need of understanding the requirement of data integration code will pop up. Click on OK and the transformation created by Instaview opens:

It is possible to modify this transformation to clean and conform to the data. Notice that the **Input** step is the same as the one that opened upon creation of the CSV Instaview. The **Output** step automatically is configured to move the data into the MonetDB database. Close the transformation and return back to Instaview.

The Model process built a Mondrian model for Analyzer to work with. Clicking on the **Edit** link will cause another warning pop up; this time around needing understanding of modeling concepts. Click on **OK** to view the model created.

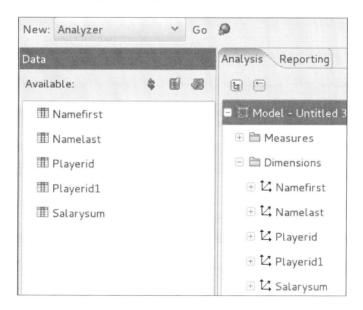

This perspective allows for the editing of models, giving advanced developers the flexibility required to build custom Mondrian cubes. Close the model and return back to Instaview.

The Data Cache process allows for the in-memory caching to be cleared, which can be done by clicking on the **Clear** link.

Pentaho Analyzer allows for a lot of different types of visualizations, from simple bar and line graphs to scatter plots, heat maps, and geolocation diagrams. While the data used for the recipe is simplistic, we are able to glean some insight through conditional formatting. The visualization options can also provide a lot of insight, depending on the type of data being analyzed.

There's more...

It is also possible to build more complicated transformations and mash data together for even greater insight as well as add more powerful capabilities to the Mondrian models automatically built by Instaview. Consider the code developed by Instaview to be the starting point. Knowledge of working with the various components is essential to get the most out of Instaview.

See also

- *Visualizing Data with AgileBI*
- The *Getting data from Hadoop* recipe in *Chapter 3, Working with Big Data and Cloud Sources*

12
Data Analytics

In this chapter, we will cover:

- ▸ Reading data from a SAS datafile
- ▸ Studying data via stream statistics
- ▸ Building a random data sample for Weka

Introduction

Data Analytics is the art of taking data and deriving information from it in order to make informed decisions. A large part of building and validating datasets for the decision making process is data integration—the moving, cleansing, and transformation of data from the source to a target. This chapter will focus on some of the tools that take Kettle beyond the normal data processing capabilities and integrate processes into analytical tools.

Reading data from a SAS datafile

SAS is one of the leading analytics suites, providing robust commercial tools for decision making in many different fields. Kettle can read files written in SAS' specialized data format known as `sas7bdat` using a new (since Version 4.3) input step called **SAS Input**. While SAS does support other format types (such as CSV and Excel), `sas7bdat` is a format most similar to other analytics packages' special formats (such as Weka's ARFF file format). This recipe will show you how to do it.

Why read a SAS file?

There are two main reasons for wanting to read a SAS file as part of a Kettle process. The first is that a dataset created by a SAS program is already in place, but the output of this process is used elsewhere in other Business Intelligence solutions (for instance, using the output for integration into reports, visualizations, or other analytic tools). The second is when there is already a standard library of business logic and rules built in Kettle that the dataset needs to run through before it can be used.

Getting ready

To be able to use the SAS Input step, a `sas7bdat` file will be required. The Centers for Disease Control and Prevention have some sample datasets as part of the *NHANES Dietary* dataset. Their tutorial datasets can be found at their website at `http://www.cdc.gov/nchs/tutorials/dietary/downloads/downloads.htm`. We will be using the `calcmilk.sas7bdat` dataset for this recipe.

How to do it...

Perform the following steps to read in the `calcmilk.sas7bd` dataset:

1. Open Spoon and create a new transformation.
2. From the input folder of the **Design** pallet, bring over a **Get File Names** step.
3. Open the **Get File Names** step. Click on the **Browse** button and find the **calcmilk. sas7bd** file downloaded for the recipe and click on **OK**.
4. From the input folder of the **Design** pallet, bring over a **SAS Input** step. Create a hop from the **Get File Names** step to the **SAS Input** step.
5. Open the **SAS Input** step. For the **Field in the input to use as filename** field, select the **Filename** field from the dropdown.
6. Click on **Get Fields**. Select the **calcmilk.sas7bd** file and click on **OK**.

 If you are using Version 4.4 of Kettle, you will receive a `java. lang.NoClassDefFoundError` message. There is a work around which can be found on the Pentaho wiki at `http://wiki.pentaho.com/display/EAI/SAS+Input`.

7. To clean the stream up and only have the `calcmilk` data, add a **Select Values** step and add a hop between the **SAS Input** step to the **Select Values** step. Open the **Select Values** step and switch to the **Remove** tab. Select the fields generated from the **Get File Names** step (`filename`, `short_filename`, `path`, and so on). Click on **OK** to close the step.

8. Preview the **Select Values** step. The data from the **SAS Input** step should appear in a data grid, as shown in the following screenshot:

Rows of step: Select values (1000 rows)

^ #	SEQN	WTDRD1	DR1TCALC	RIAGENDR	RIDAGEYR	SDMVPSU	SDMVSTRA	MILKQ	MILKCALCQ	INCOH
1	21010.0	55313.014168125	961.0	2.0	52.0	1.0	29.0	320.25	375.0	0.0
2	21031.0	50244.823473208	811.0	2.0	37.0	1.0	29.0	<null>	<null>	0.0
3	21052.0	81599.340388606	478.0	2.0	37.0	1.0	29.0	<null>	<null>	0.0
4	21070.0	52916.387266083	1149.0	2.0	31.0	1.0	29.0	<null>	<null>	0.0
5	21073.0	12226.967630579	522.0	2.0	0.0	1.0	29.0	<null>	<null>	0.0
6	21109.0	44015.266385679	892.0	1.0	25.0	1.0	29.0	<null>	<null>	0.0
7	21126.0	<null>	<null>	1.0	4.0	1.0	29.0	<null>	<null>	0.0
8	21142.0	50244.823473208	168.0	2.0	31.0	1.0	29.0	<null>	<null>	0.0

How it works...

The **SAS Input** step takes advantage of Kasper Sørensen's Sassy Reader project (`http://sassyreader.eobjects.org`). **Sassy** is a Java library used to read datasets in the `sas7bdat` format and is derived from the R package created by Matt Shotwell (`https://github.com/BioStatMatt/sas7bdat`). Before those projects, it was not possible to read the proprietary file format outside of SAS' own tools.

The **SAS Input** step requires the processed filenames to be provided from another step (like the **Get File Names** step). Also of note, while the `sas7bdat` format only has two format types (strings and numbers), PDI is able to convert fields to any of the built-in formats (dates, integers, and so on).

See also

▶ The *Data profiling with DataCleaner* recipe in *Chapter 11, Utilizing Visualization Tools in Kettle*

▶ The *Altering a data stream with Select Values* recipe in *Chapter 7, Understanding and Optimizing Data Flows*

Studying data via stream statistics

While Kettle's forte is extracting, manipulating, and loading data, there is an entire set of tools built for generating statistics and analytic style data from the data stream. This recipe will focus on several of those tools that will allow for even more insight into your data. Kettle treats the data worked on in transformations as a stream going from an input to an output. The tools discussed in this recipe will show how to learn more about the data stream through gathering statistics about the data for analysis.

Getting ready

This recipe will not be a single large process, but made up of smaller recipes around the same subject. We will be using the Baseball salary dataset that can be found on the book's website or from Lahman's Baseball Archive website, found at `http://www.seanlahman.com/ baseball-archive/statistics/`. The code for this recipe can also be found on the book's website.

The recipe will be broken into smaller recipes that will focus on three steps: **Analytic Query**, **Group by**, and **Univariate Statistics**. These steps will allow us to gain some insight into the baseball player's salaries, such as the salary change from one contract to the next, frequency of being traded, and so on.

How to do it...

Perform the following steps to learn how to use the **Analytic Query** step:

1. Create a new transformation and add a **Text file input** step from the pallet to the canvas.

2. Have the **Text file input** step point to the `Salaries.csv` file. On the **Content** tab, be sure to change the **Separator** from `;` to `,`. On the **Fields** tab, use the **Get Fields** button to get the fields of the file.

3. Click on **OK** to close the **Text file input** step.

4. Add a **Sort rows** step from the pallet to the canvas. Create a hop from the **Text file input** to the **Sort rows** step.

5. The data needs to be sorted by `playerID` in the ascending order, with `yearID` in the descending order. Your **Sort rows** step should look similar to the following:

Fields :

∧	#	Fieldname	Ascending	Ca:
	1	playerID	Y	N
	2	yearID	N	N

6. From the **Statistics** folder, select the **Analytic Query** step and add it to the canvas. Create a hop from the **Sort rows** step to the **Analytic Query** step.

7. For the **Group** field, select `playerID`. Fill in the **Analytic Functions** grid as follows:

Analytic Functions :

⌄ #	New Field Name	Subject	Type	N
1	salary_previous	salary	LEAD "N" rows FORWARD and get Subject	1

8. Add a **Calculator** step and create a hop from the **Analytic Query** step to the **Calculator** step.

9. Open the **Calculator** step. Create a new field with the following criteria:

Fields:

⌄ #	New field	Calculation	Field A	Field B	Field C	Value type
1	salary_change	A - B	salary	salary_previous		Number

10. Finally, preview the **Calculator** step. You should receive an output similar to the following:

Rows of step: Salary Change (1000 rows)

⌄ #	yearID	teamID	lgID	playerID	salary	salary_previou	salary_change
1	2012	NYA	AL	aardsda01	500000	4500000	-4000000.0
2	2011	SEA	AL	aardsda01	4500000	2750000	1750000.0
3	2010	SEA	AL	aardsda01	2750000	419000	2331000.0
4	2009	SEA	AL	aardsda01	419000	403250	15750.0
5	2008	BOS	AL	aardsda01	403250	387500	15750.0
6	2007	CHA	AL	aardsda01	387500	300000	87500.0
7	2004	SFN	NL	aardsda01	300000	<null>	<null>

Now, the salary information provides a little more detail and can show how much a player gained (or lost) over the course of their career. Now, let's look at another step that can help show even more detail around the baseball player salary dataset—**Univariate Statistics**.

Perform the following steps to learn how to use the **Univariate Statistics** step:

1. Create a new transformation and add a **Text file input** step to the canvas.

2. Have the **Text file input** step point to the `Salaries.csv` file. On the **Content** tab, be sure to change the **Separator** from `;` to `,`. On the **Fields** tab, use the **Get Fields** button to get the fields of the file. Click on **OK** to close the **Text file input** step.

3. Bring a **Univariate Statistics** step from the pallet to the canvas and create a hop from the **Text file input** step to the **Univariate Statistics** step.

4. Open the **Univariate Statistics** step. For the **Input** field, select **salary**. Set the value of **N, Mean, Std dev, Min, Max**, and **Median** to `true`.

5. Click on **OK** to close the **Univariate Statistics** step and then preview the step. A row showing the various statistics around the salary will be displayed in the preview:

Rows of step: Univariate Statistics (1 rows)						
^ #	salary(N)	salary(mean)	salary(stdDev	salary(min)	salary(max)	salary(median)
1	23141	1798885.7	2970955.9	0	33000000	500000

The data stream is processed, returning the salary statistics for the entire dataset. Now, as the last part of this recipe, let's explore the **Group by** step.

Perform the following steps to learn how to use the **Group by** step:

1. Create a new transformation and add a **Text file input** step to the canvas.

2. Have the **Text file input** step point to the `Salaries.csv` file. On the **Content** tab, be sure to change the **Separator** from `;` to `,`. On the **Fields** tab, use the **Get Fields** button to get the fields of the file. Click on **OK** to close the **Text file input** step.

3. Add a **Sort rows** step to the canvas and create a hop from the **Text file input** step to the **Sort rows** step.

4. Open the **Sort rows** step and sort the data on `playerID` in the ascending order.

5. Add a **Group by** step to the canvas and create a hop from the **Sort rows** step to the **Group by** step.

6. Open the **Group by** step. For the **Group** field, select `playerID`. Fill in the **Aggregates** data grid, as shown in the following screenshot:

gregates :			
#	Name	Subject	Type
1	salary_mean	salary	Average (Mean)
2	salary_min	salary	Minimum
3	salary_max	salary	Maximum

7. Click on **OK** to close the **Group by** step and preview the data. The data stream will be grouped by the individual players and show salary statistics per player:

Rows of step: Group by (1000 rows)

#	playerID	salary_mean	salary_min	salary_max
1	aardsda01	1322821	300000	4500000
2	aasedo01	575000	400000	675000
3	abadan01	327000	327000	327000
4	abadfe01	451500	418000	485000
5	abbotje01	246250	175000	300000
6	abbotji01	1440055	68000	2775000
7	abbotku01	470777	109000	1000000

How it works...

This recipe covered three different ways to find out more information about the data being processed, each collecting statistics about the data in ways that are reported on, but do not necessarily have to be recalculated every time a report or analysis is done. For each of the steps, there are two things to consider:

▶ The data must be sorted based on the query requirements

▶ The original data will not continue through the stream after being processed by these steps

The **Analytic Query** step provides the ability to compare multiple records through a data stream which has historically been a complicated thing to do with just SQL. Quite often, comparisons need to be made within a group of data, usually in the form of tracking changes from one record/period to the next. For our baseball salary dataset, we looked at each player as they changed from season to season and how their salaries changed.

The **Univariate Statistics** step provides common statistics for the data stream being analyzed. Having these values can be used for data validation, comparisons between data loads, and for reporting. In the baseball salary dataset, we used the **Univariate Statistics** step to see the metrics around salary (specifically the mean, min, and max salary numbers for all the records).

The **Group by** step not only provides the same types of statistics as the **Univariate Statistics** step, but also allows for grouping the data together. For the baseball dataset, we used the **Group by** step to see the metrics around the mean, min, and max salary numbers for each player.

  ▶ The *Loading data into Hadoop* recipe in *Chapter 3, Working with Big Data and Cloud Sources*

  ▶ The *Getting the value of specific cells in an Excel file* recipe found in *Chapter 2, Reading and Writing Files*

Building a random data sample for Weka

Weka is another open source tool that is officially supported by Pentaho, that focuses on data mining. Like it's cousins R and RapidMiner, Weka provides a library of statistical analysis tools that can be integrated into complex decision making systems. For this recipe, we will go over how to build a random dataset for Weka using Kettle.

Getting ready

We will be using the baseball player salaries data that can be found on the book's website or from Lahman's Baseball Archive website, found at `http://www.seanlahman.com/baseball-archive/statistics/`. The code for this recipe can also be found on the book's website.

This recipe also takes advantage of the **ARFF Output** plugin. This is available either via the **Marketplace** (for Kettle 5 and higher) or from the wiki at `http://wiki.pentaho.com/display/EAI/List+of+Available+Pentaho+Data+Integration+Plug-Ins`.

How to do it...

Perform the following steps to build a random data sample for Weka:

1. Create a new transformation and add a **Text file input** step to the canvas.

2. Have the **Text file input** step point to the `Salaries.csv` file. On the **Content** tab, be sure to change the **Separator** from `;` to `,`. On the **Fields** tab, use the **Get Fields** button to get the fields of the file. Click on **OK** to close the **Text file input** step.

3. Add a **Reservoir Sampling** step from the **Statistics** folder in the pallet to the canvas. Create a hop from the **Text file input** step to the **Reservoir Sampling** step.

4. Open the **Reservoir Sampling** step. Change the value of the **Sample size (rows)** field to `1000`. Click on **OK** to close the step.

5. Add an **ARFF Output** step to the canvas. Create a hop from the **Reservoir Sampling** step to the **ARFF Output** step.

6. Open the **ARFF Output** step. For the **File name** field, call the file `baseball_salaries`.

7. Switch to the **Content** tab. Ensure the **Format** matches the environment that you are working in (DOS for Windows, Unix for *nix).

8. Switch to the **Fields** tab. Use the **Get Fields** button to get the data stream fields into the **Fields** data grid. The step will make a best guess at the ARFF type for each data element. Click on **OK** to close the step.

9. Run the transformation. An ARFF file will be generated and can be used to work with the data within Weka.

How it works...

This recipe utilizes two steps, the first (**Reservoir Sampling**) of which can be used by anything that only needs a random data sample to process. The second one transforms the dataset into the standard format for Weka.

Reservoir Sampling takes large datasets and randomly selects records to create a smaller representative sample of the data. The two options in the step, sample size and random seed, control how big the sample set should get and how the records are randomly selected. For more details on the step, check out the Pentaho wiki at `http://wiki.pentaho.com/display/DATAMINING/Using+the+Reservoir+Sampling+Plugin`.

The **ARFF Output** step takes the data stream and stores the data in the standard format that Weka uses to process data. The first part of the file is the header, which provides the field details (name, type, and so on) and can also store the data source details (who created it, when the dataset was created, and so on). The second part fits the typical comma-separated values format, with each record's fields separated by a comma. To learn more about the format, check out the Weka wiki at `http://weka.wikispaces.com/ARFF+(stable+version)`.

There's more...

There is another Kettle plugin that will actually take advantage of a model built in Weka and return the results back for further processing within Kettle. The step is called **Weka Scoring** and is a great place to start integrating machine learning into normal data integration processes. To learn more about the plugin, check out the wiki at `http://wiki.pentaho.com/display/DATAMINING/Using+the+Weka+Scoring+Plugin`.

There is a sub forum dedicated to working with Pentaho and Weka on the forums: `http://forums.pentaho.com/forumdisplay.php?81-Pentaho-Data-Mining-WEKA`.

To learn more about Weka, check out the Weka website for tutorials and other references `http://www.cs.waikato.ac.nz/ml/weka`.

See also

▸ The *Managing plugins with the Marketplace* recipe in *Chapter 11, Utilizing Visualization Tools in Kettle*

▸ *Studying data via stream statistics*

Data Structures

This appendix describes some structures used in several recipes throughout the book.

There are two objectives in describing them here (besides keeping the explanation in a single place), one is that you understand the structure of the data being used. The second, is allowing you to create your own data in the format of your choice—database, Excel file, and so on, except of course when the data is used in a recipe that explains database steps, in which case the data should be in a database.

Books data structure

The Books database is a simple structure that holds details on a sample list of books and their authors. The recipes that use the Books database are based on you being part of a fictitious book store. In the following diagram, you can see the relationship between the authors' and books' tables, where a single author can have many books:

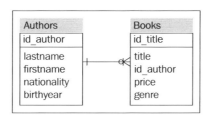

Books

The `Books` table stores the following details for each book:

Field	Description	Example
`id_title`	Identification for the book. It is a string with the format `CCC-CCC` (3 characters, a hyphen, and 3 more characters).	`123-456`
`title`	Title of the book.	`The Tommyknockers`
`id_author`	Identification for the author of a book; it references to the authors' data.	`A00002`
`price`	Price for the book. It's a decimal value.	`39.00`
`genre`	Genre of the books.	`Fiction`
		Possible values are: `Fiction`, `Non-fiction`, `Business` or `Children`

Authors

The `Authors` table stores the following details for each author:

Field	Description	Example
`id_author`	Identification for the author	`A00002`
`lastname`	Author's last name	`King`
`firstname`	Author's first name	`Stephen`
`nationality`	Author's nationality	`American`
`birthyear`	Year of author's birth. It's a numeric value.	`1947`

museums data structure

The museums database stores data about museums and the cities that they reside in. The recipes using this data source are based on you being part of a tourism company. The following diagram shows the relationship between museums and cities, where a single city can have many museums:

museums

The museums table contains the following details for each museum:

Field	Description	Example
id_museum	Identification for the museum	3
name	Museum's name	Museo de Arte Latinoamericano
id_city	Identification for the city; it references to the cities' data	1

cities

The cities table contains the following details for each city:

Field	Description	Example
id_city	Identification for the museum	1
city	City's name	Buenos Aires
country	City's country	Argentina

outdoor data structure

The outdoor database contains details on outdoor equipment and the categories they are part of. The recipes that use the outdoor dataset are based on you being part of an outdoor equipment store. The following diagram shows the relationship between the many outdoor products to their given category:

products

The products table contains the following details for each product:

Field	Description	Example
Id_product	Identification for the product	12
desc_ product	Product's description	Kelty Grand Mesa 2-Person Tent (Ruby/Tan)
price	Product's price	$107.96
Id_category	Identification for the category; it references to the categories' data	4

categories

The categories table contains the following details for each category:

Field	Description	Example
Id_category	Identification for the category	4
category	Category's description	Tents

Steel Wheels data structure

Some specific recipes use the `Steel Wheels` database included in Pentaho. This database represents the data for a fictional store named Steel Wheels. In the following diagram you can see the tables used in the recipes and how they are related:

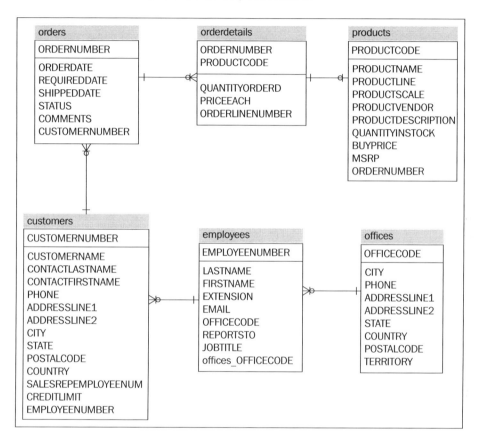

Lahman Baseball Database

The Lahman Baseball Database is one of the most comprehensive baseball statistics datasets available. While the data we work with in the recipes is with the `csv` file format dataset, it is relational data, and does come in SQL and Access formats as well. The data is provided by Sean Lahman through a Creative Commons Attribution-ShareAlike 3.0 Unported License. The following diagram shows the tables that we work with in the book:

Note that in the recipes that involve the `master` table we refer to it as `Player`, since that is the data in that source.

B
References

This appendix lists a few recommended references to other books and resources to dig deeper into the topics covered in this Cookbook. Both Pentaho and the community have pulled together a great collection of resources that assist in diving into the Pentaho stack. While some of the references refer to older versions of their particular software, they are still very much relevant in the areas they cover.

Books

▸ William D. Back, Nicholas Goodman, and Julian Hyde. *Mondrian in Action. Manning Publications* (Shelter Island), 2014.

▸ Roland Bouman and Jos Van. Dongen. *Pentaho Solutions. Wiley Publications* (Indianapolis, IN), 2009.

▸ Matt Casters, Roland Bouman, and Jos Van. Dongen. *Pentaho Kettle Solutions. Wiley Publications* (Indianapolis, IN), 2010.

▸ Will Gorman. *Pentaho Reporting 3.5 for Java Developers. Packt Publications* (Birmingham), 2009.

▸ María Carina Roldán. *Pentaho 3.2 Data Integration: Beginner's Guide. Packt Publications* (Birmingham), 2010.

▸ Ian H. Witten, Eibe Frank, and Mark A. Hall. *Data Mining. Morgan Kaufmann Publications* (Burlington, MA), 2011.

Online

▶ The Pentaho Community Wiki at `http://wiki.pentaho.com/display/COM/Community+Wiki+Home`

▶ The Pentaho Forums at `http://www.forums.pentaho.com`

▶ The Pentaho Feature and Bug-fix Tracker at `http://www.jira.pentaho.com`

▶ IRC on Freenode at `#pentaho`

▶ Pentaho Community Tools at `http://www.webdetails.pt/ctools.html`

Index

F

Feedly
   URL 167
fields
   creating, with XML structure 154, 155
   file name, using as 93-95
   fixed width fields, files reading with 70
   specifying, path notation used 137-140
   XML data 136, 137
Fields tab 374
files
   about 66
   comparing 188-190
   custom list, copying 183, 184
   custom list, deleting 185-188
   custom list, moving 183, 184
   decrypting 195-197
   deleted files, identifying 177
   detail files 78
   encrypting 195-197
   Excel file, reading 95, 96
   existence detecting, before copying 174
   fields metadata, altering 69
   fields names, altering 69
   fields order, altering 69
   format 68
   logfiles 78, 79
   master files 78
   multiple files deleting 175, 176
   multiple files, moving 172-174
   multiple files, reading at once 70-72
   multiple files with similar structure,
      generating 93
   name, providing 90-92
   name, using as field 93-95
   putting, on remote server 181, 182
   reading, with fixed width fields 70
   retrieving, from remote server 178, 179
   semi-structured files, reading 72-77
   semi-structured file, writing 87, 89
   simple file, reading 66-68
   simple file, writing 84, 86
   single file, deleting 175, 176
   single file, moving 172-174
   specifying, to transfer 180
   transferred, information retrieving 181
   with fields occupying multiple rows,
      reading 82-84
   with one field by row, reading 79-82
File Transfer Protocol (FTP) 178
File Transfer Protocol Secure. *See* **FTPS**
Filter rows step 233
findInfoRowSet() method 377
fixed width fields
   files, reading with 70
folders
   comparing 188-190
   creating 174
format
   about 69
   providing, to output fields 86
Freenode
   IRC, URL 434
FTPS
   about 181
   URL 181
FTP server
   connection, considerations 180
FULL OUTER join 261
fuzzy match algorithm
   about 219
   Damerau-Levenshtein 220
   Double Metaphone 221
   Jaro 220
   Jaro-Winkler 220
   Levenshtein 220
   Metaphone 221
   Needleman-Wunsch 220
   Pair letters Similarity 221
   Refined SoundEx 221
   SoundEx 221
Fuzzy match step 217, 219

G

GENRE parameter 107
Get a file with FTP job entry 179, 180
Get data from XML step 137, 146
Get Fields button 70, 91, 137
Get files from result step 146
getRowFrom() method 377
Get rows from result step 296

Thank you for buying
Pentaho Data Integration Cookbook
Second Edition

About Packt Publishing

Packt, pronounced 'packed', published its first book "*Mastering phpMyAdmin for Effective MySQL Management*" in April 2004 and subsequently continued to specialize in publishing highly focused books on specific technologies and solutions.

Our books and publications share the experiences of your fellow IT professionals in adapting and customizing today's systems, applications, and frameworks. Our solution based books give you the knowledge and power to customize the software and technologies you're using to get the job done. Packt books are more specific and less general than the IT books you have seen in the past. Our unique business model allows us to bring you more focused information, giving you more of what you need to know, and less of what you don't.

Packt is a modern, yet unique publishing company, which focuses on producing quality, cutting-edge books for communities of developers, administrators, and newbies alike. For more information, please visit our website: `www.packtpub.com`.

About Packt Open Source

In 2010, Packt launched two new brands, Packt Open Source and Packt Enterprise, in order to continue its focus on specialization. This book is part of the Packt Open Source brand, home to books published on software built around Open Source licences, and offering information to anybody from advanced developers to budding web designers. The Open Source brand also runs Packt's Open Source Royalty Scheme, by which Packt gives a royalty to each Open Source project about whose software a book is sold.

Writing for Packt

We welcome all inquiries from people who are interested in authoring. Book proposals should be sent to author@packtpub.com. If your book idea is still at an early stage and you would like to discuss it first before writing a formal book proposal, contact us; one of our commissioning editors will get in touch with you.

We're not just looking for published authors; if you have strong technical skills but no writing experience, our experienced editors can help you develop a writing career, or simply get some additional reward for your expertise.

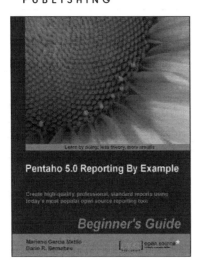

Pentaho 5.0 Reporting by Example: Beginner's Guide

ISBN: 978-1-78216-224-7   Paperback: 342 pages

Create high-quality, professional, standard reports using today's most popular open source reporting tool

1. Install and configure PRD in Linux and Windows.

2. Create complex reports using relational data sources.

3. Produce reports with groups, aggregate functions, parameters, graphics, and sparklines.

4. Install and configure Pentaho BI Server to execute PRD reports.

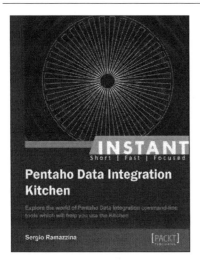

Instant Pentaho Data Integration Kitchen

ISBN: 978-1-84969-690-6   Paperback: 68 pages

Explore the world of Pentaho Data Integration command-line tools which will help you use the Kitchen

1. Learn something new in an Instant! A short, fast, focused guide delivering immediate results.

2. Understand how to discover the repository structure using the command line scripts.

3. Learn to configure the log properly and how to gather the information that helps you investigate any kind of problem.

4. Explore all the possible ways to start jobs and learn transformations without any difficulty.

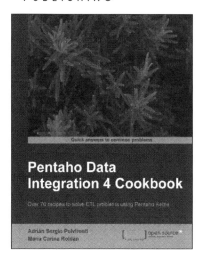

[PACKT] open source *
community experience distilled
PUBLISHING

Pentaho Data Integration 4 Cookbook

ISBN: 978-1-84951-524-5   Paperback: 352 pages

Over 70 recipes to solve ETL problems using Pentaho Kettle

1. Manipulate your data by exploring, transforming, validating, integrating, and more.

2. Work with all kinds of data sources such as databases, plain files, and XML structures among others.

3. Use Kettle in integration with other components of the Pentaho Business Intelligence Suite.

4. Each recipe is a carefully organized sequence of instructions packed with screenshots, tables, and tips to complete the task as efficiently as possible.

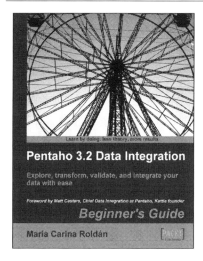

Pentaho 3.2 Data Integration: Beginner's Guide

ISBN: 978-1-84719-954-6   Paperback: 492 pages

Explore, transform, validate, and integrate your data with ease

1. Get started with Pentaho Data Integration from scratch.

2. Enrich your data transformation operations by embedding Java and JavaScript code in PDI transformations.

3. Create a simple but complete Datamart Project that will cover all key features of PDI.

Please check **www.PacktPub.com** for information on our titles

Made in the USA
Lexington, KY
12 October 2015